TravelAtlas
UNITED STATES CANADA MEXICO

Contributing Writers:

Melissa Arnold

John Boslough

John Gattuso

John A. Murray

Clark Norton

Eric Peterson

Christina Tree

Jim Yenckel

D1613768

Map Illustrations on pages A-2 through A-32 by Dave Merrill. Reference for maps on pages A-2 through A-32 courtesy of the National Scenic Byways Organization (www.byways.org).

Portions of manuscript courtesy of Exxon Mobil Travel Group.

Atlas pages 1-144 Copyright © THE NATIONAL SURVEY. Used by permission.

Photo credits for Scenic Drives and National Parks:
Accent Alaska: A-3; **Tim Bresett/New York Ausable Chasm:** A-21 (top); **Congaree National Park Service:** B-6; **Kent & Donna Dannen:** B-14 (bottom); **John Domont:** A-12 (left); **John Elk III:** A-17 (bottom); **Fort Ticonderoga:** A-21 (bottom); **Ian Adams Photography:** A-12 (right); **The Image Finders:** Mark E. Gibson, A-18 (top), A-19; Michael Lustbader, A-26; Jim Yokajty, A-5 (bottom); **Index Stock Imagery, Inc.:** A-11, A-20 (bottom); **Dewitt Jones/Bob Marshall:** B-10 (top); **Oglebay Resort:** A-13 (bottom left); **Laurence Parent:** A-8, A-9, A-14, A-15, A-16, A-22, B-8 (top); **Richmond Wayne City:** A-13 (bottom right); **State of Alabama:** A-2; **SuperStock:** A-6, A-10, A-13 (center), A-18 (bottom), A-24, A-25, B-9, B-16; **Leon Turnbull/waterfallswest.com:** A-29 (top); **Larry Ulrich:** B-5, B-15 (top); **Unicorn Stock Photos:** Robert E. Barber, B-11 (bottom); Joseph L. Fontenot, A-23 (top); Paula J. Harrington, A-27 (top); Jean Higgins, A-27 (bottom); Andre Jenny, A-23 (bottom); MacDonald Photography, A-17 (top); **George Wuerthner:** B-8 (bottom), B-11 (top).

Louis Weber, CEO
Publications International, Ltd.
7373 North Cicero Avenue
Lincolnwood, Illinois 60712

Permission is never granted for commercial purposes.

Manufactured in China.

8 7 6 5 4 3 2 1

ISBN: 1-4127-1220-3

CONTENTS

Scenic Drives
Selma to Montgomery March Byway A-2
Seward Highway A-3
Big Sur Coast Highway–
    Route 1 ....A-4
San Luis Obispo North
    Coast Byway–Route 1 ....A-6
San Juan Skyway A-7
Trail Ridge Road/Beaver
    Meadow Road......................................A-8
Creole Nature Trail A-9
Acadia Byway A-10
Historic National Road A-11
Natchez Trace Parkway A-14
Beartooth Highway A-16
Las Vegas Strip A-18
Lakes to Locks Passage,
    The Great Northeast Journey A-20
Blue Ridge Parkway A-22
North Shore Scenic Drive A-24
Hells Canyon Scenic Byway.....................A-25
Pacific Coast Scenic Byway.....................A-26
Volcanic Legacy Scenic Byway A-28
Historic Columbia River Highway A-30
A Journey Through Time
    Scenic Byway A-31
Chinook Scenic Byway A-32

Travel Atlas 1-144

National Parks
Acadia National Park................................B-1
Badlands National Park............................B-1
Arches National Park................................B-2
Big Bend National Park B-2
Biscayne National Park B-3
Bryce Canyon National Park B-3
Black Canyon of the
    Gunnison National Park.......................B-4
Canyonlands National Park.......................B-4
Capitol Reef National Park........................B-5
Channel Islands National Park B-5
Carlsbad Caverns National Park..............B-6
Congaree National Park............................B-6
Crater Lake National Park B-7
Death Valley National Park.......................B-7
Cuyahoga Valley National Park.................B-8
Dry Tortugas National Park.......................B-8
Denali National Park.................................B-9
Everglades National Park.........................B-9
Gates of the Arctic National Park B-10
Glacier National Park B-10
Glacier Bay National Park.........................B-11
Great Sand Dunes National Park B-11
Grand Canyon National Park B-12
Grand Teton National Park B-13
Great Basin National Park B-14
Guadalupe Mountains National Park.........B-14
Great Smoky Mountains National Park B-15
Haleakala National Park............................B-16
Hawai'i Volcanoes National Park...............B-16
Hot Springs National Park.........................B-17
Isle Royale National Park..........................B-17
Joshua Tree National Park........................B-18
Kenai Fjords National Park........................B-18
Katmai National Park.................................B-19
Kobuk Valley National Park B-19
Lake Clark National Park...........................B-20
Mammoth Cave National Park....................B-20
Lassen Volcanic National Park B-21
Mount Rainier National Park B-21
Mesa Verde National Park.........................B-22
North Cascades National Park...................B-22
Olympic National Park................................B-23
Redwood National Park..............................B-24
Petrified Forest National Park B-24
Rocky Mountain National Park B-25
Saguaro National Park B-26
Shenandoah National Park B-26
Sequoia National Park/Kings Canyon
    National Park...B-27
Theodore Roosevelt National Park B-28
Voyageurs National Park B-28
Wind Cave National Park B-29
Wrangell-St. Elias National Park B-29
Yellowstone National Park.........................B-30
Yosemite National Park..............................B-31
Zion National Park......................................B-32

ALABAMA

Selma to Montgomery March Byway

This historical route, rich in poignant stories, honors the memory of civil rights marchers whose efforts helped Southern African-Americans gain access to the ballot box with passage of the 1965 Voting Rights Act.

The byway that today connects these two Alabama cities has known many facets of history in its years of existence. After Dr. Martin Luther King, Jr., began leading voting rights demonstrations in Selma early in 1965, culminating with the historic Selma to Montgomery March that began on March 21, the route became internationally known.

Brown Chapel AME Church

Intrinsic Qualities

Cultural: Dr. Martin Luther King, Jr., stood in front of the stark-white state capitol in Montgomery, Alabama, and gazed at the crowd of 25,000 people on March 25, 1965. The South's largest-ever civil rights march had reached its destination after weeks of uncertainty and danger.

King did not refer to the brutal attack state troopers staged against the marchers 18 days earlier, which had come to be known as "Bloody Sunday." That attack, seen on national television, had drawn the attention of the world to this moment. Less than five months later, the 1965 Voting Rights Act was signed into law, and African-Americans throughout the South streamed into courthouses to register as voters.

Historical: Despite stiff resistance from white officials, Selma activists passionately fought for their civil rights in the early 1960s. They battled not only bureaucrats but also the intimidation tactics of Sheriff Jim Clark, who was later sued by the U.S. Justice Department for voter discrimination. Their courage attracted the attention of other African-American leaders.

Then on July 9, 1964, State Circuit Judge James Hare enjoined any group of more than three people from meeting in Dallas County. Protests and meetings came to a virtual halt. On January 2, 1965, Dr. King defied the injunction and led a rally, promising further demonstrations if voting rights were not guaranteed for African-Americans in the South. Immediately, a series of mass meetings and protest marches began with renewed momentum in Selma and nearby Marion.

On February 18, Alabama state troopers attacked African-Americans leaving a mass meeting at Zion Methodist Church in Marion. Two troopers shot Jimmie Lee Jackson at point-blank range. He died a week later.

His death angered activists, who realized that some mass nonviolent action was necessary to win the attention of political leaders and to vent the anger and frustration over Jackson's death. On Sunday,

HIGHLIGHTS

The following tour begins on the corner of Martin Luther King, Jr., Street and Jeff Davis Avenue in Selma. Twenty memorials along the route tell the stories of the individuals who came together to fight for a common cause.

Cecil B. Jackson Public Safety Building: This building served as the city and county jail in which Dr. King and other protesters were imprisoned in 1965.

Dallas County Courthouse: This was the destination of most protest marches in an effort to register to vote.

National Voting Rights Museum and Institute: Just before the Alabama River is this museum, dedicated to honoring the attainment of voting rights.

Edmund Pettus Bridge: Crossing the Alabama River is the famous landmark where "Bloody Sunday" took place on March 7, 1965.

Montgomery: From the bridge, the byway travels along Highway 80 to Montgomery, passing numerous campsites that were used by marchers in 1965.

Alabama State Capitol: On the steps of this great building, Dr. Martin Luther King, Jr., told marchers that even though the journey was through, the struggle for civil rights was far from over.

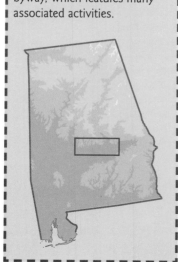

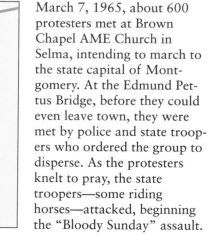

Selma to Montgomery March Byway

In Selma:
First Baptist Church
Brown Chapel AME Church
Edmund Pettus Bridge
Cecil B. Jackson Public
    Safety Building

Dallas County Courthouse
Nat'l. Voting Rights Museum and Institute

In Montgomery:
Alabama State Capitol

March 7, 1965, about 600 protesters met at Brown Chapel AME Church in Selma, intending to march to the state capital of Montgomery. At the Edmund Pettus Bridge, before they could even leave town, they were met by police and state troopers who ordered the group to disperse. As the protesters knelt to pray, the state troopers—some riding horses—attacked, beginning the "Bloody Sunday" assault.

ALASKA

Seward Highway

This southern Alaska byway offers vistas of snowcapped mountains, shimmering fjords, deep valleys, ice-blue glaciers—and glimpses of wildlife, waterfalls, or wildflowers around almost every turn.

The Seward Highway, linking Anchorage with Seward, passes through some of the most spectacular scenery in the country. For 127 miles, the road winds through a land of saltwater bays, frigid blue glaciers, knife-edged ridges, and alpine valleys. From the reflective waters of Turnagain Arm, you rapidly ascend 1,000 feet above sea level to an alpine meadow. Within the hour, you find yourself back at sea level surrounded by fjords, having just passed through a district of rivers and lakes.

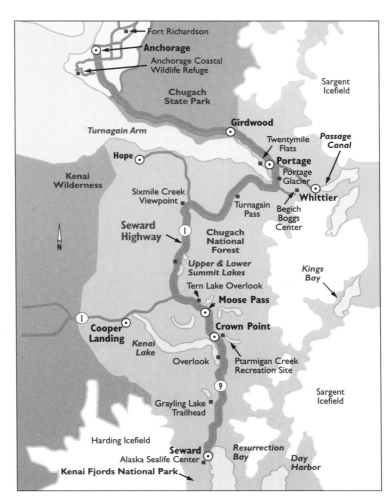

Intrinsic Qualities

Historical: Following the same early routes used by native Alaskans, the Seward Highway has evolved into a modern transportation system. Natives first used an area along the Seward Highway 9,000 years ago as a hunting camp. The region finally received its name in 1778: When shallow water forced James Cook to turn around in his quest for the Northwest Passage, he christened the sound Turnagain River. South of Anchorage, Highway 1 now follows the shore of Turnagain Arm.

In 1895, prospectors discovered gold in Hope in the Kenai Peninsula, and the rush began. Suddenly, the tiny towns of Hope and Sunrise grew into booming gold-mining towns. Sunrise was even considered for a time as a potential state capital. But by 1910, most miners had left the area in order to follow prospects of gold farther north. The privately owned town site of Sunrise is now a historic archaeological district, and the Hope Historical Society operates a small museum.

Natural: Along the highway, you may hear the honking of Canada geese, the whistle of hoary marmots, and the cry of bald eagles. Along Turnagain Arm, you may spot Dall sheep as they scale rugged mountainsides. Moose, bears, mountain goats, salmon, and a variety of birds thrive along the highway as well.

Recreational: Most of the land above the highway is within Chugach State Park or Chugach National Forest. Popular activities include hiking, windsurfing, rock climbing, rafting and canoeing, fishing, and bicycling. Once a mining town, Girdwood is now home to a world-famous ski resort that offers excellent scenery and plenty of challenges. Hope and Cooper Landing are havens for fishing.

Scenic: The trip from Anchorage to Seward is one of the most scenic drives you can take. Frequent pull-offs offer vistas of snowcapped mountains, glaciers, wildlife, and wildflowers. Side trips and hiking trails beckon adventurous explorers.

The road up Portage Valley leads into the vast Chugach National Forest and past three hanging glaciers perched in mountain canyons. But the ice here is quickly melting. Only a few bergs float in water that was once brimming with ice. The visitor center offers excellent descriptive displays of glaciers and the best chance to see ice worms, pin-size critters that burrow into glaciers and eat algae.

You can also take a day cruise along the rugged coast of Kenai Fjords National Park to see wildlife and tidewater glaciers that calve into the sea.

HIGHLIGHTS

Start in Seward, and travel north to Anchorage.

Seward: The Seward Highway begins in the town of Seward, nestled among the fjords surrounding Resurrection Bay. Nearby Kenai Fjords National Park offers the chance to see puffins, otters, whales, seals, and other marine life.

Ptarmigan Creek Recreation Site: During late July and early August, this site, 23 miles north of Seward, is an excellent place to watch thousands of red salmon head upstream to spawn.

Portage Glacier: A stop here provides an incredible opportunity to watch glacial action on fast forward.

Twentymile Flats: Farther north is Twentymile Flats, an expanse of lowlands where three river valleys empty into Turnagain Arm. Scenic views abound.

Turnagain Arm: Turnagain Arm experiences the second-highest tides in the world, often up to a 38-foot change in water level.

Anchorage: Anchorage offers a wealth of historic and cultural sites you can enjoy.

Turnagain Pass

CALIFORNIA

Big Sur Coast Highway—Route 1

With soaring redwoods, windswept cypresses, plunging waterfalls, fog-shrouded cliffs, and barking sea lions, this highway inspires awe and wonder as it winds along the California coast high above the crashing waves of the Pacific.

Route 1 from the San Luis Obispo County line north to Carmel follows some of the most spectacular and highly scenic shoreline found along California's coast. Views include rugged canyons and steep sea cliffs, granite shorelines, sea lions and other marine life, vibrant cypress trees, and majestic redwood forests.

Intrinsic Qualities

Cultural: The Big Sur is one example of an area whose culture is largely shaped by the region's geography. The awe-inspiring scenic beauty of the Big Sur has lured and inspired countless artists, authors, and poets. The Carmel area and the Salinas Valley, less rugged but no less scenic or inspiring, have also had a vital role to play in the area's culture. The area has been home to many artists, none more famous than John Steinbeck, whose novels vividly describe life in the fertile Salinas Valley.

Historical: Written histories regarding the region now known as the Big Sur began to appear in the mid-1500s, when a Portuguese ship passed by the area's coastline. New groups of European explorers approached the area throughout the late 1500s and early 1600s, many anchoring in Monterey Bay. However, it wasn't until 1770 that the first permanent settlement was established, when a Spanish group started a mission in Carmel. The Spaniards first called the area south of the Carmel settlement El Pais Grande del Sur, or "the Big Country of the South." These same Spanish settlers were quick to introduce themselves and their culture to the area natives, who had lived in the region for centuries.

Big Sur Coast Highway—Route 1

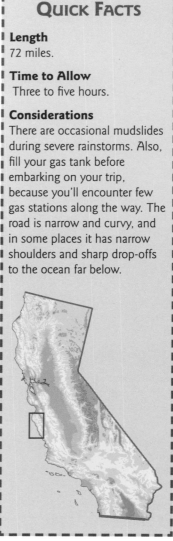

QUICK FACTS

Length
72 miles.

Time to Allow
Three to five hours.

Considerations
There are occasional mudslides during severe rainstorms. Also, fill your gas tank before embarking on your trip, because you'll encounter few gas stations along the way. The road is narrow and curvy, and in some places it has narrow shoulders and sharp drop-offs to the ocean far below.

Before the Europeans arrived at the Big Sur, the Esselen nation had thrived in the area as hunters and gatherers. By the early 18th century, other Spanish missions followed the Carmel Mission. In the late 1700s, the Spanish missionaries and soldiers forced many of the Esselen and other native peoples to leave their villages and move into the missions. Smallpox, cholera, and other European diseases almost completely wiped out the Esselen people. Those who were left mixed with other natives in the missions. As a result, very little is known today about the Esselen way of life.

Until the late 1800s, a small, rough trail served as the best overland route to Monterey from the Big Sur. Eventually, the trail widened into a road of sorts, which was still frequently lost in landslides. This widening allowed the journey to Monterey to be made in just 11

Bixby Bridge

Pacific coastline

hours, as opposed to the three or four days it had taken previously. After many years of difficult passage over poor roads between the Big Sur and the rest of central California, Route 1 was completed in 1937. By its completion, 15 years of labor and $9 million had been expended.

Natural: The allure of the Big Sur Coast Highway comes not just from the sea and the mountains but also from the convergence of the sea with the mountains. The ocean has helped to carve out the tanta-

lizing craggy rock inlets along the corridor, which are often havens for marine mammals.

The byway enables you to experience the Pacific Ocean in its natural state. Unlike most other coastlines, the endless blue horizon at Big Sur is usually void of any floating vessels. Travelers are actually more likely to witness a massive whale surfacing for air or some sea otters playing than to see a freighter waiting to port.

The San Lucia coastal mountains, on the other side of the highway, are a paradise of cypress and redwood

forests, waterfalls, and meadows full of colorful wildflowers, such as lupines and poppies. The mountains also host one of the byway's unique natural elements: the giant redwood tree. Redwood trees thrive in the specific climate along this area and are not native to any other region in the world. Many of the oldest trees are around 2,000 years old, and the tallest have reached heights of 350 feet.

Recreational: The Big Sur's beaches offer a wide variety of recreational possibilities. Even during the summer, beaches are subject to generally cool weather. Sunny days are sporadic because a blanket of seasonal fog often hugs the coastline, dropping the temperature in the process. Several state park and U.S. Forest Service beaches are open to the public year-round. These beaches are recommended due to easy access and breathtaking scenery.

Scenic: The Big Sur Coast Highway affords you fantastic views of one of the nation's most stunning coastlines. At certain points along the byway, the only way to get any closer to the Pacific would be to get in it! Luckily, scenic overlooks are plentiful, providing you with a plethora of breathtaking views from safe pull-offs.

If the vast blue waters of the Pacific aren't enough for you, direct your eyes inland, taking in the beautiful coastal hills and breathtaking mountains.

Carmel Mission

HIGHLIGHTS

The Big Sur Coast Highway runs north along Route 1 from northwest of San Simeon to Carmel.

Ragged Point: On a promontory 400 feet above the Pacific, Ragged Point has incredible ocean views; a waterfall; a steep trail to a secluded beach; and a restaurant, gas station, and motor inn complex.

Lucia: Northwest of Ragged Point is the tiny hamlet of Lucia. Lucia has an incredible vantage point looking out over the Pacific.

Limekiln State Park: Not far after Ragged Point, the byway enters Los Padres National Forest, traveling north to Limekiln State Park, which has campsites in the redwoods and wonderful coastal views.

Julia Pfeiffer Burns State Park: Julia Pfeiffer Burns State Park has trails through the redwoods and a short trail to a spectacular waterfall that plunges 80 feet into the Pacific.

Pfeiffer Beach: Secluded Pfeiffer Beach is one popular stop for those who can find it. Watch for paved but unmarked Sycamore Canyon Road, located on the western side of Route 1 one mile south of Pfeiffer Big Sur State Park. The road leads 2½ miles to gloriously golden sand.

Pfeiffer Big Sur State Park: Pfeiffer Big Sur State Park makes a good central base for exploring the area. The park has a lodge and campgrounds in the redwoods, while hiking trails follow the Big Sur River to an inland waterfall.

Andrew Molera State Park and Point Sur State Historic Park: Next up is Andrew Molera State Park, the largest park along the Big Sur Coast, where a mile-long trail crosses rugged headlands to a stretch of wild beach. Just north is Point Sur State Historic Park, site of the historic Point Sur Light Station.

Bixby Bridge: The Bixby Bridge follows Point Sur. Built in 1932 and spanning a 100-foot-wide canyon, it's one of the ten highest single-span bridges in the world at 260 feet above the sea.

Carmel: In addition to a picture-perfect beach and intriguing shops, the resort town of Carmel is known for its beautiful Spanish-style mission, which was founded in 1770 by Father Junipero Serra.

Point Lobos Reserve: Often called the "crown jewel" of the state park system, Point Lobos has rocky headlands to hike, hidden coves, and rich marine life, including sea otters and sea lions.

CALIFORNIA

San Luis Obispo North Coast Byway—Route 1

Pastoral countryside, golden beaches, rocky coves, serene hills, clean air, the blue Pacific, even an American castle in the sky—this California coastal byway is an enchanted pathway for daydreamers and nature lovers.

Just south of the Big Sur Coast Highway, Route 1 in north San Luis Obispo County winds past some of the finest views in the western United States. The byway blends the rural beauty associated with much of Route 1 in the northern portion of the state with the convenience and amenities found in the more populated southern sections of California.

Morro Bay

Intrinsic Qualities

Historical: The city of San Luis Obispo began with the 1772 founding of the Mission San Luis Obispo de Tolosa. Built on a knoll beside a sparkling creek, the mission became the hub of a growing settlement.

During the 1880s, the Southern Pacific Railroad built a railroad south from San Jose. After a five-year delay, the railroad came to San Luis Obispo in 1894. Construction of the railroad helped bring both industry and variety to the small community and changed the face of the city.

Natural: The San Luis Obispo North Coast Byway's prominent resource is the ocean, including its sea life and nationally recognized bays: Morro Bay and Morro Bay National Estuary. The bays are home to otters, seals, sea lions, and whales. The estuary supports many species of migratory birds. There are breeding colonies of elephant seals near Piedras Blancas Point, easily viewed from the byway. The byway skirts the Morro Peaks and the Santa Lucia coastal mountain range and traverses the state's southernmost native Monterey pine forest.

Recreational: The San Luis Obispo corridor is blessed with year-round opportunities for outdoor recreation. Visitors often hike, cycle, surf, ride horses, watch birds, windsurf, hang glide, kayak, and fly kites. The highway itself generally has generous shoulders and makes for a great bike ride.

Just north of the California beach community of Cayucos on rural Route 1, the Harmony Coast contains unique opportunities to kayak into rocky coastal inlets that are extensive tide pool habitat areas.

Scenic: The harbors and bays found along the byway have served as inspiration for artistic seascape paintings. Morro Bay, a working fishing village and a protected harbor, is also home to Morro Rock, abruptly rising more than 500 feet above the bay. Softly sculptured hills ring the city, the remains of ancient volcanoes, called *morros*.

The spectacular shoreline of the San Luis Obispo North Coast Byway is backed by a series of coastal terraces that rise to the foothills and then to the high ridges of the Santa Lucia Range. In spring, these areas are mantled in the lush green of new growth, followed by vibrant displays of orange California poppy, purple lupine, and other colorful native wildflowers.

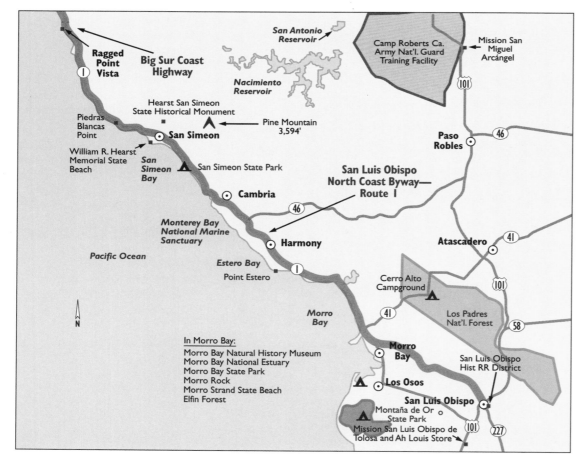

Colorado

San Juan Skyway

Mountain passes, cliff dwellings, spring waterfalls, winter skiing, and fall splendor mark this "Million Dollar Highway" as it journeys to the top of the world and back in time.

Discover history and new heights on the San Juan Skyway. The byway passes through the heart of five million acres of national forest, over mountain passes, and through quaint towns.

HIGHLIGHTS

The following tour begins in Mesa Verde National Park and ends in the town of Ouray.

Mesa Verde National Park: At this park, explore cliff dwellings made and inhabited by the Anasazi Indians. The cliffs were mysteriously abandoned in approximately A.D. 1300.

Durango: Founded in 1880, Durango still retains its Old-West and Victorian charm. Restored historic landmarks line downtown streets, while nearby ski resorts beckon to adventurous winter travelers.

Silverton: This remote historic mining community can be reached either by taking the historic Durango and Silverton Narrow Gauge Railroad or by driving over the 10,910-foot Molas Divide Pass.

Ghost towns: The ghost towns of Howardsville, Eureka, and Animas Forks are all located within 14 miles of Silverton.

Million Dollar Highway: This scenic section of highway from Silverton to Ouray was so named for the immense amounts of silver and gold that were carted through these passes.

Intrinsic Qualities

Archaeological: Among this byway's many archaeological sites, Mesa Verde National Park is arguably the most outstanding. Mesa Verde reflects more than 700 years of history. From approximately A.D. 600 to 1300, native people lived and flourished in elaborate cliff dwellings in the sheltered alcoves of the canyon walls. In the late 1200s and within only one or two generations, they left their homes and moved away.

Historical: The discovery of precious metals led to the exploration and settlement of areas along the San Juan Skyway during the late 19th century. Narrow-gauge railroads played an important role during the mining era.

With their rails set three feet apart as opposed to the standard gauge of nearly five feet, the narrow-gauge lines made it possible for trains to operate in mountainous country with tight turns and steep grades. One narrow-gauge railroad, the Durango and Silverton, continues to operate as a tourist line, offering scenic vistas and the experience of riding an authentic coal-fired, steam-powered railroad.

Natural: The already spectacular San Juan Skyway takes on especially vibrant beauty in the fall. The lush green of deciduous vegetation on the mountainsides is transformed into shades of gold, red, bronze, and purple. The aspen trees are the first to turn shades of gold and rosy red. The cottonwood trees, located along rivers and creeks, are next to turn gold, and a variety of shrubs complement the scene with their fall hues of red, purple, bronze, and orange.

Recreational: Summer activities include hiking, mountain biking, kayaking, hunting, and fishing. Winter activities include snowshoeing, snowmobiling, and skiing. Durango Mountain Resort offers downhill skiing and a Nordic center. In summer, the lift takes visitors up for mountain biking, sightseeing, and wildflower viewing.

Scenic: This byway is known as the Million Dollar Highway not only for its connection to gold and silver mining, but also for the first-class scenery it provides. The brawny and pine-furrowed Rockies lounge around this byway, and their uneven ridges yield to tree-packed forests, flashing streams, and slate blue lakes.

QUICK FACTS

Length 233 miles.

Time to Allow One to two days.

Considerations Be prepared for changing weather both while driving and while hiking. If you are not accustomed to high altitudes, get plenty of rest during your first two days at high altitude. Mountain passes are sometimes closed for an hour or two (sometimes even a day or two) in the case of heavy snowstorms or slides during the winter. The road has many hairpin switchbacks and a tunnel, includes tremendous drop-offs with no railings or shoulders, and offers few places to pass. Some curves are signed at 10 mph.

Mesa Verde National Park

COLORADO

Trail Ridge Road/Beaver Meadow Road

The highest continuous paved road in the United States, this byway on the roof of the Rockies offers stirring vistas at every overlook as it climbs through Rocky Mountain National Park.

This road is defined by its many overlooks bestowing stirring vistas of the towering mountains, many of which measure more than 14,000 feet above sea level. The clear atmosphere of this alpine tundra makes seeing the night sky from one of the overlooks incomparable. Constellations, planets, meteor showers, and phases of the moon seem brighter than ever and just beyond arm's reach.

Intrinsic Qualities

Historical: The first Europeans to see this area were French fur traders. A few others had settled in this rugged county by 1909 when Enos Mills—a naturalist, writer, and conservationist—began to campaign for preservation of the pristine area, a portion of which became Rocky Mountain National Park in 1915.

Natural: A full one-third of the park is above the timberline, and the harsh, fragile alpine tundra predominates. In the sublime valleys and meadows below, forests of spruce and fir take over in a subalpine ecosystem. Openings in these cool, dark forests expose wildflower gardens of rare beauty and luxuriance in which the blue Colorado columbine reigns. The park's resident wildlife includes black bear, elk, deer, and bighorn sheep.

Recreational: The recreational opportunities include hiking, horseback riding, camping, fishing, rock climbing, and numerous winter activities. Several campgrounds are open year-round. The Rocky Mountain National Park maintains dozens of hiking and equestrian trails (over 350 miles in all) and also offers a variety of challenging ascents throughout the year for climbers. Winter brings cross-country skiing in the lower valleys and winter mountaineering in the high country.

Scenic: The highest continuous paved road in the United States, this route affords an almost-too-rapid sequence of scenic overlooks as it skips along the continental divide at elevations over 12,000 feet. From these wind-scoured peaks, you can gaze out to the dark masses of other Rockies, posed like hands of cards in the distance. Right next to the road, the tundra is also beautiful in its own rugged way. The twisted, ground-creeping trees, crusted snow, and hard-faced boulders seem like they belong to a colder, more distant world.

Rocky Mountain National Park

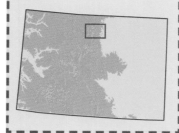
HIGHLIGHTS

While visiting Rocky Mountain National Park, you can take a self-guided tour. This route enters the park from the east and moves west and then south.

Rainbow Curve Overlook: At 10,829 feet, this overlook is more than two miles above sea level. At this elevation, every exposed tree is blasted by wind, ice, and grit into distinctive flag shapes.

Forest Canyon Overlook: Here, the erosive force of glacial ice is unmistakable. With the grinding of a giant rasp, the ice scoured the valley into the distinctive U-shape of today.

Alpine Visitor Center and Fall River Pass: Beside the visitor center, there is a gift shop and a short trail to an overlook at 12,003 feet.

Milner Pass: Here, Trail Ridge Road crosses the Continental Divide, where snowmelt and other water enters either the Atlantic or Pacific drainages. The Rockies divide these two great watersheds, but the Continental Divide may be a mountaintop, a ridge, or a pass. From this point, a short trail leads past Poudre Lake, headwaters of the Cache La Poudre River, and up to Old Fall River Road, the original road over the Continental Divide. The trail then connects with another trail leading to Mount Ida, the summit of which sits at 12,880 feet. This is a 4½-mile hike.

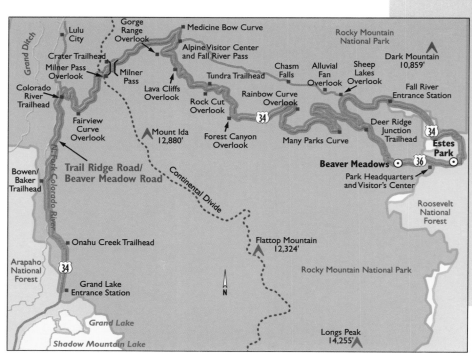

LOUISIANA

Creole Nature Trail

In this unique world of water, encompassing thousands of acres of wetlands, explore three wildlife refuges and a bird sanctuary. Along the way, try your hand at crabbing, and keep an eye open for alligators.

The Creole Nature Trail travels through thousands of acres of untouched wetlands that traverse the edge of the Gulf of Mexico. The combination of fresh and saltwater areas provides a unique habitat for many of the plants and creatures that live along the byway.

Intrinsic Qualities

Archaeological: Comparatively large concentrations of Native American archaeological finds, such as pots, shards, and arrowheads, have been unearthed throughout Cameron Parish, and burial mounds were found on Little Chenier, indicating that the earlier civilizations in the region must have been large and widespread.

Cultural: The culture along the Creole Nature Trail has been mixing and evolving for hundreds of years. Spanish, French, and African influences have all collided in this coastal outback where alligators roam and hurricanes are known to swallow entire villages. The people of south-west Louisiana understand the place where they live, and they revel in it. Throughout the year more than 75 festivals celebrate living on the Creole Nature Trail. Visitors might learn how to skin an alligator or enjoy some real Cajun cooking.

Shrimp boats and ships in the Cameron Ship Channel reflect the importance of the ocean in the area. Shrimp, crabs, oysters, and a host of fresh and saltwater fish are harvested daily. Visitors can sample these delicacies at area restaurants or purchase fresh seafood for their own recipes.

Historical: The pirate Jean Lafitte made a huge profit in the early 1800s from capturing Spanish slave ships and selling the slaves to Louisiana cotton and sugar cane planters. It is rumored that he buried riches and treasure chests all along the Calcasieu River.

Natural: The marshlands of coastal Louisiana teem with wildlife. They are a bird-watcher's paradise and a photographer's dream. These marshes are filled with the songs of the cardinal and blackbird, the quacking and honking of ducks and geese, the chatter of squirrels, the croaking of frogs, and the bellowing of alligators.

Marshes and other wetlands can be viewed in the Sabine National Wildlife Refuge, the Rockefeller Wildlife Refuge, and the Cameron Prairie National Wildlife Refuge.

As a coastal prairie, much of the land along the byway displays beautiful wildflowers throughout the warmer months. Many of the flowers have memorable names, such as maypop passionflower and duck potato. Unique plants can be found everywhere along the byway. Cordgrass grows where nothing else will, and a plant called alligator weed is a food source for deer, herons, and egrets.

Recreational: The fishing on Louisiana's coastline is excellent. Visitors will catch more than just fish. Crabs, shrimp, and oysters are popular items to pull from the sea.

Even on the Creole Nature Trail, you may want a taste of civilization every now and then. Visitors love to stop in places such as Lake Charles or Cameron Parish just to take a look at the historic sites that make each town memorable.

Scenic: The Creole Nature Trail provides scenery just as it should be in an outback wilderness—pristine, untamed, and a bit mysterious. These characteristics are preserved in the way wetland birds roam freely across the countryside and ocean waves curl into the salt marshes. The Creole Nature Trail provides extraordinary natural scenery formed from the interactions of the Gulf of Mexico and the Louisiana lowlands.

Mineral soils and higher ground form cheniers. The most significant of these ridges is Blue Buck Ridge. The chenier ridges are where the live oaks grow, offering a habitat for songbirds.

HIGHLIGHTS

This tour begins in Sulphur, Louisiana, heads south to the Gulf of Mexico, and turns east toward the Cameron Prairie National Wildlife Refuge.

Sulphur: At Sulphur, the area is characterized by rolling pastureland that gradually turns to wetland.

Hackberry: In Hackberry, you find an abundance of shrimp and crab houses along Kelso Bayou. Here, seafood is cheap and plentiful. There are also numerous bait shops and outfitters that offer gear and advice for anglers.

Sabine National Wildlife Refuge: The refuge includes the 1½-mile self-guided Marsh Trail with interpretation stations, an observation tower, and panoramic view of marsh terrain.

Holly Beach: Also known as the Cajun Riviera, Holly Beach provides 25 miles of year-round beaches, campsites, accommodations, and a variety of outdoor recreation.

Sabine Pass Lighthouse

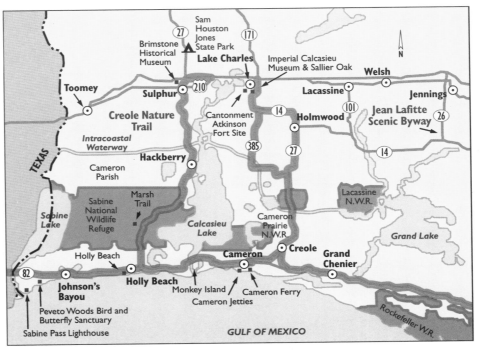

MAINE

Acadia Byway

Acadia National Park spreads across much of Mount Desert, a mainland-hinged island. The Loop Road hugs the ocean and shore, accessing hiking trails, bicycle paths, and the top of Cadillac Mountain.

Fog is a common sight along this byway, muting the landscape with its romantic gray mists. In the midday sun, the sea's bright blue surface is studded with colorful lobster buoys. Seen at sundown from Cadillac Mountain, the sea glows in soft pinks, mauves, and golds.

QUICK FACTS

Length 40 miles.

Time to Allow Three hours.

Considerations
The Park Loop Road is closed from late November to mid-April. Other roads can be closed during extreme weather conditions.

Intrinsic Qualities

Archaeological: Deep shell heaps suggest Native American encampments dating back 6,000 years in Acadia National Park. The Wabanaki Indians called Mount Desert Island *Pemetic,* or "the sloping land." They built bark-covered conical shelters and traveled in delicately designed birch bark canoes.

Cultural: Perhaps the best-known sights along the coast are the lobster traps and colorful buoys. Catching lobster has been a profitable activity in Maine since the 1840s. While the lobster boats are not the same wooden dories originally used, they are still a unique sight along the waters.

Historical: Samuel de Champlain led the French expedition that landed on Mount

Bar Harbor

Desert on September 5, 1604. The land was in dispute between the French to the north and the English to the south. After British troops triumphed at Quebec in 1759, lands along the Maine coast opened for English settlement. Soon, an increasing number of settlers homesteaded on Mount Desert Island. By 1820, farming and lumbering vied with fishing and shipbuilding as major occupations. Outsiders—artists and journalists—revealed and popularized the island to the world in the mid-1800s.

Mount Desert, still remote from the cities of the East, became a retreat for prominent people of the times. The Rockefellers, Morgans, Fords, Vanderbilts, Carnegies, and Astors chose to spend their summers on the island.

Natural: Acadia Byway runs right along Acadia National Park, home to a menagerie of wildlife that captivates the most experienced nature watcher. Whether you yearn to catch a glimpse of whales and seals or native and migratory birds, Acadia offers it all.

Although finback, minke, and right whales can be seen in the Gulf of Maine, humpbacks are among the most playful whales. They are known for spy hopping (sticking their heads out of the water to look around), lobe tailing (throwing the lower half of their bodies out of the water), and tail slapping.

Acadia is an especially fertile area for bird sightings. In fact, 338 species—some migratory and some native—frequent the area.

Recreational: Relatively small at only 13 miles wide and 16 miles long, Acadia National Park offers a multitude of activities. Acadia maintains 45 miles of carriage roads for walking, riding, biking, and skiing and more than 100 miles of trails just for hiking. Situated right along the coast, the area is perfect for boating, sailing, and kayaking.

Scenic: Park Loop Road, constructed specifically to take visitors through the variety of sights that Acadia has to offer, leads you along a path of breathtaking delight. The views from Acadia's mountaintops encompass shadowy forests, gleaming lakes, hushed marshes, bold rocky shores, and coastal islands.

HIGHLIGHTS

This tour begins at the north end of the national park and travels south along the coastline.

Visitor Center: Pick up some brochures at the visitor center near Hull's Cove. If you're planning to hike, you'll want to know how difficult each hiking trail is so that you can plan according to your level of expertise.

Bar Harbor: Spend time in the city of Bar Harbor, soaking in the relaxed atmosphere, eating at a charming restaurant, and exploring a few of the hundreds of specialty shops or the nightlife.

Dorr and Champlain Mountains and The Tarn: Spend the day hiking around Dorr and Champlain Mountains and The Tarn.

Thunder Hole, Otter Cliffs, Otter Point, and Cranberry Islands: Make sure to hit these simply remarkable sights. You can also hop a ferry for whale-watching.

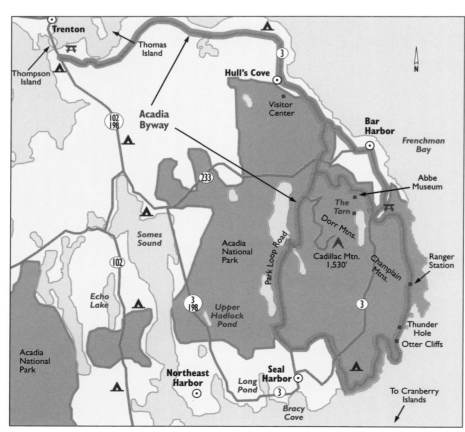

MARYLAND, WEST VIRGINIA, PENNSYLVANIA, OHIO, INDIANA, AND ILLINOIS

Historic National Road

Once nothing more than a buffalo trace, the National Road became the nation's first interstate route in the early 19th century. Follow in the footsteps of George Washington and Daniel Boone over one of the most historic roads in America.

As America entered the 19th century, the young nation faced one of its first challenges: how to link the people and cities along the Eastern Seaboard to those on the frontiers west of the Allegheny Mountains. The solution was the National Road, which ultimately passed through six states on its way from the Atlantic Ocean to the Mississippi River.

Cahokia Mounds State Historic Site

Intrinsic Qualities

Archaeological: Prehistoric civilizations once dominated the land surrounding what is now known as the Historic National Road. The Cahokia Mounds State Historic Site bisects the Historic National Road in Illinois. This remarkable World Heritage Archaeological Site consists of the largest mound buildings constructed by Native Americans on the continent.

Native Americans found flint for tools at Ohio's Flint Ridge State Memorial. Flint from Ohio has been found from the Atlantic Seaboard to Louisiana. Flint was so important, in fact, that it was made the state gem of Ohio.

Historical: The National Road was the first federally funded highway in the United States. Conceived by President Thomas Jefferson and authorized by Congress in 1806, the road ran from Cumberland, Maryland, west to Vandalia, Illinois. Designed to connect with the terminus of the C&O Canal in Cumberland, the National Road gave agricultural goods and raw materials from the interior direct access to the eastern seaboard. It also encouraged Americans to settle in the fertile plains west of the Appalachians. For the first time in the United States, a coordinated interstate effort was organized and financed to survey and construct a road for both transportation purposes and economic development.

The major engineering marvels associated with the National Road may have been the bridges that carried it across rivers and streams. These bridges came in a wide variety of styles and types and were made of stone, wood, iron, and later, steel. As this diversity indicates, an amazing variety of skills were used to build the road: Surveyors laid out the path; engineers oversaw construction; carpenters framed bridges; and masons cut and worked stones for bridges and milestones.

Cultural: The route of the Historic National Road is a road of history. The National Road was developed from existing Native American pathways and, by the 1840s,

Continued on page A-13

HIGHLIGHTS
This tour begins in Baltimore, Maryland, and ends in Collinsville, Illinois.

MARYLAND:
B&O Railroad Museum: America's first commercial railroad was chartered in Baltimore in 1827, an event commemorated by the B&O Railroad Museum.

Antietam National Battlefield: Fought on September 17, 1862, as Confederate General Robert E. Lee attempted to invade the North, the Battle of Antietam has entered the history books as the bloodiest day of the Civil War.

Chesapeake and Ohio Canal National Historical Park: A popular hiking and bicycling route, the towpath of the Chesapeake and Ohio Canal parallels the Potomac River for 184½ miles from Washington, D.C., to Cumberland.

PENNSYLVANIA:
Fort Necessity National Battlefield: This is the site of George Washington's only military surrender.

Fallingwater: One of the most celebrated buildings of the 20th century, architect Frank Lloyd Wright's Fallingwater perches dramatically above a small waterfall on Bear Run. Built in the 1930s as a vacation retreat, it aptly illustrates Wright's concept of "organic architecture."

WEST VIRGINIA:
Wheeling Custom House: Completed as the Civil War began, the stately Wheeling Custom House has been dubbed "the birthplace of West Virginia."

OHIO:
National Road/Zane Grey Museum: Mile markers, a 136-foot diorama, vehicles, and films tell the tale of the Historic National Road, as a collection of memorabilia interprets the life of area native and western novelist, Zane Grey.

QUICK FACTS

Length 825 miles.

Time to Allow Two to nine days.

Considerations
High seasons are spring and fall. Blooming flowers and plants make spring quite colorful. Fall has its own colors, of course, and may offer community festivals along the way. Some delays may be experienced during severe weather, and seasonal storms may increase driving times.

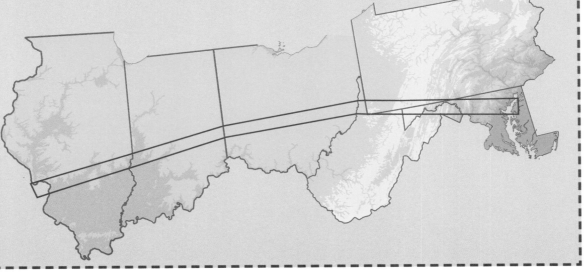

Historic National Road

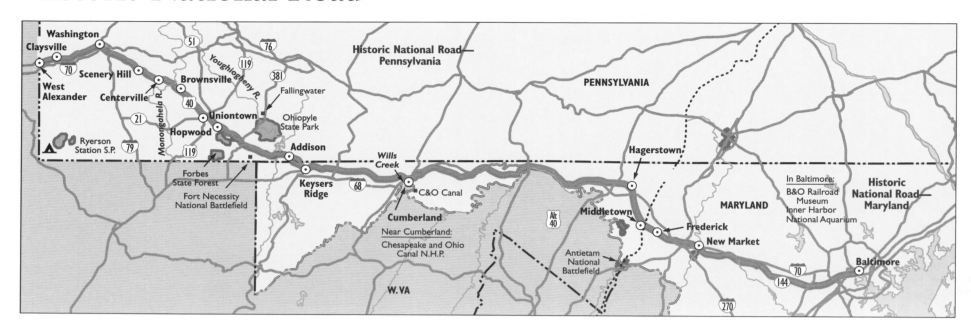

Greenfield, Indiana

Brick Road

was the busiest transportation route in America. Over its miles lumbered stagecoaches, Conestoga wagons with hopeful settlers, and freight wagons pulled by braces of mules—along with peddlers, caravans, carriages, foot travelers, and mounted riders. In response to demand, inns, hostels, taverns, and retail trade sprang up. The National Road is now lined with later automobile-era structures, such as gas stations, diners, and motels.

Natural: First a Native American trail cutting through the mountains and valleys, and then a primitive wagon trail to the first federal highway, the National Road is surrounded by views of pristine hardwood forests blanketing rolling hills, vintage homes and barns, historic farmlands, orchards, and hunting grounds.

The road starts with the picturesque shores of the Chesapeake Bay and the towering mountains surrounding Cumberland, then makes its way west into West Virginia and Pennsylvania. In Ohio, the diverse byway traverses steep wooded hills and valleys in the east and gently rolling farmland in the west. Different species of wildlife make their homes along the route, and fish are plentiful in the many lakes and rivers. The mighty Mississippi River lies at the road's west end in Illinois.

Recreational: The byway offers many recreational opportuni-

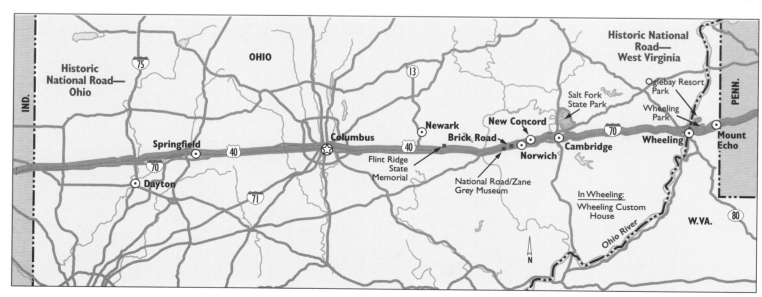

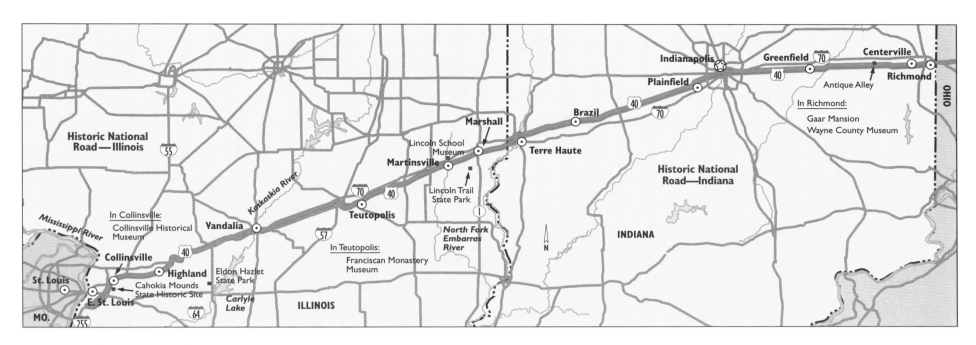

Fallingwater

ties. Along portions of the byway, you can hike, camp, fish, hunt, and picnic, while relishing the various species of local flora and fauna. Numerous state parks allow you to enjoy the natural characteristics of the byway; many of the towns have parks and recreational facilities. In Ohio, for example, more than 50,000 acres of state parks, forests, and wildlife areas are easily accessible from the byway. West Virginia offers Oglebay Resort, a major regional recreation center that is also home to a zoo, a mansion museum, and a glass museum.

Scenic: The Historic National Road is a combination of scenes from rural communities, small towns, and a metropolitan city. This combination makes the byway a scenic tour along one of the most historically important roads in America. Small-town antique shops and old-fashioned gas pumps dot the byway. Broad views of cultivated fields, distant barns and farmhouses, and grazing livestock dominate the landscape. In other areas, courthouse towers, church steeples, and water towers signal approaching communities that draw you from the open areas into historic settlements. The topography of the land affords vistas down the corridor and glimpses into natural areas that sit mostly hidden in the rural landscape.

HIGHLIGHTS

Continued from page A-11

Brick Road: This one-mile stretch of the National Road's former path in Norwich offers a glimpse into the past. Paved entirely with bricks, a popular pavement in the early 20th century, the road is open to cars.

INDIANA:
Centerville: One of the first pike towns to develop along the National Road, this historic community is in the middle of Indiana's Antique Alley. It is home to 100 structures listed in the National Register, many of which are connected by brick archways.

Greenfield: The small town, rich with local flavor, is revitalizing its downtown. Historic buildings are preserved, with new construction underway.

Indianapolis: The center of Indiana's National Road is also its state capital. Downtown Indianapolis offers a growing array of activities and attractions.

ILLINOIS:
Lincoln School Museum: This quality museum is located near Martinsville. The building itself was built in 1888, and the school is open to groups for an interpretation of early pioneer days.

Franciscan Monastery Museum: Dating to 1858, this historic monastery has a wonderful museum that displays artifacts from early settlers as well as the Franciscan Fathers.

The Bissonnette Gardens at Oglebay Resort

Lantz House in Centerville, Indiana

MISSISSIPPI, ALABAMA, AND TENNESSEE

Natchez Trace Parkway

Part of a 445-mile, three-state route, the scenic parkway follows the historic late 18th- and early 19th-century footpath north from Natchez to the Ohio River Valley. This multistate byway starts in Mississippi and runs through Alabama and Tennessee.

At first, the Natchez Trace Parkway was probably a series of hunters' paths that slowly came together to form a trail leading from the Mississippi River over the low hills into the Tennessee Valley. Over time, these paths were gradually linked and used for transportation, communication, and trade. By 1785, Ohio River Valley farmers searching for markets had begun floating their crops and products down the rivers to Natchez or New Orleans. Since the late 1930s, the National Park Service has been constructing a modern parkway that closely follows the course of the original trail.

commemorate the historical significance of the Old Natchez Trace as a primitive trail that stretched some 500 miles through the wilderness from Natchez, Mississippi, to Nashville, Tennessee. Although generally thought of as one trail, the Old Natchez Trace was actually a number of closely parallel routes. These probably started as game trails that were adopted by the region's early human inhabitants.

Natural: The Natchez Trace Parkway encompasses a diversity of natural resources. The motor road cuts through six major forest types and four major watersheds. Within the parkway's land, approximately 800 species of plants help to support 57 species of mammals, 216 species of birds, 57 species of reptiles, 36 species of amphibians, and a variety of other animals.

Recreational: Take in one of the many museums located on

Rosalie House

Vicksburg National Military Park

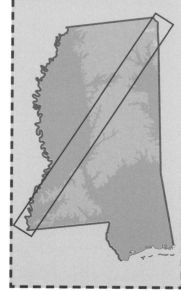
Intrinsic Qualities

Archaeological: Archaeological sites in this area date from the Paleo-Indian period (about 12,000–8000 B.C.) through historic Natchez, Choctaw, and Chickasaw settlements (A.D. 1540–1837). Campsites, village sites, stone quarry sites, rock shelters, shell heaps, and burial sites are among the numerous archaeological treasures that have been uncovered here.

Cultural: The people who live along this parkway embody its rich culture. Southern traditions and hospitality are apparent as you meander through the heart of Dixie. From Natchez to Nashville, the people along the Natchez Trace Parkway are a diverse lot who embrace a number of traditions, from great home cooking and barbecue to some of the best-sounding blues music on the planet.

Historical: The Natchez Trace Parkway was established to

Old Natchez Trace

HIGHLIGHTS

Start in Natchez, Mississippi, and end in Nashville, Tennessee.

Natchez: The historic Mississippi River port of Natchez boasts a number of palatial homes that are open to the public, such as Rosalie House or Melrose, a national historical park site and former home of John McMurran, a prominent northern lawyer before the Civil War.

Emerald Mound: Dating to A.D. 1250, Emerald Mound is, at 35 feet tall, the second-largest Native American temple in the country and a national historic site. It covers eight acres.

Mount Locust: Take a quick tour of Mount Locust. Dating back to the 1780s, it is a rustic inn, or "stand," one of the first that provided food and shelter along this trail.

Sunken Trace: Here are three sections of the original trace that show what the route was like long before the asphalt era.

Rocky Springs Site: A church and cemetery mark the site of the once prosperous town of Rocky Springs. In the 1790s, the rural community grew to more than 2,600 residents. But by 1920, the Civil War, yellow fever, the boll weevil, and erosion had devastated the town. Now a ghost town, it is still worthy of a stop.

Vicksburg National Military Park: Vicksburg's major attraction is this national military park, where on July 4, 1863, Union General Ulysses S. Grant's army captured the city and its bluffs overlooking the Mississippi River.

Jackson: Mississippi's state capital is an attractive river city with fine museums and parks. Of particular note is the Old Capitol, a Greek Revival landmark that was the state's seat of power from 1838 to 1903.

Jeff Busby Site: The campground at Jeff Busby Site is named for Thomas Jefferson Busby, who introduced a bill in Congress that led to the creation of the Natchez Trace Parkway.

Tupelo National Battlefield: Fought on July 13–15, 1864, the battle resulted in a Union victory over the guerrilla troops of General Nathan Bedford Forrest.

Elvis Presley Birthplace: The king of rock 'n' roll was born in a humble two-room abode in sleepy Tupelo on January 8, 1935. The house is now a museum with a variety of exhibits.

Freedom Hills Overlook: A steep quarter-mile trail in the midst of a wildlife management area climbs to the highest point on the parkway—800 feet.

the byway, or take a hike among the dogwood groves. The byway is also home to many historic battlefields, which allow visitors a glimpse into the region's Civil War history. Another approach is to pack a picnic and tour a few of the many Southern mansions along the route or hunt for souvenirs in one of the many quaint shops along the way.

Scenic: From blossoming flowers and trees to historical Native American earthen mounds, the Natchez Trace Parkway offers scenic vistas at every turn.

Coon Dog Memorial Graveyard: An Alabama curiosity, more than 100 coon dogs—and only coon dogs—have been buried here since 1937.

Buzzard Roost Spring: Levi Colbert, a Chickasaw Indian chief, operated an inn, or "stand," nearby. His story is told in exhibits.

Colbert Ferry Park: In the trace's heyday, George Colbert operated an inn and a river ferry here. There are facilities for swimming, fishing, and boating.

Rock Spring: A short trail follows Colbert Creek. It is one of many easy trails along the trace that offer motorists a chance to climb from behind the wheel.

McGlamery Stand: This village still bears the name of an old stand that has long since disappeared.

Sweetwater Branch Nature Trail: A swift, crystalline stream runs along the route of this short trail of about a mile.

Napier Mine: This 19th-century open pit mine was worked for iron ore.

Metal Ford: Travelers crossed the Buffalo River here; an ironworks and McLish's Stand were nearby.

Meriwether Lewis Monument: A campground, picnic area, ranger station, and the grave of Meriwether Lewis (of Lewis and Clark fame) are here.

Old Trace: Here the trace marked the boundaries of the Chickasaw lands ceded to the United States in 1805 and 1816.

Tobacco Farm: Exhibits at the farm and barn explain tobacco growing.

Sheboss Place: This is the site of another of the stands that once served travelers on the trace.

Jackson Falls: Named for Andrew Jackson, the falls are on the intermittent Jackson Branch that empties into the Duck River.

Tennessee Valley Divide: When Tennessee joined the Union in 1796, this watershed was the boundary between the United States and the Chickasaw nation.

Garrison Creek: Named for a nearby 1801–1802 U.S. Army post, this area is a trailhead for horseback riders and hikers.

Nashville: The "Country Music Capitol of the World" has plenty of diversions, including the Grand Ole Opry, the Parthenon, and the Country Music Hall of Fame.

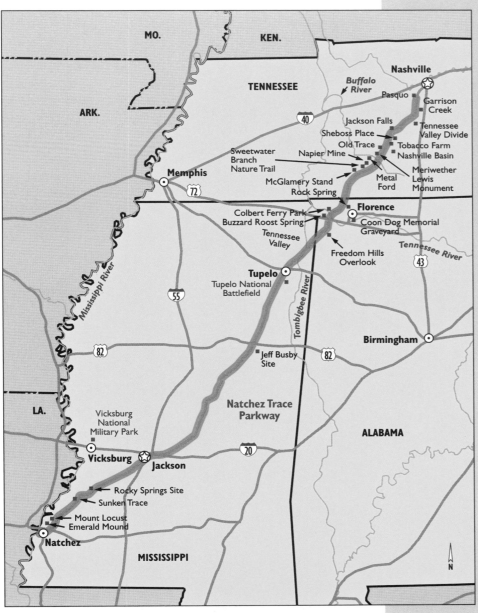

MONTANA AND WYOMING

Beartooth Highway

With the rugged peaks of the glacier-flanked Beartooth Range as a backdrop, this stunning highway travels through three national forests to Yellowstone National Park.

Since its completion in 1936, the Beartooth Highway has provided millions of visitors with a rare opportunity to see the transition from a lush forest ecosystem to alpine tundra in the space of a few miles. The Beartooths are one of the most rugged areas in the lower 48 states, with 20 peaks higher than 12,000 feet in elevation and plenty of glaciers. This byway journeys into parts of the Custer, Shoshone, and Gallatin National Forests.

Historical: The first recorded travel across the Beartooth Pass area occurred in 1882, when General Philip Sheridan and a force of 129 soldiers and scouts (and 104 horses and 157 mules) pioneered and marked a route across the mountains from Cooke City to Billings. A year later, a packer named Van Dyke modified the trail and located a route off the Beartooth Plateau into Rock Creek and Red Lodge. Van Dyke's trail was the only direct route between Red Lodge and Cooke City until the Beartooth Highway was constructed in 1934 and 1935. Remnants of Van Dyke's trail are visible from the Rock Creek Overlook parking lot, appearing as a Z on the mountain.

Natural: A variety of theories exist concerning the formation of the Beartooth Mountains, but geologists generally agree that the mountains resulted from an uplifting of eroded metamorphic rocks. Glaciers shaped the Beartooths into the range they are today. Along the Beartooth Front, the Pal-

QUICK FACTS

Length 69 miles.

Time to Allow Three hours.

Considerations Driving from Red Lodge to Cooke City (east to west) in the morning and west to east in the afternoon reduces glare. The alpine climate is rigorous, and severe weather conditions can occur any month of the year. Summer temperatures range from the 70s on sunny days to below freezing during sudden snowstorms. Snow conditions might close sections of the drive. The byway is generally closed due to snow from October through April.

Intrinsic Qualities

Archaeological: Even though Native Americans dwelt in various places throughout present-day Montana and Wyoming, archaeological evidence from the Beartooth Mountains is somewhat limited. The high elevation most likely restricted anyone from living there on a permanent basis. There is only a short time during the summer to hunt and gather plants specially adapted to high elevations before the cold returns. The rest of the year, deadly weather conditions contribute to making it a hostile environment. The fact that Native Americans came here nonetheless, rather than staying in the fertile and more comfortable plains in the low country, can mean only that the steep mountains held deep significance for them.

Shoshone National Forest

HIGHLIGHTS

The following itinerary begins in Red Lodge and journeys west to Cooke City.

Red Lodge: Red Lodge was a boomtown of the late 1880s, growing quickly after coal was discovered and mines started popping up throughout the area. Although mining coexisted with ranching and agriculture for a number of years, that industry closed down by the middle of the 20th century. Today tourism feeds the economy, which sees people from around the world arrive in search of skiing and the sights of Yellowstone National Park.

Vista Point Scenic Overlook: The Rock Creek Vista Point Scenic Overlook is packed with information. Interpretive panels portray the history of the Beartooth road and mining in the Rock Creek Valley. They also provide details about alpine wildlife and ecosystems. Follow the short hiking trail to a ridge that will provide you with an outstanding view.

Beartooth Plateau: Traversing the Beartooth Plateau will take you to the Beartooth Pass, which is 10,947 feet above sea level. Enjoy the beautiful scenery of the Shoshone National Forest to the south. Don't forget, you are a relative newcomer to this area—the earliest recorded travel through this pass occurred in 1882.

Absaroka Range: On the north side of the highway looms the Absaroka and Beartooth mountain ranges. Keep a lookout for Granite Peak, Montana's highest point at 12,799 feet. Absaroka is the name the Crow nation had for themselves. Much of south-central Montana was inhabited by the Crow prior to the arrival of Europeans.

Clay Butte Lookout: An old fire lookout, this site now affords panoramic vistas of dozens of mountains over 11,000 feet and the overall Beartooth Plateau. Inside the lookout, there are interpretation displays of the 1988 wildfires.

Crazy Creek Campground: Picnicking and camping facilities are available at Crazy Creek Campground. Directly across the highway from the campsite, crystal clear water spills out of the high country from hundreds of lakes in the Beartooths at the Crazy Creek Cascade.

Pilot and Index Overlook: Take in the view of Pilot and Index peaks. These two mountains got their names because the Crow nation, trappers, and other travelers used them to keep their bearings. This overlook also provides great views into the Absaroka-Beartooth Wilderness Area.

Cooke City: Another town founded on mining—this time gold—Cooke City is only a few miles from Yellowstone National Park.

Beartooth Lake

isades are sedimentary rocks originally deposited as flat-lying beds in an ancient sea. Thrust skyward, they have become conspicuous spires.

The Stillwater Complex, a body of igneous magma formed along the northern edge of the mountain range 2.7 billion years ago, is one of the most unusual and least understood geologic occurrences in the world. It is the site of the only source of the platinum group of metals in the United States. At the highway's end, Yellowstone National Park has been an active volcanic center for more than 15 million years.

Recreational: Recreational opportunities abound near the Beartooth Highway. You can cross-country ski on the snowfields nearly year-round or hike across the broad plateaus and on trails. Camping, fishing, and wildlife watching are top endeavors.

Visitors can also visit a guest ranch, take a guided horseback trip from Cooke City, bicycle, and downhill ski at Red Lodge.

Scenic: The spire known as the Bears Tooth at Beartooth Pass was carved in the shape of a large tooth by glacial ice gnawing inward and downward against a single high part of a rocky crest. Beartooth Butte is a remnant of sedimentary deposits that once covered the entire Beartooth Plateau. The snowbanks often remain until August near Beartooth Pass, and remnants of some drifts may remain all summer.

In these treeless areas, near or above the timberline, vegetation is often small—a characteristic that is vital to the survival of the plants at this elevation. Wildflowers, often as tiny as a quarter-inch across, create a carpet of color during the 45-day-or-shorter growing season. Mid-July is generally the optimum time for wildflower viewing.

Wildlife varies from the largest American land mammal, the moose, to the smallest land mammal, the shrew. Other animals commonly seen are mule deer, white-tail deer, marmots, elk, and pine squirrels. Birds include the golden eagle, raven, Clark's nutcracker, Steller's mountain bluebird, and falcon.

Mountain overlook

NEVADA

Las Vegas Strip

The most glittering, neon-lit drive in America explodes with visual delights as it leads past exotic and lavish casino resorts. It's the only byway in the country that's more scenic by night than by day.

Often referred to as the Jewel of the Desert, Las Vegas has long been recognized as the entertainment vacation capital of the country. More than 35 million visitors from around the world are drawn to the lights of the strip each year.

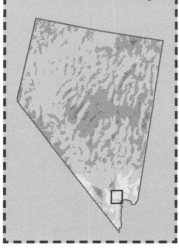
Intrinsic Qualities

Cultural: While Las Vegas is perhaps best known for its gaming culture, the Las Vegas Strip possesses many other outstanding cultural amenities. Some of the world's most talented architects have created complex fantasylands all along the strip. Just a few of the more recent projects include reproductions of the streets of New York, a bayside Tuscan village, the canals of Venice, and replicas of the Eiffel Tower and the Arc de Triomphe.

Many resorts on the Strip also feature world-class art galleries full of paintings by world-renowned artists, such as Renoir, Monet, and Van Gogh. Other resorts hold galleries of unique items, such as antique automobiles or wax figures. The Guinness World of Records Museum offers an interesting array of the unusual, and the World of Coca-Cola features an interactive storytelling theater.

New York–New York Casino

Various hotels on the Las Vegas Strip feature a variety of top-caliber theatrical and dance shows. Several hotels and casinos host world-class sporting events and concerts featuring top-name entertainers.

Historical: The Las Vegas Strip, world-renowned for its neon glitter, possesses an equally colorful historical past. Gambling was legalized in Nevada in 1931, and the first casino opened downtown that same year. Competition was intense, and casino builders were soon looking at land outside the city limits just south of downtown along Highway 91, the area now known as the Las Vegas Strip.

Most of the Las Vegas Strip is not really located within the Las Vegas city limits, but along a corridor of South Las Vegas Boulevard located in unincorporated Clark County. The area was sparsely developed until 1938, when the first resort property was built four miles south of downtown Las Vegas.

In 1941, El Rancho Vegas resort opened for business at the corner of San Francisco Avenue and Highway 91. It introduced a new style of recreation and entertainment to the Nevada desert by combining lodging, gambling, restaurants, entertainment, shops, a travel agency, horse-

Las Vegas Strip

HIGHLIGHTS

This tour of the southern end of Las Vegas Strip begins at Las Vegas Boulevard and Russell Road.

Little Church of the West: The famous "Welcome to Fabulous Las Vegas" sign announces that you're on the right track. On the east side of the strip, you see the Little Church of the West, the site of many celebrity weddings past.

Mandalay Bay: Park the car at the free parking garage at Mandalay Bay (most of the large hotels offer plenty of covered free parking). Explore the tropical-themed hotel, including a fun sand and surf beach. Mandalay Bay is one of the newest hotels on the strip (built in 1999), and that makes it a popular attraction.

Luxor: From Mandalay Bay, you can walk north to Luxor, the great black glass pyramid. (If you prefer, hop on the free tram that takes you right to the front doors of Luxor—you may want to save your energy for later in the trip.) While at this resort, don't

miss the King Tut Tomb exhibit, which is an exact replica of the ancient Egyptian pharaoh's tomb. A rotating IMAX film experience is also a popular attraction here. This unique hotel is amazing. Be sure you don't miss one of the largest atriums in the world.

Excalibur: Take as long as you'd like at Luxor, and then hop on the tram that takes you over to Excalibur. This is the place for an exciting dinner and show. The majestic castle offers adventure at its Fantasy Faire Midway, an arena of games appropriate for everyone in the family.

New York–New York: After spending time at the medieval castle, cross the walkway over the street into New York–New York, inspired by the Big Apple. Billed as "the Greatest City in Las Vegas," New York-New York has attractions that are all themed to the New York life. Park Avenue shopping, a fast-paced Manhattan roller coaster, and Greenwich Village eateries help keep the theme intact.

Monte Carlo: It's not time to stop yet. The Monte Carlo, just north of New York–New York, is just as classy, but with a purely European twist. Stroll through the Street of Dreams to find a taste of France in the cobblestone shopping promenade.

Bellagio: After a jaunt to Monte Carlo, walk farther north, getting close to the halfway point. The big lake and fantastic fountains are part of Bellagio, a hotel that strives for utter perfection. Check out the art gallery here; it houses some fantastic pieces. The gallery has original paintings by Van Gogh, Monet, Renoir, Cezanne, and other masters.

Paris: Now, at Flamingo Road, cross the street to Paris. This is the midpoint of the tour, and this area is full of places to sit and rest or to grab a bite to eat. While at Paris, tour the Eiffel Tower. This is an exact replica, in half scale, of the original in France. The plans for the original were lent to the developers of the hotel so they could be as accurate as possible.

There's also a two-thirds-scale replica of the Arc de Triomphe near the hotel entrance—complete with Napoleon's victories inscribed on it.

MGM Grand: Head back south to the next stop on this tour, the MGM Grand. This very large hotel strives to make visitors feel like stars. Elegance abounds at this hotel. Don't miss the Lion Habitat here: a walk-through tour that showcases beautiful lions, some of which are descendants of Metro, the MGM marquee lion. The only thing separating you and the lions is a glass wall.

Tropicana: Just south of the MGM Grand is the famous Tropicana, home to the longest-running show on the strip: Folies Bergere.

Southern Las Vegas Strip: Finish off the tour of the Southern Las Vegas Strip by driving north back past the Tropicana and MGM Grand and beyond. The drive provides amazing views that you may have missed on the walk.

back riding, and swimming in one resort. Although this resort lasted only two decades, Las Vegas has continued to build on its legacy, developing newer and more elaborate resorts every few years like clockwork.

Recreational: The simplest and easiest recreation on the strip is strolling and sight-seeing along the boulevard. For the more adventuresome, roller coasters featured at several hotels provide rides that twist, loop, and turn for your delight. Other resorts provide 3-D ride films appealing to the senses of sight, sound, and motion. Anyone driving the byway can stop to

see erupting volcanoes, dueling pirate ships, dancing fountains, circus acts, and lush tropical gardens.

Scenic: As one of the most geographically isolated major cities in the continental United States, Las Vegas provides you with an extraordinary visual experience. The strip's incredible array of resorts are constructed

around themes that transport visitors to different exotic realms, including a medieval castle, the Parisian Eiffel Tower, a lakeside Italian village, and a pyramid in ancient Egypt. Day or night, the Neon Trail provides a fascinating foray past spectacular resorts that offer a variety of visual delights to pedestrians and motorists alike.

Bellagio Hotel and Casino

New York

Lakes to Locks Passage, The Great Northeast Journey

Running along Lake Champlain, east of the Adirondacks, the Lakes to Locks Passage transports visitors through a land rich in both old history and new adventures. Come by car, but be sure to carry your bike, kayak, or hiking boots.

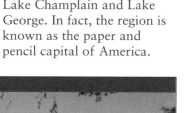

Driving through the villages and hamlets of the Lakes to Locks Passage, travelers are swept into a place of history. State parks and preserves offer hiking trails, lakeside beaches, and wildlife-spotting opportunities.

Lake Champlain

Intrinsic Qualities

Cultural: Residents along the Lakes to Locks Passage look at their part of the country as a working land; the seasons harmonize with the agricultural activities that take place along the byway. From sugar in the winter to strawberries in the summer, the land along the passage is continually productive. This productivity began long ago with the Iroquois and Abenaki, who were able to develop strategies of survival there. The culture along the byway today is one that cherishes resources both agricultural and natural.

During the Industrial Revolution, the rich iron deposits and the forests of the Adirondacks fueled the country. Later, another resource was discovered. Remember that yellow pencil you chewed on in elementary school? Ticonderoga was the name written on the side of the pencil, and it was made from the rich graphite deposits found along the shores of Lake Champlain and Lake George. In fact, the region is known as the paper and pencil capital of America.

Historical: When Samuel de Champlain arrived in the area in 1609, he found people there who loved the land and who struggled for it. The Iroquois were battling against the Algonquin and Huron, who were joined by the French. By 1709, the British had settled the southern end of the passage, while the French had settled the northern end. This separation played a part in the French and Indian War as several different nations fought for control of the land.

The war ended in 1763, when the French ceded Canada to Great Britain. In 1775, American colonists began the Revolutionary War and changed the country forever. The battles at Saratoga were a turning point as the rebels gained control and a new country was formed.

Natural: The natural lakes and rivers of the byway flow through a landscape dotted with mountains. Chasms and forests create scenic places for hiking and adventure. Lake Champlain and its connecting

Lake George

Ausable Chasm

waterways are on the east side, while the Adirondack Mountains are on the west side.

Today, Lake Champlain is one of the largest freshwater lakes in the United States, full of many varieties of trout, bass, perch, pike, and other fish. And fish aren't the only kind of wildlife along the byway. The Lakes to Locks Passage is host to a natural migration via the Atlantic Flyway. From Canada geese to red-winged blackbirds, creatures with feathers are well represented on the byway.

Recreational: Lake Champlain offers a vast array of superb boating and fishing opportunities. Boaters, kayakers, and windsurfers can all find communities with marinas, supplies, and plenty of places to relax. Trout, bass, pike, or perch are the prime angling targets.

The sights beneath the surface of Lake Champlain also interest visitors to the byway. America's best collection of freshwater shipwrecks can be found at the bottom of Lake Champlain, and diving is the best way to see them. Your dive may even include Champ, the legendary Lake Champlain Monster.

At water's edge, Lake Champlain Bikeway is one of the best cycling spots in the country. The route is 363 miles long and goes through many parts of the byway and into Quebec.

Scenic: The passage begins where canals and rivers converge, and then it follows the path of the Champlain Canal where visitors and residents are boating and canoeing. Mount Defiance offers an incredible vista of Lake Champlain, Fort Ticon-

deroga, and Mount Independence in Vermont. At Point Au Roche State Park, the Lake Shore Road guides you through scenic farmland and views of the northern lake islands.

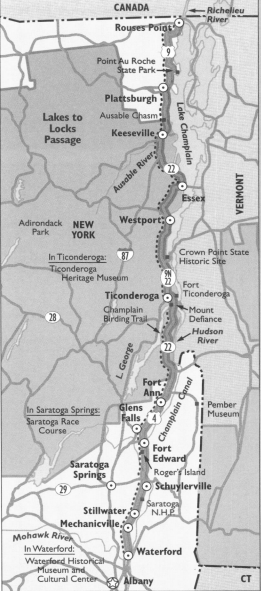

Crown Point State Historic Site

HIGHLIGHTS

Begin the Lakes to Locks Passage in Waterford, and make your way north to Plattsburgh and Rouses Point.

Waterford Historical Museum and Cultural Center: Before you leave Waterford, stop at the Waterford Historical Museum and Cultural Center, located in an 1830 Greek Revival mansion overlooking the Mohawk River and the old Champlain Canal. The museum has exhibits about Waterford, the oldest continually incorporated village in the United States.

Saratoga National Historical Park: The site of a 1777 American victory that marked a key turning point of the Revolutionary War, Saratoga National Historical Park offers a ten-mile auto tour that runs through the battlefield.

Saratoga Springs: To visit the historic resort town of Saratoga Springs, take Route 29 west from Route 4. Saratoga Springs is the site of the beautiful Saratoga Race Course, the nation's oldest thoroughbred racetrack, and a public spa where the rich and famous have long taken the waters.

Adirondack Park: Continue north on Route 4 to Route 22 north. Off to the left are the southeastern fringes of 6.1-million-acre Adirondack Park, the largest park in the lower 48 states. The multiuse park covers much of eastern upstate New York, encompassing dozens of towns as well as recreational lands that include 46 mountain peaks more than 4,000 feet high, some 1,000 miles of rivers, and more than 2,500 lakes and ponds. The byway passes near the eastern shores of resort-lined Lake George and then continues north along the eastern edges of the park for much of the rest of the route.

Fort Ticonderoga and Mount Defiance: Occupying a strategic location at the outlet of Lake George and above the southern tip of Lake Champlain is Fort Ticonderoga, built in 1755 by the French. Americans later captured it from the British in 1775, the first major victory of the Revolutionary War. Daily ceremonies (May to mid-October) feature fife and drum parades and cannon firings. A scenic road leads from the fort up to the summit of Mount Defiance, for great views stretching into Vermont.

Lake Champlain: East of the byway lies Lake Champlain, the sixth largest freshwater lake in the United States. The byway continues along its western shores for most of the rest of the route. The lake is a natural wonderland, ideal for fishing, boating, scuba diving, bird-watching, and bicycling.

Crown Point State Historic Site: Farther north just off Route 9N/22 is Crown Point State Historic Site, where the ruins of two Colonial era forts, St. Frederic and Crown Point, are preserved. They were occupied by a succession of French, British, and American soldiers during the French and Indian War and the American Revolution.

Ausable Chasm: Continue north to Ausable Chasm, a tourist attraction since 1870. The chasm, nearly two miles long and up to 50 feet wide and 200 feet deep, was carved by the Ausable River, which plunges in falls and rapids past sandstone cliffs and huge rock formations. Paths and bridges crisscross and line the chasm, and river rafting trips are available.

Plattsburgh: Near the Canadian border, the city of Plattsburgh is worth a stop. Among the historic homes is the Kent-Delord House Museum, which served as British officers' quarters during the Battle of Plattsburgh in the War of 1812. North of town, ferries leave for Vermont from Cumberland Head 24 hours a day year-round.

NORTH CAROLINA

Blue Ridge Parkway

Unhampered by stop signs and stoplights, this parkway glides along mountain ridge tops, offering nonstop views right and left of quilted fields and toylike towns far below.

The Blue Ridge Parkway is a scenic drive that crests the southern Appalachian Mountains and takes you through a myriad of natural, cultural, and recreational places. The route appeals to both history buffs and outdoor fans.

Intrinsic Qualities

Archaeological: There are many signs of Native American culture and influence along the Blue Ridge Parkway, including that of the Cherokee. Many of the fields still visible at the base of the mountains date back centuries to ancient Native American agricultural methods of burning and deadening the trees and underbrush to provide needed land for grazing and growing. In North Carolina, the parkway enters the Qualla Reservation just southeast of Great Smoky Mountains National Park. Remnants of early European settlements and homesteads are also found along the parkway.

Cultural: Mountain handicrafts are one of the most popular attractions along the byway, and traditional and contemporary crafts and music thrive in the Blue Ridge Mountains. Along the parkway in North Carolina are several places to view and purchase locally made items. The Folk Art Center in Asheville also offers an impressive collection of crafts. Festivals and events occur regularly in local towns and communities, their subject matter ranging from sports to outdoor adventure to drama to folk art.

Historical: The parkway was conceived as a link between the Shenandoah National Park in Virginia and the Great Smoky Mountains National Park in North Carolina and Tennessee. The vision came to slopes of the mountain, the Linn Cove Viaduct, a 1,200-foot suspended section of the parkway, was designed and built. Considered an engineering marvel, it represents one of the most successful fusions of road and landscape on the parkway. The Blue Ridge Parkway was officially dedi-

Mount Mitchell

fruition in 1935. The idea to build the parkway resulted from a combination of many factors, the primary one being the need to create jobs for those people suffering from the Great Depression and for poor mountain families.

World War II halted construction, but work on the parkway resumed soon after the war ended. By 1968, the only task left was the completion of a seven-mile stretch around North Carolina's Grandfather Mountain. In order to preserve the fragile environment on the steep

cated in 1987, a full 52 years after ground was first broken.

Natural: The creation of the Blue Ridge Mountains hundreds of millions of years ago was violent and dramatic. Today, you can witness the flip side to the mountain-building story—the gradual destruction of the world's oldest mountain range. The slow, steady forces of wind, water, and chemical decomposition have reduced the Blue Ridge from proportions along the lines of California's Sierra Nevada range to the low profile seen today.

Linville Falls

HIGHLIGHTS

Although the Blue Ridge Parkway extends north well into Virginia, only the section in North Carolina has so far been designated an All-American Road. This route travels southwest from the Virginia border to the entrance of Great Smoky Mountains National Park.

Cumberland Knob: Cumberland Knob, at 2,885 feet, is where construction on the parkway began in 1935. Today it is a great spot to walk through fields and woodlands.

Brinegar Cabin: This log cabin was built by Martin Brinegar about 1880 and occupied until the 1930s. It is open for tours and is the site of regular craft demonstrations.

Northwest Trading Post: The Northwest Trading Post keeps alive the old crafts within North Carolina's 11 northwestern counties.

Moses H. Cone Memorial Park: This park has 25 miles of carriage roads, ideal for hiking and horseback riding.

E. B. Jeffress Park: E. B. Jeffress Park has a self-guided trail to the Cascades and another trail to the old cabin and church.

Linn Cove Viaduct: Linn Cove Viaduct, a highlight of the parkway and a design and engineering marvel, skirts the side of Grandfather Mountain.

Linville Falls: Linville Falls roars through a dramatic, rugged gorge. Take trails to overlooks.

Museum of North Carolina Minerals: This museum has a display of the state's mineral wealth.

Mount Mitchell State Park: This park has a picnic area and a lookout tower. At 6,684 feet above sea level, Mount Mitchell is the highest point east of the Mississippi River.

Folk Art Center: This center offers sales and exhibits of traditional and contemporary crafts of the Appalachian Region.

Biltmore Estate: This is George Vanderbilt's impressive 250-room mansion and grounds landscaped by Frederick Law Olmstead, designer of New York's Central Park.

Mount Pisgah: Part of the Biltmore Estate became home to the first U.S. forestry school. That tract of land is the nucleus of the Pisgah National Forest.

Devil's Courthouse: Devil's Courthouse is a rugged exposed mountaintop rich in Cherokee legends. A walk to the bare rock summit yields a spectacular view.

Richland Balsam Trail: This trail takes you through a remnant spruce-fir forest. It's the highest point on the parkway at 6,047 feet.

Waterrock Knob: Waterrock Knob provides a panorama of the Great Smokies, as well as a trail, exhibits, and comfort station.

Museum of the Cherokee Indian: Located in the town of Cherokee, near Bryson City, this facility presents the rich history of the Cherokee Indian through a combination of high-tech exhibits and collections of low-tech artifacts.

The biodiversity of the Appalachian Mountains is impressive. Biologists have identified 1,250 kinds of vascular plants, 25 of which are rare or endangered. The reasons for this wide diversity are many. Elevation is a key factor, with parkway lands as low as 650 feet above sea level and as high as 6,047 feet above. The parkway is also oriented on a north-south axis, with its two ends far apart.

Beginning at the parkway's lowest elevations and climbing up to its highest, there are numerous transitions among a variety of forest types. Interspersed among these various kinds of forests are small habitats, such as mountain bogs and "heath balds," where shrubs have taken over altogether, creating jumbled areas that are too overgrown for trees to survive. Many species of animals find their niche in these small pockets of habitat. Bog turtles and Gray's lily, for instance, thrive in mountain bogs. Sheltered, wet coves are excellent homes for amphibious salamanders. A hemlock grove provides a great habitat for the red squirrel.

For birding enthusiasts, the parkway not surprisingly offers a never-ending supply of beautiful birds. Black-capped chickadees replace the Carolina chickadees as you climb up toward the spruce-fir forest. The Blue Ridge Mountains are also home to mountain lions, eagles, and bears.

Recreational: The very nature of the Blue Ridge Parkway allows for outstanding recreational opportunities, such as camping, hiking, cycling, horseback riding, and kayaking. Top outdoor destinations include Moses H. Cone Memorial Park and Mount Mitchell State Park, as well as the parkway's western endpoint in Great Smoky Mountains National Park.

Scenic: The parkway combines awesome natural beauty with the pioneer history of gristmills, weathered cabins, and split-rail fences en route to the country's most popular national park. It encompasses a world of mountain forests, wildlife, and wildflowers thousands of feet above a patchwork of villages, fields, and farms.

Moses H. Cone Memorial Park

MINNESOTA

North Shore Scenic Drive

The North Shore Scenic Drive is home to the Superior Hiking Trail, a 200-mile recreation trail connecting all eight of Minnesota's state parks.

The North Shore of Lake Superior, the world's largest freshwater lake, is 154 miles of scenic beauty and natural wonders. It has what no other place in the Midwest can offer—an inland sea, a mountain backdrop, and an unspoiled wilderness.

Intrinsic Qualities

Historical: It is believed that the first people to settle the North Shore region arrived about 10,000 years ago. These Native Americans entered the region during the final retreat of the Wisconsin glaciation. The first Europeans reached Lake Superior country around 1620. By 1780, fur-trading posts had been established at the mouth of the St. Louis River and at Grand Portage. The late 1800s saw a rise in commercial fishing and mining along the North Shore. Lumber barons moved into the region between 1890 and 1910 and cut millions of feet of red and white pine from the hills in the area.

Natural: The North Shore Scenic Drive follows the shore-line of the world's largest freshwater lake, Lake Superior, which contains 10 percent of the world's freshwater supply. Northeastern Minnesota is the only part of the country where the expansive northern boreal forests dip into the lower 48 states. This environment supports beaver, otter, timber wolf, white-tailed deer, coyote, red fox, black bear, and moose. Federally listed threatened species of bald eagle, gray wolf, and peregrine falcon also have populations here.

Recreational: The North Shore is a primary destination for recreation in the Midwest, with facilities for outdoor activities including camping, hiking, biking, skiing, snow-mobiling, fishing, and canoeing. You might also try touring some of the area's classic historical sites. The Minnesota Historical Society takes care of the Split Rock Lighthouse and provides interpretive programs.

Scenic: The North Shore Scenic Drive offers splendid vistas of Lake Superior and its rugged shoreline, as well as views of the expansive North Woods. The road crosses gorges carved out by cascading rivers, offering views of waterfalls and adding diversity to the landscape. The falls at Gooseberry Falls State Park make this the most visited state park in Minnesota.

Split Rock Lighthouse

Oregon

Hells Canyon Scenic Byway

This Oregon trail is a feast for the senses and opens up endless opportunities for four-season recreation, both tranquil and thrilling. Come along as the byway loops through a landscape dramatically sculpted by nature's artistry.

Leave the fast pace and fenced-in views of Interstate 84, and follow the contours of the land into wilder places. After passing through lush valleys rimmed by snow-tipped mountains, stand next to the majestic Snake River as it begins its tumbling course through North America's deepest canyon.

Wallowa Lake

QUICK FACTS

Length 218 miles.

Time to Allow Eight hours.

Considerations
You won't find any services between Joseph and Halfway, so make sure you have plenty of gas before leaving La Grande or Baker City. Be prepared for both hot and cold temperatures. Wallowa Mountain Loop USFS Road 39, between Joseph and Halfway, is closed from November through February due to heavy snow.

HIGHLIGHTS

The following scenic tour gives you a chance to enjoy the highlights of this byway in a semicircle from west to east and back again.

Wallowa Mountains Visitor Center: Start your summer tour at midday so you can go to this facility about half a mile northwest of Enterprise to get current and detailed information about camping in the mountains or beside the Imnaha River.

Wallowa Lake: This lake, created millennia ago by glaciers, is just the place to relax for a few hours of swimming, fishing, boating, or hiking.

Hells Canyon Overlook: About 30 miles along the byway from the lake, the overlook offers a staggering view, 5,400 feet above the canyon floor.

Snake River: In Copperfield, visitors can take a jet boat tour on the Snake River or rent rafts for a slower-paced look.

Hole-in-the-Wall Slide: This landslide once dammed the Powder River and now covers the original road on the opposite side of the river from the current road.

Intrinsic Qualities

Archaeological: Extremes in the land have dictated the course of the area's natural and cultural history. Relatively mild winters and an abundance of wildlife drew people to the canyon more than 7,000 years ago. Extensive archaeological evidence, ranging from rock art to winter "pithouse" villages, can be found in the Snake River corridor.

Cultural: Northeastern Oregon looks far removed from metropolitan area amenities, but you may be surprised by the availability of arts and culture. Plays, concerts, and living-history productions can be enjoyed in Baker City. The small town of Joseph has earned a national reputation for its bronze foundries and galleries. Eastern Oregon University, located in La Grande, offers theatrical productions and concerts. The historic Elgin Opera House in Elgin is another crowd-pleaser.

Historical: The picturesque Wallowa Valley is the beloved homeland of the Nez Perce Indians. By winter of 1877, settlement conflicts drove young Chief Joseph to make a harrowing attempt to reach Canada with a group of 250 men, women, and children. They struggled to within 24 miles of safety before being captured in Montana and sent to reservations. This area remains a significant religious and cultural center for the Nez Perce.

Natural: Millions of years ago, the Wallowa Mountains formed the coast of what would eventually be called Oregon. Uplifted layers of limestone on the peaks harbor fossilized shells that once sat at the bottom of the ocean. Eons of volcanic action and faulting pushed the masses of rock upward while new land formed to the west. The Coast Range, Cascade Mountains, and upland desert of central Oregon now separate the Wallowas from the ocean by hundreds of miles.

Recreational: The Wallowa–Whitman National Forest, along with county and state parks departments, operates numerous campgrounds, trail systems, viewpoints, and picnic facilities along or near the route. Many visitors hike or mountain bike into the high country.

Spring and summer are great times to fish for steelhead or trout on the region's myriad rivers. In autumn, you can hunt wild animals or capture them on film. Winter's dry, powdery snow adorns area ski resorts and turns backcountry hiking trails into snowshoeing and cross-country skiing routes.

Scenic: The magnificent Snake River twists and churns over boulders and past towering cliffs. Lush valleys lie at the feet of magnificent mountain ranges with peaks that tower to nearly 10,000 feet. Fields of hay, wheat, grass, mint, and canola color the valley floor. Historic barns and houses bring human warmth and scale to the dramatic scenery.

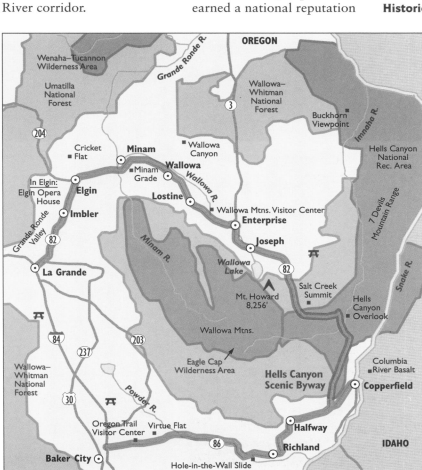

OREGON

Pacific Coast Scenic Byway

This byway by the sea passes fishing ports, oceanfront resorts, rugged cliffs, sandy beaches, dairy farms, windswept dunes, and the occasional migrating whale.

As it travels the length of the Oregon coast, this byway parallels the Lewis and Clark Trail. It makes stops in such spots as the resort town of Seaside, famous for its beachfront promenade, and the city of Tillamook, where the famous brand of cheese is produced.

Intrinsic Qualities

Archaeological: The relics and structures located in this area indicate that people have lived and prospered here for several millennia. Archaeologists have found remnants of spears, knives, and other hunting equipment, as well as bones near campsites.

Cultural: Go to Lincoln City to soar a colorful kite alongside the locals; after that, visit some of Lincoln City's many art galleries. Another popular destination is Bandon, a charming town famous for its lighthouse, its giant sea stacks, its cheese factory, and the cranberry harvest. You might stop in Tillamook and see Oregon's largest cheese factory for a taste-testing tour. This impressive factory has been around for more than 100 years.

Historical: Historical sites on the byway include Fort Clatsop National Memorial, a life-size replica of Lewis and Clark's 1805–1806 winter

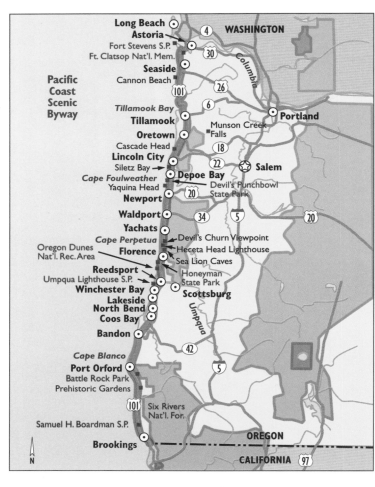

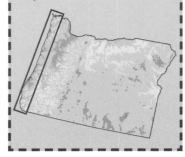

QUICK FACTS

Length 363 miles.

Time to Allow 10 to 12 hours.

Considerations
Slides and floods caused by extreme weather conditions sometimes temporarily disrupt access. Temperatures are comfortably in the 60s and 70s in the summer and rarely drop below freezing in the winter. Be prepared for fog, drizzle, or rain showers any time of year, but mainly in the winter and spring. Steady breezes are common most of the year. At the Oregon Dunes National Recreation Area, temperatures are at their highest and winds are at their lowest during the early fall.

outpost; historic Battle Rock Park in Port Orford, one of Oregon's oldest incorporated towns; and Yaquina Head's lighthouse, a testament to the area's historical shipping industry. Astoria is one of the most historic towns on the Pacific Coast.

Natural: The byway runs along the coastline, bringing highway travelers to the sea and away again, winding by estuarine marshes, clinging to exposed seaside cliffs, passing through gentle agricultural valleys, and brushing against wind-sculpted dunes. Travelers encounter the scenic splendor of sea-stack rock formations that are eroding under constant surf, as well as a plethora of unusual plants and animals that provide natural wonder.

Munson Creek Falls, the highest waterfall in the Coast Range at 266 feet, is an easy side trip from the byway, seven miles southeast of Tillamook. Waysides and state parks along the coast make excellent vantage points for observing gray whales that migrate between December and May.

Recreational: Beaches along the byway are open to public use. In addition, many state

Heceta Head Lighthouse

View from Ecola State Park

HIGHLIGHTS

Consider taking the Pacific Coast Scenic Byway's must-see tour.

Astoria: You will pass through Long Beach and go on to the city of Astoria, the oldest American settlement west of the Rockies. Astoria offers more points of historical interest than any other place on the Oregon coast.

Fort Clatsop National Memorial: For a glimpse into life on one of the most important expeditions in the nation's history, travel three miles east on Alternate (Old) 101 to Fort Clatsop Road and follow signs to the memorial. It is operated by the National Park Service on the site where the Lewis and Clark Expedition spent the winter of 1805–1806.

Seaside: Next you will reach the city of Seaside, which was Oregon's first seashore resort. The Turnaround there is the location of the statue designating the end of the Lewis and Clark Trail. At the south end of the Promenade, you will find the Lewis and Clark Salt Cairn, where members of the expedition made salt from seawater.

Cannon Beach: Cannon Beach, just south of Ecola State Park, is the site of the famous annual Sandcastle Building Contest in early June. The beach was named for the wreckage of the schooner *Shark* that washed ashore in 1846.

Lincoln City: Lincoln City has miles of ocean beaches known for fine agates and other minerals. There are also ocean cruises and whale-watching trips out of Depoe Bay and Newport.

Yaquina Head Lighthouse: The lighthouse, built in 1872 and 1873, has a museum. At 93 feet, it's Oregon's tallest.

Devil's Churn Viewpoint: The basalt that forms the shore here is penetrated by a split in the rock that narrows to a few feet before finally disappearing into the cliff. Fascinating in summer, it is awe-inspiring during winter storms and is an excellent spot for photographers.

Heceta Head Lighthouse State Scenic Viewpoint: This pretty little cove is a great place to see a lighthouse up close.

Sea Lion Caves: These natural caves are home to Steller's sea cows.

parks can be found on the byway and provide public access to beaches. An abundance of public campsites, motels, beach houses, and eateries along the byway corridor ensure a delightful extended stay along Oregon's Pacific Coast Scenic Byway.

Florence is the gateway to the Oregon Dunes National Recreation Area, a 47-mile sandbox with areas designated for bird-watching and dune riding. Visitors can camp, arrange a tour, take an exhilarating off-highway vehicle ride, or just walk along tranquil lakes, forest trails, and beaches.

Tucked in among some of the highest coastal dunes in the world, you'll find plenty of fishing and boating opportunities in small communities such as Winchester Bay and Lakeside. The dunes end near the cities of North Bend and Coos Bay, the coast's largest urban area. As Oregon's deepest natural harbor, Coos Bay has long been a major shipping port for the timber industry and a haven for sport-fishing enthusiasts. Depoe Bay also offers fishing and whale-watching excursions from the world's smallest navigable harbor.

Flying large, beautiful kites is a common practice all along the coast and is especially popular in Lincoln City, which was recognized by *KiteLines* magazine as one of the best places to fly a kite in North America. Annual

Cannon Beach

spring and fall kite festivals draw kite enthusiasts from all over. Get out your kite, and watch with the crowds as the delicate crafts are lofted up into the sky by the strong coastal winds.

Scenic: Keep your camera close at hand so that you can capture the Oregon coast's most photographed seascape, Cape Foulweather and the churning waves at Devil's Punchbowl. The superb scenery continues through Waldport and Yachats to Cape Perpetua. Here, you can

watch the waves rush in and out of Devil's Churn, or you can hike on trails high above it. As the rugged cliffs give way to graceful sand dunes, you'll arrive in Florence, a city that explodes with wild rhododendrons in the spring. The drive into Brookings saves some of the byway's best scenery for last. For example, Samuel H. Boardman State Park shows off nine miles of rocky viewpoints and quiet beaches. The Pacific Coast Scenic Byway ends in redwood country at the California border.

Florence: There are many delightful shops, restaurants, and galleries near the Siuslaw River in this town.

Oregon Dunes National Recreation Area: The Oregon Dunes NRA extends from Florence to North Bend with many access points off the byway.

Umpqua River: The Umpqua River Bridge is one of the historic coast bridges. The Umpqua is a major river in Oregon and is navigable by fairly large vessels upstream as far as Scottsburg.

Cape Blanco: Five miles west of the byway, Cape Blanco was discovered by the Spanish explorer Martin de Aguilar in 1603. The lighthouse is located at the westernmost point in Oregon.

Prehistoric Gardens: In the rainforest atmosphere of the Oregon coast, life-size replicas of dinosaurs fit in nicely.

OREGON AND CALIFORNIA

Volcanic Legacy Scenic Byway

This remarkably varied volcano-to-volcano route leads to lava fields, snowcapped peaks, mountain lakes, historic towns, wildlife refuges, forest vistas, and year-round recreation.

The Volcanic Legacy Scenic Byway stretches from Oregon's Crater Lake to California's Mount Lassen. The volcanic activity of the past has created unique geological formations, such as wavy lava flows and lava tube caves.

Intrinsic Qualities

Archaeological: This byway is rich with ancient Native American artifacts. The Favell Museum of Western Art and Indian Artifacts houses some 100,000 of them in its collections of basketry, beadwork, stone tools, and pottery covering 12,000 years of history.

Cultural: The Klamath nations are an integral part of the communities along the byway because they lived here before anyone can remember. Also, the determination and grit they have demonstrated to survive the changes of years, famine, and new settlers have affected positively the attitudes of other groups who have lived in the area, including the groups who caused their setbacks.

Historical: The Volcanic Legacy Scenic Byway is dotted with historic towns, many of which began as logging communities. McCloud is one example, with the still-functioning McCloud Railway evidence of its logging history. The Weed Historic Lumber Town Museum helps to reveal the part the town of Weed played in the logging industry of the time. Other historical towns along the byway include Westwood, one of the largest company towns in the West during the early to mid-1900s, and Mount Shasta.

Mount Shasta is another site of historical significance along this byway. It has a spiritual history. Native Americans of the area believed Mount Shasta to be the abode of the Great Spirit.

Out of respect, the natives never ascended past the timberline. Fort Klamath, Crater Lake Lodge, and Captain Jack's Stronghold (in Lava Beds National Monument) are structures of historic importance on the byway.

Natural: Six national wildlife refuges have been established in the area: Lower Klamath, Tule Lake, Clear Lake, Bear Valley, Upper Klamath, and Klamath Marsh. These refuges are diverse; they include freshwater marshes, open waters, grassy meadows, coniferous forests, sagebrush, juniper grasslands, agricultural lands, rock cliffs, and slopes. More than 400 different species have been identified in the refuges.

The Volcanic Legacy Scenic Byway allows you to experience the effects of the geological and volcanic history of the region. Lassen Volcanic National Park is located in the southern portion of the byway. The park contains Lassen Peak, one of the largest plug dome volcanoes in the world. Lassen Peak was a major source of the many

geological formations of the area. Lava Beds National Monument, located along the northern part of the byway near California's border with Oregon, is the site of the largest concentration of lava tube caves in the United States. Capping this volcano-to-volcano journey is devastatingly beautiful Crater Lake National Park.

Recreational: The Volcanic Legacy Scenic Byway's length and vast diversity of landscapes provide a wide variety of year-round recreational opportunities. In the summer, you can fish, camp, visit a horse and cattle ranch, whitewater raft, or hike. You can tour a lighted lava tube or spelunk on your own at Lava Beds National Monument, see bubbling mud pots and steam vents at Lassen Volcanic National Park, or drive to an elevation of 7,900 feet on Mount Shasta to view the surrounding landscape. You can also tour the scenic shores of the Upper Klamath Canoe Trail by canoe. Crater Lake National Park is especially good for camping and hiking.

Scenic: The volcanic landscape of the Volcanic Legacy Scenic Byway includes distinctive features of mountain lakes and streams, three volcanoes (all nationally recognized), lava flows, and lava tube caves. However, the

Crater Lake

HIGHLIGHTS

When traveling the byway from north to south, consider following this tour of scenic viewpoints.

Walker Mountain: The view from the fire lookout near Chemult extends from Mount Jefferson in central Oregon to Mount Shasta in northern California. There, you're surrounded by a sea of forest land. The mountain is accessible by high-clearance vehicle only.

Crater Lake National Park: Located 65 miles north of Klamath Falls on Highways 97 and 62, here are the world-renowned views you've seen on postcards and in magazines. Many viewpoints are accessible by wheelchair; some are found at the ends of hiking trails.

Ouxkanee Overlook: A short drive off Highway 97 leads to a picnic area with a stunning overlook of the Williamson River Valley and the surrounding landscape. Scan the horizon as far as Mount Shasta in northern California.

Calimus Butte: This historic, cupola-style lookout was built by the Bureau of Indian Affairs in 1920 and overlooks the scene of the 48-square-mile Lone Pine fire in 1992, as well as Klamath Marsh and Sprague River Valley. It is accessible by high-clearance vehicle only.

Pelican Butte: The summit offers breathtaking views of Upper Klamath Lake and Sky Lakes Wilderness. Old-growth timber lines the narrow, rough road to the top, which takes about an hour and is accessible only by high-clearance vehicle and by foot.

Herd Peak: A gravel road off Highway 97 leads to Herd Peak, where a fire lookout is staffed during the summer months and is open to the public. The summit offers breathtaking views of Mount Shasta and the surrounding area.

Klamath Basin National Wildlife Refuges: Straddling Oregon and California are these refuges, home to a remarkable array of bird life. Those making this drive in October or November can watch for skies filled with geese and ducks; from mid-December to February, hundreds of bald eagles; and in springtime, huge flocks of waterfowl and shorebirds.

Lava Beds National Monument: Lava Beds National Monument, south of Tule Lake National Wildlife Refuge, has weirdly shaped lava formations, cinder and spatter cones, and undulating beds of volcanic rock. It is honeycombed with nearly 400 lava tube caves (two dozen of which are easily accessible to visitors).

Mount Shasta: Now double back to Highway 97. Vistas on the route south are dominated by mighty Mount Shasta, a 14,162-foot snow-capped volcano. At the town of Mount Shasta (where the byway has briefly joined with Interstate 5), consider a side trip up the mountain on the Everitt Memorial Highway.

McArthur–Burney Falls Memorial State Park: Theodore Roosevelt called Burney Falls the "Eighth Wonder of the World." Two cascades spill 100 million gallons of water a day into a deep emerald pool. A mile-long nature trail loops around the park, where there are campgrounds, picnic areas, and a lake.

Lassen Volcanic National Park: The alpine scenery here rivals that of Yosemite, but it's far less crowded. Don't miss Bumpass Hell, where boardwalk trails lead past bubbling mud pots. Hikers find a challenging trail five miles round-trip to the summit of Lassen Peak, which towers over the park at almost 10,500 feet. The trail gains 2,000 feet of elevation and has 40 steep switchbacks.

Lake Almanor: Twenty miles southeast of Lassen Peak along Highway 89 lies Lake Almanor, a good place to relax with fishing, skiing, and several resorts.

volcanic landscape is visible throughout the entire byway. The byway offers extended views of majestic volcano peaks, an abundance of beautiful forest vistas, and up-close views of crisp mountain lakes and streams.

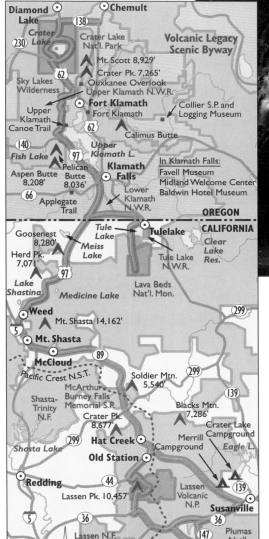

Burney Falls

Mount Shasta

OREGON

Historic Columbia River Highway

Designed to offer incomparable views as it navigates the Columbia River Gorge past waterfalls and wildflowers, this engineering marvel is both a scenic highway and historic landmark.

The Historic Columbia River Highway is exquisite: Drive through the Columbia River Gorge for nearly 50 miles, then encounter a spectacular river canyon that you can often view from the tops of 900-foot cliffs. This is the first scenic highway in the United States to gain the distinction of National Historic Landmark.

Intrinsic Qualities

Historical: Beyond being on the National Register of Historic Places, the Historic Columbia River Highway is also a National Historic Civil Engineering Landmark. The historic district includes several bridges, lodges, viewpoints, and waterfall areas.

Natural: The Columbia River Gorge is a spectacular canyon, 80 miles long and up to 4,000 feet deep, cutting the only sea-level route through the Cascade Mountains. Bald eagles, peregrine falcons, Snake River salmon, and Larch Mountain salamanders also reside here. Wildflower tours of this route are common in the spring.

Recreational: Recreational facilities in the Columbia River Gorge National Scenic Area have national significance, including the three major highways (Historic Columbia River Highway, Interstate 84, and Washington State Route 14) that are used extensively for pleasure driving. The highways provide access to many hiking trails, windsurfing sites, and the Mount Hood Railroad, a scenic and historic passenger and freight route up the Hood River Valley.

Scenic: The corridor contains some of the most dramatic views available anywhere in the country, including the Columbia River, with basalt cliffs and canyon walls; Multnomah Falls, a 620-foot, two-tiered waterfall that is the most-visited natural attraction in the state of Oregon; and giant basalt cliffs and monoliths, including Crown Point, a National Natural Landmark.

QUICK FACTS

Length 70 miles.

Time to Allow Three to five hours.

Considerations Midweek sees the fewest crowds along the byway. Fall has the best weather; spring provides the best time to view the waterfalls. Some attractions are closed in the winter. Also, the byway is narrow and winding, so you may want to consider traveling in a car instead of an RV.

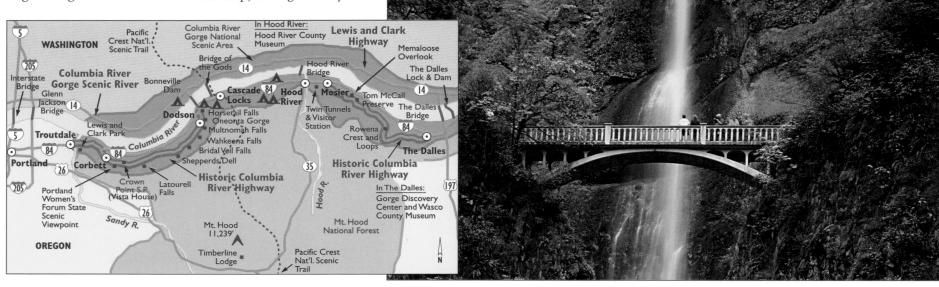

Multnomah Falls

Begin your must-see tour in Troutdale, the western entry point to the Historic Columbia River Highway.

Sandy River: An old iron bridge crosses the river at this point. You can take a side trip to the north to visit Lewis and Clark Park.

Portland Women's Forum State Scenic Viewpoint: This stunning scenic vista is about ten minutes from Troutdale.

Crown Point and Vista House: Take a stroll around the point, and enjoy another wonderful view of the river and the Columbia River Gorge.

Multnomah Falls: Scattered throughout the next few miles are many waterfalls, each with its own history and qualities. The tallest is Multnomah Falls, which plunges more than 620 feet. Take the hike for a closer view.

Oneonta Gorge: Back on the highway, you shortly encounter Oneonta Gorge. This narrow canyon and its associated stream are a cool, dark, and shady hike.

Bridge of the Gods at Cascade Locks: Continuing east, you rejoin the interstate for a while. The Bridge of the Gods at Cascade Locks connects Oregon to Washington.

Hood River: The city of Hood River is the windsurfing capital of the world. Stop and watch expert windsurfers from the riverside or from vantage points along the river.

Memaloose Overlook: This overlook gives you a feel for the transition from the rain forest of the gorge into the drier, wide rolling plains west of Rowena and The Dalles.

Tom McCall Preserve: This preserve, owned by the Nature Conservancy, produces great spring wildflower displays and features two hiking trails.

Gorge Discovery Center and Wasco County Museum: Beyond the switchbacks of the Rowena Loops, this museum offers interpretive exhibits about the human and natural history of the Columbia River Gorge.

The Dalles: End your trip on the Historic Columbia River Highway at The Dalles. You can view the nearby Dalles Lock and Dam or tour the historic district of this city.

UTAH

A Journey Through Time Scenic Byway

As it winds its way through rugged and colorful canyons lying between two national parks, this byway showcases a land of ancient cultures, pioneers, and explorers—with a piece of history beckoning around every turn.

Driving through this byway that connects Bryce Canyon National Park and Capitol Reef National Park, you are treated to enticing views and stops, along with a kaleidoscope of color. Byway towns in between offer a flavor of simple life in the middle of a fantastic wilderness.

QUICK FACTS

Length 124 miles.

Time to Allow One to three days.

Considerations Several stretches of this road are quite isolated and rugged, some with 12-percent grades. The road climbs to 8,000 feet as it crosses Boulder Mountain, rising and falling in steep switchbacks through Escalante Canyons and Boulder Mountain. The Aquarius Plateau/Boulder Mountain segment receives heavy accumulations of winter snow and may be closed temporarily during heavy snowstorms. The Hogsback is narrow and can be windy.

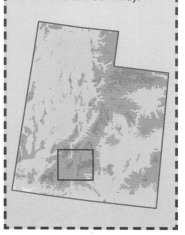

HIGHLIGHTS

This tour starts in the vicinity of Bryce Canyon on the western end of the byway.

Bryce Canyon National Park: This 56-square-mile park is filled with colorful, fantastic cliffs and pinnacles created by millions of years of erosion.

Kodachrome Basin State Park: This state park is home to strange, vividly colored stone pinnacles, believed to be ancient fossilized geysers.

Escalante State Park: The next stop is a petrified forest with mineralized wood and dinosaur bones. The park has a reservoir for swimming, fishing, and boating as well as hiking trails, picnicking, birdwatching, and camping.

Anasazi Indian Village State Park: Near Boulder is this partially excavated village, with a museum that tells the story of the Anasazi people.

Capitol Reef National Park: Off the northeastern end of the byway is 378-square-mile Capitol Reef National Park, where red sandstone cliffs are capped with domes of white sandstone. A 25-mile round-trip scenic drive leads through the park.

Intrinsic Qualities

Archaeological: The Anasazi, Fremont, and Utes all left their mark on the rugged and challenging land. The structures that the Anasazi left behind astound travelers and archaeologists alike. Alcoves high in the rocks hold ancient stone granaries for food storage.

Cultural: The archaeological remains and artwork of the Fremont Indians and the Anasazi enable modern-day experts and visitors to specu-

Escalante River

late about what these people must have been like. These cultures had a belief system of legends and histories that explained the landforms that surrounded them. Mormon pioneers established communities more than a century ago and brought a new collection of stories and histories.

Historical: The first explorers were Spanish and claimed the land for Spain in 1776. The name of the town Escalante comes from one of the priests who was on the expedition, Silvestre Velez de Escalante. John Wesley Powell more thoroughly explored the land nearly 100 years later in 1869 on a treacherous journey on which he lost several of his company. By the time he explored the area, Mormon pioneers had already begun to inhabit the region.

Natural: Red Canyon, Bryce Canyon, and Kodachrome Basin offer some of the strangest geological sites. The walls of Bryce Canyon are lined with singular, humanlike pinnacles that protrude from

the rock. Red Canyon displays a range of orange and red colors in the rock, and trails lead to natural arches. In Kodachrome Basin, evidence of another natural wonder from millions of years ago is in the strange pinnacles of stone. Geologists believe that the towers of stone there are actually fossilized geysers.

Recreational: Some of the most captivating hikes in Utah are located just off A Journey Through Time Scenic Byway in the slot canyons of the Grand Staircase. Red Canyon and its accompanying canyons offer trails for hikers, bikers, horseback riders, and ATV enthusiasts.

Scenic: Spanning a route of more than 120 miles, this byway travels through some of the most diverse and ruggedly beautiful landscapes in the country. The surrounding red rock formations, slickrock canyons, pine and aspen forests, alpine mountains, national and state parks, and quaint rural towns all contribute in making Highway 12 a unique route in terms of scenery.

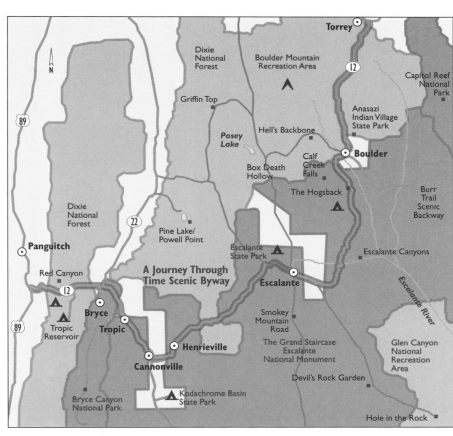

WASHINGTON

Chinook Scenic Byway

Glacier-covered Mount Rainier is the star attraction of this scenic corridor through the Cascades. Ride to what can be a summer playground or a winter wonderland, or just stop to gaze along the way at the regal 14,410-foot volcano.

The Chinook Scenic Byway is possibly the most scenic route crossing the Cascade Mountain Range, and it is the most accessible road for viewing Mount Rainier. At Chinook Pass, the roadway descends dramatically through the Wenatchee National Forest before ending near the fertile valleys of Yakima County.

Intrinsic Qualities

Archaeological: Even though only about 3.5 percent of Mount Rainier National Park has been systematically surveyed for archaeological remains, there are more than 75 known sites in the park, of which 62 have been fully documented and recorded. One dates between 2,300 and 4,500 years ago. Sites just outside of the park hint at much earlier occupation, perhaps as much as 8,000 years. In more modern times, the Nisqually, Puyallup, Muckleshoot, Yakama, and Taidnapam nations came to the area in the summer and early fall to hunt and to collect resources.

Historical: Part of this byway has been designated a National Historic Landmark District. In the 1920s, officials at the park developed a master plan. This was a significant development because it was the first and most complete national park plan developed by the National Park Service Landscape Division. Today the Mount Rainier National Historic Landmark District is one of the nation's finest collections of "national park rustic" architecture.

Natural: Rainier's 25 glaciers form the largest single-peak glacier system in the United States outside of Alaska; the glacier-carved canyon of the Rainier fork of the American River is geologically rare; and the mountain meadows are without parallel in the Cascades or Pacific volcano system. Some 50 species of mammals and 130 species of birds live here. Deer, hawks, owls, and bald eagles all thrive in the forests.

The farther up the mountainside, the wetter and colder. The delicate and elusive calypso orchid blooms here in the spring, and patches of huckleberry bushes abound. Black bears are one of this area's large predators. Above the timberline is a world of extremes. On a summer day, the sun can shine warm and bright, but in just moments clouds can bring a sudden snow or lightning storm.

Recreational: The area surrounding the Chinook Scenic Byway is rife with recreational activities. There are great opportunities for fishing, hunting, hiking, biking, and rafting. Snow sports also abound, given that Mount Rainier and its surrounding area is one of the snowiest places on Earth. Skiing and snowshoeing are among the most popular wintertime activities.

Scenic: The Chinook Scenic Byway takes you through picturesque mountain towns and historical sites and guides you past 14,410-foot Mount Rainier, "the shining jewel of the Northwest." Rainier is the tallest volcano in the 48 continental states and is the largest mountain in the Cascade chain of volcanoes extending from California to the Canadian border.

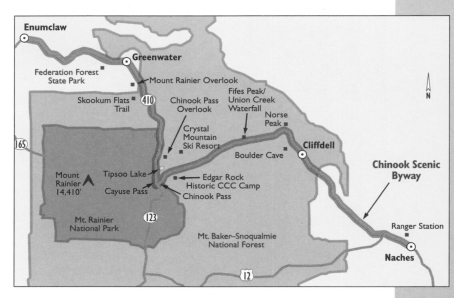

Mount Rainier National Park

QUICK FACTS

Length 85 miles.

Time to Allow Two to three hours.

Considerations Weather can be unpredictable, especially in the winter and spring. Park entrance fees are $10 per car for a week or $5 for those on foot or two wheels.

HIGHLIGHTS

These Chinook Scenic Byway attractions are listed from east to west.

Boulder Cave National Recreation Trail: This short hike leads past a number of different falls on route to Boulder Cave and offers great views of Norse Peak.

Fifes Peak: Here, the road changes to a southwesterly course and passes through old-growth environments that surround Fifes Peak. Union Creek Waterfall can also be found in this area.

Chinook Pass: Edgar Rock Historic CCC Camp is located at Chinook Pass, where the parkway resumes its northwestern direction. Tipsoo Lake is on the eastern side of the parkway shortly after the pass, followed by the Chinook Pass Overlook and Crystal Mountain Ski Resort.

Mount Rainier National Park: Soon after Chinook Pass, you enter Mount Rainier National Park. This national park is known for its recreational, scenic, and natural resources. Goats, chipmunks, and marmots are some wildlife you might see here.

UNITED STATES.........4-5

ALABAMA............6-7
Birmingham..................7
Mobile............7
Montgomery............7
Huntsville.........7
ALASKA............ 8-9
Aleutian Islands............ 8
Anchorage............ 9
Fairbanks............9
Juneau............ 9
ARIZONA............10-11
Flagstaff............ 10
Nogales............11
Phoenix............11
Tucson............11
Yuma............11
ARKANSAS............ 12-13
Little Rock............ 12
Fayetteville............13
Ft. Smith............93
CALIFORNIA............14-17
Bakersfield............15
Fresno............15
Los Angeles/San Diego..18
Los Angeles Downtown..18
Lake Tahoe............ 15
Monterey............16
Palm Springs............17
Sacramento............15
San Diego............18
San Francisco Area........19
San Francisco/
Downtown............15
San Bernadino............18
San Jose............ 19
Santa Barbara............18
Stockton............15
COLORADO............20-21
Colorado Springs............20
Denver............ 20
CONNECTICUT............ 22
Bridgeport............ 22
Hartford............ 22
New Haven............ 22
Danbury............23
Stamford............ 23
DELAWARE............ 23
Dover............ 23
Wilmington............ 23
FLORIDA............24-25
Daytona Beach............ 27
Florida Keys............ 25
Ft. Lauderdale............ 27
Jacksonville............26
John F. Kennedy
Space Center............24
Miami/Miami Beach......26
Orlando............26
Pensacola............ 26
St. Augustine............ 27
Tallahassee............ 26
Tampa/St. Petersburg... 26
West Palm Beach............ 27
GEORGIA............ 28-29
Atlanta............27
Augusta............27
Brunswick/Jekyll Island...27
Columbus............28
Macon............27
Savannah............ 27
HAWAII............30-31
Hilo............30
Honolulu............30
Kahului/Wailuku............ 31
IDAHO............32-33
Boise/Nampa/Caldwell.. 32
Pocatello............ 32
Idaho Falls............32
Lewiston............32
Twin Falls............ 32
ILLINOIS............34-35
Chicago............36
Champaign............37
Decatur............ 37
Peoria............ 37
Rockford............ 37
Rock Island............37
Springfield............ 37
INDIANA............38-39
Evansville............ 36
Fort Wayne............ 36
Indianapolis............ 36
South Bend............ 36
Terre Haute............ 36
IOWA............ 40-41
Cedar Rapids............41
Davenport............37
Des Moines............ 41
Waterloo............37
KANSAS............ 42-43
Kansas City............63
Topeka............42
Wichita............42

KENTUCKY............44-45
Frankfort............ 44
Kentucky Lakes Region.. 44
Lexington............44
Louisville............ 44
Owensboro............44
LOUISIANA............ 46-47
Baton Rouge............46
New Orleans............ 46
French Quarter............ 46
Shreveport............46
MAINE............48-49
Augusta............48
Bangor............48
Lewiston/Auburn............ 48
Portland............ 48
Waterville............49
MARYLAND............50-51
Annapolis............51
Baltimore............50
Cumberland............50
Frederick............ 51
Hagerstown............51
Salisbury............ 51
MASSACHUSETTS............54-55
Boston Downtown............53
Boston & Vicinity............53
Lowell............54
New Bedford............ 54
Pittsfield............54
Springfield............ 54
Worcester............55
MICHIGAN............ 56-57
Detroit............59
Battle Creek............58
Flint............58
Grand Rapids............58
Jackson............58
Kalamazoo............58
Lansing............ 58
Saginaw............58
Sault St. Marie............ 59
Upper Peninsula............58
MINNESOTA............ 60-61
Minneapolis/St.Paul......62
Duluth............62
Rochester............ 62
MISSISSIPPI............ 64-65
Gulfport/Biloxi............65
Hattiesburg............64
Jackson............64
Natchez............64
Vicksburg............65
MISSOURI............66-67
Branson............63
Columbia............63
Jefferson City............ 63
Joplin............63
Kansas City............63
St. Joseph............ 63
St. Louis............63
Springfield............ 63
MONTANA............ 68-69
Billings............69
Great Falls............69
Helena............69
Missoula............68
NEBRASKA............70-71
Grand Island............70
Lincoln............ 71
Omaha/Council Bluffs....71
NEVADA............72
Carson City............ 72
Lake Tahoe............ 15
Las Vegas............72
Las Vegas Strip............ 72
Reno............72
NEW HAMPSHIRE............73
Concord............ 73
Manchester............ 73
Nashua............ 73
Portsmouth............ 73
NEW JERSEY............74-75
Atlantic City............75
Cape May............ 75
Toms River............74
Trenton............75
NEW MEXICO............ 76-77
Albuquerque............77
Las Cruces............ 77
Santa Fe............ 77
NEW YORK............ 80-83
Albany............82
Buffalo............82
Long Island............ 81
Manhattan............78
New York City............78
Niagara Falls............82
Rochester............82
Syracuse............82
Utica............82
Watertown............83
NORTH CAROLINA............ 84-85
Asheville............ 84
Charlotte............ 85

Fayetteville............86
Raleigh/Durham/
Chapel Hill............ 86
Winston-Salem/
Greensboro............86
Wilmington............86
NORTH DAKOTA............87
Bismarck............87
Fargo............87
Grand Forks............87
OHIO............88-91
Akron............ 89
Canton............ 89
Cincinnati............91
Cleveland............88
Columbus............91
Dayton............91
Mansfield............ 89
Sandusky............ 89
Springfield............ 89
Toledo............88
Warren............89
Youngstown............89
OKLAHOMA............92-93
Lawton............93
Oklahoma City............ 92
Tulsa............92
OREGON............94-95
Columbia River Area.......96
Eugene............96
Medford............96
Portland............ 96
Salem............96
PENNSYLVANIA............ 98-101
Allentown/
Bethlehem............97
Altoona............97
Erie............97
Greensburg............97
Harrisburg............97
Hershey............96
Johnstown............97
Newcastle............97
Reading............97
Penn Dutch Country/
Lancaster............97
Philadelphia............ 102
Philadelphia
Downtown............102
Pittsburgh............96
Scranton............97
State College............97
Wilkes-Barre............97
York............96
RHODE ISLAND............ 103
Newport............ 103
Providence............ 103
SOUTH CAROLINA............ 104
Charleston............104
Columbia............103
Florence............ 104
Greenville............103
Myrtle Beach............104
Spartanburg............103
SOUTH DAKOTA............ 105
Black Hills Area............105
Pierre............105
Rapid City............105
Sioux Falls............105
TENNESSEE............ 106-107
Chattanooga............106
Knoxville............ 106

Memphis............106
Nashville............106
TEXAS............108-111
Abilene............111
Amarillo............109
Austin............112
Beaumont............ 111
Corpus Christi............111
Dallas/Ft. Worth............112
El Paso............77
Galveston............111
Houston............ 112
Laredo............111
Lubbock............109
San Antonio............ 112
Texarkana............110
Waco............111
UTAH............112-113
Ogden............112
Provo............112
Salt Lake City............113
VERMONT............114
Burlington............114
Montpelier............ 114
VIRGINIA............116-117
Charlottesville............116
Danville............116
Fredericksburg............116
Hampton Roads............115
Lynchburg............116
Norfolk............115
Richmond/Petersburg...115
Roanoke............116
WASHINGTON............118-119
Olympia............118
Seattle/Tacoma............ 118
Spokane............118
Yakima............120
WASHINGTON DC............52
Downtown............52
Vicinity............ 50
WEST VIRGINIA............ 120
Charleston............121
Wheeling............121
Huntington............121
Morgantown............121
WISCONSIN............ 122-123
Appleton............121
Madison............123
Green Bay............122
Milwaukee............123
Oshkosh............121
Racine/Kenosha............ 122
Sheboygan............122
WYOMING............124-125
Casper............124
Cheyenne............124

CANADA............ 126-127

BRITISH COLUMBIA...128-129
Vancouver/Victoria......128
Vancouver Area............128
Victoria............128
ALBERTA............130-131
Calgary............131
Edmonton............130
SASKATCHEWAN......132-133
Regina............132
Saskatoon............ 132
MANITOBA............ 135
Brandon............ 134

Winnipeg............ 134
NEW BRUNSWICK............140
Fredericton............140
Saint John............ 141
**NEWFOUNDLAND/
LABRADOR............ 141**
Saint John's............ 141
**NORTHWEST
TERRITORIES............9**
NOVA SCOTIA............140-141
Halifax............140
ONTARIO............136-137
Hamilton............136
North Bay............134
Ottawa............136
Sudbury............ 134
Thunder Bay............134
Toronto............ 136
PRINCE EDWARD ISLAND.. 140
Charlottetown............140
QUEBEC............138-139
Quebec............139
Montreal............139
YUKON TERRITORY............9

MEXICO............142-143
Acapulco............143
Guadalajara............143
Mexico City............ 143

PUERTO RICO............143

NATIONAL PARKS
Acadia National Park, ME.. 48
Arches National Park, UT......115
Bryce Canyon
National Park, UT............ 115
Colonial National
Historical Park, VA............ 116
Crater Lake
National Park, OR............ 96
Gettysburg National
Military Park, PA............ 97
Grand Canyon National
Park Village, AZ............ 11
Great Smoky Mountains
National Park, NC/TN......86
Hot Springs
National Park, AR............ 13
Kings Canyon/Sequoia
National Park, CA............ 15
Lassen Volcanic
National Park, CA............ 15
Mammoth Cave
National Park, KY............ 44
Mount Rainier
National Park, WA............ 120
Yosemite
National Park, CA............ 15
Rocky Mountain
National Park, CO............ 20
Hawaii Volcanoes National Park
(Kilauea Caldera), HI............ 31
Waterton-Glacier International
Peace Park, MT/AB............ 32
Yellowstone/Grand Teton
National Park, WY............ 124
Zion National Park, UT............115

REFERENCE
Driving Distances............3
Mileage Table............ 2
U.S. County Index............ 144

MAP LEGEND

ROADS, BOUNDARIES

EXIT NUMBER 405 / INTERCHANGE — CONTROLLED ACCESS	MILEAGE NUMBER / MILEAGE MARKER 5 — PRIMARY UNDIVIDED	- - - - - - TIME ZONE
TOLL CONTROLLED ACCESS	ARTERIAL UNDIVIDED	·········· TRAIL
PRIMARY DIVIDED	STREET, MINOR	— - — - — COUNTY BOUNDARY
▪▪▪▪▪ UNDER CONSTRUCTION	~~~~~ UNPAVED	STATE BOUNDARY
ARTERIAL DIVIDED	· · · · · SCENIC ROUTE	INT'L BOUNDARY

HIGHWAY SYMBOLS

INTERSTATE SHIELDS	U.S. HWY SHIELD	STATE HWY SHIELD	COUNTY HWY SHIELD	INDIAN HWY SHIELD	FOREST HWY SHIELD	AUTOROUTE SHIELD
275 95 BUS 95	101 41	299 60	550 39	5	5	5

SYMBOLS & FILLS

▲ STATE/LOCAL PARK	✈ COMMERCIAL AIRPORT	▲▲△ REST AREAS	⚙ CUSTOM STATION
▲ FOREST	■ POINT OF INTEREST	ⓘ INFORMATION CTR	✸ STATE CAPITAL
☆ WILDLIFE REFUGE	+ PHYSICAL FEATURE	⛷ SKI AREA	◉ COUNTY SEAT
▲ CAMPGROUND	Mt. Olympus	)(MOUNTAIN PASS	• CITY, TOWN

Distances are shown in miles

Routes used to determine these mileages are not always the shortest distance between cities, but are generally considered the easiest route to drive.

This page contains a large triangular distance matrix between North American cities. The cities listed (both as row and column headers) are:

ALBANY, NY; ALBUQUERQUE, NM; ATLANTA, GA; BALTIMORE, MD; BILLINGS, MT; BIRMINGHAM, AL; BOISE, ID; BOSTON, MA; BUFFALO, NY; CHARLESTON, WV; CHARLOTTE, NC; CHEYENNE, WY; CHICAGO, IL; CINCINNATI, OH; CLEVELAND, OH; COLUMBUS, OH; DALLAS, TX; DENVER, CO; DES MOINES, IA; DETROIT, MI; EL PASO, TX; HARTFORD, CT; HOUSTON, TX; INDIANAPOLIS, IN; JACKSON, MS; KANSAS CITY, MO; LAS VEGAS, NV; LITTLE ROCK, AR; LOS ANGELES, CA; LOUISVILLE, KY; MEMPHIS, TN; MIAMI, FL; MILWAUKEE, WI; MINNEAPOLIS, MN; MOBILE, AL; MONTGOMERY, AL; NASHVILLE, TN; NEW ORLEANS, LA; NEW YORK, NY; NORFOLK, VA; OKLAHOMA CITY, OK; OMAHA, NE; ORLANDO, FL; PHILADELPHIA, PA; PHOENIX, AZ; PITTSBURGH, PA; PORTLAND, ME; PORTLAND, OR; RALEIGH, NC; RENO, NV; RICHMOND, VA; ST. LOUIS, MO; SALT LAKE CITY, UT; SAN ANTONIO, TX; SAN DIEGO, CA; SAN FRANCISCO, CA; SEATTLE, WA; SPOKANE, WA; TAMPA, FL; TORONTO, ON; WASHINGTON, DC; WICHITA, KS; WINNIPEG, MB; YELLOWSTONE, N.P.; YOSEMITE VILLAGE

[This is a standard North American city-to-city driving-distance mileage table. The dense triangular numeric matrix contains the mileages between each pair of the cities listed above. The individual cell values are too densely printed and too numerous to reliably transcribe each to its correct row/column intersection.]

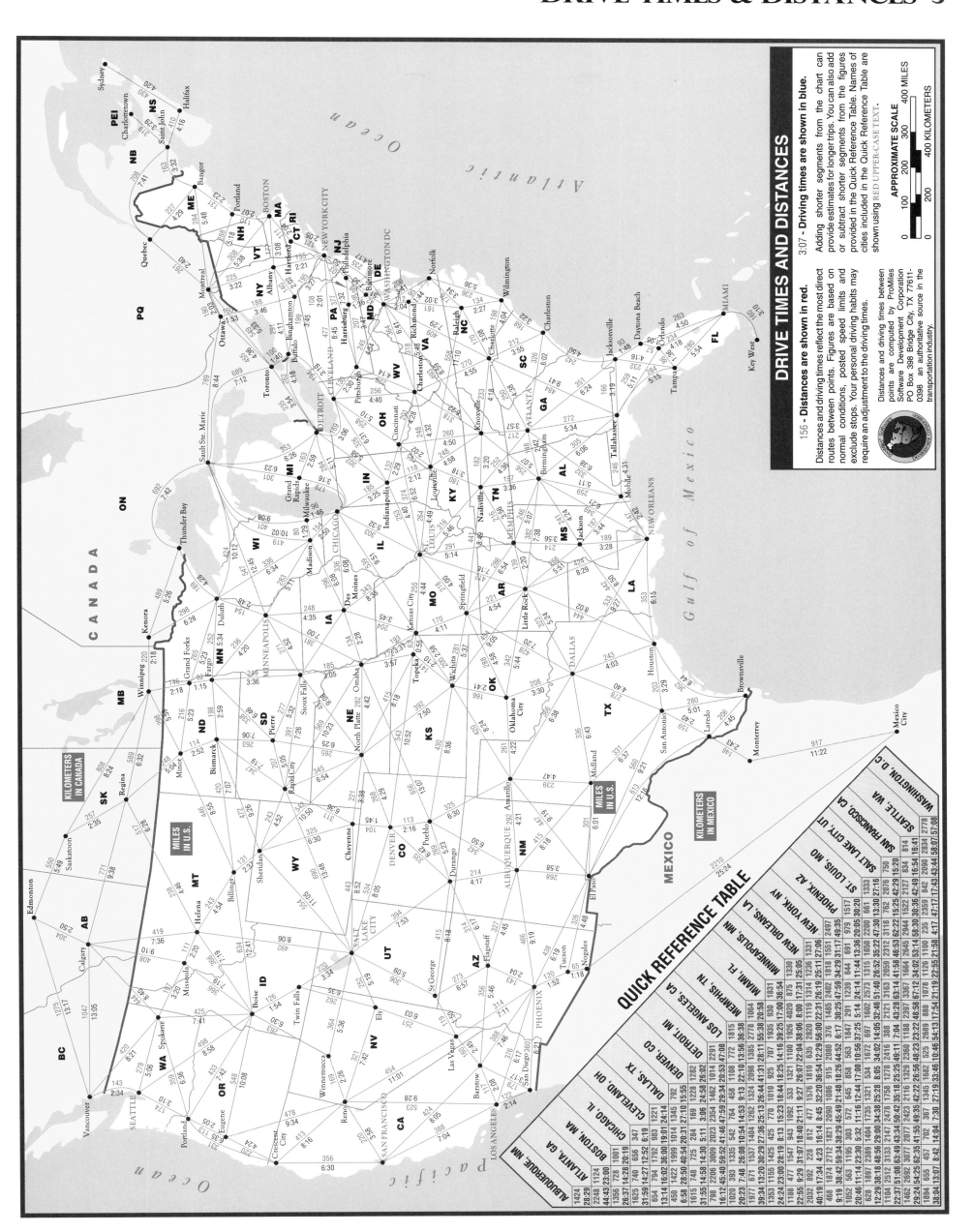

DRIVE TIMES AND DISTANCES

156 – Distances are shown in red.

Distances and driving times reflect the most direct routes between points. Figures are based on normal conditions, posted speed limits and exclude stops. Your personal driving habits may require an adjustment to the driving times.

3:07 – Driving times are shown in blue.

Adding shorter segments from the chart can provide estimates for longer trips. You can also add or subtract shorter segments from the figures provided in the Quick Reference Table. Names of cities included in the Quick Reference Table are shown using RED UPPER-CASE TEXT.

Distances and driving times between points are computed by ProMiles Software Development Corporation PO Box 398 Bridge City, TX 77611-0398 an authoritative source in the transportation industry.

APPROXIMATE SCALE

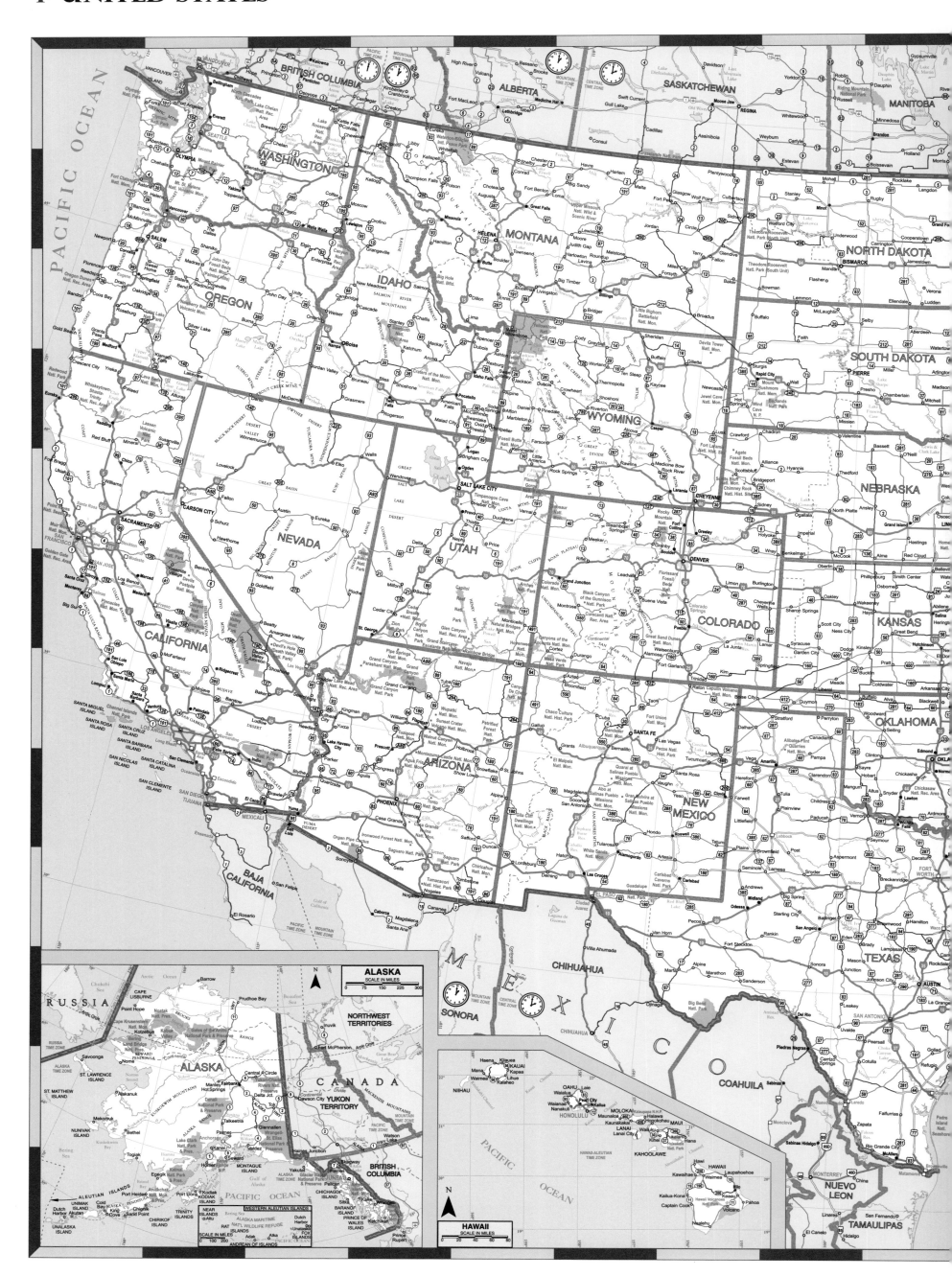

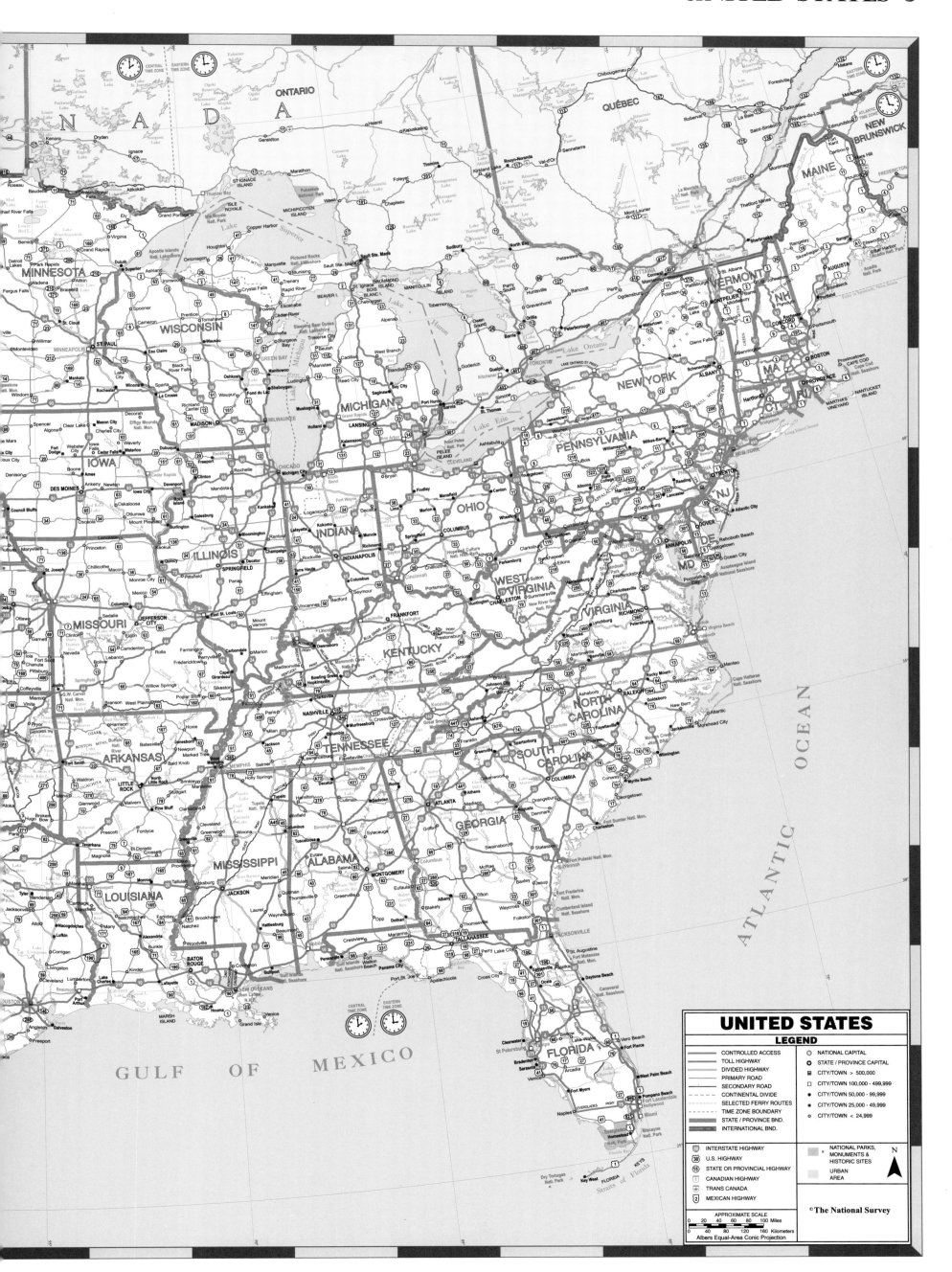

6 ALABAMA

	ANNISTON	BIRMINGHAM	DECATUR	DOTHAN	FLORENCE	GADSDEN	HUNTSVILLE	LIVINGSTON	MOBILE	MONTGOMERY	TUSCALOOSA
BIRMINGHAM	65	0	84	198	120	63	104	116	263	105	60
HUNTSVILLE	105	104	26	299	67	74	0	216	364	194	159
LIVINGSTON	179	116	196	243	188	178	216	0	156	143	63
MOBILE	283	263	344	199	380	321	364	156	0	173	228
MONTGOMERY	110	93	174	105	210	151	194	143	173	0	107

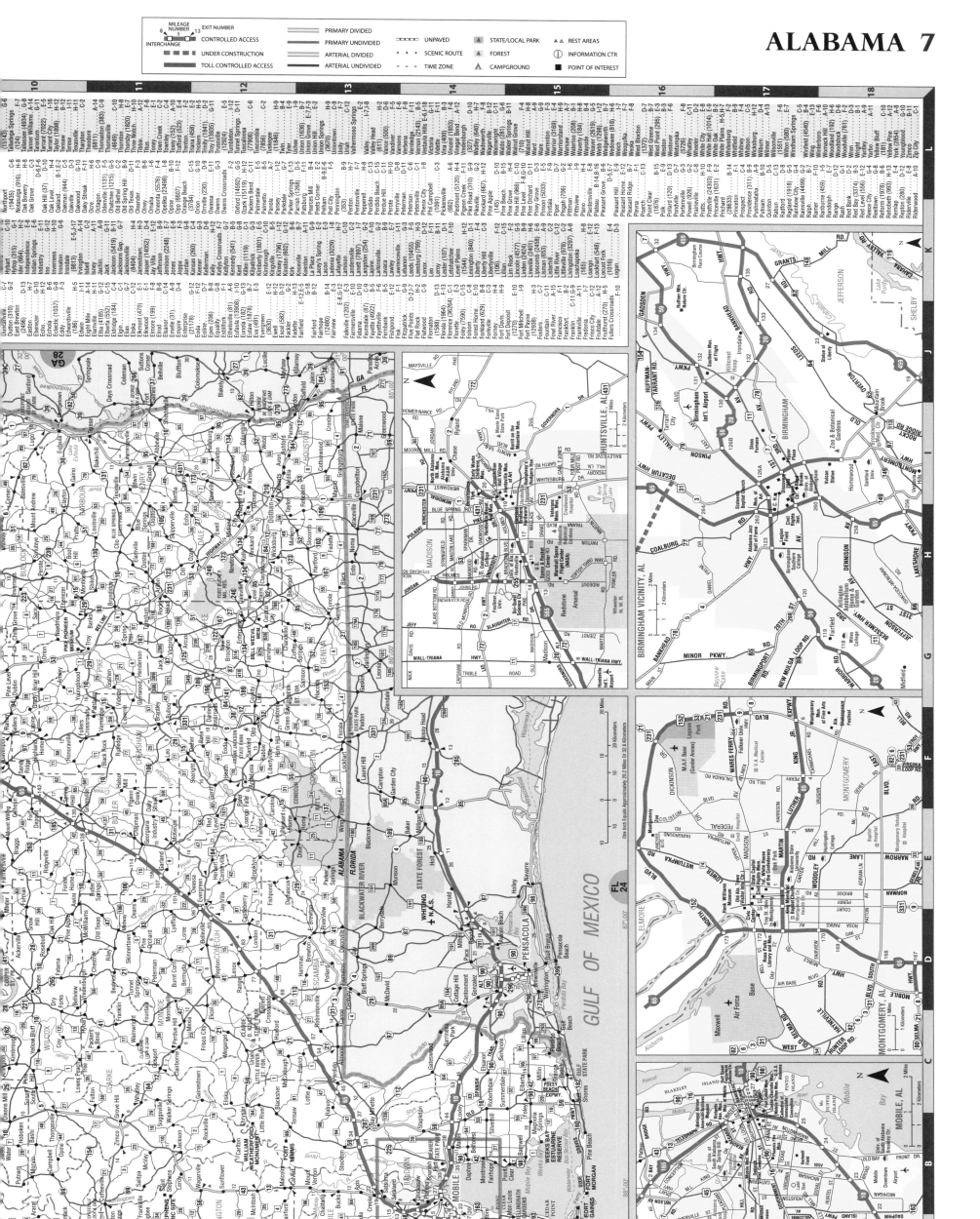

	ANCHORAGE	FAIRBANKS	GULKANA	HOMER	JUNEAU	SEWARD	TOK	VALDEZ
ANCHORAGE	0	355	211	226	864	126	339	315
FAIRBANKS	353	0	221	577	742	477	216	349
JUNEAU	864	742	653	1086	0	986	526	781

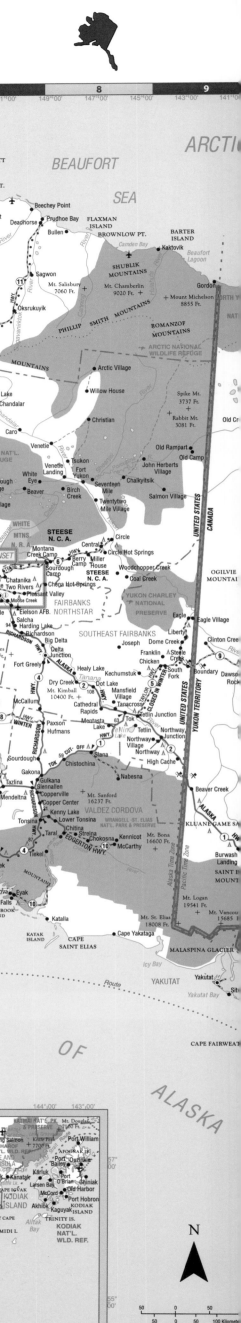

	CASA GRANDE	FLAGSTAFF	GR. CANYON VIL.	HOLBROOK	KINGMAN	NOGALES	PHOENIX	SPRINGERVILLE	TUCSON	YUMA
FLAGSTAFF	192	0	80	92	147	324	143	180	263	326
GRAND CANYON VIL.	277	80	0	172	174	410	228	260	348	412
PHOENIX	50	143	228	234	184	182	0	221	120	188
TUCSON	72	263	348	241	305	71	120	240	0	246

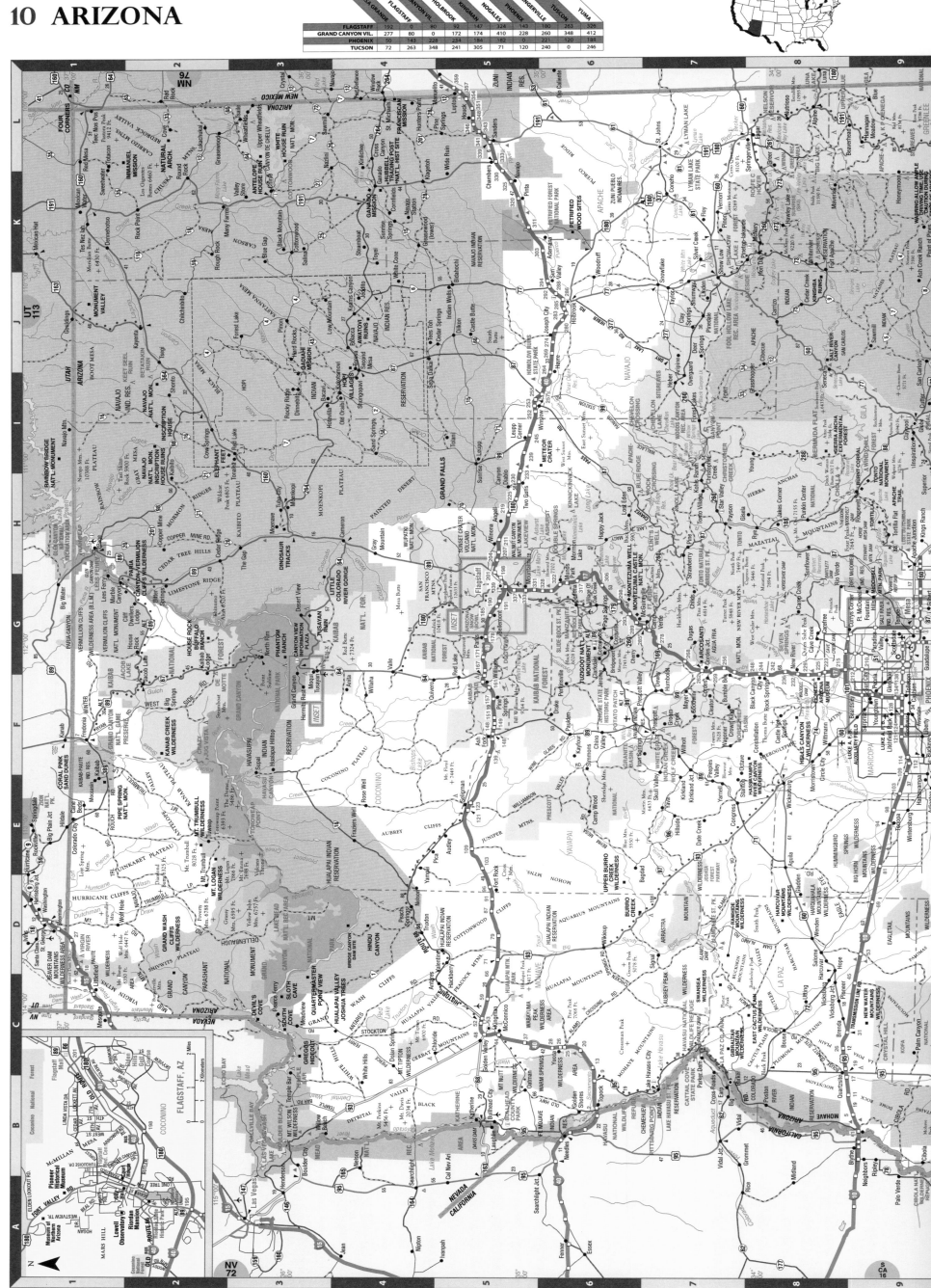

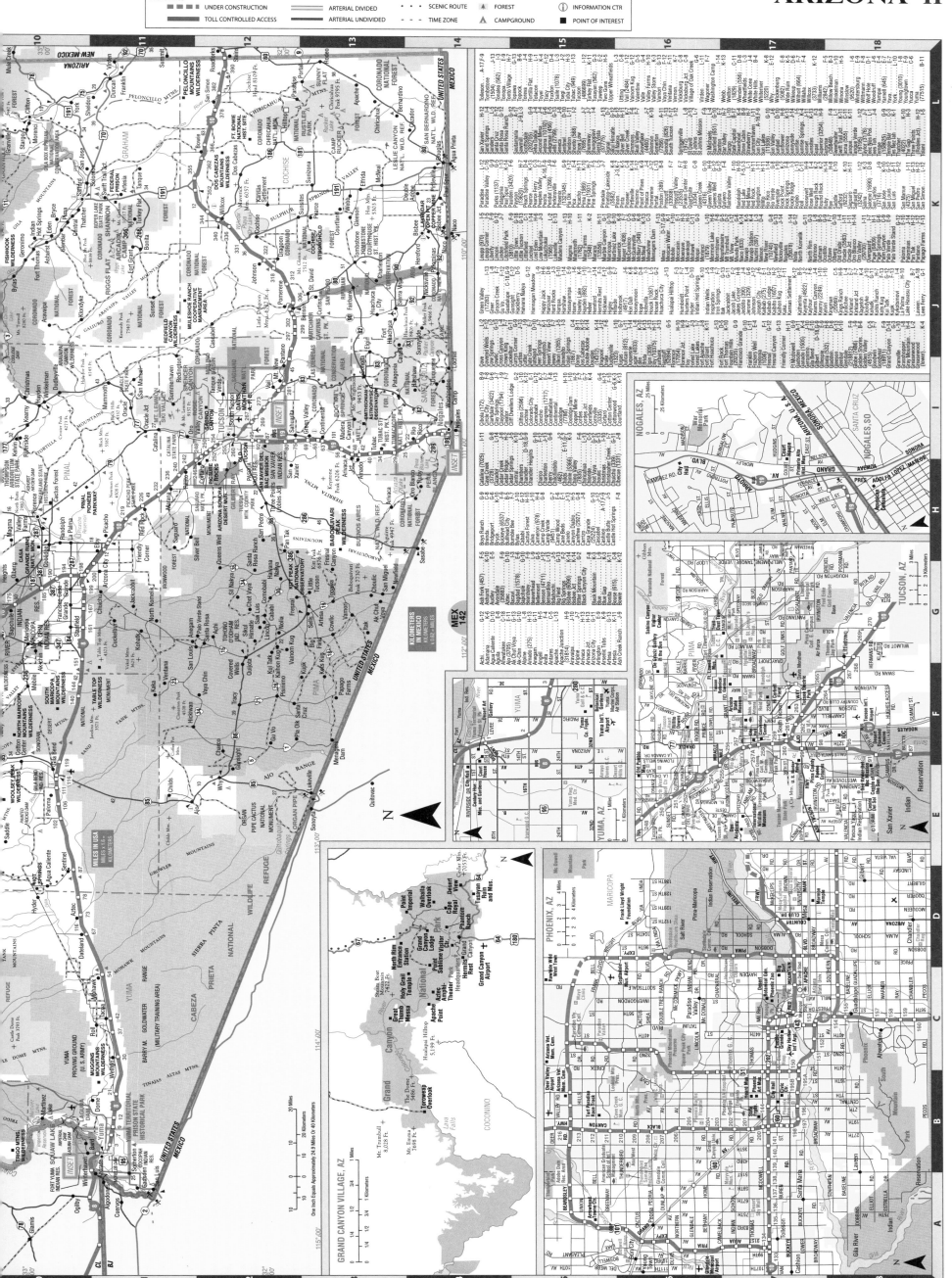

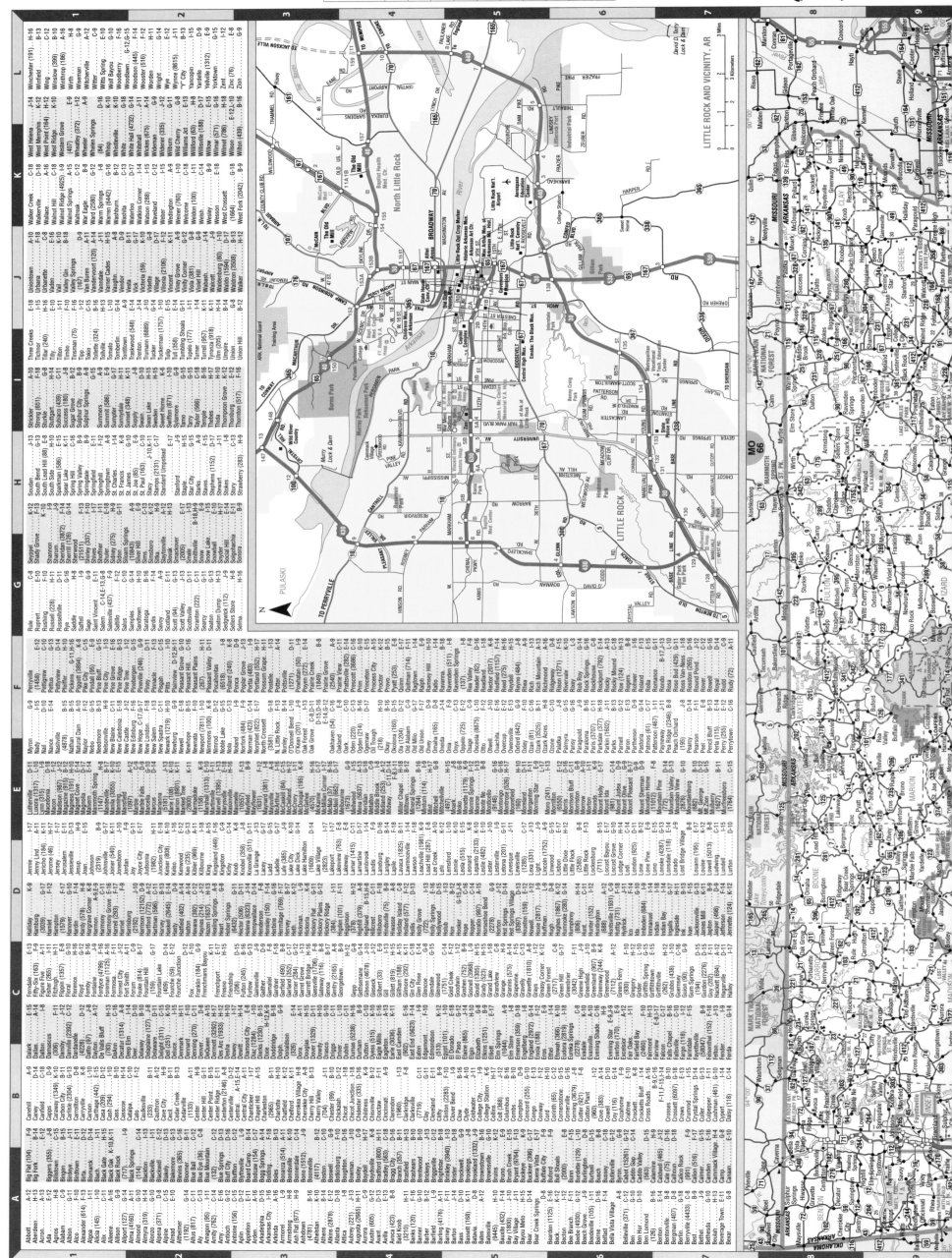

MILEAGE NUMBER
EXIT NUMBER
CONTROLLED ACCESS
INTERCHANGE
UNDER CONSTRUCTION
TOLL CONTROLLED ACCESS

PRIMARY DIVIDED
PRIMARY UNDIVIDED
ARTERIAL DIVIDED
ARTERIAL UNDIVIDED

UNPAVED
SCENIC ROUTE
TIME ZONE

STATE/LOCAL PARK
FOREST
CAMPGROUND

REST AREAS
INFORMATION CTR
POINT OF INTEREST

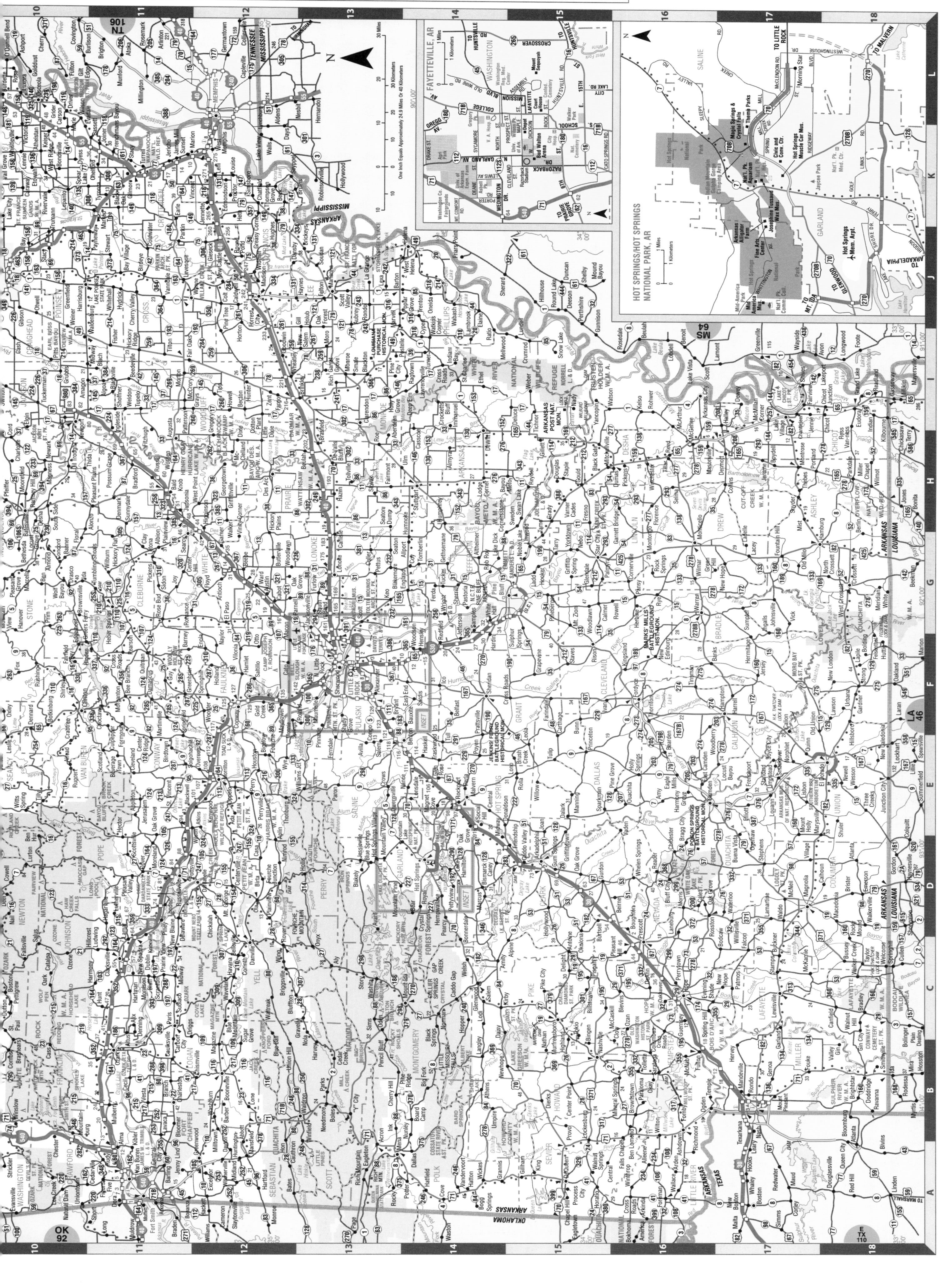

FAYETTEVILLE, AR

HOT SPRINGS/HOT SPRINGS NATIONAL PARK, AR

CALIFORNIA-
Northern

	BAKERSFIELD	CRESCENT CITY	DEATH VALLEY	FRESNO	LOS ANGELES	SACRAMENTO	SAN BERNARDINO	SAN DIEGO	SAN FRANCISCO	SAN JOSE	SANTA BARBARA	YOSEMITE VILL.
LOS ANGELES	115	735	272	223	0	391	61	122	388	343	96	316
SACRAMENTO	282	361	506	173	391	0	443	513	90	121	401	167
SAN DIEGO	237	857	384	345	122	513	110	0	510	465	218	438
SAN FRANCISCO	287	356	438	189	388	90	439	510	0	51	331	185
SANTA BARBARA	150	683	332	259	96	401	149	218	331	282	0	352

PACIFIC
OCEAN
GULF OF THE FARALLONES
OREGON
CALIFORNIA NORTH
NEVADA
SAN FRANCISCO
Sacramento
Redding
Eureka
Chico
Stockton
Modesto
Oakland
San Jose
Santa Cruz
Monterey
Yosemite Village
Klamath Falls
Reno
Carson City
PG. 19
INSET
One Inch Equals Approximately 26.2 Miles Or 42.1 Kilometers
FOR ADJOINING AREA SEE PAGES 16-17

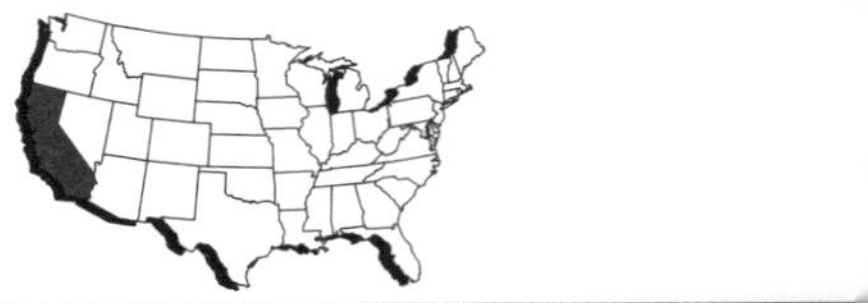

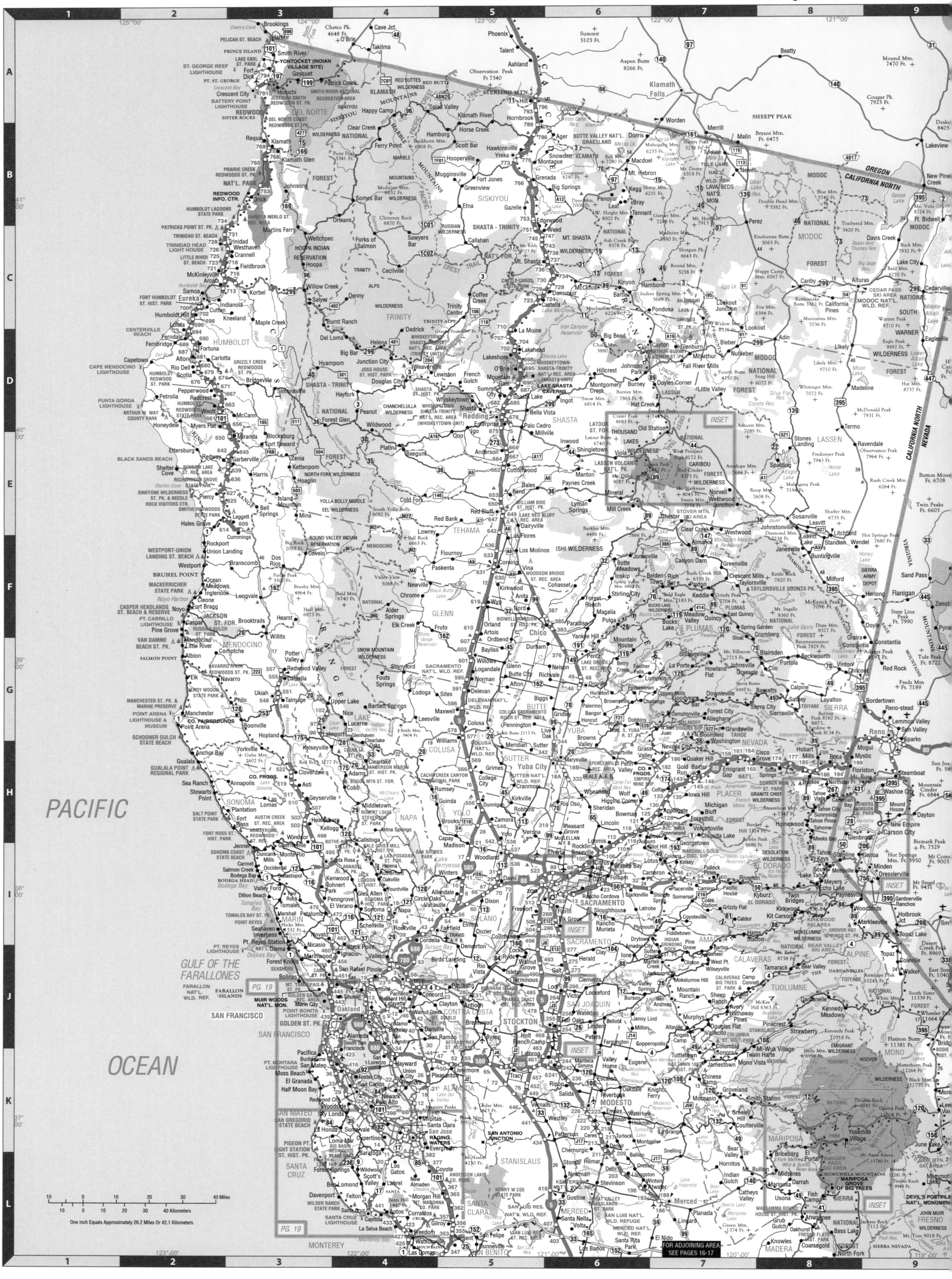

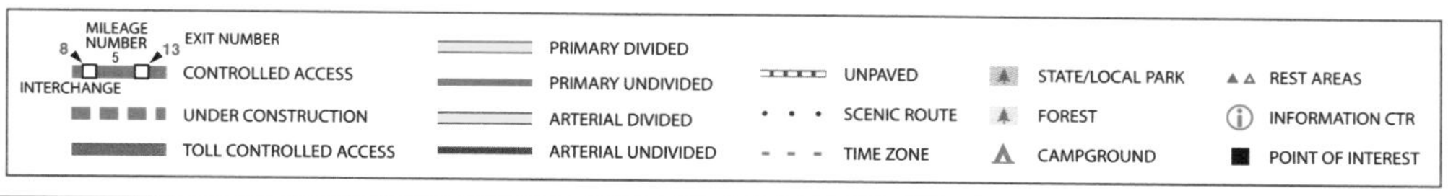

MILEAGE NUMBER — EXIT NUMBER
INTERCHANGE — CONTROLLED ACCESS
UNDER CONSTRUCTION
TOLL CONTROLLED ACCESS
PRIMARY DIVIDED
PRIMARY UNDIVIDED
ARTERIAL DIVIDED
ARTERIAL UNDIVIDED
UNPAVED
SCENIC ROUTE
TIME ZONE
▲ STATE/LOCAL PARK
♠ FOREST
▲ CAMPGROUND
▲ REST AREAS
ⓘ INFORMATION CTR
■ POINT OF INTEREST

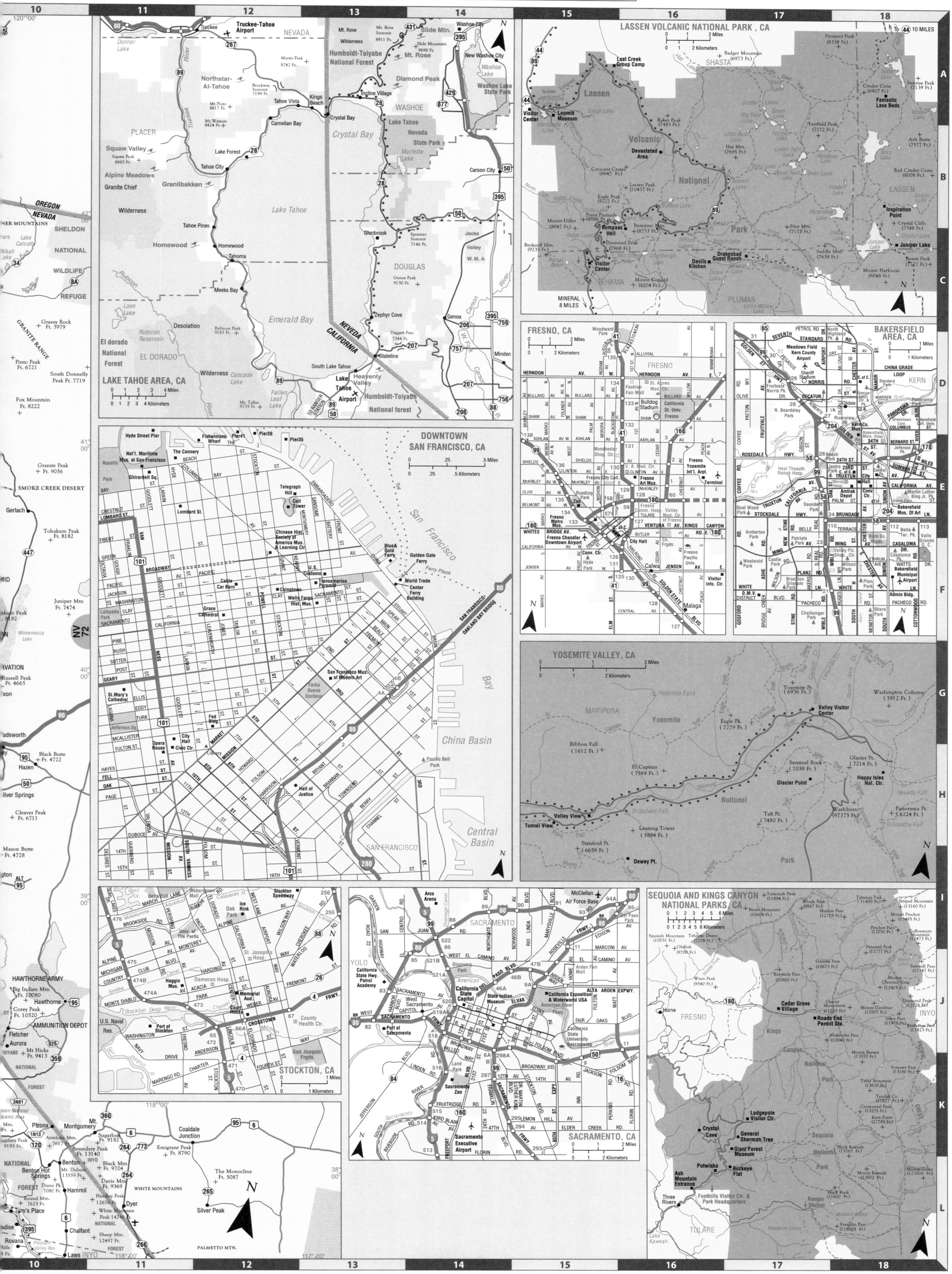

LASSEN VOLCANIC NATIONAL PARK, CA

SHASTA
Lassen
Volcanic
National
Park
TEHAMA
PLUMAS
LASSEN

Lake Tahoe Area, CA

OREGON
NEVADA
CALIFORNIA
Donner Lake
Truckee-Tahoe Airport
NEVADA
WASHOE
Mt. Rose
Humboldt-Toiyabe National Forest
Lake Tahoe
Crystal Bay
Lake Tahoe Nevada State Park
Washoe Lake State Park
Carson City
PLACER
Squaw Valley
Alpine Meadows
Tahoe City
DOUGLAS
Emerald Bay
EL DORADO
El dorado National Forest
South Lake Tahoe
Heavenly Valley
Lake Tahoe Airport
Humboldt-Toiyabe National forest

DOWNTOWN SAN FRANCISCO, CA

Hyde Street Pier
Fisherman's Wharf
Pier 39
Nat'l. Maritime Mus. at San Francisco
The Cannery
Ghirardelli Sq.
Telegraph Hill
Coit Tower
Lombard St.
Chinese Hist. Society of America Mus. & Learning Ctr.
Blue & Gold Ferry
Golden Gate Ferry
Ferry Plaza
Transamerica Pyramid
Cable Car Barn
Chinatown
Grace Cathedral
Wells Fargo Hist. Mus.
U.S. Customs
World Trade Center Ferry Building
San Francisco Mus. of Modern Art
Yerba Buena Gardens
St. Mary's Cathedral
Opera House
City Hall / Civic Ctr.
Library
Hall of Justice
Pacific Bell Park
SAN FRANCISCO
San Francisco Bay
China Basin
Central Basin
San Francisco Oakland Bay Bridge

FRESNO, CA
HERNDON AV.
BULLARD AV.
SHAW AV.
ASHLAN AV.
SHIELDS AV.
CLINTON AV.
McKINLEY AV.
OLIVE AV.
BELMONT
VENTURA
KINGS CANYON RD.
Fresno Yosemite Int'l. Arpt.
Fresno Chandler Downtown Airport
City Hall

BAKERSFIELD AREA, CA
Meadows Field Kern County Airport
KERN
CHINA GRADE LOOP
ROSEDALE
CALIFORNIA AV.
Bakersfield Municipal Airport

YOSEMITE VALLEY, CA
MARIPOSA
Yosemite Falls
Yosemite Pt. (6936 Ft.)
Washington Column (5912 Ft.)
Valley Visitor Center
Eagle Pk. (7779 Ft.)
Ribbon Fall (1612 Ft.)
El Capitan (7569 Ft.)
Sentinel Rock (7038 Ft.)
Glacier Pt. (7214 Ft.)
Glacier Point
Happy Isles Nat. Ctr.
Bridalveil Fall
Valley View
Tunnel View
Leaning Tower (5884 Ft.)
Taft Pt. (7480 Ft.)
Washburn (7373 Ft.)
Panorama Pt. (6224 Ft.)
Stanford Pt. (6659 Ft.)
Dewey Pt.
National Park

STOCKTON, CA
Stockton Speedway
Univ. of The Pacific
St. Josephs Hosp.
Haggis Mus.
Dameron Hosp.
Port of Stockton
U.S. Naval Res.
San Joaquin Frgds.
YOLO

SACRAMENTO, CA
McClellan Air Force Base
Arco Arena
SACRAMENTO
California State Hwy. Patrol Academy
California State Capitol
State Indian Museum
California Expo. & Cal Expo/American River USA
West Sacramento
Port of Sacramento
California State University
Sacramento Zoo
Sacramento Executive Airport
YOLO

SEQUOIA AND KINGS CANYON NATIONAL PARKS, CA
FRESNO
INYO
Cedar Grove Village
Roads End Permit Sta.
Kings
TULARE
Lodgepole Visitor Ctr.
Crystal Cave
General Sherman Tree
Giant Forest Museum
Ash Mountain Entrance
Foothills Visitor Ctr. & Park Headquarters
Three Rivers
Sequoia National Park

Legend

MILEAGE NUMBER	EXIT NUMBER	
INTERCHANGE	CONTROLLED ACCESS	
	UNDER CONSTRUCTION	
	TOLL CONTROLLED ACCESS	

PRIMARY DIVIDED
PRIMARY UNDIVIDED
ARTERIAL DIVIDED
ARTERIAL UNDIVIDED
UNPAVED
SCENIC ROUTE
TIME ZONE

STATE/LOCAL PARK
FOREST
CAMPGROUND

REST AREAS
INFORMATION CTR
POINT OF INTEREST

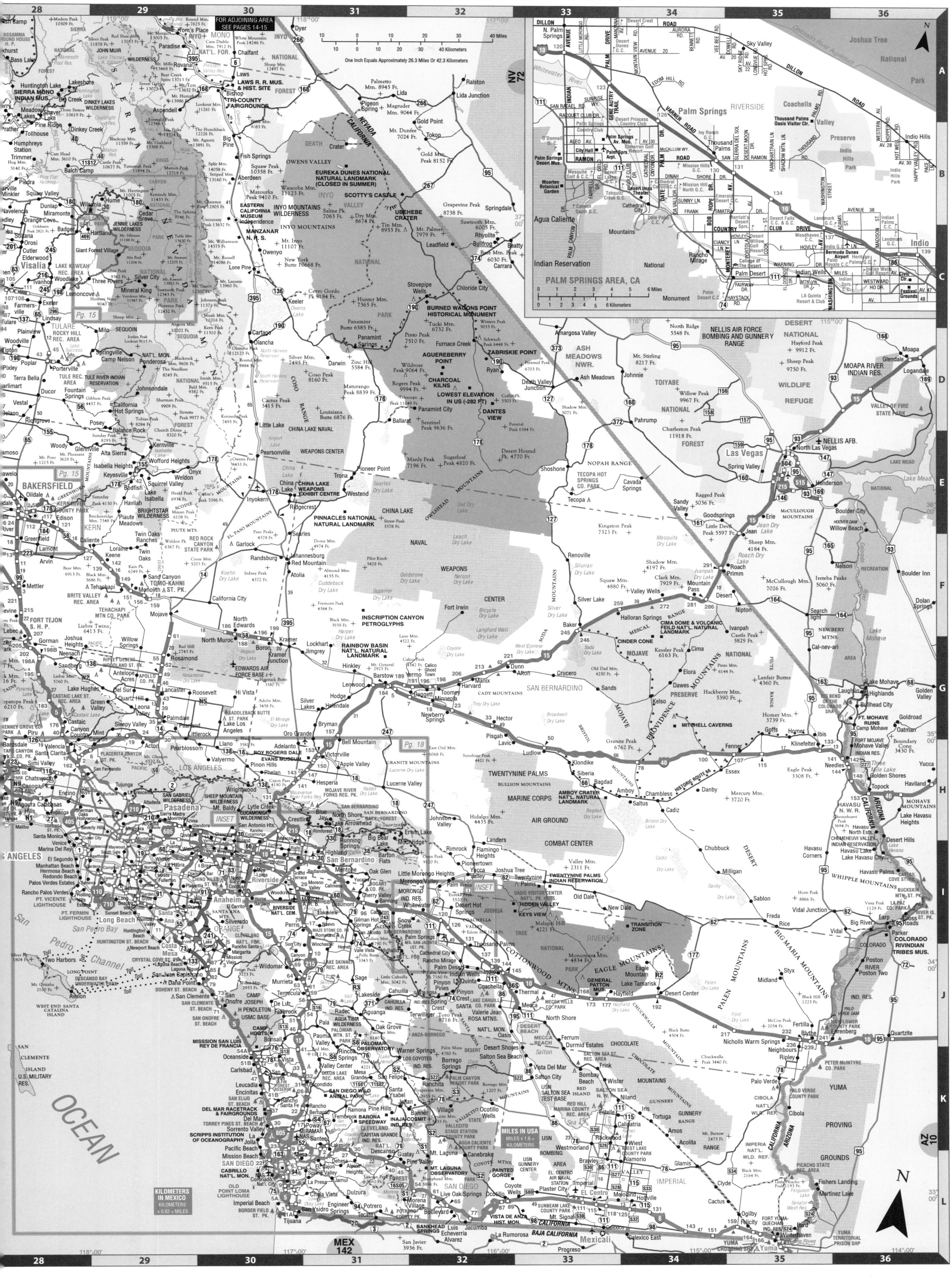

FOR ADJOINING AREA
SEE PAGES 14-15

One Inch Equals Approximately 26.3 Miles Or 42.3 Kilometers

PALM SPRINGS AREA, CA

OCEAN

MEX 142

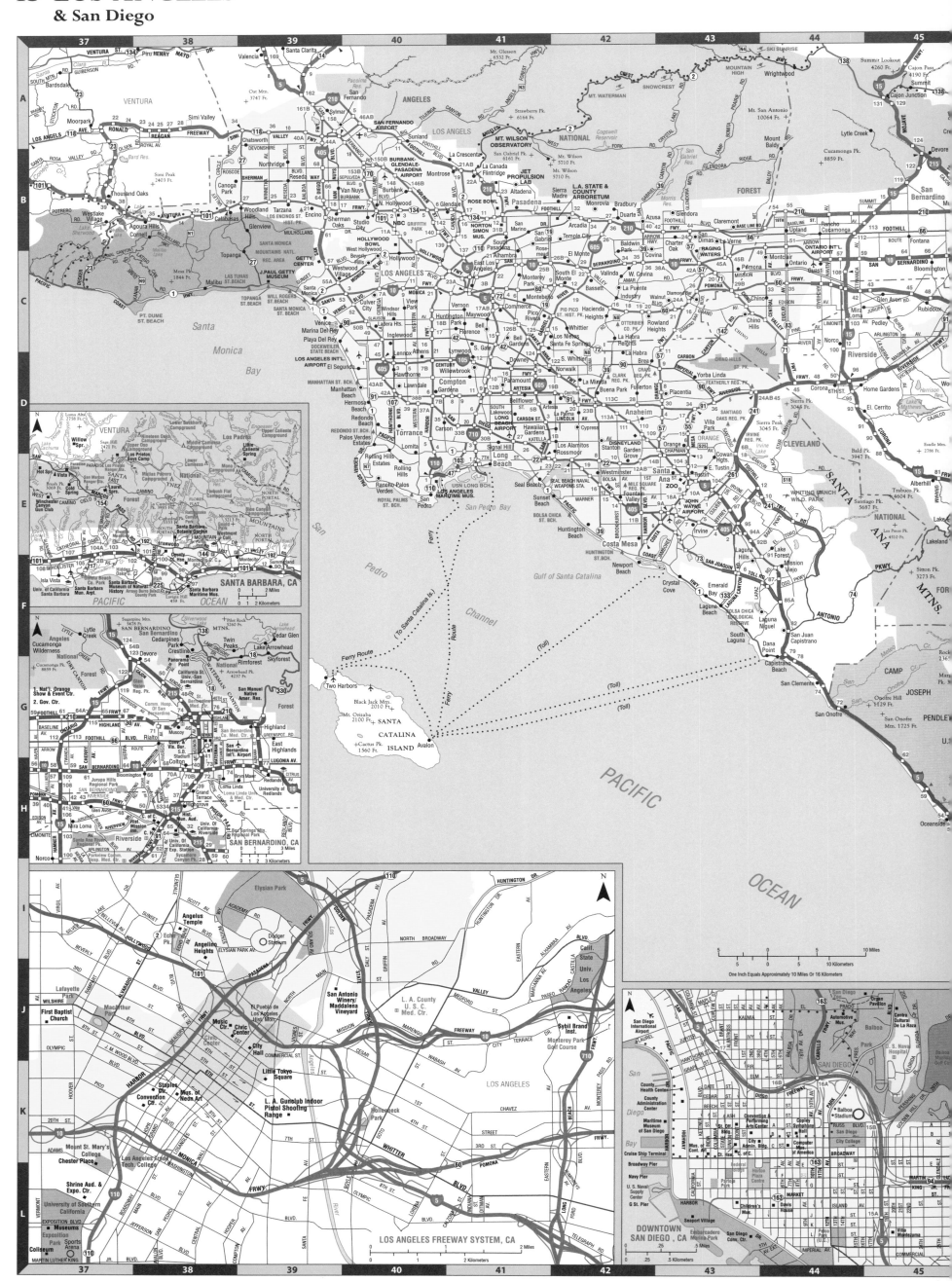

LOS ANGELES FREEWAY SYSTEM, CA

SANTA BARBARA, CA

SAN BERNARDINO, CA

DOWNTOWN SAN DIEGO, CA

Legend:
MILEAGE NUMBER — EXIT NUMBER — INTERCHANGE — CONTROLLED ACCESS — UNDER CONSTRUCTION — TOLL CONTROLLED ACCESS — PRIMARY DIVIDED — PRIMARY UNDIVIDED — ARTERIAL DIVIDED — ARTERIAL UNDIVIDED — UNPAVED — SCENIC ROUTE — TIME ZONE — STATE/LOCAL PARK — FOREST — CAMPGROUND — REST AREAS — INFORMATION CTR — POINT OF INTEREST

SAN FRANCISCO, CA

0 1 2 3 4 5 Miles
0 1 2 3 4 5 Kilometers

San Pablo Bay · CONTRA COSTA · Point Pinole Reg. Shoreline · Tara Hills · Pinole · Hercules · Rodeo · Crockett · Benicia Capitol S.H.P. · Port Costa · Benicia · MARTINEZ BRIDGE · Suisun Bay · Martinez · John Muir Nat'l. Hist. Site · Buchanan Field · Concord · Pleasant Hill · Walnut Creek · Lafayette · Orinda · Sibley Volcanic Reg. Preserve · Eugene O'Neill Nat'l. Hist. Site · Las Trampas Regional Wilderness · Danville · Diablo · Alamo · Diablo Foothills Reg. Park · Mt. Diablo · St. Park And Game Refuge · Castle Rock Reg. Park · Behring Auto Museum · San Ramon · Dublin · Pleasanton · Camp Parks Reg. Park · Tassajara Creek Reg. Park · Livermore · Del Valle Reg. Park · Lake Del Valle

Muir Beach · Mill Valley · Corte Madera · San Quentin · RICHMOND-SAN RAFAEL BRIDGE · North Richmond · Richmond · El Sobrante · El Cerrito · Kensington · Tilden Reg. Park · Berkeley · Univ. of California Berkeley · Albany · San Pablo Reservoir · Briones Regional Park · Briones Reservoir

GOLDEN GATE · Golden Gate National Rec. Area · Sausalito · Tiburon · Belvedere · ANGEL I. · Angel Island Reg. Park · TREASURE ISLAND · ALCATRAZ I. · Fisherman's Wharf · SAN FRANCISCO · Golden Gate Pk. · Univ. of San Fran. · JFK University · Emeryville · Oakland · Children's Hosp. · Naval Supply Center · Alameda Naval Air Station · Convention Center · Piedmont · Oakland Mus. · Redwood Reg. Park · Moraga · Canyon · Lake Chabot Reg. Park · San Leandro

PACIFIC OCEAN · GULF OF THE FARALLONES · Daly City · Broadmoor · Colma · Brisbane · Pacifica · Pacifica St. Beach · Sweeney Ridge · San Bruno · Candlestick Park · Hunters Point Naval Shipyard · Crown Mem. State Beach · Network Associates Coliseum · Oakland-Alameda Co. Arena · San Leandro Bay Reg. Shoreline · Oakland Int'l. Arpt. · ALAMEDA · Hayward Reg. Shoreline · San Lorenzo · Castro Valley

South San Francisco · San Francisco Int'l. Arpt. · Millbrae · Burlingame · Hillsborough · San Mateo · Foster City · Bay Meadows Racetrack · Belmont · San Carlos · Upper Crystal Springs Res. · Huddart Co. Pk. · SAN MATEO BRIDGE · Hayward Air Terminal · Hayward · Cal. State Univ. - Hayward · Union City · Garin Reg. Park · Coyote Hills Reg. Park · Fremont · San Francisco Bay N.W.R. · Newark · DUMBARTON BRIDGE · Mission San Jose · Mission Peak Reg. Park · Sunol · Sunol Regional · Ohlone Regional Wilderness

Fish and Game Refuge · Redwood City · North Fair Oaks · Atherton · Menlo Park · East Palo Alto · Woodside · Wunderlich Co. Park · Stanford · Stanford Univ. · Palo Alto · Ladera · Portola Valley · Los Altos Hills · Los Altos · Moffett Field N.A.S. · Mountain View · Sunnyvale · Milpitas · Calaveras Reservoir · Del Valle Regional Pk.

SAN JOSE, CA

0 1 2 Miles
0 1 2 Kilometers

Alviso Park · Baylands · Moffett Field N.A.S. · Sunnyvale Municipal Golf Course · Great America · Santa Clara Golf & Tennis · Agnew's St. Hosp. East Annex · River Oaks Park · Columbia Park · Fair Wood Park · Mission College · Central · El Camino · Washington Park · Sylvan Park · Cuseta Park · El Camino Hospital · Las Palmas Park · Ponderosa Park · Serra Park · San Antonio Park · Ortega Park · Municipal Golf Course · Kaiser Permanente Med. Ctr. · Central Park · San Jose International Airport · Santa Clara University · Mission Santa Clara · Santa Clara · Reid-Hillview of Santa Clara Co. Airport · Rancho San Antonio County Park · Juniperp Memorial Park · Farm Golf Course · McClellan Ranch Park (Site) · De Anza College · Deep Cliff Golf Course · Linda Vista Park · Mise Park · Winchester Mystery House · Pruneridge Golf Club · Valley Fair · Santa Clara Valley Med. Center · Good Samaritan Hosp. · Stevens Creek County Park · Saratoga Country Club · Hakone Gardens · La Rinconada Country Club · Villa Montalvo Arboretum · West Valley College · Allendale Ave · Campbell · Oak Hill Mem. Cem. · Santa Clara Co. Fairgrounds · Kelley Park · Pleasant Hills Golf & Country C. · Guadalupe Oak Grove Park · Almaden · Los Gatos

SAN BERNARDINO · Round Mtn. 5272 Ft. · Luna Mtn. 5967 Ft. · RIM OF THE WORLD DR. · Fawnskin · Baldwin Lake · Big Bear Lake · SNOW VALLEY · Delmar Mtn. 8398 Ft. · Erwin Lake · Arrowbear Lake · Running Springs · Angelus Oaks · Harrison Mtn. 4743 Ft. · NATIONAL · SAN BERNARDINO · FOREST · Green Valley Lake · Cedar Glen · Lake Arrowhead · Blue Jay · Rim Forest · Twin Peaks · Arrowhead Pk. 4237 Ft. · Keller Pk. 7882 Ft. · Mr. Russel 2704 Ft.

Highland · E. Highlands · Mentone · Redlands · Loma Linda · Bryn Mawr · Yucaipa · Calimesa · Cherry Valley · Beaumont · Banning · MORONGO INDIAN RESERVATION · MORENO VALLEY · Moreno Valley · Perris · SAN JACINTO · San Jacinto · Hemet · SOBOBA INDIAN RES. · SAN BERNARDINO NATIONAL FOREST · Gilman Hot Springs · Lake Perris · CLEVELAND · Quail Valley · Sun City · Menifee · Winchester · Bell Mtn. 1448 Ft. · Romoland · Homeland · Nuevo · Canyon Lake · Lake Elsinore · Murrieta Hot Springs · Murrieta · Temecula · Rancho California · PECHANGA INDIAN RES. · AQUA TIBIA WILDERNESS · Mt. Olympus 2224 Ft. · Monserate Mtn. 1567 Ft. · Pala · PALA INDIAN RESERVATION · Gavilan Mtn. 1831 Ft. · Rainbow · Fallbrook · Bonsali · Eagle Crag 5077 Ft. · Wild Horse 3277 Ft. · High Pt. 6140 Ft. · Boucher Hill 5436 Ft. · Birch Hill 5710 Ft. · PALOMAR OBSERVATORY · LA JOLLA INDIAN RES. · Pine Mtn. 4221 Ft. · RIVERSIDE · Oak Mtn. 2706 Ft. · Bachelor Mtn. 2555 Ft. · Diamond Valley Lake · Vail Lake · CAHUILLA INDIAN RESERVATION · CLEVELAND FOREST · Valley Center · SAN PASQUAL INDIAN RES. · Burnt Mtn. 2135 Ft. · Vista · San Marcos · Escondido · San Pasqual · Rancho Santa Fe · Rancho Bernardo · Poway · BARONA RANCH INDIAN RES. · CAPITAN GRANDE INDIAN RES. · Ramona · San Vicente Lake · El Capitan Lake · Loveland Res. · LEGOLAND CALIFORNIA · Carlsbad · Agua Hedionda · Encinitas · Cardiff By The Sea · Solana Beach · Del Mar · Lake Hodges · Lakeside · Glenview · Harbison Canyon · Alpine · NATIONAL FOREST

SCRIPPS INSTITUTION OCEANOGRAPHY · La Jolla · Pacific Beach · Mission Beach · Ocean Beach · SEA WORLD · MISSION BAY AQUATIC PARK · Linda Vista · La Mesa · Santee · El Cajon · Spring Valley · Jamul · FT. ROSECRANS NAT'L. CEMETERY · CABRILLO NATIONAL MONUMENT · VISITORS CENTER · NAVAL BASE · Point Loma · SAN DIEGO · Coronado · National City · Bonita · San Miguel Mtn. 2565 Ft. · Sweetwater Res. · Upper Otay Lake · Honey Springs · Dulzura · MONTGOMERY AIRPORT · MARINE CORPS AIR STATION MIRAMAR · KNOTT'S SOAK CITY U.S.A. · ARCO OLYMPIC TRAINING CTR. OF THE US OLYMPIC COMMITTEE · COORS AMPHITHEATER · MARINE CORPS RECRUIT DEPOT · SILVER STRAND STATE BEACH · U.S. NAVAL AMPHIBIOUS BASE · SUNSET CLIFFS PARK · FT. LOMA · NAVAL STATION SAN DIEGO · Chula Vista · Imperial Beach · BORDER FIELD STATE PARK · San Ysidro · TIJUANA · MEXICO · U.S.A. · MEX 142

PACIFIC OCEAN

MILES IN USA — MILES × 0.62 = KILOMETERS
KILOMETERS IN MEXICO — KILOMETERS × 1.6 = MILES

	ALAMOSA	COLORADO SPGS	CORTEZ	DENVER	DURANGO	GRAND JUNCTION	GREELEY	LAMAR	PONCHA SPRINGS	PUEBLO
COLORADO SPRINGS	166	0	356	72	312	303	134	164	110	46
DENVER	236	71	374	0	330	236	65	206	138	116
DURANGO	147	312	52	330	0	167	391	349	194	266
PUEBLO	121	46	310	116	266	346	178	120	96	0

Abarr..... E-17
Adams City..... I-3
Agate..... F-15
Aguilar (593)..... K-13
Akron (1711)..... D-16
Alamosa (7960)..... K-11
Allenspark..... E-12,H-5
Allison..... L-8
Alma (179)..... G-11
Almont..... H-9
Amherst..... C-18
Antero Jct...... H-11
Anton..... E-16
Antonito (873)..... L-11
Arapahoe..... G-18
Arboles (232)..... L-8
Arlington..... I-16
Aroya..... G-16
Arriba (244)..... F-16
Arriola..... K-6
Arvada..... E-12,I-1
Aspen (5914)..... G-9
Atwood (195)..... D-16
Ault (1432)..... D-13
Aurora..... F-13,J-4
Austin..... H-7

Avon (5561)..... F-10
Avondale (754)..... I-14
Bailey..... F-12
Barnesville..... D-13
Bartlett..... K-18
Basalt (2681)..... G-9
Battlement Mesa..... F-7
Baxter..... I-14
Bayfield (1549)..... L-8
Bedrock..... I-8
Bellvue..... D-12
Bennett (2021)..... F-14
Berthoud (4839)..... E-12
Beshoar Jct...... K-14
Bethune..... F-17
Beulah..... I-13
Black Forest..... B-1
Black Hawk..... E-12
Blanca (391)..... K-12
Blue River (685)..... F-11
Bonanza (14)..... H-10
Boncarbo..... K-13
Bond..... E-10
Boone (323)..... I-14
Boulder (94673)..... E-12

Bowie..... H-8
Boyero..... G-16
Brandon..... H-17
Branson (77)..... L-15
Breckenridge..... F-11
Breen..... L-7
Briggsdale..... C-14
Bristol..... I-18
Broadmoor..... B-1
Broomfield (38272)..... E-13
Brush (5117)..... D-16
Buckingham..... C-14
Buena Vista..... H-11
Buffalo Creek..... F-12
Buford..... E-8
Burns..... E-9
Byers (1233)..... F-14
Caddoa..... K-18
Cahone..... K-6
Calhan (896)..... G-14
Cameo..... F-7
Campion..... E-13
Campo (150)..... M-17
Canon City..... I-12
Capulin..... K-11

Carbondale..... G-9
Carlton..... G-12
Carr..... C-13
Cascade..... A-1
Castle Rock..... F-13
Cedaredge (1854)..... H-7
Cedarwood..... J-13
Center (2392)..... J-10
Central City..... E-12
Chama..... L-11
Cheney Center..... J-18
Cheraw (211)..... I-15
Cherry Hills Village
Cheyenne Wells..... G-18
Chimney Rock..... L-8
Chipita Park..... A-1
Chivington..... H-17
Chromo..... L-9
Cimarron..... H-8
Clark..... C-5
Clarkville..... D-17
Climax..... G-11
Coal Creek (303)..... I-12
Coalmont..... D-10

Cokedale (139)..... L-13
Collbran (388)..... G-7
Colorado City..... J-13
Colorado Springs (360890)..... I-13
Columbine..... C-9
Commerce City..... I-3
Como..... G-11
Conejos..... L-11
Conifer..... F-12
Cope..... E-16
Copper Mountain..... F-11
Cortez (7977)..... K-6
Cotopaxi..... I-12
Cowdrey..... C-10
Craig (9189)..... D-8
Crawford (366)..... H-8
Creede (377)..... J-9
Crested Butte..... H-9
Crestone (73)..... J-11
Cripple Creek..... H-12
Crook (128)..... C-17
Crowley (187)..... I-15
Cuchara..... K-13
Dacono (3015)..... E-13
Dailey..... C-17

De Beque..... G-7
Deckers..... G-12
Deer Ridge..... D-11
Deer Trail (598)..... F-14
Del Norte (1705)..... J-10
Delhi..... J-15
Delta (6400)..... H-7
Denver..... L-3
Dillon (802)..... F-11
Dinosaur (319)..... L-5
Divide..... G-12
Dolores (857)..... K-6
Dotsero..... F-9
Dove Creek (698)..... J-6
Dowd..... F-10
Doyleville..... H-10
Drake..... D-12
Dunton..... J-7
Duport..... H-2
Durango (13922)..... K-7
Eads (747)..... H-17
Eagle (3032)..... F-9
Eaton (2690)..... D-13
Eckley (278)..... D-17
Edgewater..... J-2
Edwards..... F-10,J-2
Egnar..... J-5

El Moro..... K-14
Elbert..... F-13
Elizabeth (1434)..... F-13
Elk Springs..... D-6
Ellicott..... H-14
Empire (355)..... F-11
Englewood..... L-3
Erie (6291)..... E-13
Estes Park..... D-12,E-5
Evans (9514)..... D-13
Evergreen..... F-12
Fairplay (610)..... G-11
Falcon..... G-13
Farisita..... J-13
Federal Heights..... H-1
Firestone (908)..... E-13
Firstview..... G-17
Fleming (426)..... C-16
Florence (3653)..... I-12
Florissant..... H-12
Fort Collins (118652)..... D-12
Fort Garland..... K-12
Fort Lewis..... L-7
Fort Lupton..... E-13
Fort Lyon..... I-16

Fort Morgan (11034)..... D-15
Fountain..... H-13
Fowler (1206)..... I-15
Foxton..... F-12
Franktown..... F-13
Fraser (910)..... F-11
Frederick..... E-13
Frisco (2443)..... F-11
Fruita (6478)..... G-6
Galatea..... H-16
Galeton..... D-13
Garcia..... L-12
Gardner..... J-12
Garo..... G-11
Gateway..... H-5
Genoa (211)..... F-15
Georgetown..... F-11
Gilcrest (1162)..... D-13
Gill..... D-13
Glade Park..... G-6
Gladstone..... J-8
Glendevey..... C-11,K-3
Glenwood Springs (7691)..... F-8
Golden (17159)..... F-12

Goodrich..... D-14
Gould..... D-11
Granada (1525)..... I-18
Grand Junction (41986)..... G-6
Grand Lake..... D-11,G-1
Grant..... F-11
Great Divide..... D-7
Greeley (76930)..... D-13
Green Mountain Falls
Grover (153)..... C-14
Guffey..... H-12
Guiluire..... K-13
Gunnison (5409)..... H-9
Gypsum (3654)..... F-9
Hahns Peak..... C-5
Hale (747)..... H-17
Hartman..... D-8
Hartman (111)..... I-18
Hasty..... J-17
Haswell (84)..... H-16
Hawley..... J-15
Haxtun (982)..... C-17

Hayden (1634)..... D-7
Heartstrong..... E-17
Heeney..... F-10
Herford..... C-14
Hermosa..... L-7
Hesperus..... L-7
Hideaway (254)..... D-9
Hillside..... I-12
Hoehne..... K-14
Holly (1048)..... I-18
Holyoke (2261)..... C-18
Homelake..... J-10
Hooper (123)..... J-11
Hotchkiss (968)..... H-8
Howard..... I-12
Hoyt..... E-15
Hudson (1513)..... E-14
Hugo (885)..... F-16
Hygiene..... E-12
Idaho Springs..... F-11
Idalia..... F-18
Iliff (213)..... C-16
Ignacio (669)..... L-8
Jansen..... K-14

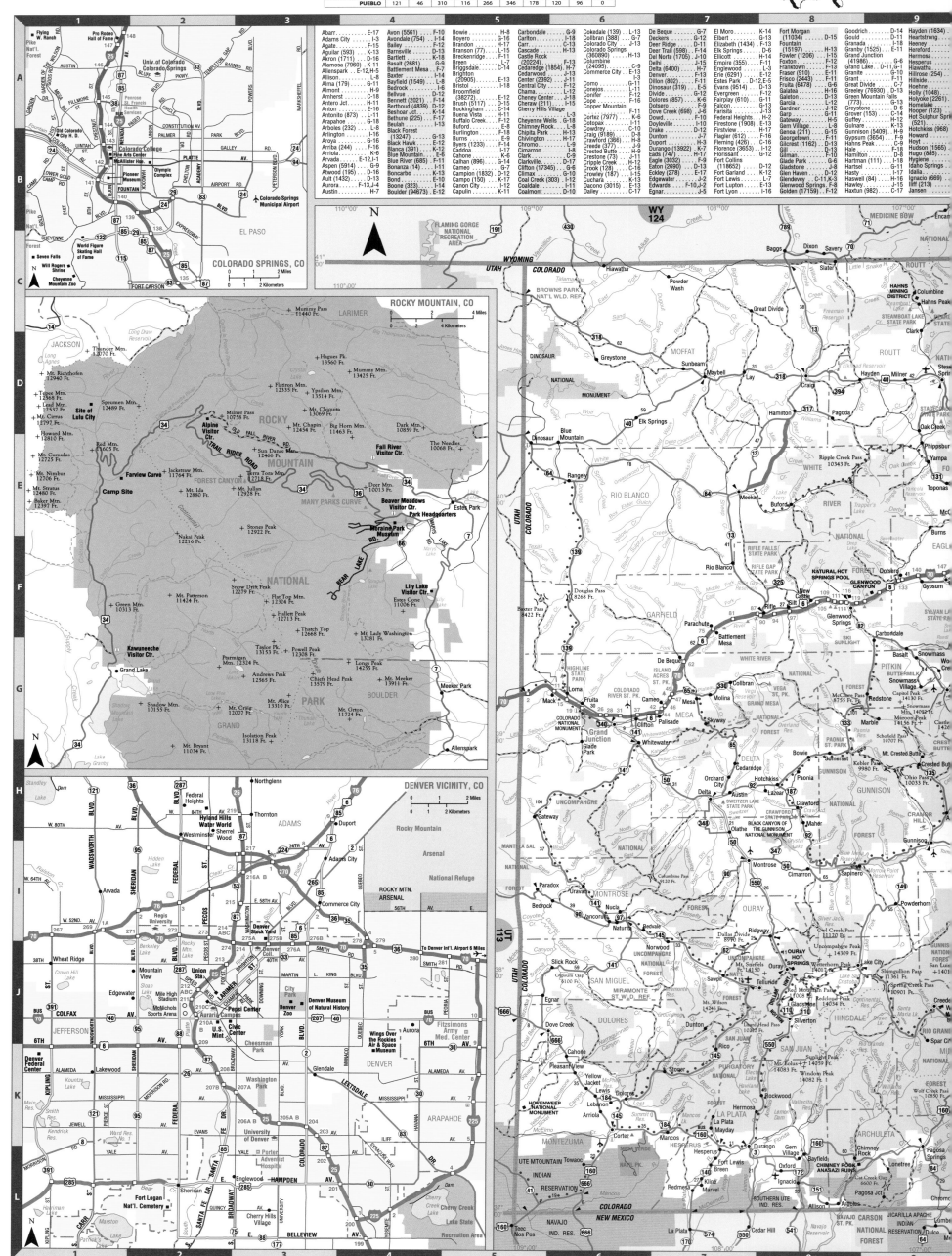

ROCKY MOUNTAIN, CO

COLORADO SPRINGS, CO

DENVER VICINITY, CO

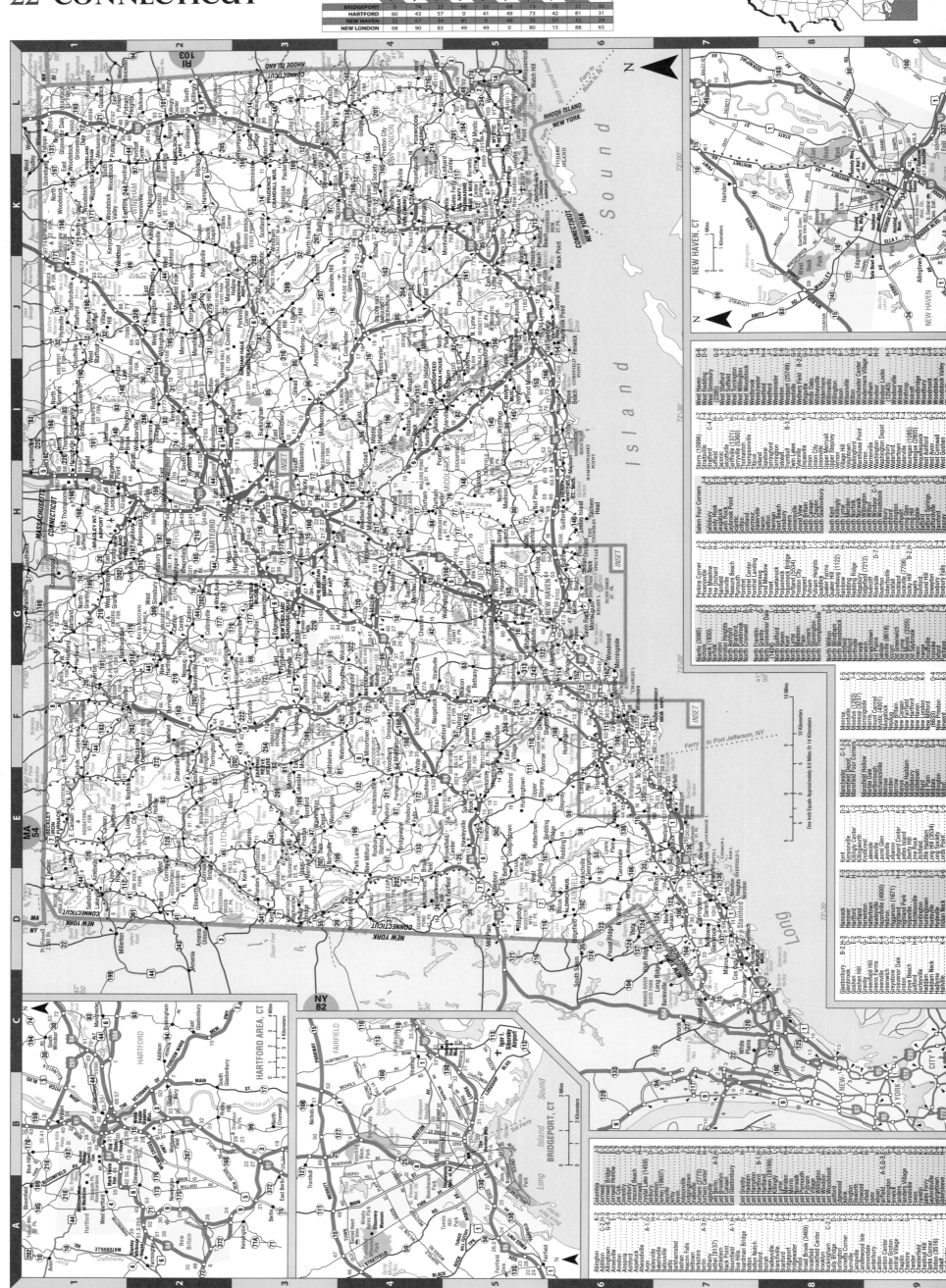

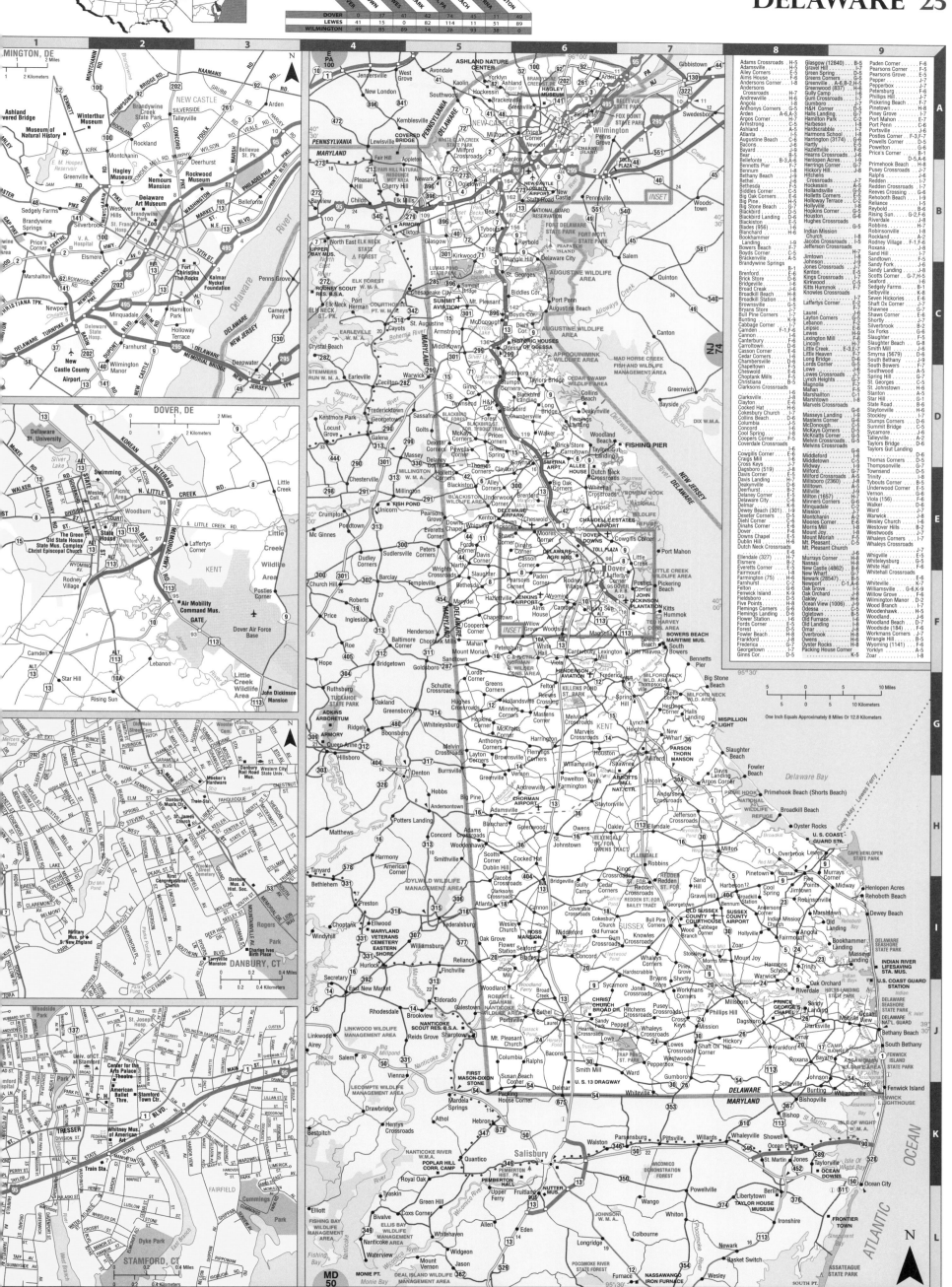

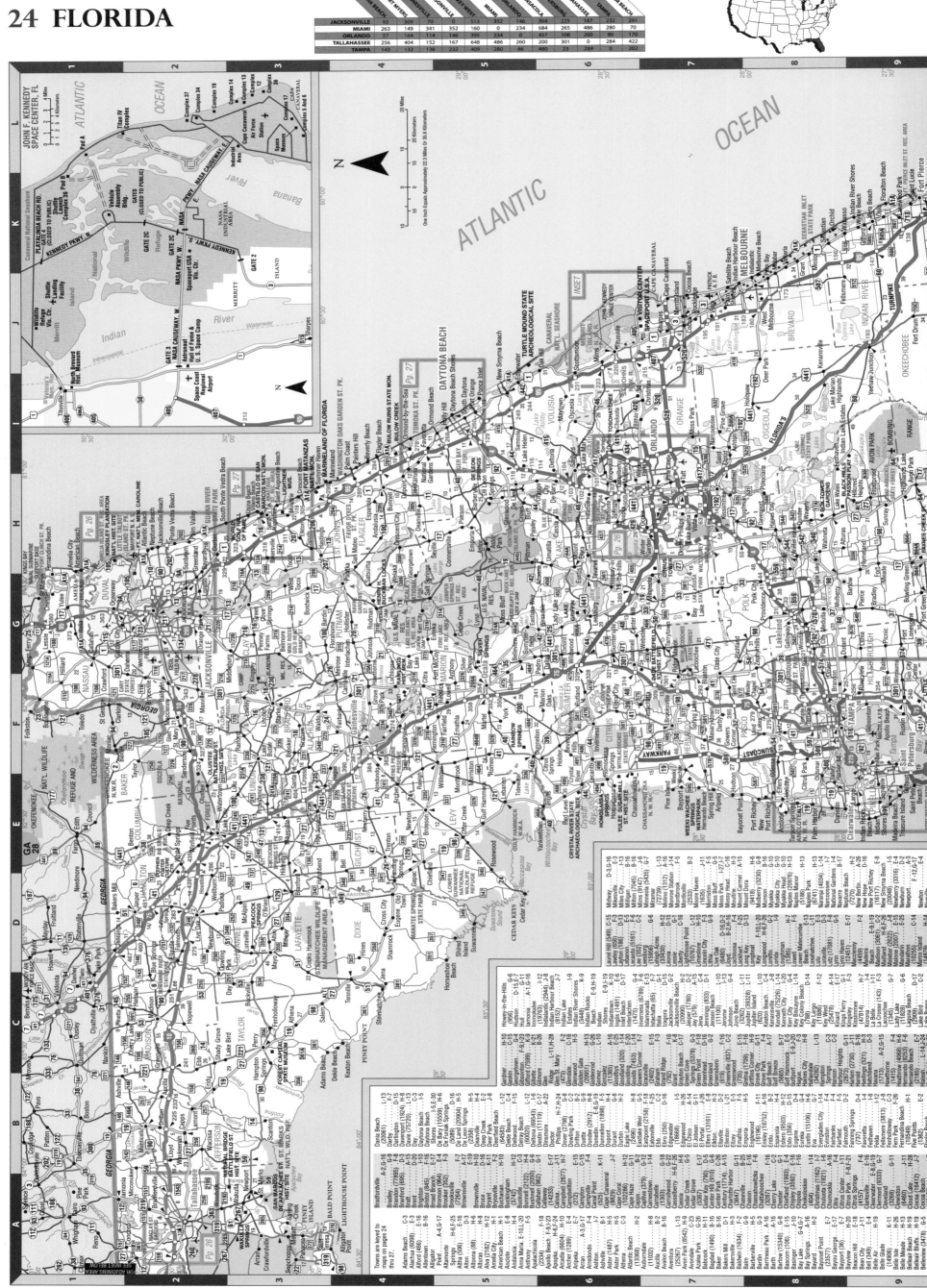

Towns are keyed to maps on pages 24 thru 27

MILEAGE NUMBER — EXIT NUMBER — INTERCHANGE — CONTROLLED ACCESS — UNDER CONSTRUCTION — TOLL CONTROLLED ACCESS

PRIMARY DIVIDED — PRIMARY UNDIVIDED — ARTERIAL DIVIDED — ARTERIAL UNDIVIDED — UNPAVED — SCENIC ROUTE — TIME ZONE

STATE/LOCAL PARK — FOREST — CAMPGROUND — REST AREAS — INFORMATION CTR — POINT OF INTEREST

Western FLORIDA

Florida Keys

GULF OF MEXICO

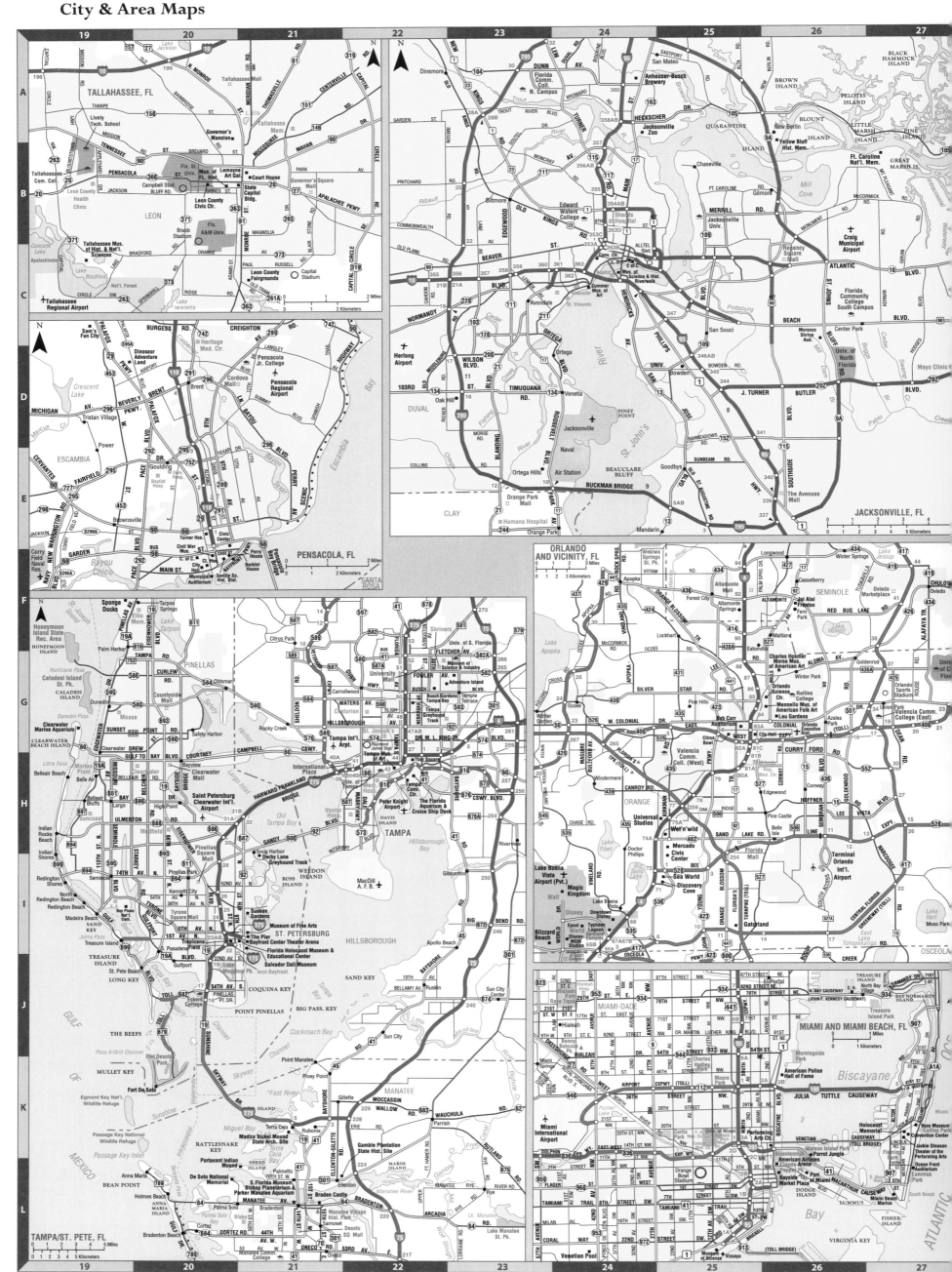

ST. AUGUSTINE, FL

DAYTONA BEACH, FL

ST PALM BEACH AREA, FL

FT. LAUDERDALE, FL

ATLANTA AND VICINITY, GA

AUGUSTA, GA

SAVANNAH, GA

MACON, GA

BRUNSWICK, GA

28 GEORGIA

	ALBANY	ATHENS	ATLANTA	AUGUSTA	BRUNSWICK	COLUMBUS	MACON	ROME	SAVANNAH	STATESBORO	TIFTON	VALDOSTA
ALBANY	0	206	186	233	176	87	108	260	228	190	42	89
ATLANTA	186	72	0	151	312	105	85	70	252	214	183	231
AUGUSTA	233	98	151	0	106	251	123	223	129	81	190	230
COLUMBUS	87	173	109	251	254	0	100	151	251	213	135	184
MACON	108	99	85	125	228	100	0	160	168	130	105	153

Towns with star (*) are keyed to maps on page 27.

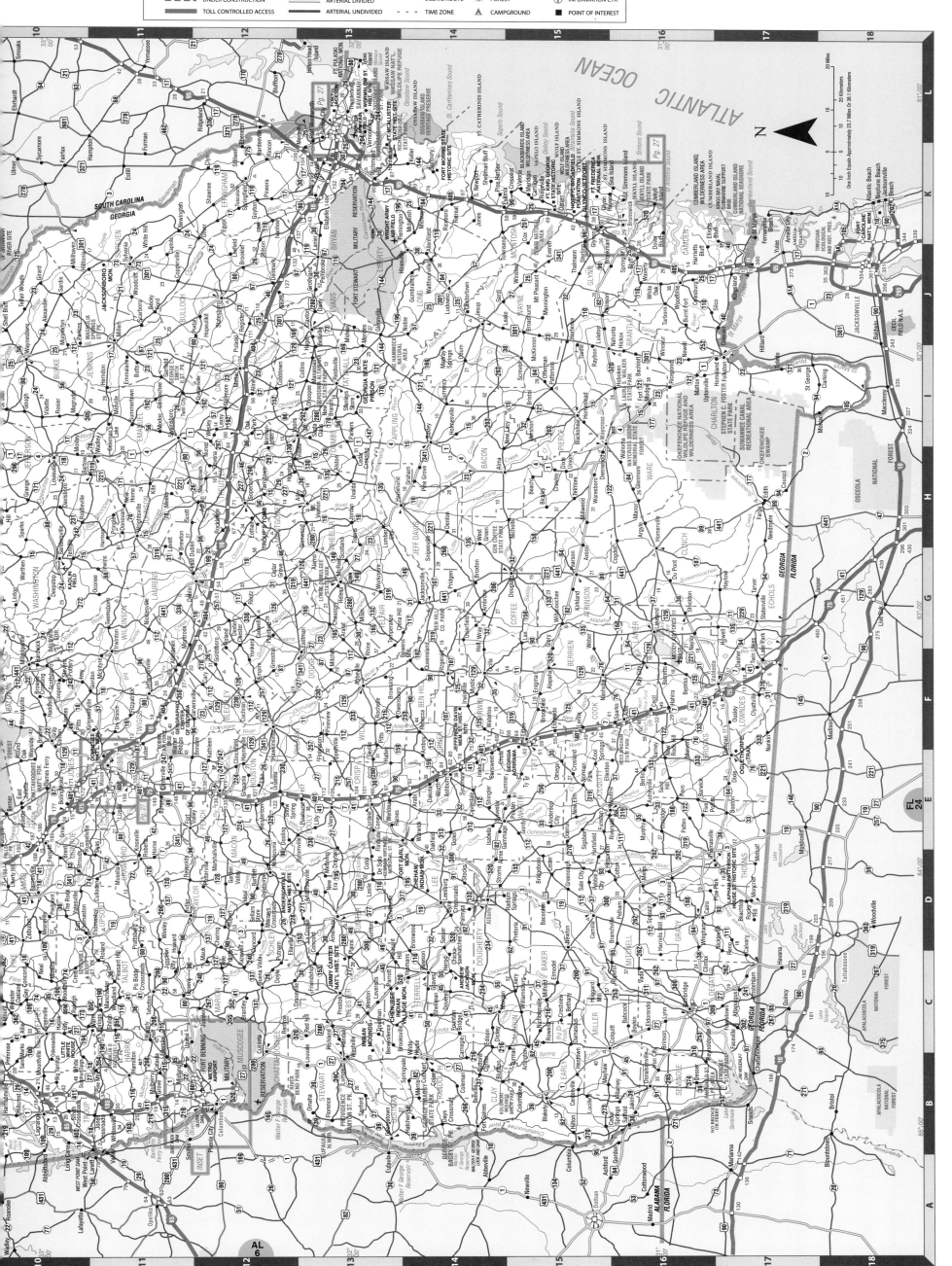

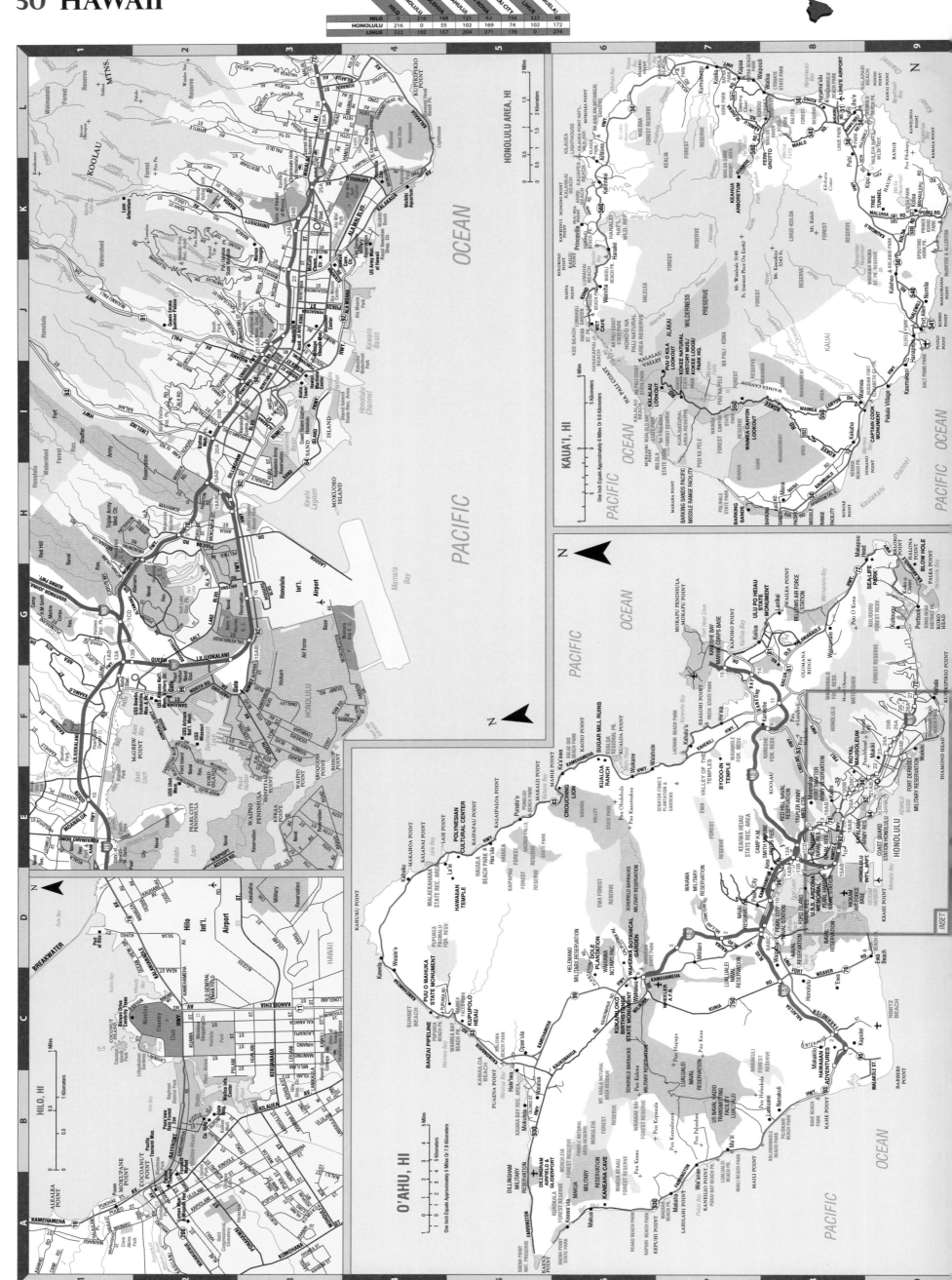

	HILO	HONOLULU	HOOLEHUA	KAHULUI	KAILUA KONA	LANAI CITY	WAIMEA (KAMUELA)	LIHUE
HILO	0	216	168	121	62	156	322	45
HONOLULU	216	0	55	102	169	74	102	172
LIHUE	322	102	157	204	271	176	0	274

HONOLULU AREA, HI

KAUA'I, HI

O'AHU, HI

HILO, HI

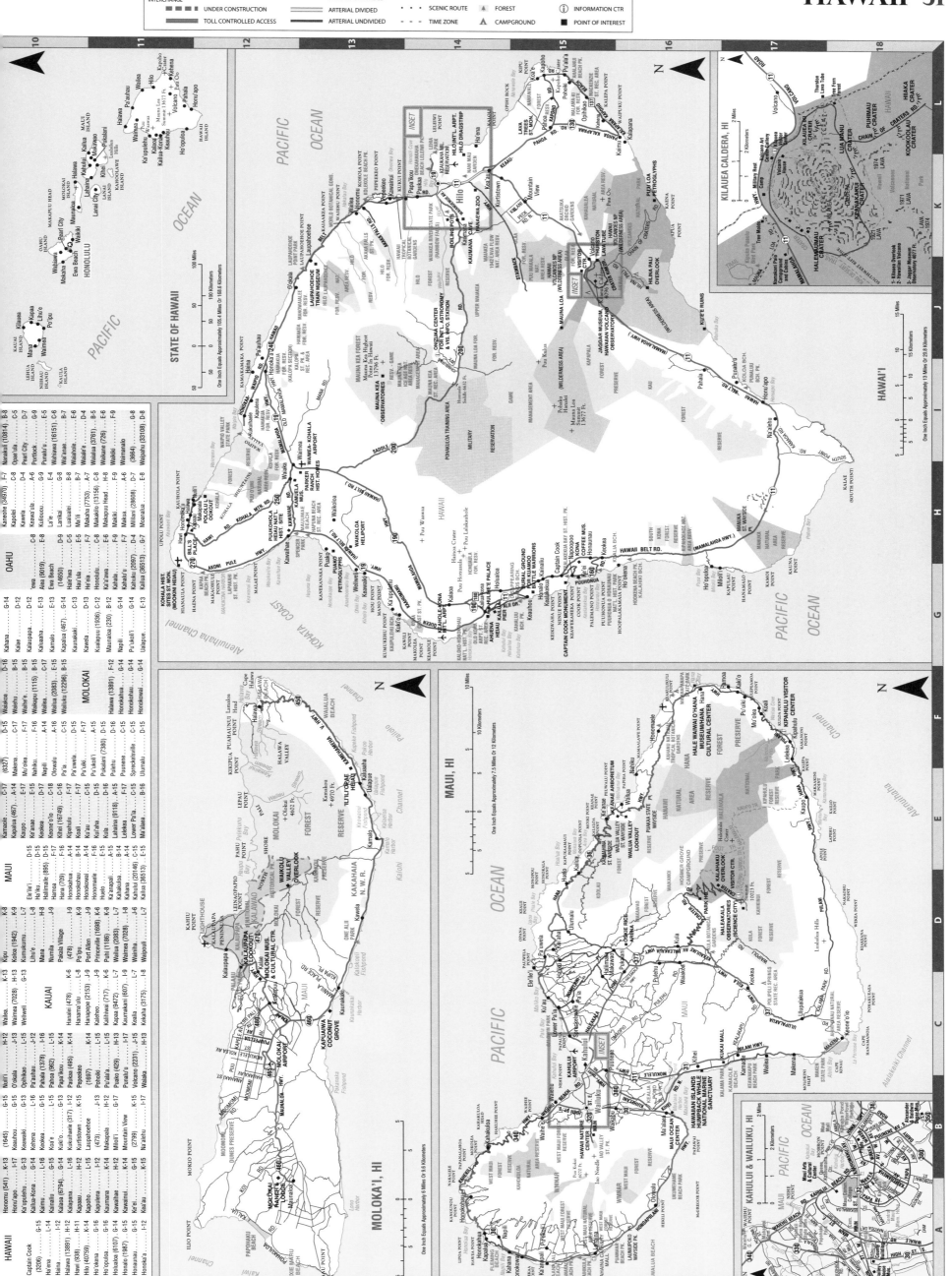

MILEAGE
NUMBER   EXIT NUMBER
8   13
         CONTROLLED ACCESS
INTERCHANGE
5

PRIMARY DIVIDED
PRIMARY UNDIVIDED
ARTERIAL DIVIDED
ARTERIAL UNDIVIDED
UNDER CONSTRUCTION
TOLL CONTROLLED ACCESS
UNPAVED
SCENIC ROUTE
TIME ZONE
STATE/LOCAL PARK
FOREST
CAMPGROUND
REST AREAS
INFORMATION CTR
POINT OF INTEREST

STATE OF HAWAII

KILAUEA CALDERA, HI

KAHULUI & WAILUKU, HI

MOLOKA'I, HI

MAUI, HI

HAWAI'I

	BOISE	COEUR D'ALENE	IDAHO FALLS	LEWISTON	MISSOULA MT	POCATELLO	SPOKANE WA	TWIN FALLS
BOISE	0	457	281	268	351	235	425	126
POCATELLO	235	528	53	504	369	0	562	116
TWIN FALLS	126	580	161	394	477	116	547	0

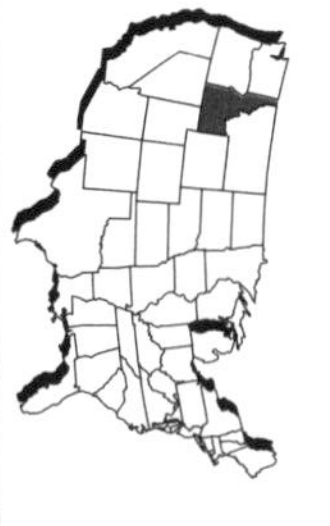

POCATELLO, ID

IDAHO FALLS, ID

BOISE-NAMPA-CALDWELL, ID

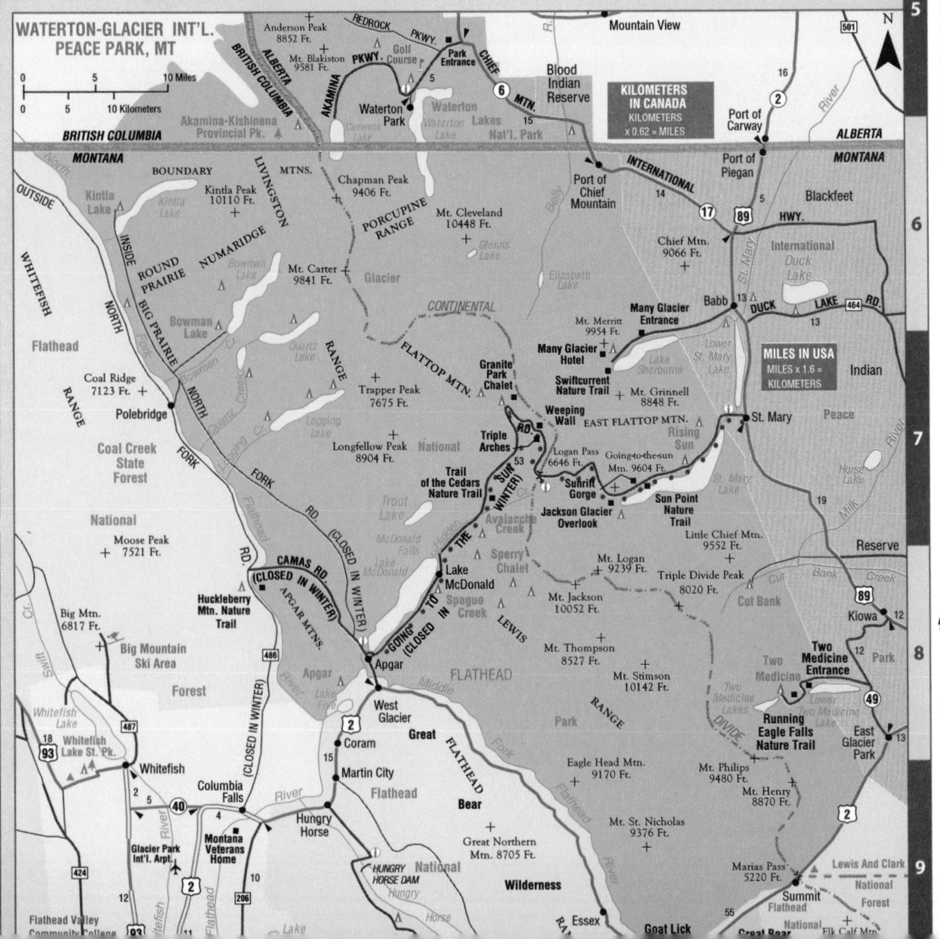

WATERTON-GLACIER INT'L. PEACE PARK, MT

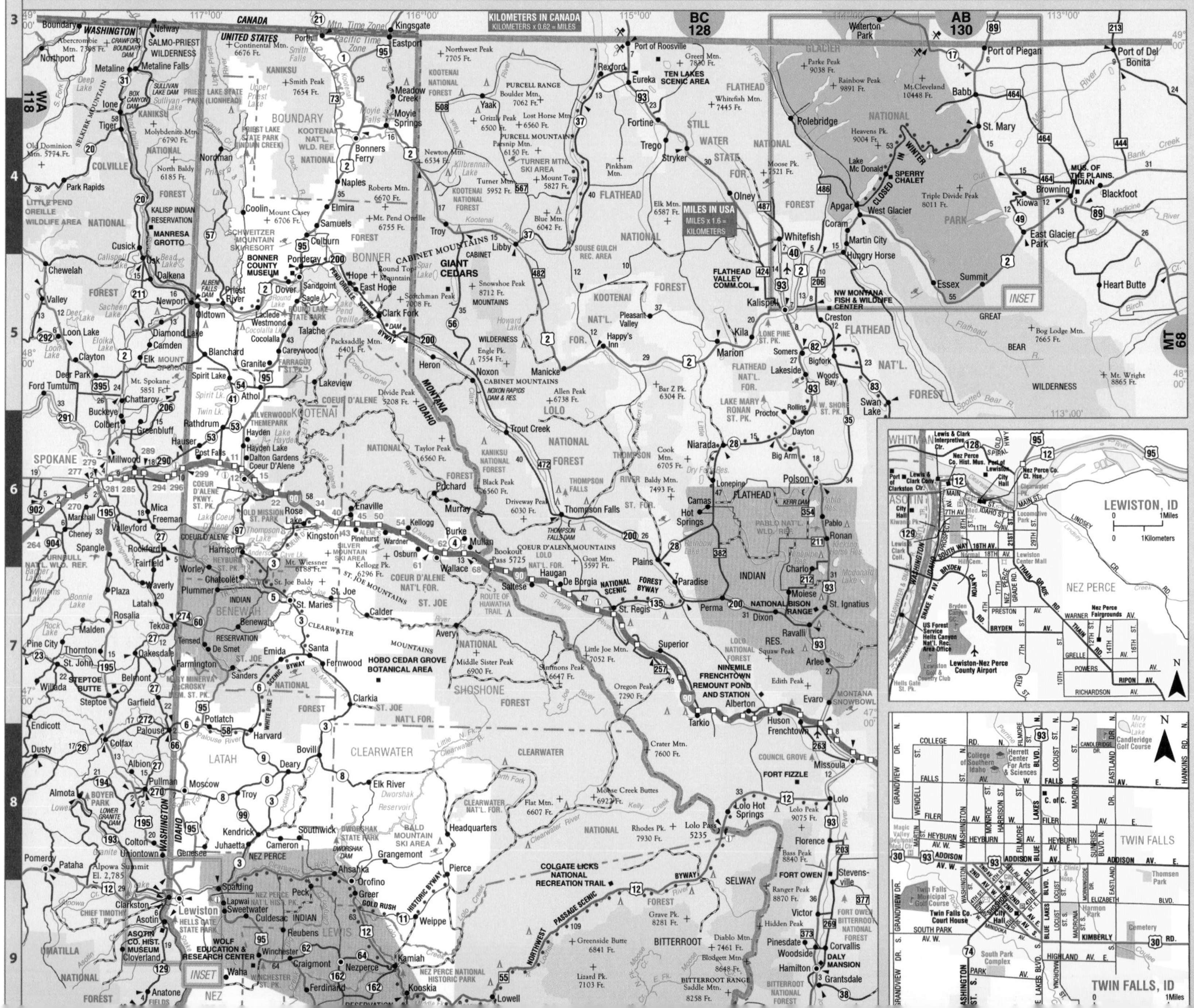

LEWISTON, ID

TWIN FALLS, ID

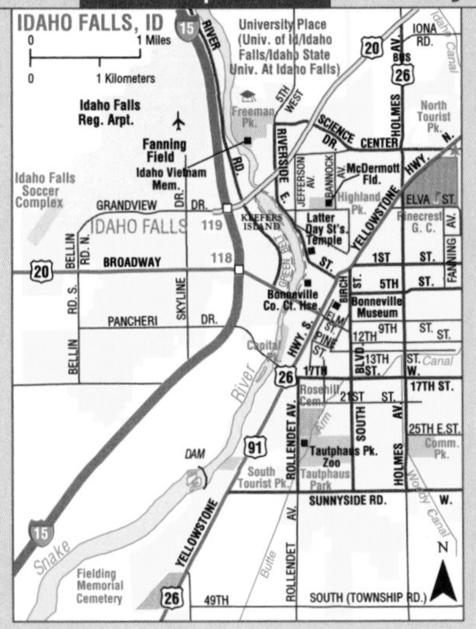

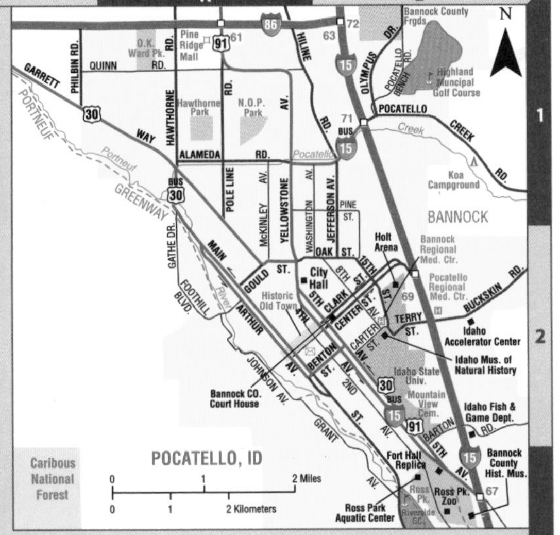

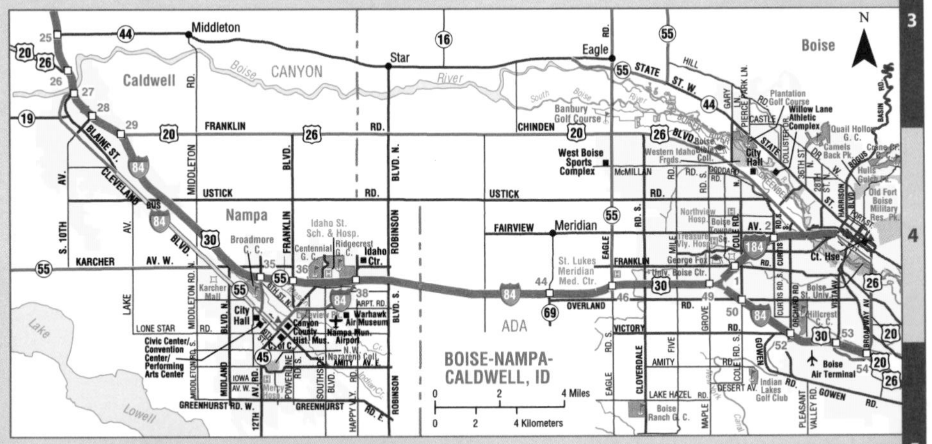

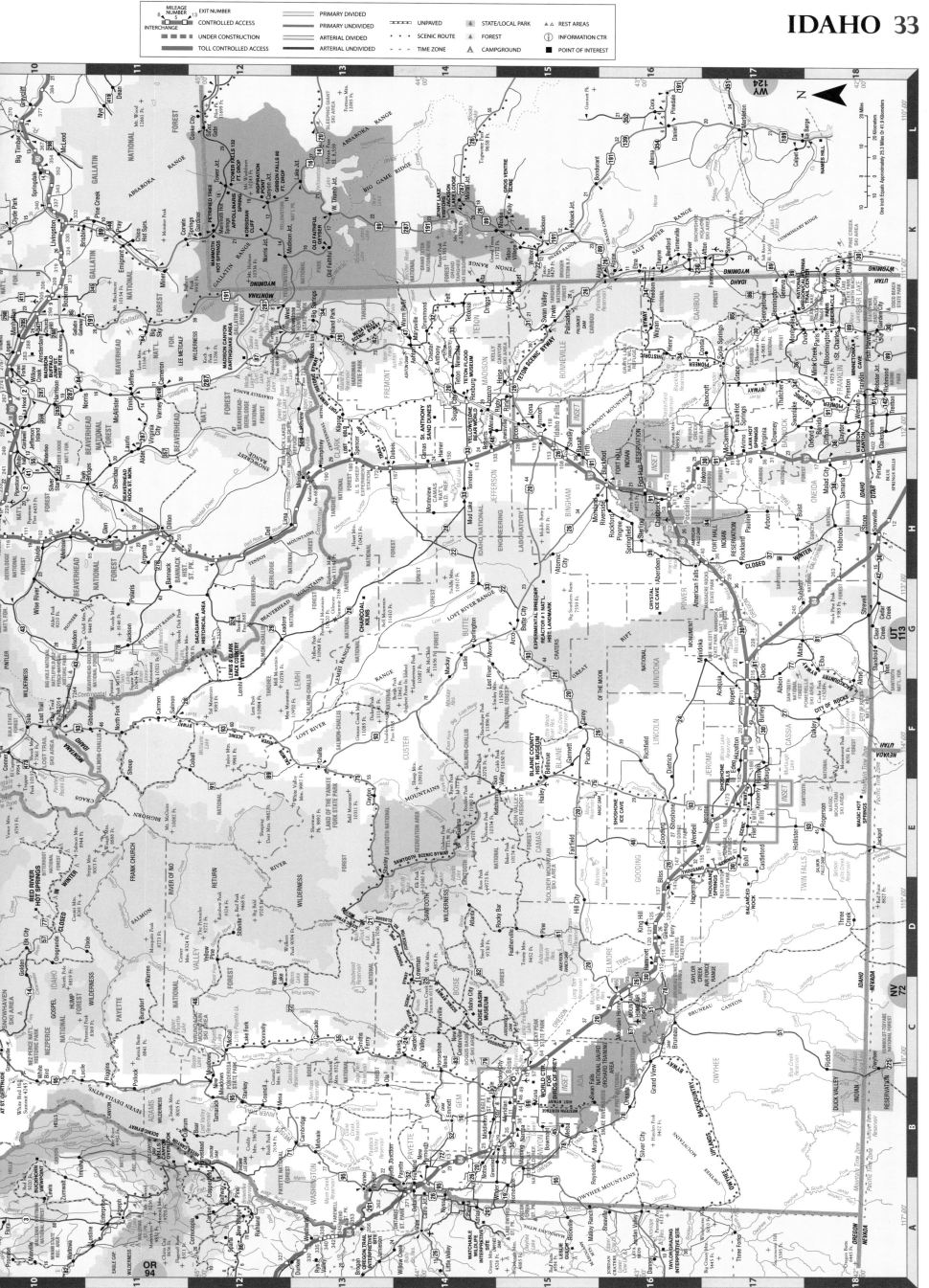

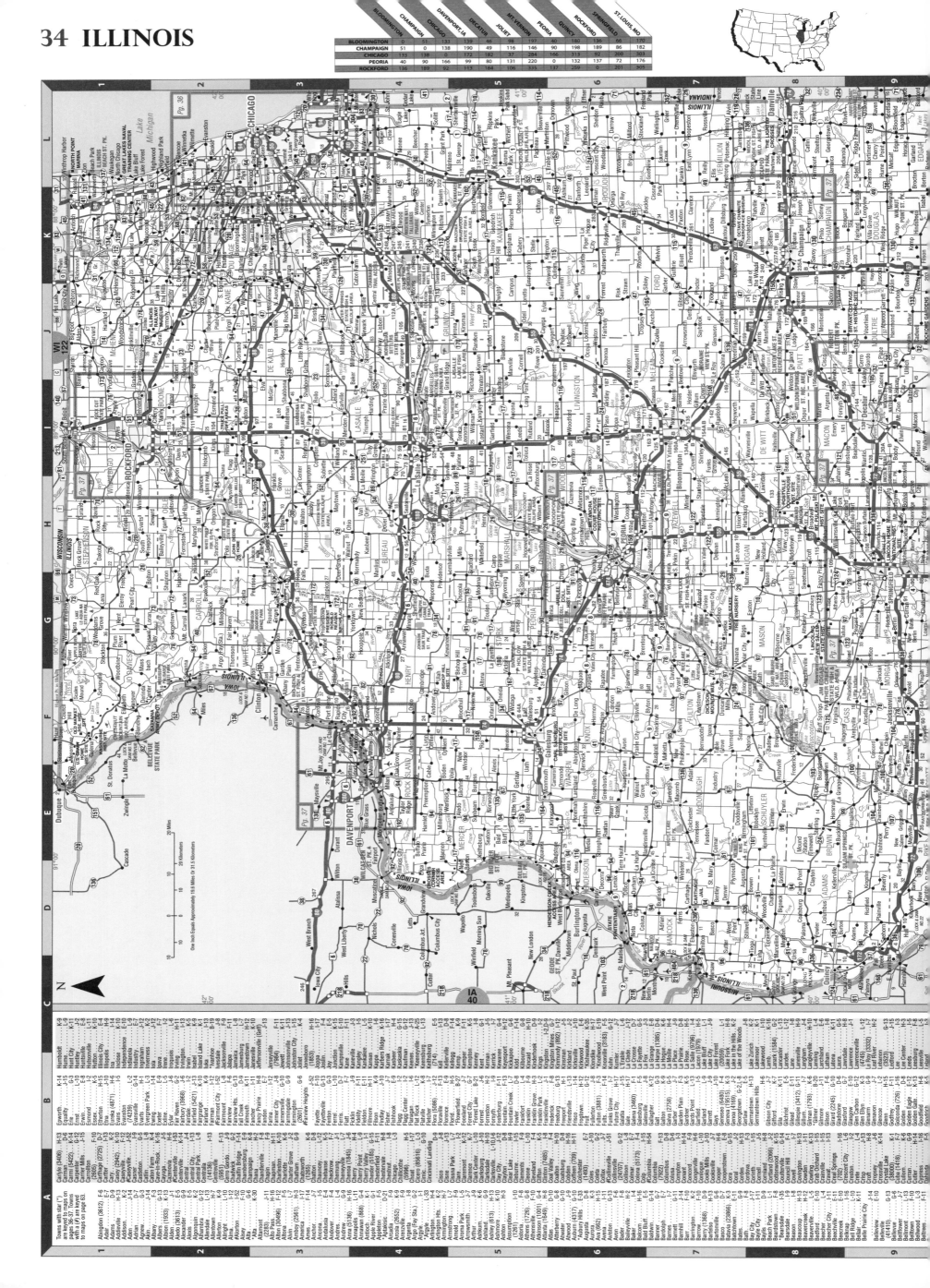

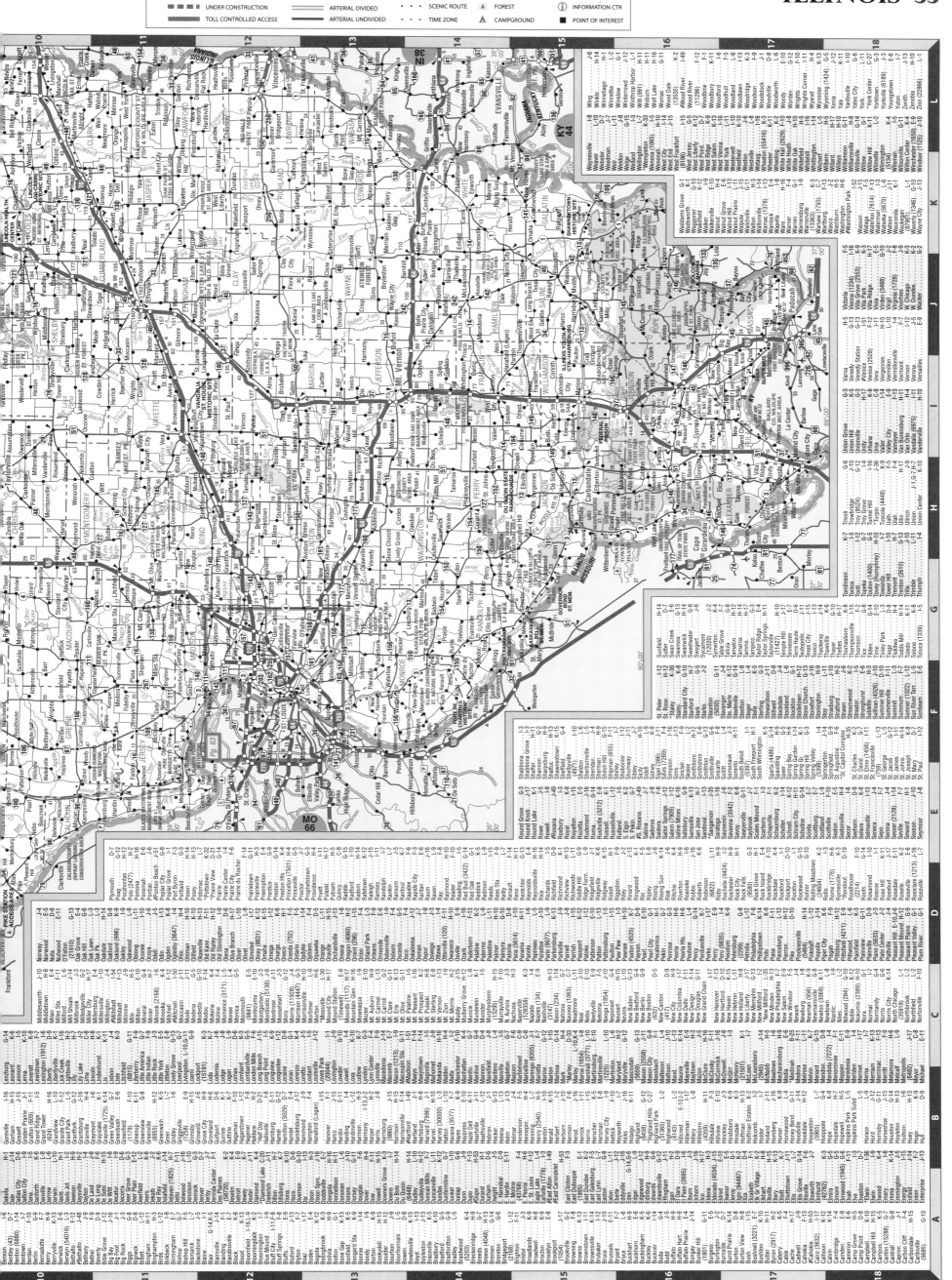

	CHICAGO, IL	CINCINNATI, OH	COLUMBUS	EVANSVILLE	FORT WAYNE	INDIANAPOLIS	LAFAYETTE	LOUISVILLE, KY	MICHIGAN CITY	RICHMOND	SOUTH BEND	TERRE HAUTE
FORT WAYNE	176	197	173	306	0	128	113	242	156	84	211	
INDIANAPOLIS	185	132	48	178	128	0	66	116	178	75	146	82
MICHIGAN CITY	57	308	226	314	116	114	290	0	248	42	189	
RICHMOND	254	65	115	248	110	75	135	184	248	0	183	153
TERRE HAUTE	182	203	120	122	211	82	90	190	189	153	195	0

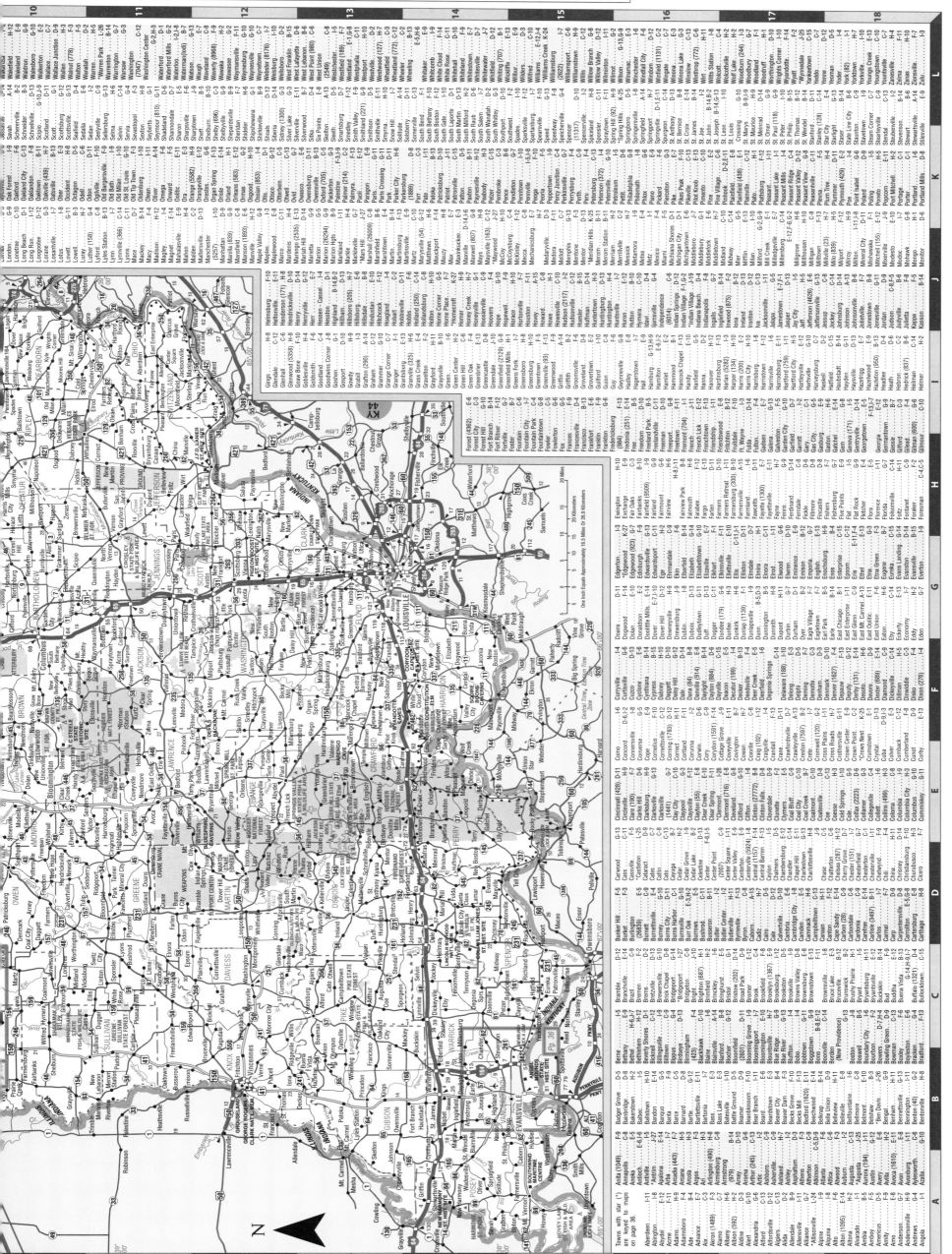

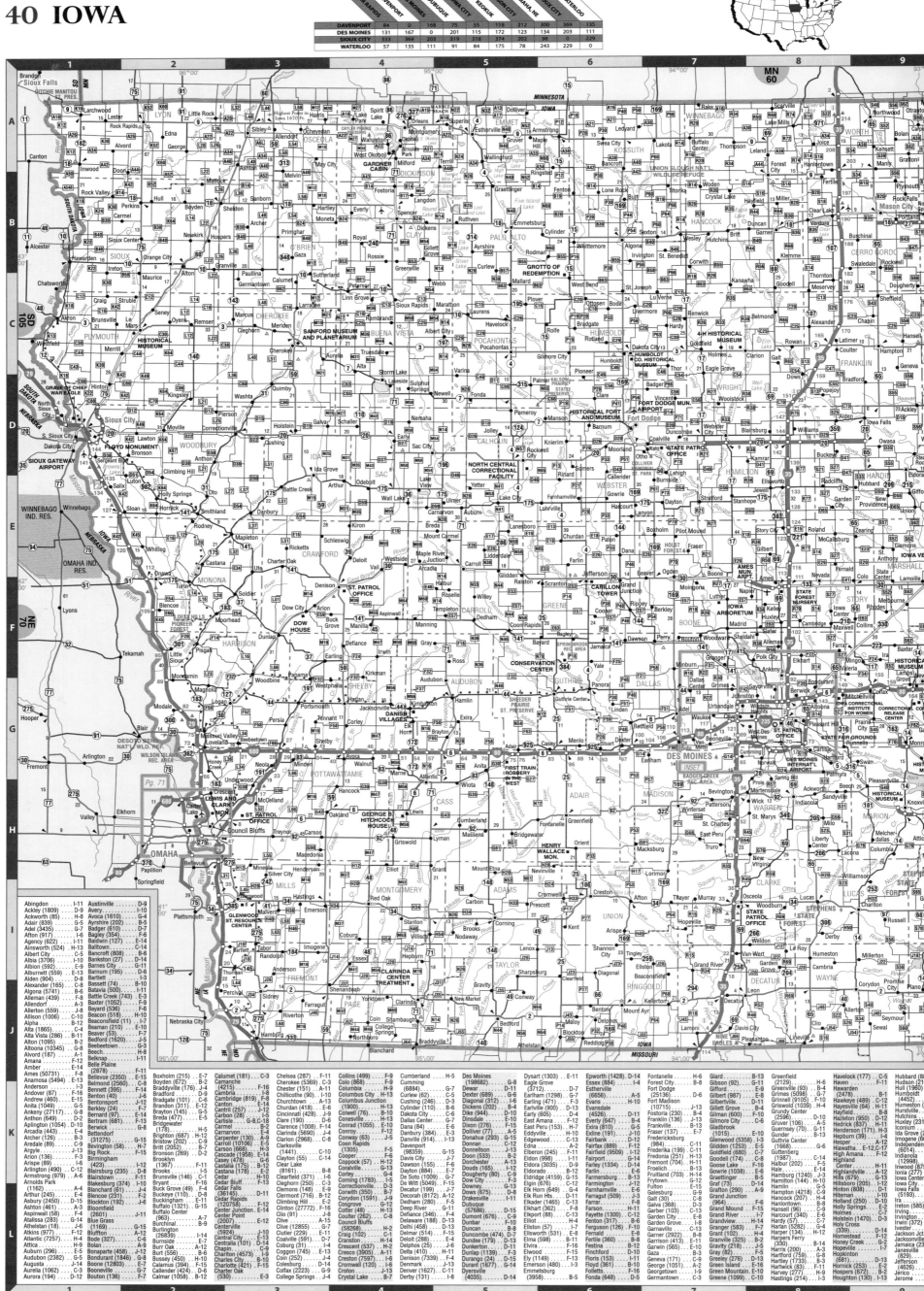

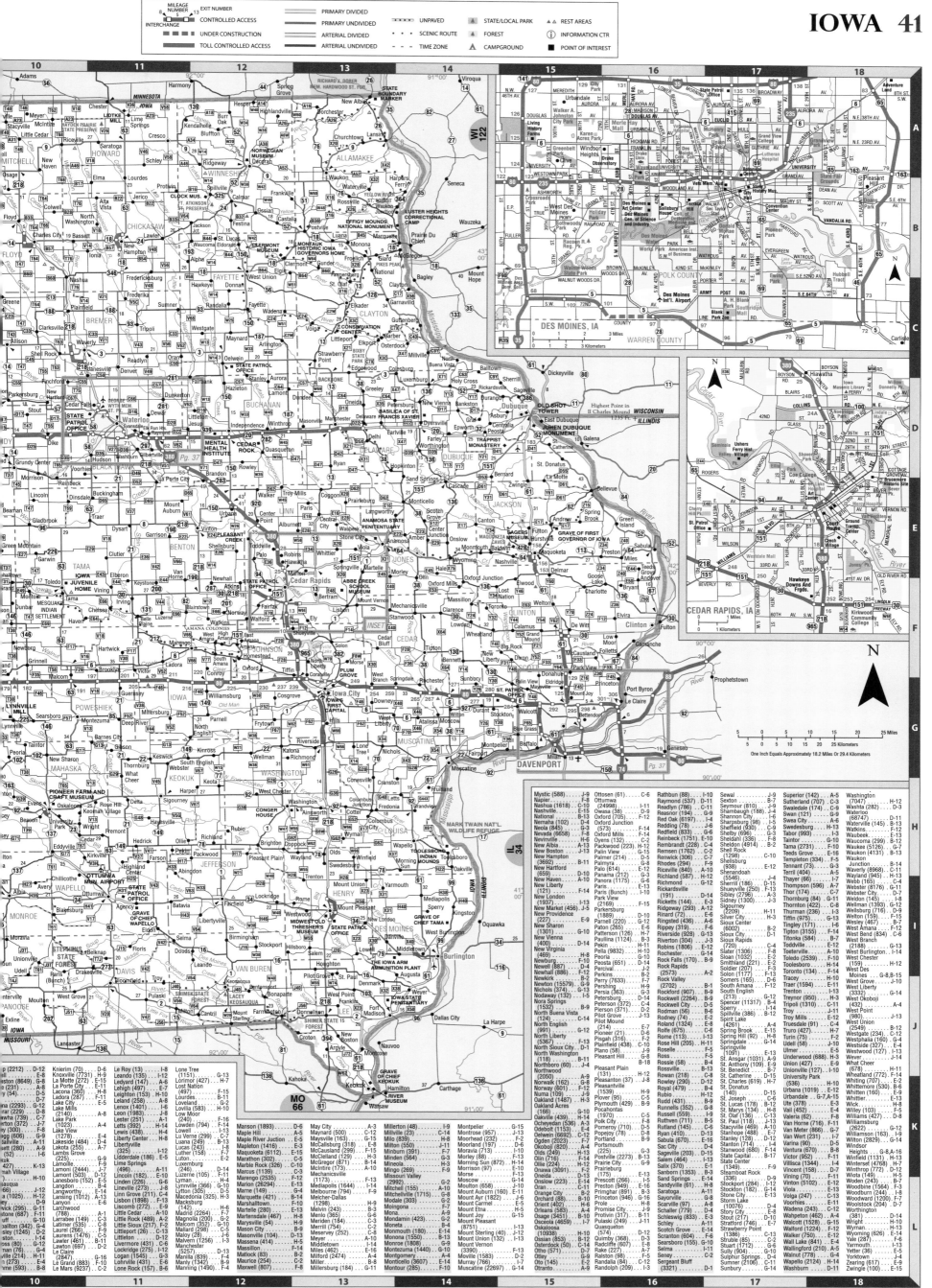

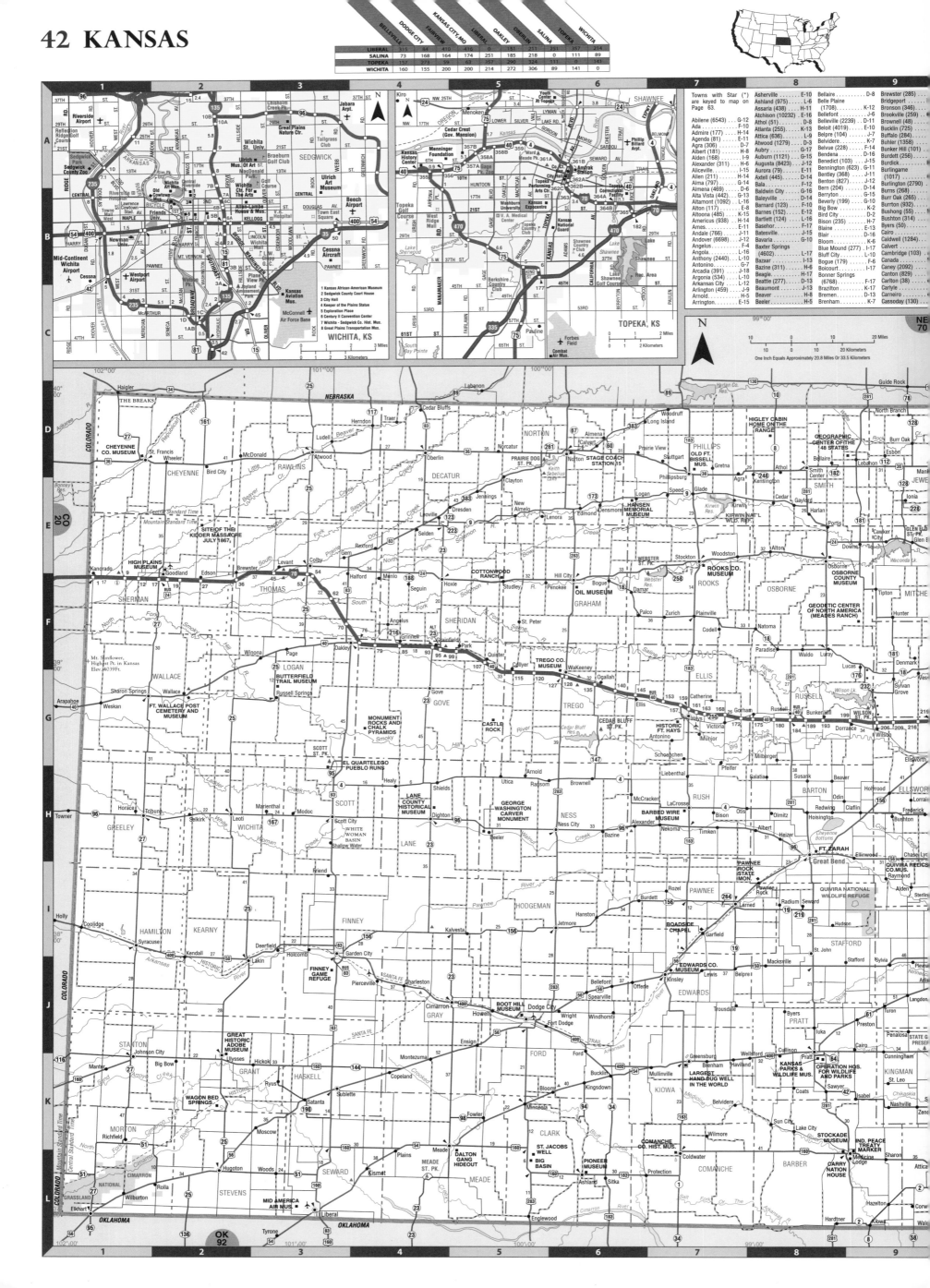

Mileage chart	MELLEVILLE	DODGE CITY	FAIRVIEW	KANSAS CITY, MO	LIBERAL	OAKLEY	OBERLIN	SALINA	TOPEKA	WICHITA
LIBERAL	315	64	410	416	0	151	211	251	357	214
SALINA	73	168	164	174	251	185	218	0	111	89
TOPEKA	157	273	59	63	357	290	324	111	0	141
WICHITA	160	155	200	200	214	272	306	89	141	0

WICHITA, KS

1 Kansas African-American Museum
2 Sedgwick County Court House
3 City Hall
4 Keeper of the Plains Statue
5 Exploration Place
6 Century II Convention Center
7 Wichita - Sedgwick Co. Hist. Mus.
8 Great Plains Transportation Mus.

TOPEKA, KS

NE 70

Towns with Star (*) are keyed to map on Page 63.

Asherville E-10
Ada (6543) G-12
Admire (177) H-14
Agenda (81) E-11
Agra (306) D-7
Albert (181) H-6
Alden (168) I-9
Alexander (311) H-6
Aliceville I-15
Allen (211) H-14
Alma (797) G-14
Almena (469) D-6
Alton (117) E-8
Altamont (1092) L-16
Altoona (485) K-15
Americus (938) H-14
Ames E-11
Andale (766) J-11
Andover (6698) J-12
Angelus F-4
Angola I-14
Anthony (2440) L-11
Antonino G-7
Arcadia (396) L-16
Argonia (534) L-10
Arkansas City (12062) L-12
Arlington (459) J-9
Arnold H-5
Arrington E-15

Ashland (975) L-6
Assaria (438) H-11
Athol (51) D-8
Atlanta (255) K-13
Atchison (10232) E-16
Atwood (1279) D-3
Auburn (1121) G-15
Aubry G-17
Augusta (8423) J-12
Aurora (79) E-11
Axtell (445) D-14
Bala F-12
Baldwin City G-16
Baleyville L-10
Barnard (123) F-10
Bazaar J-13
Bazine (311) H-6
Basehor F-17
Bison (235) H-7
Batesville J-15
Beagle G-15
Beattie (277) D-13
Beaumont (17) J-18
Beaver (534) L-10
Beeler H-5

Bellaire D-8
Belle Plaine (1708) K-12
Bellefont J-6
Belleville (2239) D-11
Beloit (4019) E-10
Belpre (104) J-7
Belvidere K-7
Belvue (228) F-14
Bendena D-16
Benedict (103) J-15
Bennington (623) G-11
Bentley (363) J-11
Benton (827) J-12
Bern (204) D-14
Berryton G-15
Beverly (199) G-10
Big Bow K-2
Bird City D-2
Blue Mound (277) L-16
Bloom K-6
Blair D-16
Bluff City L-10
Bogue (179) F-6
Boicourt I-17
Bonner Springs (6768) F-17
Brazilton K-17
Bremen D-13
Brenham K-7

Brewster (285) E-3
Bridgeport H-11
Bronson (346) J-16
Brownell (48) H-5
Brookville (259) G-11
Buffalo (284) J-15
Buhler (1358) J-10
Bunker Hill (101) G-7
Burdett (256) I-6
Burdick H-13
Burlingame (1017) G-15
Burlington (2790) H-15
Burns (268) J-13
Burr Oak (265) D-9
Burrton (932) J-11
Bushong (50) H-14
Bushton (314) H-9
Byers (50) J-7
Cairo H-7
Caldwell (1284) L-11
Calvert E-7
Cambridge (103) K-13
Canada J-12
Caney (2092) L-15
Canton (829) H-11
Carlton (38) H-12
Carlyle J-16
Carneiro G-9
Cassoday (130) J-13

CO 20

OK 92

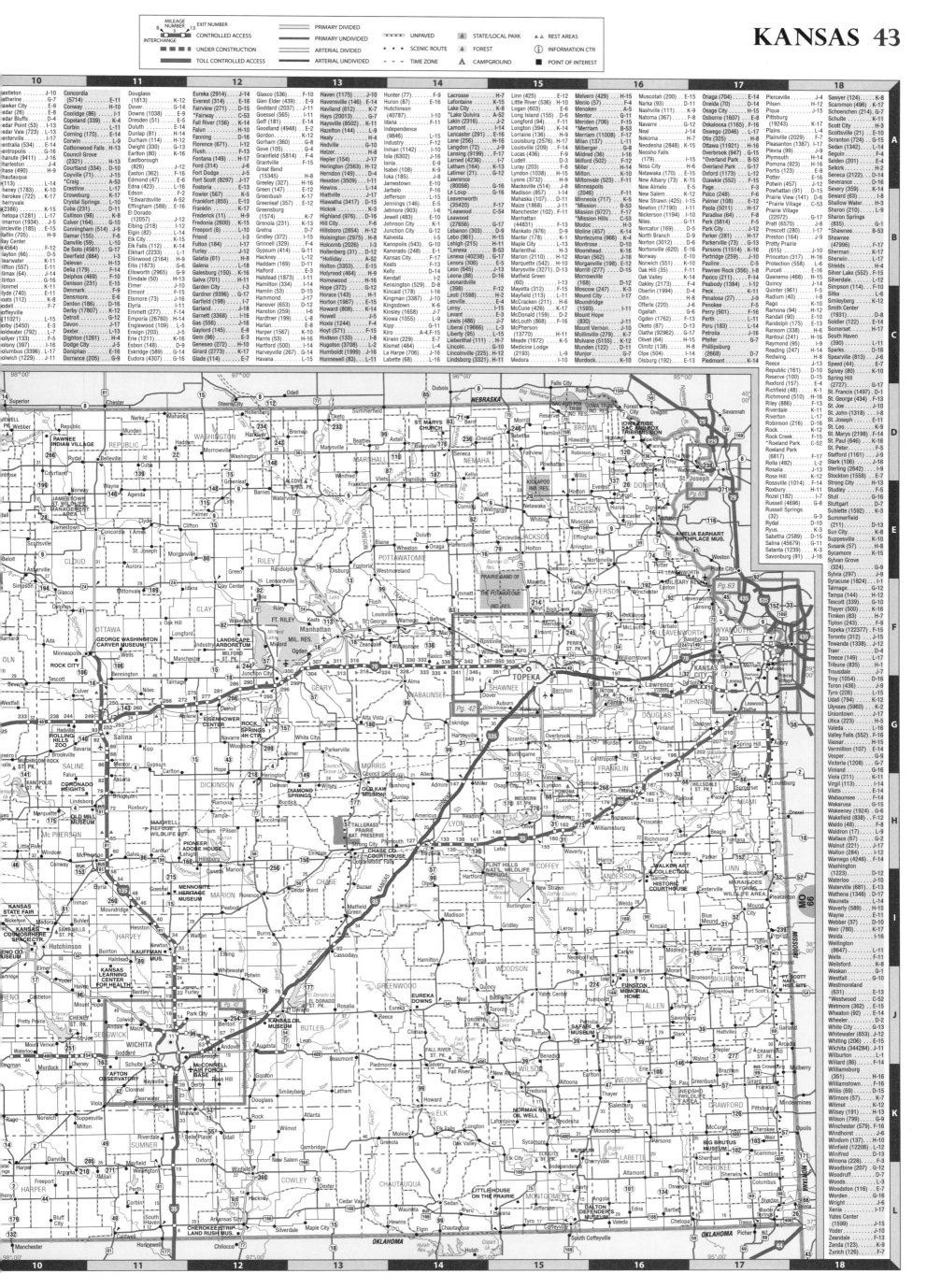

	ASHLAND	BOWLING GREEN	CINCINNATI, OH	CORBIN	EVANSVILLE, IN	FRANKFORT	LEXINGTON	LOUISVILLE	MADISONVILLE	MIDDLESBORO	OWENSBORO	PADUCAH
CINCINNATI, OH	138	223		175	224	94	87	105	262	220	212	325
EVANSVILLE, IN	309	114	224	267		173	195	119	51	312	41	109
FRANKFORT	142	159	94	116	173		28	54	198	161	162	261
LEXINGTON	118	156	87	90	195	28		76	195	135	183	258
LOUISVILLE	191	117	105	165	119	54	76		168	209	108	226

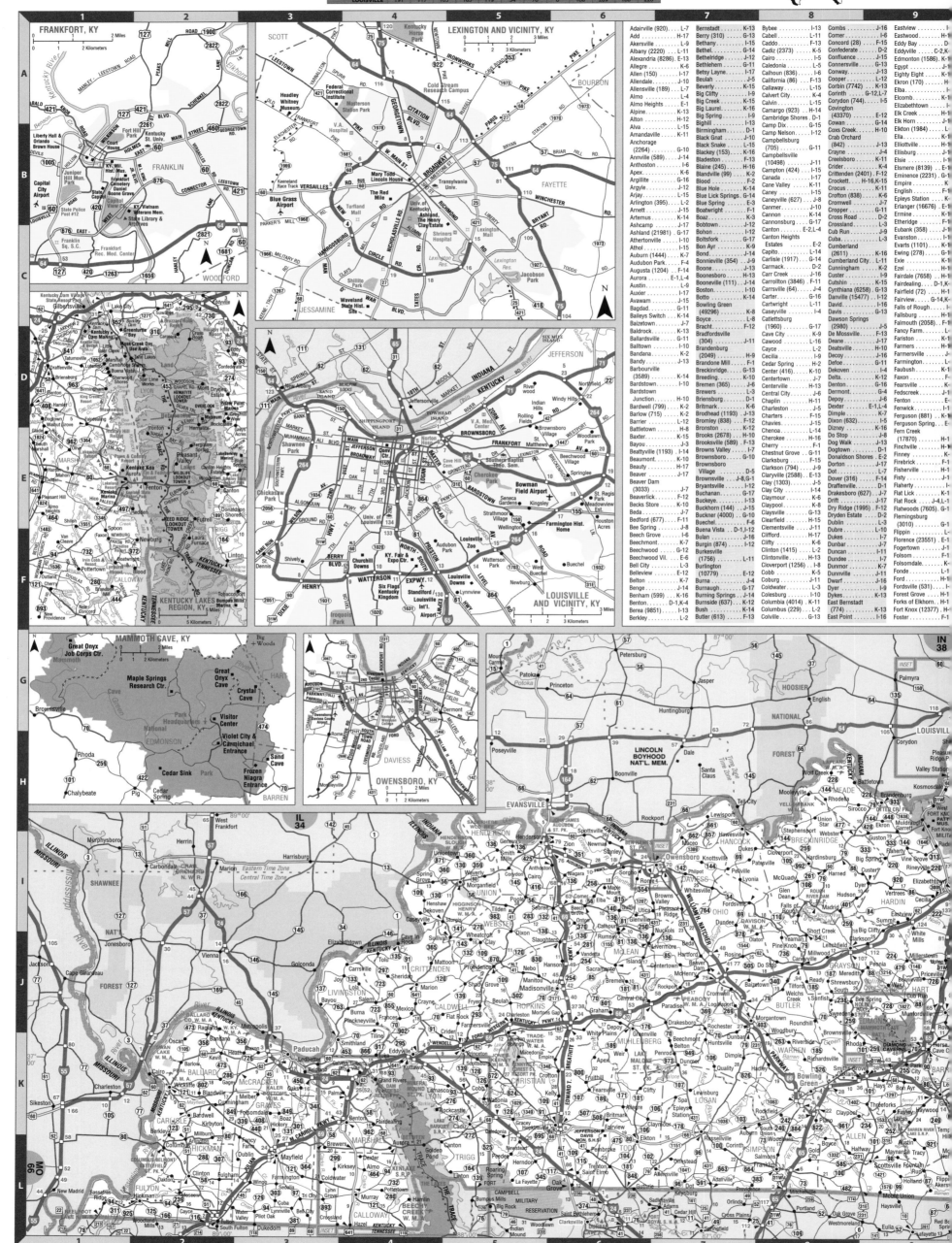

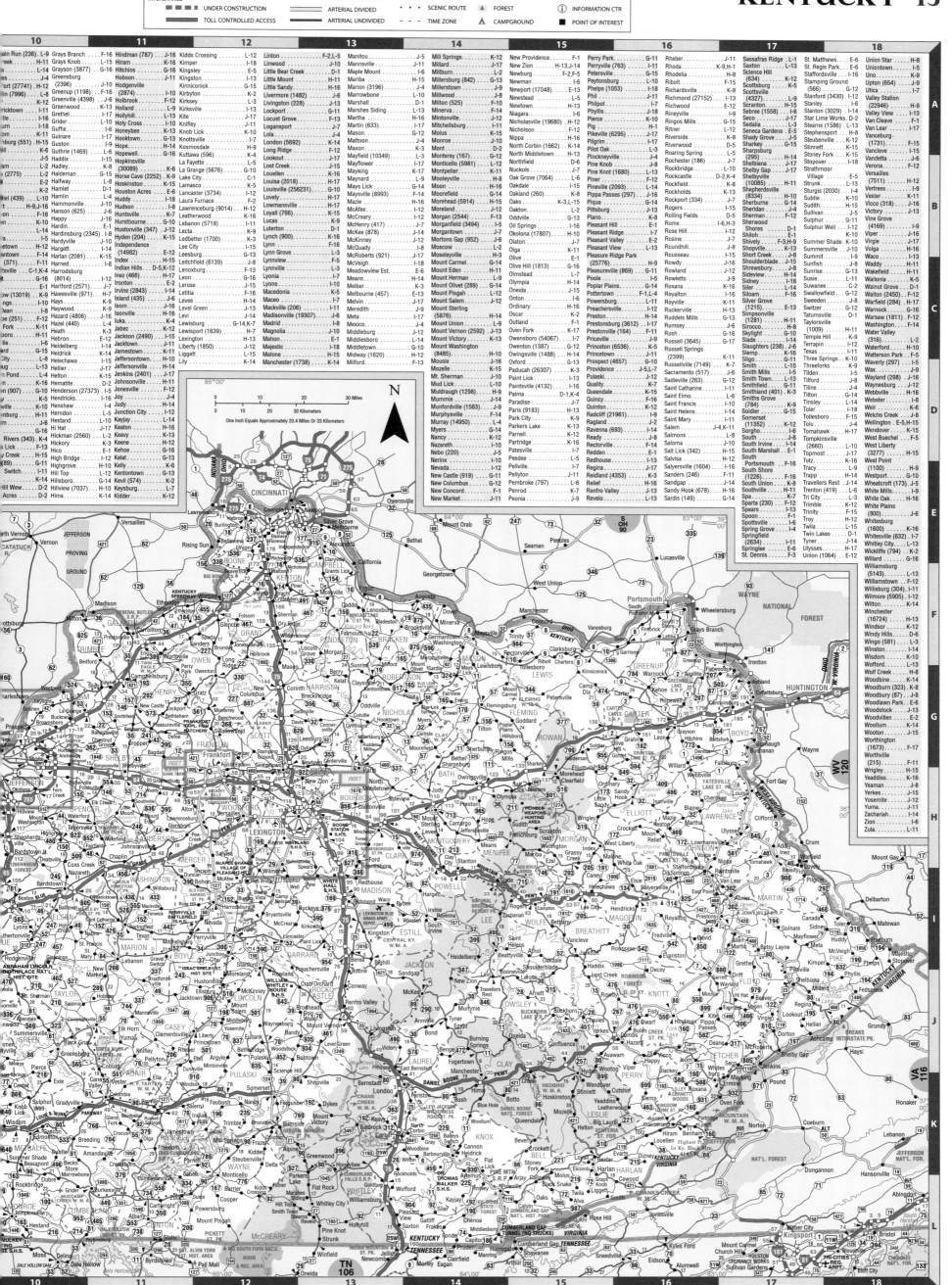

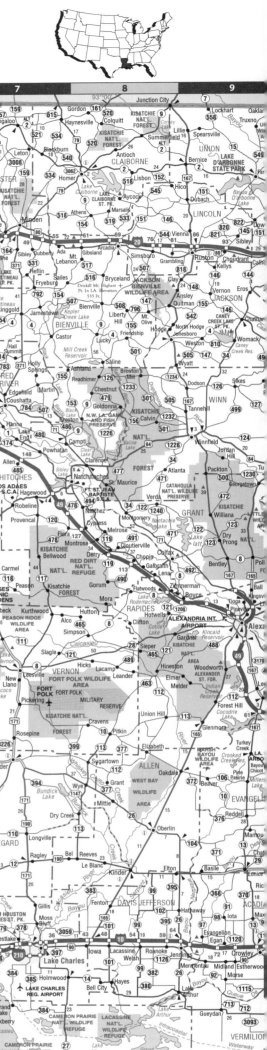

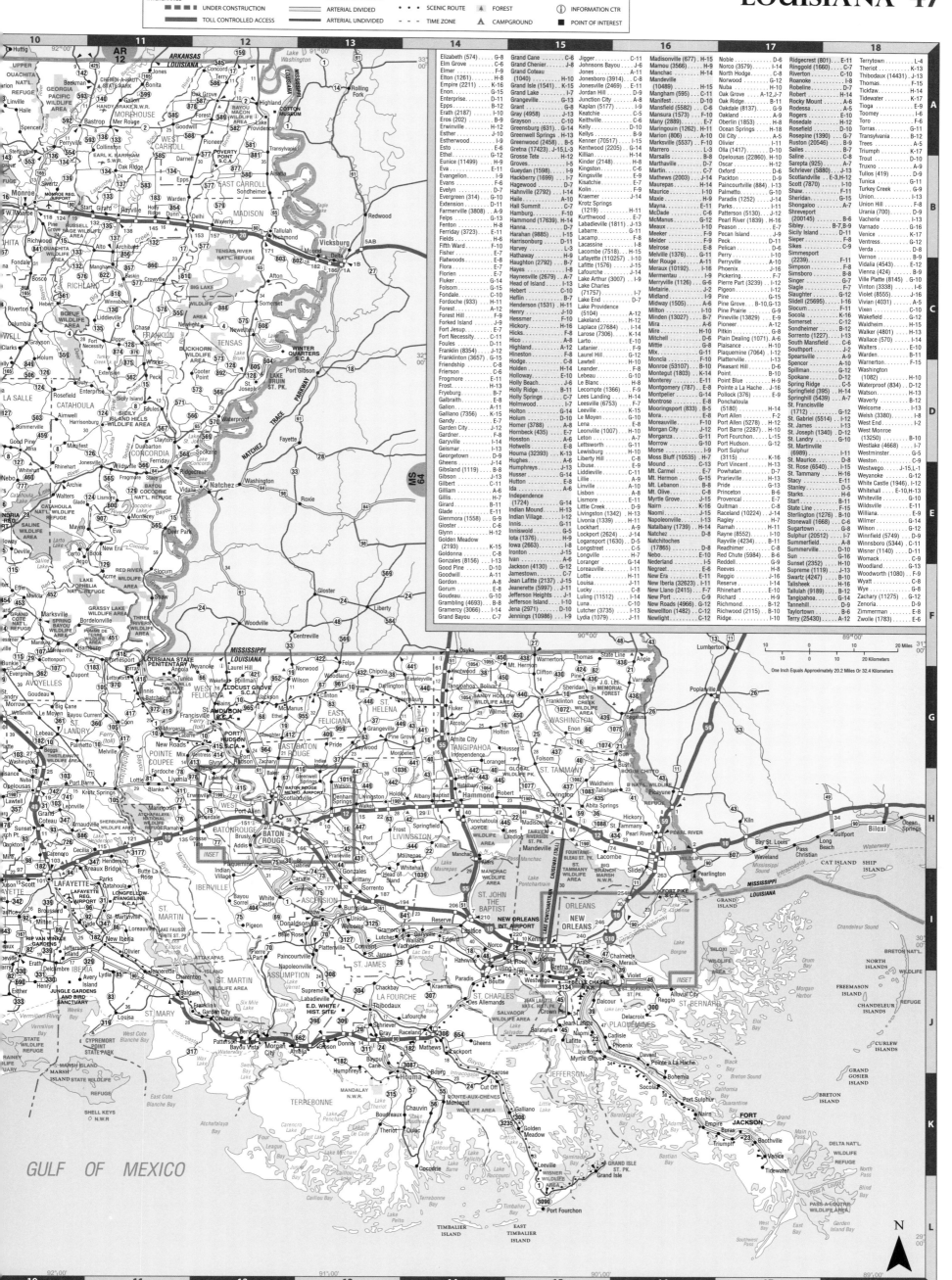

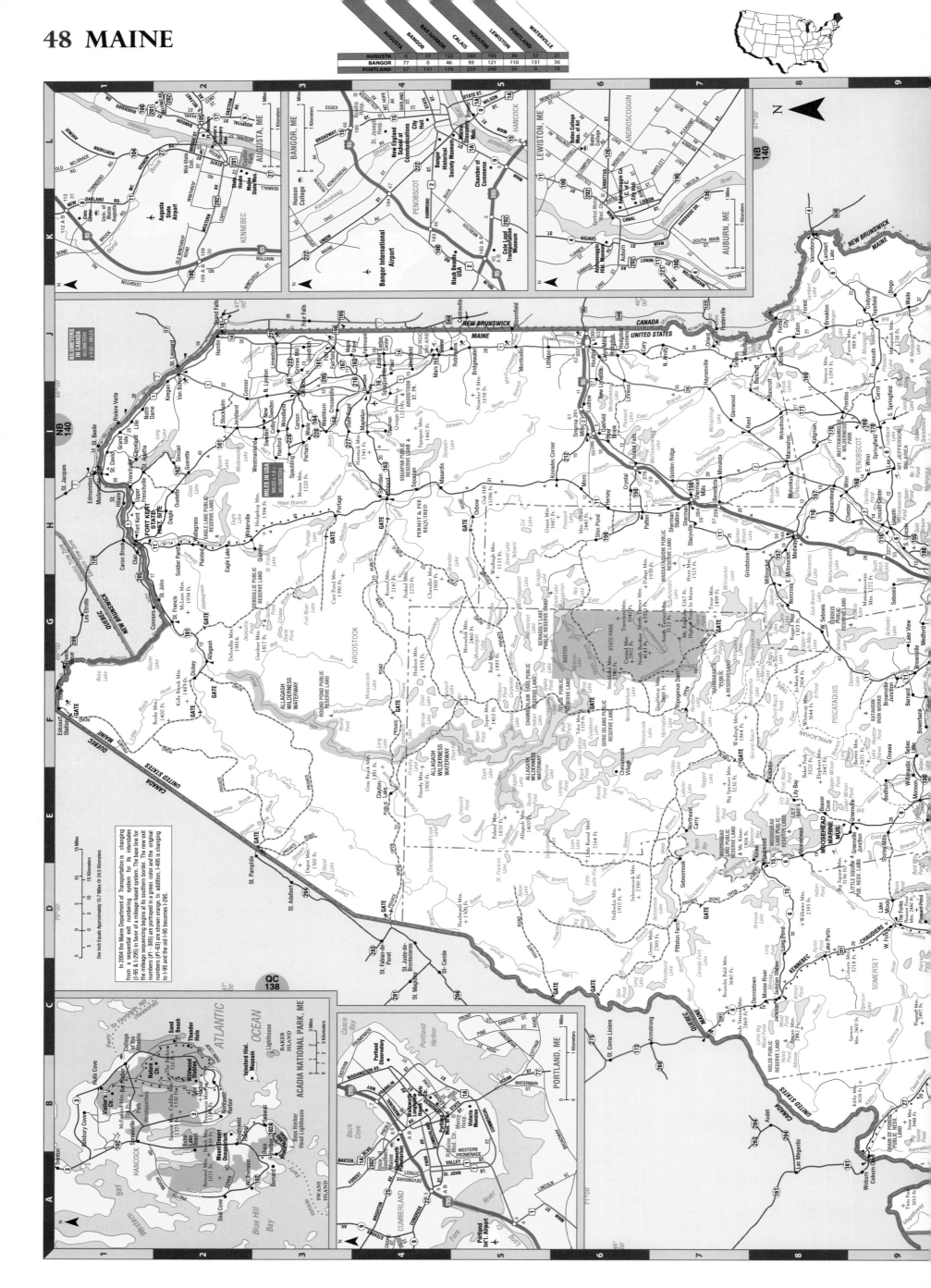

	AUGUSTA	BANGOR	BAR HARBOR	CALAIS	HOULTON	LEWISTON	PORTLAND	WATERVILLE
AUGUSTA	0	77	122	169	195	36	57	21
BANGOR	77	0	46	93	121	110	131	56
PORTLAND	57	131	176	223	249	35	0	75

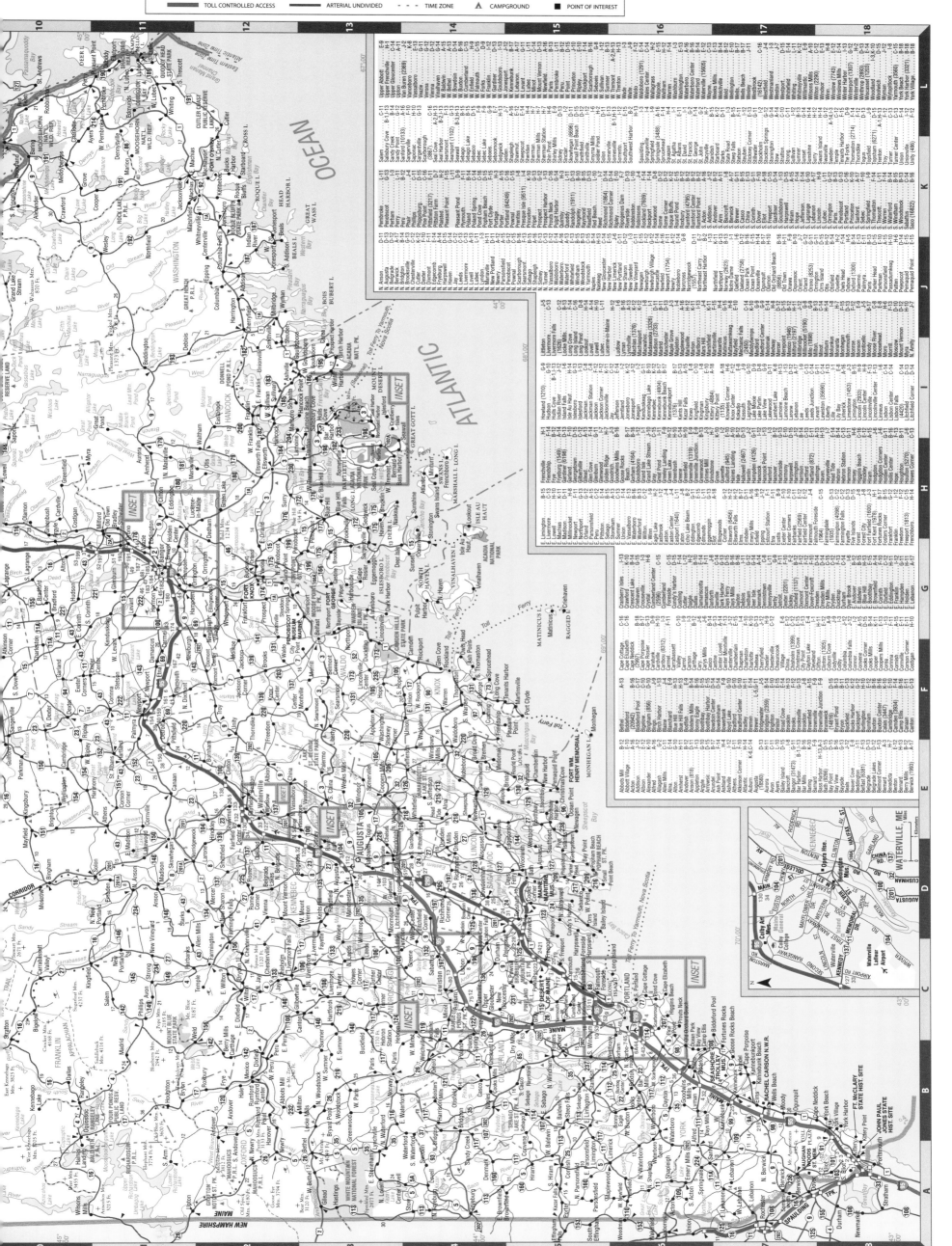

	ANNAPOLIS	BALTIMORE	CUMBERLAND	FREDERICK	HAGERSTOWN	OCEAN CITY	SALISBURY	WASHINGTON, D.C.
ANNAPOLIS	0	28	159	67	93	106	88	33
BALTIMORE	28	0	140	48	74	128	110	42
WASHINGTON, D.C.	33	42	134	44	68	138	120	0

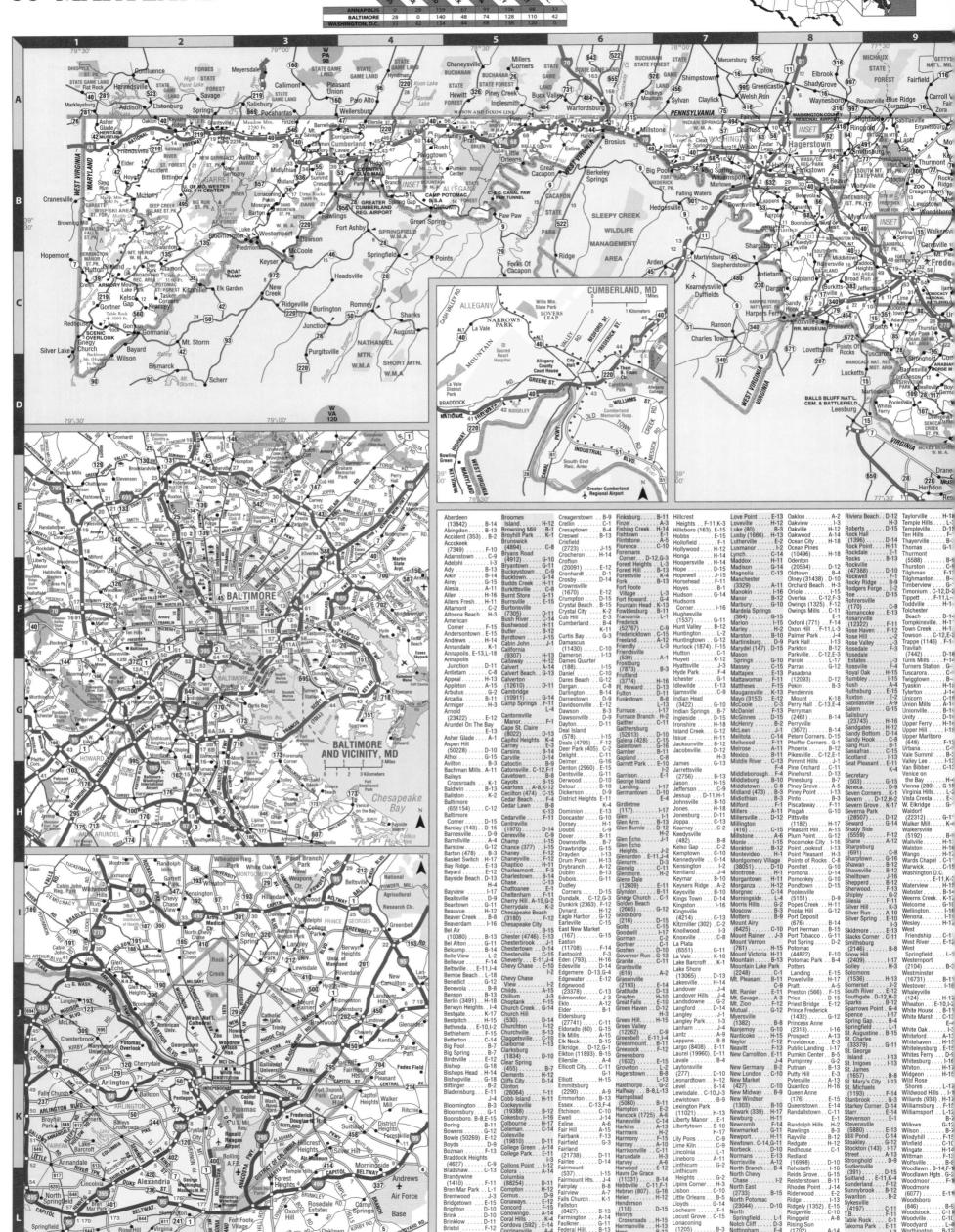

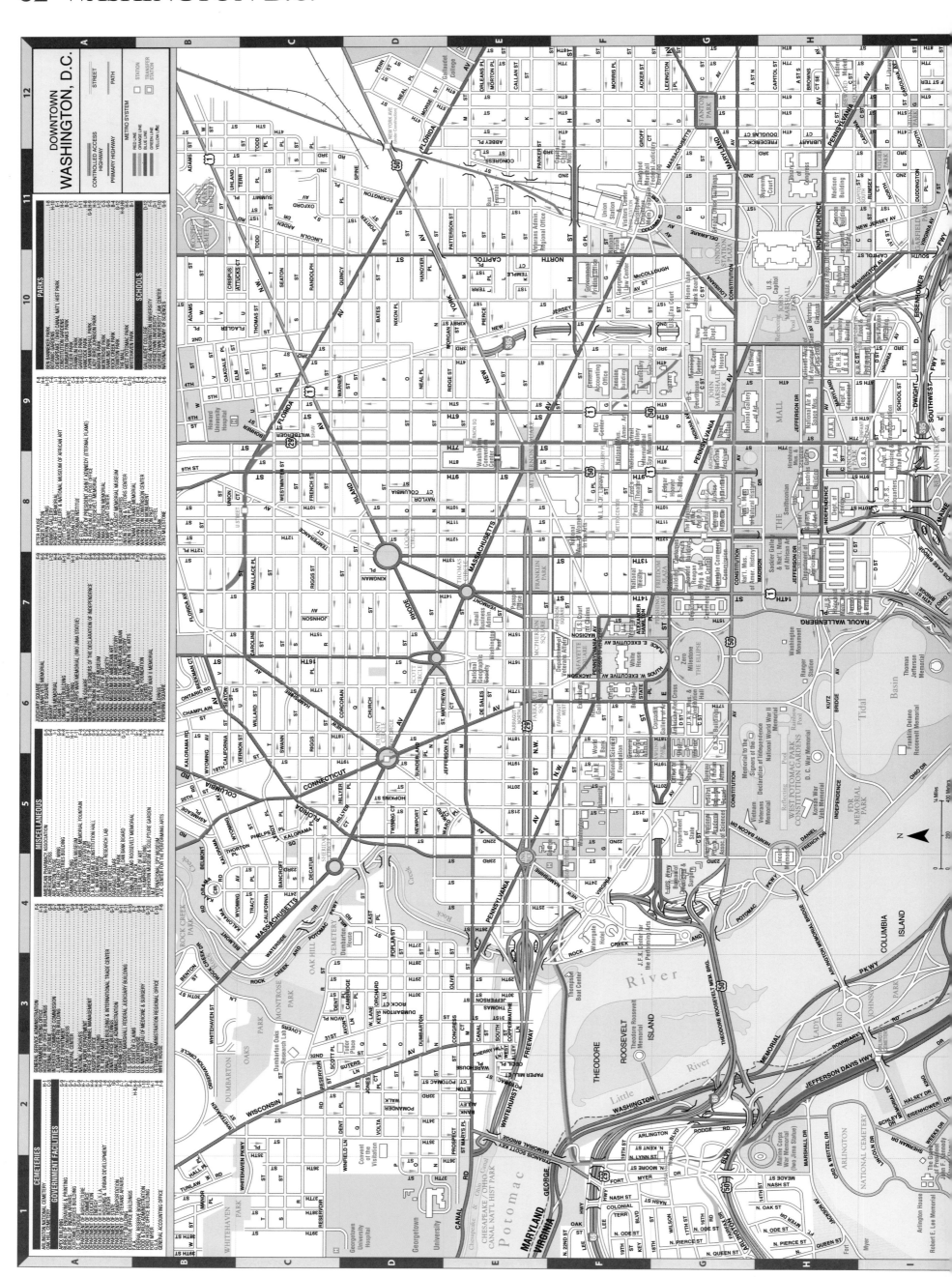

BOSTON & VICINITY, MA

One Inch Equals Approximately 1.6 Miles Or 2.6 Kilometers

BOSTON AND VICINITY PLACES OF INTEREST
1. STEPHEN PHILLIPS MEMORIAL TRUST HOUSE I-20
2. WITCH HOUSE I-20
3. PEABODY ESSEX MUSEUM I-20
4. SALEM WITCH MUSEUM I-20
5. HOUSE OF SEVEN GABLES I-20

	GREAT BARRINGTON	BOSTON	NEW BEDFORD	NEWBURYPORT	PLYMOUTH	PROVINCE TOWN	SAGAMORE	SPRINGFIELD	WILLIAMSTOWN	WORCESTER
BOSTON		60	147	60	40	111	72	100	137	53
NEW BEDFORD	176	60		111	34	93	32	128	184	82
SPRINGFIELD		100	53	128	127	124	197	137		90	52
WORCESTER	53	99	82	76	77	150	90	52	110	0

LOWELL, MA

PITTSBURG, MA

SPRINGFIELD, MA

NEW BEDFORD, MA

One Inch Equals Approximately 9.4 Miles Or 15.03 Kilometers

Towns with star (*) are keyed to the maps on page 53.

Abington (14605).....F-13
Acton.....C-11
Acushnet.....H-14
Adams (5784).....B-3
Adamsville.....B-5
*Braintree.....D-29
Agawam (28144).....E-2
Alford.....E-2
Allerton.....D-14
*Allston.....J-26
Amesbury (12327).....A-13
Amherst.....D-6
Andover (7900).....B-12
Annisquam.....F-7
Aquinnah (Gay Head).....J-14
*Arlington.....D-23
Arlington (42389).....C-12
Arlington Heights.....C-23
Asbury Grove.....N-14
Ashburnham.....B-9
Ashby.....B-9
Ashfield.....C-4
Ashland.....D-11
Ashley Falls.....F-2
Assinippi.....E-13
Assonet.....G-13
Athol (8370).....C-7
Attleboro (42068).....G-12
Auburn.....E-10
Avon.....E-13
Ayer (2960).....B-10
Bancroft.....D-4
Barnstable (47821).....H-17
Barre (1150).....D-8
Barre Plains.....D-8
Barrowsville.....G-12
Becket.....D-4
Bedford.....C-12
Belchertown.....D-6
Bellingham (4497).....F-11
Belmont (24194).....C-12
Berkley.....G-13
Berlin.....D-10
Bernardston.....B-5
*Beverly.....I-19
Beverly (39862).....C-14
Billerica.....C-11
Blackstone.....F-11
Blandford.....E-4
Bolton.....D-10
Bondsville (1876).....E-7

Boston (589141).....D-13
Bourne (1443).....H-15
Bourndale.....H-15
Boxborough.....C-11
Boxford (2340).....B-13
Boylston.....D-10
*Brainttree.....D-29
Braintree (33698).....E-13
Braintree Highlands.....G-30
Brant Rock.....F-15
Brewster (2212).....H-18
Bridgewater (6664).....F-13
Briggs Corner.....G-12
Briggsville.....B-3
*Brighton.....D-25
Brockton (94304).....F-13
*Brookline.....D-25
Brookline (57107).....D-13
Buckland.....B-4
Burlington (22876).....C-12
Buzzards Bay (3549).....H-15
Byfield.....F-7
*Cambridge.....D-24
Cambridge (101355).....D-13
Canton.....E-13
Carlisle.....C-11
Carver (2960).....G-14
Centerville.....H-16
Central Village.....I-13
Charlemont.....B-4
Charlton.....E-9
Charlton City.....E-9
Charlton Depot.....E-9
Chartley.....G-12
Chatham (1667).....H-18
*Chelsea.....F-24
Chelsea (35080).....D-13
Cheshire.....C-3
Chester.....D-4
*Chestnut Hill.....C-26
Chicopee (54653).....E-6
Chilmark.....J-15
Clarksburg.....A-3
*Cliftondale.....D-22
Clinton (7884).....D-10
Cochesett.....E-13
Cohasset.....E-14
Coldbrook Springs.....D-8

Colrain.....B-5
Concord.....C-11
Conway.....C-5
Cordaville (2515).....E-11
Cotuit.....I-16
Cummaquid.....C-4
Cuthrunk.....J-14
Dalton.....C-3
*Danvers.....H-19
Danvers (25212).....C-11
*Danversport.....H-19
Dartmouth.....I-13
Dedham (23464).....E-12
Deerfield.....C-5
Dell.....B-4
Dennis (2798).....H-17
Dennis Port (3612).....H-17
*Dorchester.....F-27
Dorchester (2459).....E-2
*Dover.....A-28
Dover (2216).....E-12
Dracut (28701).....B-11
Dudley.....F-9
Dunstable.....B-11
Dwight.....D-6
Easton (20770).....F-13
*East Boston.....F-24
East Braintree.....H-29
East Brewster.....G-18
East Brookfield.....E-8
East Brookfield (1410).....E-8
East Dedham.....C-28
*East Douglas (2319).....F-10
East Falmouth (6615).....I-15
East Freetown.....H-13
East Lexington.....B-23
*East Longmeadow.....F-3
East Lynn.....H-22
East Orleans.....G-18
East Otis.....E-4
East Princeton.....D-9
East Sandwich (3720).....H-16
East Shelburne.....B-5
East Windsor.....B-5
Eastham.....G-18
Easthampton (15994).....E-5

Easton.....F-13
Edgartown.....J-16
Egremont.....E-2
Elmwood.....F-13
Endicott.....C-29
Erving.....C-6
Essex (1426).....B-14
*Everett.....E-23
Everett (38037).....D-13
Fairhaven.....H-14
Fall River (91938).....H-13
Falmouth (4115).....I-15
Falmouth Heights.....I-15
Farnumsville.....E-10
*Feeding Hills.....F-3
Feltonville.....D-9
*Fields Corner.....F-27
Fitchburg (39102).....C-9
Florence.....D-5
Florida.....B-4
Forestdale (3992).....H-16
Forge Village.....C-11
Foxborough (5509).....F-12
Framingham (66910).....E-11
Franklin (29560).....F-11
Freetown.....H-13
Gardner (20770).....C-8
Georgetown.....B-13
*Germantown.....D-30
Gibbs Crossing.....E-7
Gilbertville.....D-7
Gill.....B-6
Gleasonville.....D-11
*Glendale.....D-25
Gloucester.....B-15
Goshen.....D-5
Gosnold.....J-14
Grafton.....E-10
Granby (1344).....E-6
Granville.....F-4
Great Barrington (2459).....E-2
*Green Harbor.....E-14
Greenfield (13716).....C-6
*Greenwood.....D-21
Griswoldville.....B-5
Groton (1113).....B-10
Groveland.....B-13
Hadley.....D-6
Halifax.....F-14
Hamilton.....B-14
Hampden.....F-6

Hancock.....C-2
Hanover.....E-14
Hanson (2044).....F-14
Hardwick.....D-7
Hartsville.....E-2
Harvard.....C-10
Harwich.....H-18
Harwich Port (1809).....H-18
Hatfield (1298).....D-5
Haverhill (58969).....A-13
Hawley.....C-4
Haydenville.....D-5
Heath.....B-4
*Hingham.....E-14
Hingham (5352).....E-14
Hinsdale.....D-3
Hixville.....H-13
Hockanum.....E-6
Holbrook (10785).....E-13
Holden.....D-9
Holland (1444).....F-7
Holliston.....E-11
Holyoke (39838).....E-6
Hopedale (4158).....F-11
*Houghs Neck.....H-27
Housatonic (1335).....E-2
Hubbardston.....C-8
Hudson (14388).....D-11
*Hull.....J-26
Hull (11050).....E-14
Huntington.....D-4
Hyannis (14048).....H-17
Hyannis Port.....H-17
*Hyde Park.....D-28
Ipswich (4161).....B-14
*Jamaica Plain.....D-26
Kingston (5380).....F-14
*Lakeview.....A-24
Lakeville.....G-14
Lancaster.....C-10
Lanesborough.....B-3
Lawrence (72043).....B-13
Lebanon Mills.....G-12
Lee (2021).....D-3
Leeds.....D-5
Leicester.....E-9
Lenox (1667).....D-3
Leominster (41303).....C-9
*Lexington.....B-22

Lexington (30355).....C-12
Leyden.....B-5
Lincoln.....C-12
Lithia.....D-4
*Little Nahant.....H-23
Littleton.....C-11
Lowell (105167).....B-11
Locks Village.....C-6
Loudville.....E-5
*Lower Mills.....E-27
Ludlow.....E-6
Ludlow Center.....E-6
Lunenburg (1695).....C-9
Lynn (89050).....C-13
*Lynnfield.....C-22
Lynnfield (11542).....C-12
Lynnhurst.....G-21
Madaket.....K-17
Magnolia.....B-14
*Malden.....E-23
Malden (56340).....D-13
Manchester-by-the-Sea.....C-14
Manomet.....G-15
Mansfield.....F-12
Marblehead (20377).....C-14
Marion.....H-14
Marlborough (36255).....D-11
Marshfield (4246).....F-15
Marstons Mills.....H-16
Mashpee.....H-16
*Mattapan.....F-27
Mattapoisett.....H-14
Maynard (10433).....D-11
Medfield (5676).....E-12
Medford (57074).....D-12
Medway.....E-11
Melrose (27134).....C-13
Menemsha.....J-15
Merrimac.....A-13
Methuen (43789).....B-13
Middleborough (6979).....G-14
Middlefield.....D-4
Middleton.....B-13
Milford (24230).....E-11
Mill River.....F-2
Millbury.....E-10
Millers Falls (1072).....C-6

Millville.....F-10
*Milton.....E-28
Milton (26062).....E-13
Monroe.....B-4
Monponsett.....F-14
Monson.....F-7
Montague.....C-6
Montague City.....C-6
*Montclair.....F-27
Monterey.....E-3
Montgomery.....E-5
Mount Auburn.....D-24
Mount Hermon.....B-6
Mount Washington.....E-1
Myricks.....G-13
*Nahant.....G-13
Nahant (3632).....C-14
Nanlasket.....D-14
Nantucket (3830).....K-18
Natick.....D-11
*Neponset.....E-27
New Ashford.....C-3
New Bedford (93768).....H-14
New Boston.....F-3
New Braintree.....D-8
New Marlborough.....E-3
New Salem.....C-7
New Seabury (815).....I-16
Newbury.....A-14
Newburyport (17189).....A-14
*Newton.....C-25
Newton (83829).....D-12
*Newton Lower Falls.....A-26
*Newton Upper Falls.....B-26
Nichewaug.....D-7
Nobscot.....D-11
Norfolk.....E-12
North Abington.....E-12
North Adams (16681).....B-3
North Amherst (6019).....D-6
North Andover.....B-13
North Attleborough.....F-12
North Brookfield (2527).....E-8
*North Cambridge.....C-24
North Carver.....G-14
North Chelmsford.....B-11
Peru.....D-3

North Eastham (1915).....G-18
North Easton.....E-13
North Egremont.....E-2
North Grafton.....E-10
North Hadley.....D-6
Montague.....C-6
Monson.....F-7
*North Leominster.....C-9
*North Lexington.....B-22
North Middleborough.....G-14
North Otis.....E-4
North Oxford.....E-9
North Plymouth.....F-14
*North Quincy.....D-27
*North Reading.....B-12
North Reading.....C-12
North Rehoboth.....G-12
North Rochester.....H-13
*North Salem.....H-19
*North Saugus.....G-21
North Truro.....F-20
North Weymouth (28974).....D-27
Northborough.....D-10
Northbridge.....E-10
Northfield (1141).....B-6
Norton.....F-12
Norwell.....E-14
*Norwood.....C-29
Norwood (28587).....E-12
Oak Bluffs.....J-16
*Oak Hill.....C-26
Oakdale.....D-9
*Oak Island.....G-23
Old Furnace.....E-7
Old Town.....E-14
Onset (1460).....H-15
Orange (3945).....C-7
Osterville.....I-16
Otis.....E-4
Otter River.....C-8
Oxford (5899).....E-9
Oxford (1141).....E-9
Palmer (3900).....E-7
Paxton.....D-9
Peabody (48129).....C-13
Pelham.....D-6
Pembroke.....F-14
Pepperell (2517).....B-10
Peru.....D-3

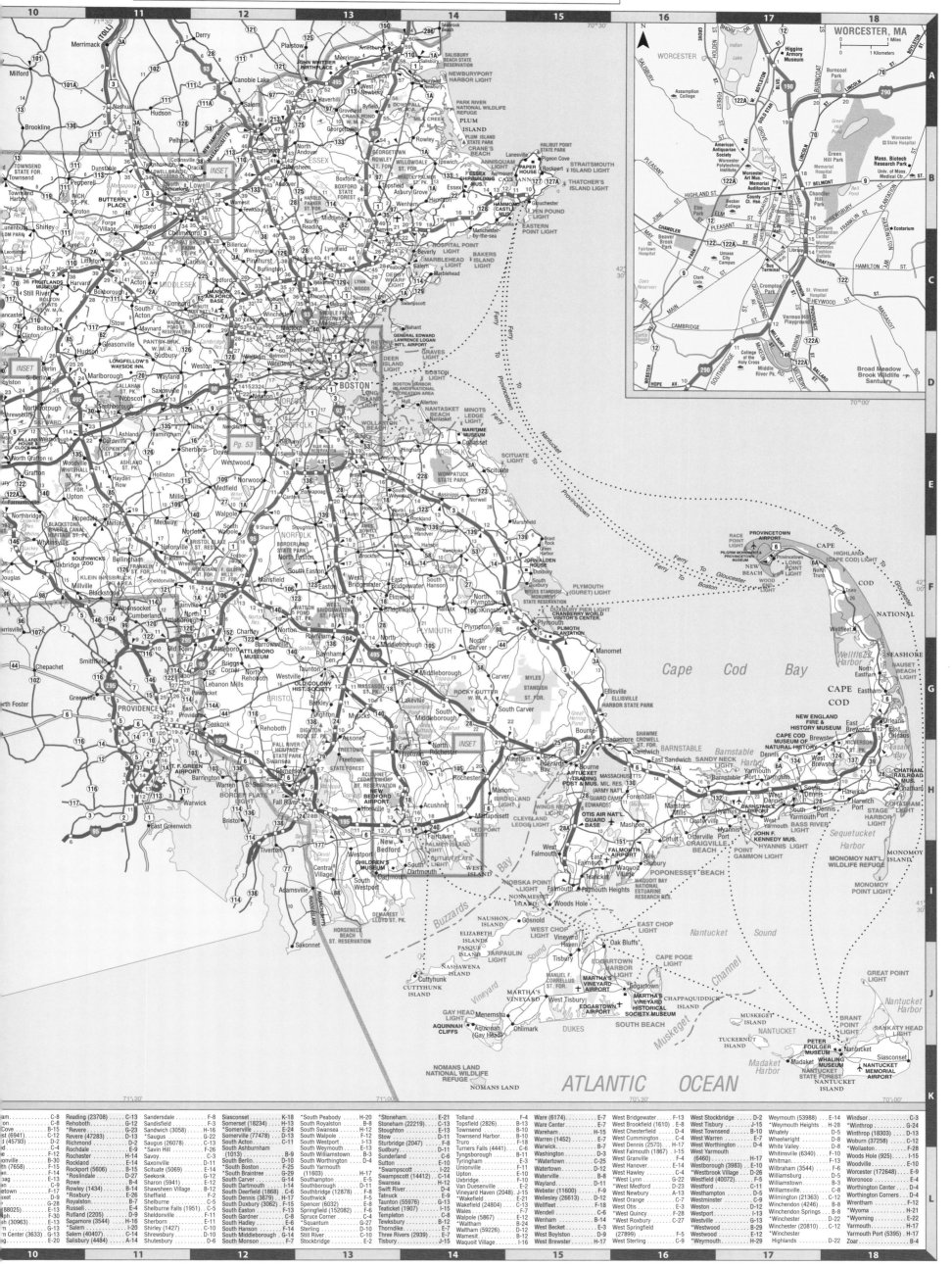

...am. C-8	Reading (23708) C-13	Sandersdale F-8	Siasconset K-18	*South Peabody H-20
on. C-8	Rehoboth G-12	Sandisfield F-3	Somerset (18234) H-13	*Stoneham (22219) C-13
Cove B-15	*Revere (47283) C-12	Sandwich (3058) H-16	Somerville (77478) D-13	Stoughton E-13
(6941) C-12	Richmond D-2	Saugus G-22	*Somerville D-13	Stow D-11
(45793) B-15	Rochdale E-8	Saugus (26078) C-13	South Acton D-11	Sturbridge (2047) F-8
onville F-12	Rochester H-14	*Savin Hill F-26	South Ashburnham B-9	Sudbury D-11
(7658) F-15	Rockland D-14	Savoy C-3	South Berlin D-10	Sunderland C-6
ille F-14	Rockport (5606) B-15	Saxonville D-11	*South Boston F-25	Sutton E-9
Rosindale D-27	Scituate (5069) E-14	South Carver G-14	Swampscott (14412) C-14
-13	Rowe B-4	Sharon (5941) E-13	South Deerfield (1868) C-6	Swansea G-12
own E-17	Rowley (1434) B-13	Shawsheen Village B-12	South Dennis (3679) H-17	Swift River D-7
-9	*Roxbury E-26	Sheffield F-2	South Duxbury (3062) F-15	Taunton (55976) G-12
xet H-2	Royalston B-8	Shelburne E-11	Southfield E-11	Teaticket (1907) I-15
E-13	Russell E-4	Shelburne Falls (1951) C-5	South Easton F-13	Templeton B-8
(88025) E-13	Rutland (2205) D-9	Sherborn E-11	South Gardner B-8	Tewksbury B-12
(30963) E-13	Sagamore (3544) H-16	Shirley (1427) C-10	South Hadley E-6	Three Rivers (2939) E-7
Center (3633) G-13	Salem (40407) C-14	Shrewsbury D-10	South Hanson E-14	Thorndike F-7
-20	Salisbury A-14	Shutesbury D-6	South Middleborough G-14	Tisbury J-15
			South Monson E-7	Still River C-10	Stockbridge E-2

Tolland F-4	Ware (6174) E-7	West Bridgewater F-13	West Stockbridge D-2
Topsfield (2826) B-13	Ware Center E-7	West Chesterfield D-4	*West Tisbury J-15
Townsend B-10	Wareham H-15	West Chesterfield D-4	*Weymouth Heights H-28
Townsend Harbor B-10	Warren (1452) E-8	West Cummington C-4	West Townsend B-10
Truro F-18	Warwick B-7	West Dennis (2570) H-17	West Warren E-8
Turners Falls (4441) C-6	Washington D-3	West Falmouth (1867) I-15	West Yarmouth H-17
Tyngsborough B-11	Watertown D-12	West Granville F-4	(6460) H-17
Uxbridge E-9	*Watertown D-12	West Hanover E-14	Westborough (3983) D-10
Unionville E-11	Waterville B-8	West Hawley C-4	*Wrentham (3544) F-10
Upton E-10	Wayland D-11	*West Lynn G-22	Worcester (172648) E-9
Van Duesenville F-2	Webster (11600) F-9	West Medford G-22	Woronoco E-4
Vineyard Haven (2048) J-15	Wellesley (26613) D-12	West Newbury A-13	Worthington D-4
Wakefield (24804) C-13	Wellfleet F-18	West Orange C-7	Worthington Corners D-4
Wakefield (24804) C-13	Wendell C-6	Westminster C-8	Wrentham F-10
Wales E-8	Wenham B-14	Westminster C-8	*Wyoming H-21
Walpole (5867) E-11	West Becket E-3	Weston D-12	*Wyoming E-22
Waltham (59226) D-12	West Boylston D-9	Westport H-12	Yarmouth H-17
Warnesit B-12	West Brewster H-17	*Westwood B-29	Yarmouth Port (5395) H-17
Wauquoit Village I-16		West Springfield F-5	Zoar B-4
		*West Weymouth H-29	
		Highlands D-22	

	BATTLE CREEK	BAY CITY	DETROIT	ESCANABA	FLINT	GRAND RAPIDS	IRONWOOD	LANSING	MARQUETTE	MUSKEGON	PORT HURON	SAULT STE MARIE
DETROIT	120	113	69	444	69	163	611	95	546	202	62	351
FLINT	111	48	69	379	0	117	546	57	396	156	68	286
GRAND RAPIDS	64	132	163	302	117	0	548	70	483	43	184	300
LANSING	55	99	95	383	57	70	550	0	400	109	124	290
MUSKEGON	108	146	202	407	156	43	596	109	424	0	223	314

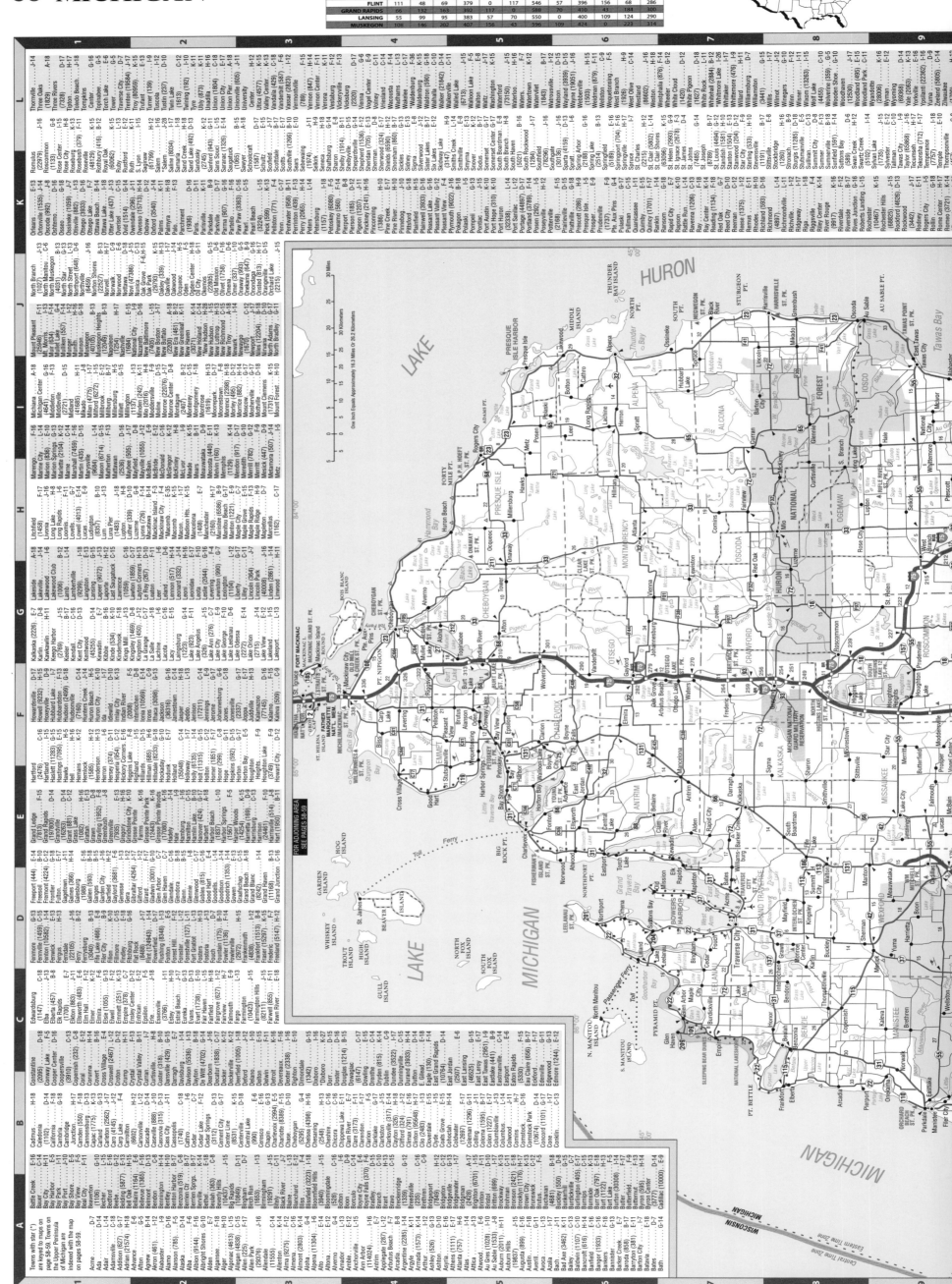

Legend:

- MILEAGE NUMBER — EXIT NUMBER
- INTERCHANGE
- CONTROLLED ACCESS
- UNDER CONSTRUCTION
- TOLL CONTROLLED ACCESS
- PRIMARY DIVIDED
- PRIMARY UNDIVIDED
- ARTERIAL DIVIDED
- ARTERIAL UNDIVIDED
- UNPAVED
- SCENIC ROUTE
- TIME ZONE
- STATE/LOCAL PARK
- FOREST
- CAMPGROUND
- REST AREAS
- INFORMATION CTR
- POINT OF INTEREST

	BATTLE CREEK	BAY CITY	DETROIT	ESCANABA	FLINT	GRAND RAPIDS	IRONWOOD	LANSING	MARQUETTE	MUSKEGON	PORT HURON	SAULT STE MARIE
DETROIT	120	113	0	444	69	163	611	95	461	202	62	351
FLINT	111	48	69	379	0	117	546	57	396	156	68	286
GRAND RAPIDS	66	132	163	392	117	0	588	70	410	43	184	300
LANSING	55	99	95	383	57	70	550	0	400	109	124	290
MUSKEGON	108	146	202	407	156	43	596	109	424	0	223	314

ISLE ROYALE NATIONAL PARK
LAKE
LAKE MICHIGAN
CANADA
UNITED STATES
FOR ADJOINING AREA SEE PAGES 56-57
SAGINAW, MI
FLINT, MI
KALAMAZOO, MI
BATTLE CREEK, MI
JACKSON, MI
GRAND RAPIDS, MI
LANSING, MI

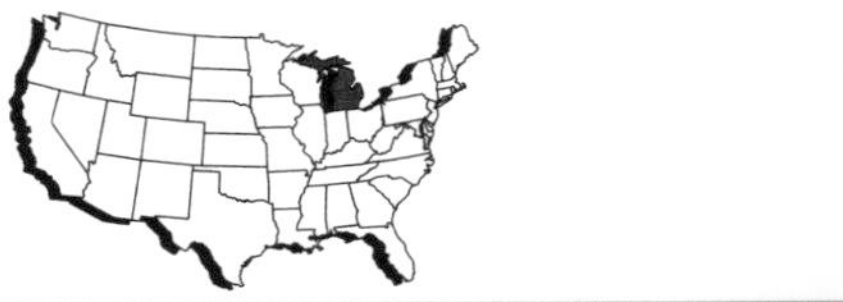

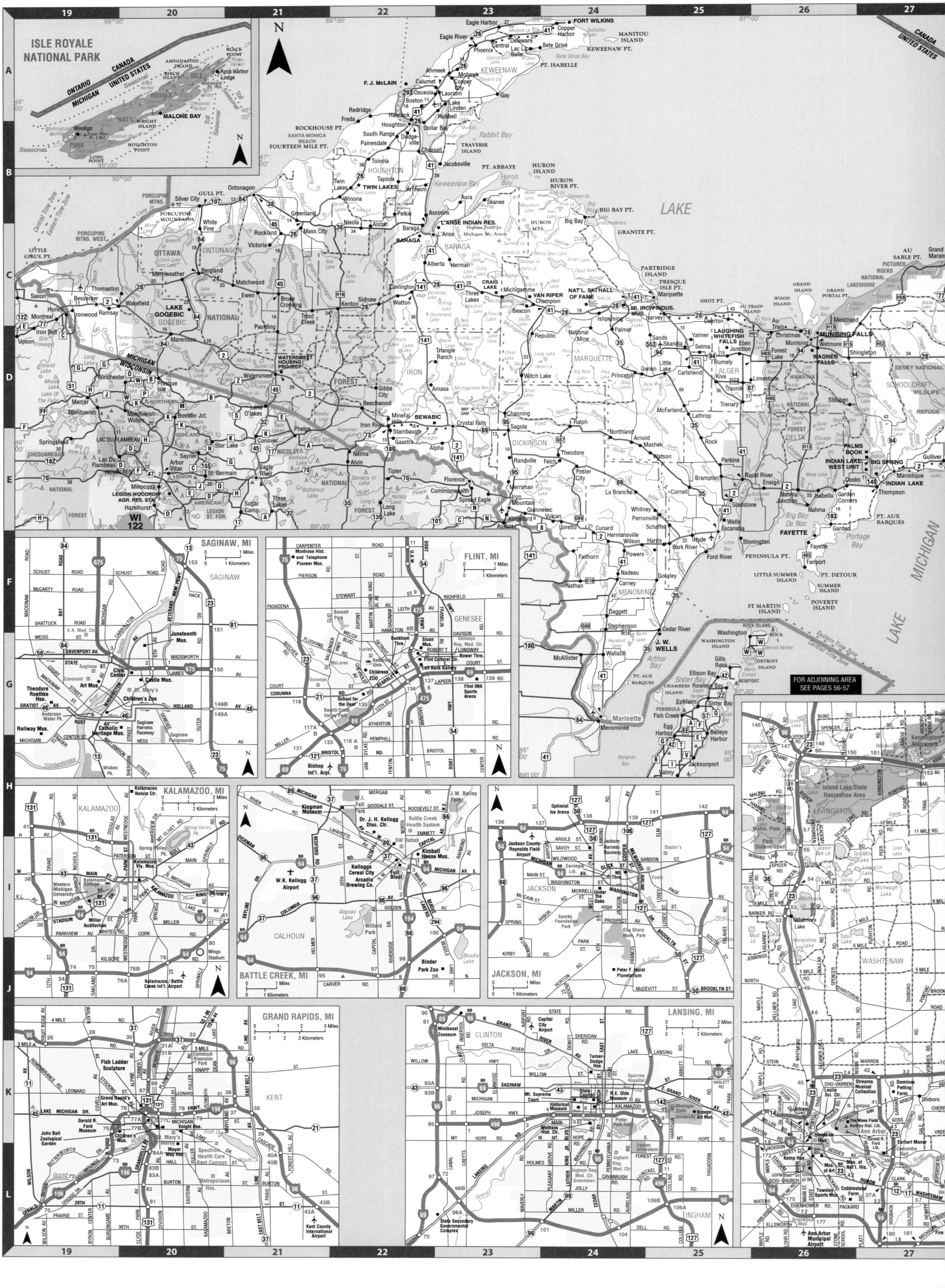

Legend

MILEAGE NUMBER	EXIT NUMBER
INTERCHANGE	CONTROLLED ACCESS
	UNDER CONSTRUCTION
	TOLL CONTROLLED ACCESS
PRIMARY DIVIDED	UNPAVED
PRIMARY UNDIVIDED	SCENIC ROUTE
ARTERIAL DIVIDED	TIME ZONE
ARTERIAL UNDIVIDED	
STATE/LOCAL PARK	REST AREAS
FOREST	INFORMATION CTR
CAMPGROUND	POINT OF INTEREST

Scale

One Inch Equals Approximately 22.5 Miles Or 36.2 Kilometers

KILOMETERS IN CANADA — Kilometers x 0.62 = Miles

MILES IN USA — Miles x 1.6 = Kilometers

Place Index

Place	Grid	Place	Grid
Advance	G-29	Champion	C-23
Afton	G-30	Channing	D-23
Ahmeek (157)	A-23	Charlevoix (2994)	G-29
Alanson (785)	F-30	Chassell	B-22
Alberta	C-22	Cheboygan (5295)	F-30
Allenville	F-30	Christmas	B-25
Aloha	E-30	Clarion	F-30
Alpha (198)	E-23	Conway Lake	F-30
Alston	C-22	Cooks	E-26
Alverno	F-31	Copper City	A-23
Amasa	E-24	Copper Harbor	A-24
Arnheim	C-22	Cornell	E-25
Arnold	E-24	Covington	C-22
Assinins	B-22	Cross Village	F-29
Au Train	B-25	Crystal Falls (1791)	D-23
Aura	C-22	Cunard	D-24
Baraga (1285)	C-22	Curtis	D-28
Barbeau	D-31	Dafter	D-31
Bark River	F-25	Daggett (270)	F-24
Bay Harbor	F-30	De Tour Village	E-31
Bay Mills	C-30	Deer Park	B-30
Bay Shore	G-29	Deerton	C-25
Bay View	G-30	Delaware	A-23
Beacon	C-23	Dollar Bay	B-22
Beechwood	D-22	Dollarville	D-29
Bergland	C-20	Donaldson	D-31
Bessemer (2148)	C-19	Drummond	E-32
Bete Grise	A-23	Eagle Harbor	A-23
Big Bay (265)	B-24	Eagle River	A-23
Blaney Park	D-28	Eben Junction	C-25
Bliss	F-30	Eckerman	D-29
Boston	A-22	Engadine	D-28
Boyne City	E-29	Ensign	E-26
Brampton	E-25	Epoufette	D-29
Brevort	E-29	Epsilon	G-30
Brimley	D-30	Escanaba (13140)	E-25
Bruce Crossing	C-20	Ewen	C-21
Brutus	F-30	Fairbanks	F-27
Burt Lake	F-30	Fairport	F-24
Calumet (879)	A-23	Fayette	E-26
Carlshend	D-25	Fibre	D-31
Carney (225)	F-24	Fenton	G-29
Carp Lake	F-30	Ford River	F-25
Cedar River	F-25	Forest Lake	D-24
Cedarville	E-31		
Central	A-23		

Place	Grid	Place	Grid
Foster City	E-24	L'Anse (2107)	C-22
Freda	B-22	La Branche	E-24
Gaastra (339)	E-23	Lac La Belle	A-23
Garden (30047)	E-26	Lake Linden (1081)	A-23
Garden Corners	E-26	Lathrop	D-25
Garnet	D-28	Laurium (2126)	A-23
Gay	A-23	Levering	F-30
Germfask	D-27	Limestone	D-25
Gibbs City	E-23	Little Lake	D-25
Gladstone (5032)	E-25	Loretto	E-24
Goetzville	E-31	Mackinac Island (523)	E-31
Good Hart	F-29	Mackinaw City	E-30
Gould City	E-28	Manistique (3583)	D-27
Gourley	C-21	Marenisco	C-20
Grand Marais	B-27	Marquette (19661)	C-25
Greenland	C-21	Mashek	C-23
Gulliver	D-27	Mass City	C-21
Gwinn (1965)	D-24	Matchwood	C-21
Hancock (4323)	B-22	Mc Carron	D-31
Harbor Springs	F-29	McFarland	C-25
Harris	F-25	McMillan	D-28
Harvey (1321)	C-25	Melstrand	C-27
Helmer	D-28	Menominee (9131)	G-24
Herman	C-23	Merriman	D-29
Hermansville	F-24	Merriweather	C-20
Hessel	E-31	Michigamme (287)	C-23
Hilton Beach	D-32	Milford Haven	E-32
Homestead	D-31	Millecoquins	D-28
Horton Bay	G-29	Mineral Hills (214)	D-23
Houghton (7010)	B-22	Mohawk	A-23
Hubbell (1105)	A-23	Moran	E-30
Hulbert	D-29	Mullet Lake	F-30
Hyde	F-25	Munising (2539)	C-26
Indian River (2008)	F-30	Munuscong	D-31
Iron Mountain (8154)	E-23	Nadeau	F-25
Iron River (1929)	D-22	Nahma	E-26
Ironwood (6293)	C-19	Nahma Junction	E-26
Isabella	E-23	Nathan	F-25
Ishpeming (6686)	C-24	National Mine	C-24
Jacobsville	B-23	Naubinway	D-28
Kelden	D-31	Negaunee (6686)	C-24
Kenton	C-22	Newberry (2686)	D-28
Kincheloe	D-30	Nisula	C-22
Kingsford (5549)	E-23	Northland	D-25
Kinross	D-30	Norwood	G-29
Kiva	D-25	Ontonagon (1769)	B-21

Place	Grid	Place	Grid
Osceola	A-23	South Range	B-22
Ozark	E-31	St. Ignace (2678)	E-30
Painesdale	B-22	St. James	F-28
Palmer (449)	D-24	Stalwart	E-31
Paradise	C-30	Stambaugh (1243)	E-22
Paulding	C-21	Stephenson	F-24
Pelkie	B-22	Steuben	C-26
Pellston (771)	F-30	Stirlingville	D-31
Perkins	E-25	Stonington	F-25
Perronville	E-25	Strongs	D-30
Petoskey (6080)	F-29	Stutsmanville	F-29
Phoenix	A-23	Taploa	F-24
Pickford	D-31	Theodore	E-24
Pine Stump Jct.	C-28	Thomaston	C-20
Pleasant View	F-30	Thompson	D-27
Powers (430)	F-24	Three Lakes	C-23
Princeton	D-24	Toivola	C-21
Pte. Aux Pins	F-30	Topinabee	D-30
Quinnesec (1187)	E-23	Traunik	D-25
Raber	E-31	Trenary	D-25
Raco	D-30	Triangle Ranch	C-21
Ralph	D-24	Trout Creek	C-21
Ramsay	C-19	Trout Lake	D-29
Randville	C-23	Twin Lakes	B-22
Rapid River	E-25	Two Heart	C-29
Redridge	A-23	Vulcan	E-24
Republic (614)	D-23	Wakefield (2085)	C-19
Rexton	D-29	Wallace	G-24
Richards Landing	D-31	Walloon Lake	G-30
Riggsville	F-30	Watersmeet	D-21
Rock	E-25	Watson	D-25
Rockland	C-21	Watton	E-23
Rudyard	D-30	Wells	E-25
Rumely	C-25	Wequetonsing	F-29
Sagola	E-23	White Pine	C-20
Sands	D-25	Whitefish Point	C-31
Sault Ste. Marie (16542)	C-31	Whitney	E-25
Schaffer	C-25	Wilson	F-24
Selma	D-25	Winona	C-22
Seney	D-27	Witch Lake	D-23
Shingleton	C-26	Wolverine (359)	G-30
Sidnaw	C-22	Yalmer	D-25
Silver City	B-20		
Skandia	D-25		
Skanee	B-23		
Soo Junction	D-29		

INTERNATIONAL BRIDGE SEE PANEL FOR TOLL RATES.

DETROIT AREA, MI

SAULT STE. MARIE, ON / SAULT STE MARIE, MI

	ALBERT LEA	BEMIDJI	DULUTH	FARGO ND	INT'L FALLS	MINNEAPOLIS	ROCHESTER	ST. CLOUD	ST. PAUL	SIOUX FALLS-SD
DULUTH	260	151	0	252	161	154	234	145	152	433
INTERNATIONAL FALLS	398	112	161	244	0	293	372	246	290	476
MINNEAPOLIS	100	220	154	236	293	0	90	68	10	271
ROCHESTER	66	308	234	324	372	90	0	156	77	237

FOR ADJOINING AREA SEE INSET BELOW

Legend

MILEAGE NUMBER — EXIT NUMBER — CONTROLLED ACCESS — INTERCHANGE

PRIMARY DIVIDED	UNPAVED
PRIMARY UNDIVIDED	SCENIC ROUTE
ARTERIAL DIVIDED	TIME ZONE
ARTERIAL UNDIVIDED	
UNDER CONSTRUCTION	STATE/LOCAL PARK
TOLL CONTROLLED ACCESS	FOREST
	CAMPGROUND
	REST AREAS
	INFORMATION CTR
	POINT OF INTEREST

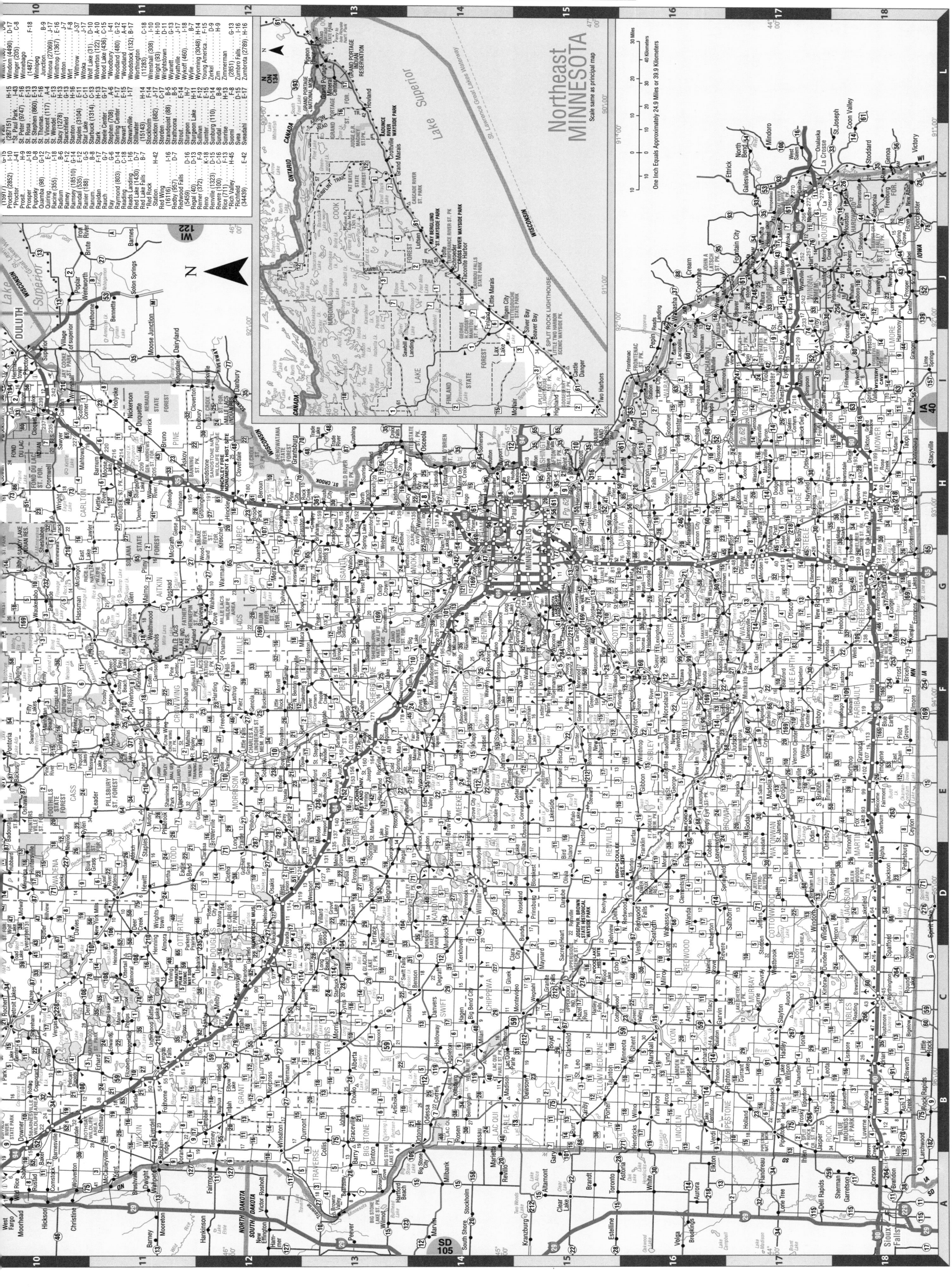

Northeast MINNESOTA
Scale same as principal map

Lake Superior

CANADA • ONTARIO

WISCONSIN

One Inch Equals Approximately 24.9 Miles or 39.9 Kilometers

DULUTH

Grand Marais
Grand Portage
Two Harbors
Silver Bay
Finland
Tofte

JEFFERSON CITY, MO

SPRINGFIELD, MO

LOCATION OF HOSPITALS
1. Barnes-Jewish-North Hospital
2. Barnes-Jewish-South Hospital
3. St. Louis Childrens Hospital
4. St. Louis University Hospital

COLUMBIA, MO

ST. LOUIS VICINITY,
MISSOURI & ILLINOIS

BRANSON, MO

LOCATION OF MAJOR ATTRACTIONS
1. Baldknobbers Jamboree Theatre
2. Buck Trent Breakfast Theatre
3. Country Tonite Theatre
4. Dixie Stampede
5. The Dutton Family Theatre
6. The Grand Palace
7. The Hughes Brothers Celebrity Theatre
8. Jim Stafford's American Jake Box
9. Legends Family Theatre
10. Mickey Gilley Theatre
11. Moe Bandy Theatre
12. Owens Theatre
13. Presley's Country Jubilee Theatre
14. Remington Theatre
15. Shoji Tabuchi Theatre
16. Showtown
17. Starlite Theatre
18. Yakov's American Pavilion

KANSAS CITY VICINITY

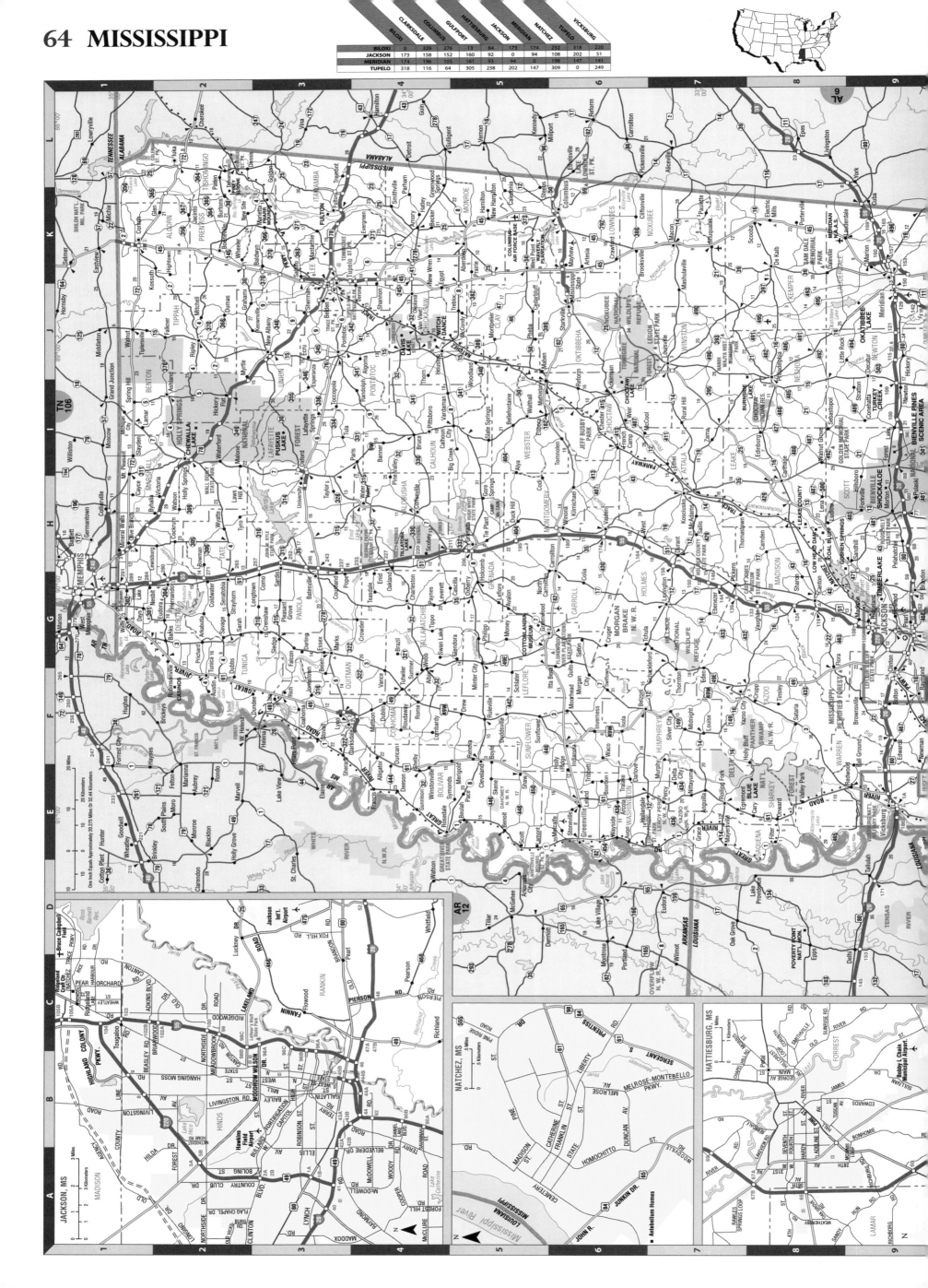

	BILOXI	CLARKSDALE	COLUMBUS	GULFPORT	HATTIESBURG	JACKSON	MERIDIAN	NATCHEZ	TUPELO	VICKSBURG
BILOXI	0	329	276	13	84	173	174	232	318	220
JACKSON	173	158	152	160	92	0	94	108	202	51
MERIDIAN	174	196	105	161	93	94	0	198	147	141
TUPELO	318	116	64	305	238	202	147	309	0	249

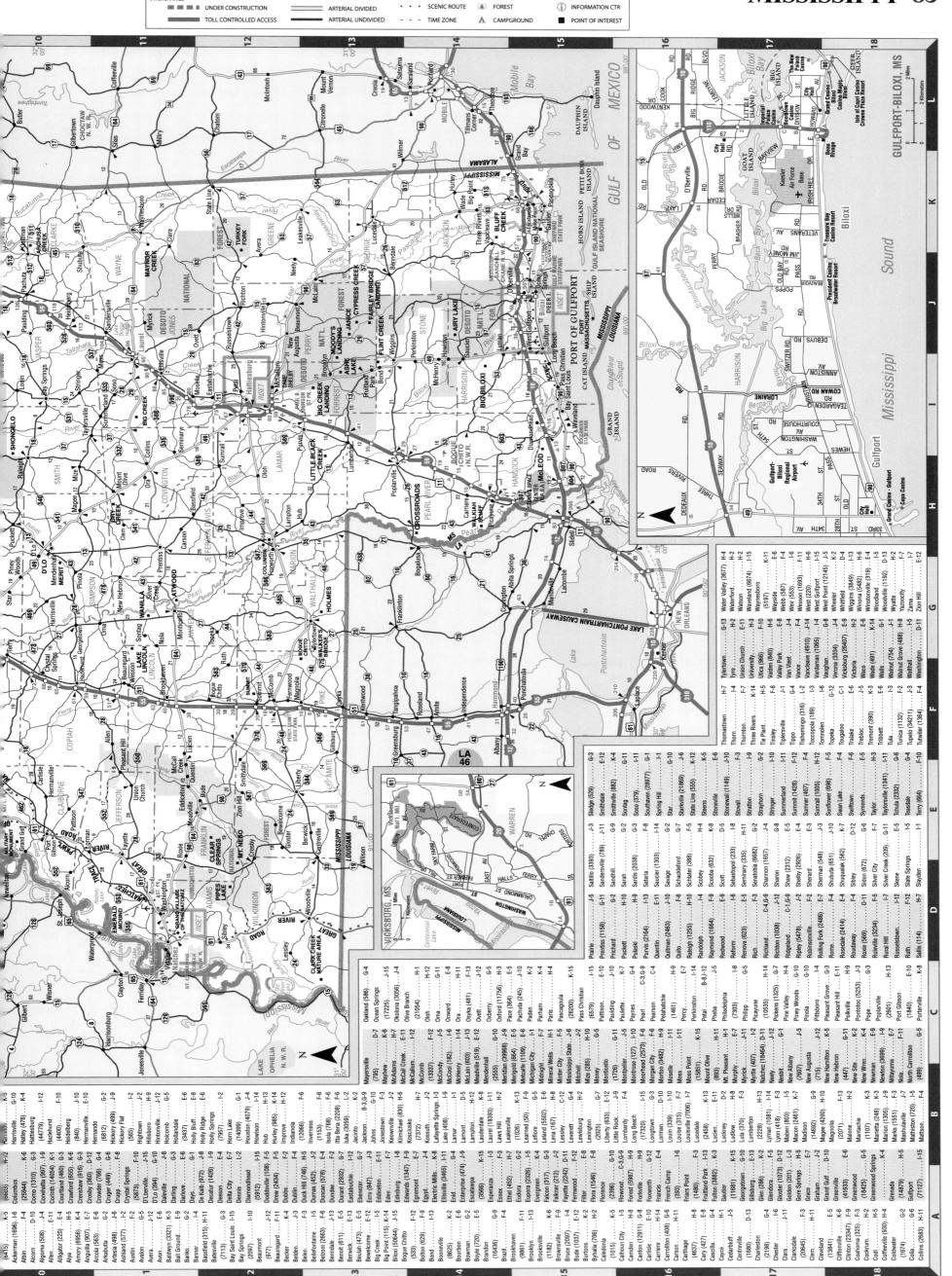

	BRANSON	COLUMBIA	JOPLIN	JEFFERSON CITY	KANSAS CITY	POPLAR BLUFF	SIKESTON	SPRINGFIELD	ST. JOSEPH	ST. LOUIS
KANSAS CITY	215	129	163	149	0	392	383	170	60	255
SIKESTON	245	259	309	252	383	49	0	239	442	150
SPRINGFIELD	45	173	71	140	170	194	239	0	228	218
ST. LOUIS	256	130	288	127	255	158	150	218	313	0

Towns with Star (*) are keyed to the maps on page 63.

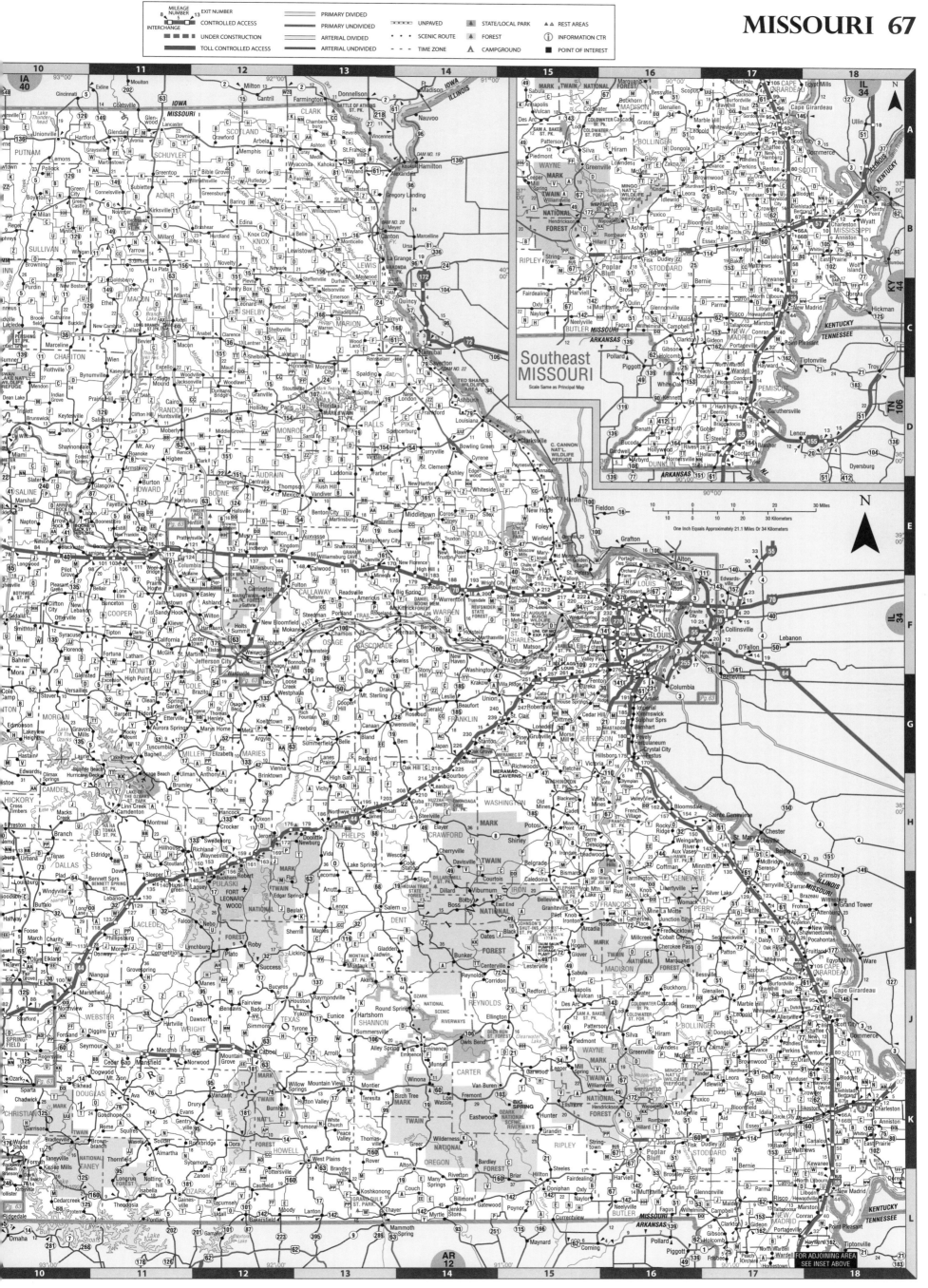

Southeast MISSOURI
Scale Same as Principal Map

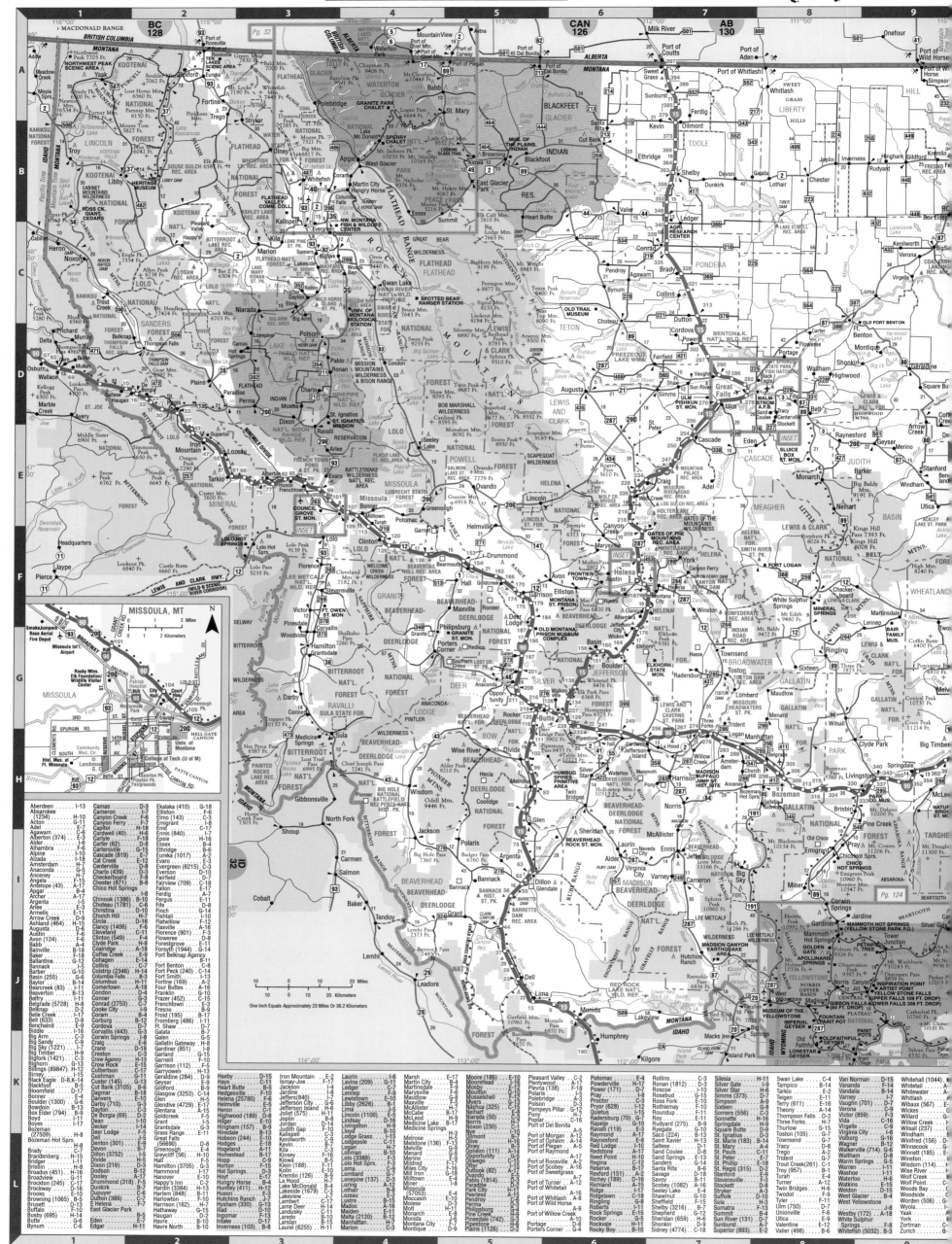

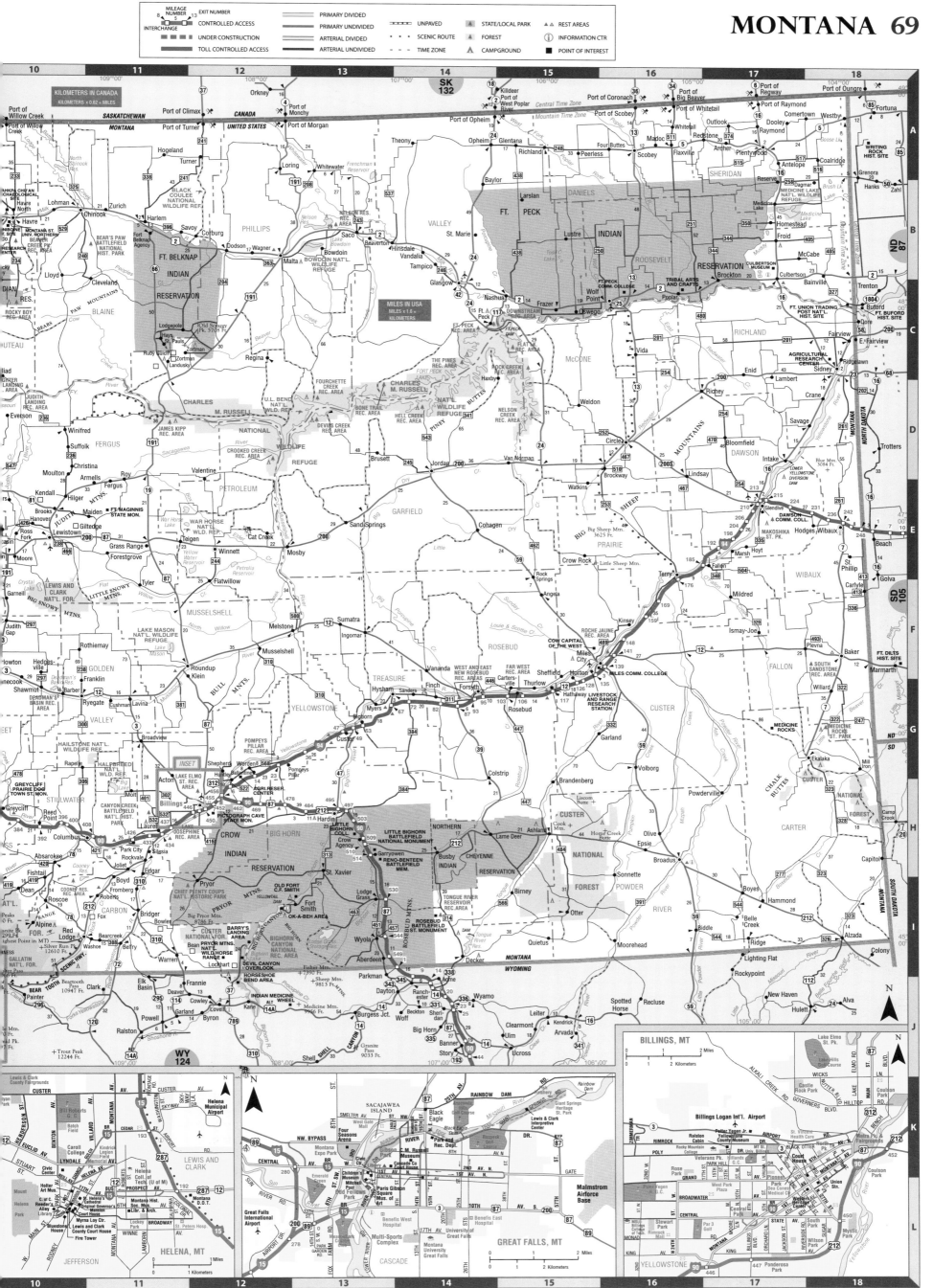

	COLUMBUS	GRAND ISLAND	LINCOLN	NORTH PLATTE	OMAHA	SCOTTSBLUFF	SIOUX CITY, IA	VALENTINE
LINCOLN	79	104	0	233	62	408	156	316
NORTH PLATTE	210	145	233	0	282	177	376	134
OMAHA	85	153	62	282	0	457	98	302

Abie (108) I-15
Adams (489) . . . K-16
Agnew. I-15
Ainsworth (1862). E-9
Albion (1797) . . H-13
Alda (652) J-12
Alexandria (216) K-14
Allen (411) F-15
Alliance (8959). . . F-3
Alma (1214). . . . L-10
Almeria G-10
Aloys G-15
Alvo (142) J-16
Amelia F-11
Ames H-16
Amherst (277) . . J-10
Angora. G-3
Angus K-13
Anoka (10). D-11
Anselmo (159). . . H-9
Ansley (520) I-10
Antioch G-4
Arapahoe (1028) . K-9
Arcadia (359). . . H-11
Archer. I-13
Arlington (1197) H-16
Arnold (630) H-8
Arthur (145) H-5
Ashby G-5
Ashland (2262) . . I-16
Ashton (237). . . . I-11
Aten E-14
Atkinson (1244) . E-11
Atlanta (130) . . . K-10
Auburn (3350) . . K-17
Aurora (4225) . . J-13
Avoca (270) J-17
Axtell (696) K-11
Ayr (98) K-12
Bancroft (520) . . G-16
Barada (28) K-18
Barneston (122). L-16
Bartlett (128). . . G-12
Bartley (355) K-8
Bassett (743) . . . E-10
Battle Creek (1158) G-14
Bayard (1247) . . . G-2
Bazile Mills (26) . E-13
Beatrice (12496) K-15
Beaver City L-9
Beaver Crossing (457) J-14
Bee (223) I-15
Beemer (773) . . G-15
Belden (131) . . . F-14
Belgrade (134). . H-13
Bellevue (44382). I-17
Bellwood (446) . . I-14
Belmont E-2
Belvidere (98) . . K-14
Benedict (278) . . I-14
Benkelman (1006) L-6
Bennet (570) . . . J-16
Bennington (937) H-17
Bertrand (786) . . K-10
Berwyn (134) . . . I-10
Big Springs (418) . I-5
Bingham G-5
Bladen (291) . . . K-12
Blair (7512) H-17
Bloomfield (1126) E-13
Bloomington (124) L-11
Blue Hill (867) . . K-12
Blue Springs (383) L-16
Boelus. I-11
Bonner. G-3
Boone H-13
Bostwick L-12
Bow Valley E-14
Bradshaw (336) . J-13
Brady (366). I-8
Brainard (351) . . I-15
Brandon J-5
Breslau. F-13
Brewster (29) . . . G-9
Bridgeport (1594) H-3
Bristow (88). . . . E-12
Broadwater (140) H-3
Brock (162) K-17
Broken Bow (3491) H-10
Brownlee F-8
Brownson I-2
Brule (372) I-5
Bruning (300) . . K-14
Bruno (112) I-15
Brunswick (179). F-13
Burchard (103) . L-16
Burr (66) K-16
Burton (11) D-10
Burwell (1130) . G-11
Bushnell (162) . . . I-1
Butte (366) D-11
Byron (144) L-13
Cadams L-13
Cairo I-12
Callaway (637) . . . I-9
Cambridge (1041) K-8
Campbell (387) . K-11
Carleton (136) . . K-14
Carroll (238). . . . F-14
Cedar Bluffs (615) H-16
Cedar Rapids . . . H-13
Center (90). E-13
Central City I-13
Ceresco (920) . . . I-16
Chadron (5634) . . D-3
Chambers (333) . F-11
Champion K-5
Chapman (341) . . I-12
Chappell (983) . . . I-4
Chester (294) . . . L-14
Clarks (361) I-13
Clarkson (685). . H-15
Clatonia (275) . . K-15
Clay Center (861) K-13
Clearwater (384) F-12
Clinton (30) E-4
Cody (149) D-6
Coleridge (541) . E-14
Colon (138). I-16
Columbus (20971) H-14
Comstock (110). H-10
Concord (160) . . F-15
Cook (322). K-17
Cordova (127) . . J-14
Cornlea (41) . . . H-14
Cortland (488) . . K-15
Cotesfield (66) . . I-12
Cowles (48) L-12
Cozad (4163) J-9
Crab Orchard (49) K-16
Craig (241) G-16
Crawford (1107) . E-2
Creighton (1270) F-13
Creston (215) . . H-14
Crete (6028). . . . J-15
Crofton (754) . . . E-14
Crookston (98) . . D-7
Crowell G-15
Culbertson (594) . L-7
Cummingsville. . G-12
Curtis (832) J-8
Cushing (31). . . . I-12
Dakota City. F-16
Dalton (332) H-3
Danbury (127) . . . L-8
Dannebrog (352). I-12
Dannevirke I-11
Darr J-9
Davenport (339) K-13
Davey (153) I-16
David City I-15
Dawson (209) . . L-17
Daykin (177) . . . K-14
De Witt (572). . . K-15
Decatur (618) . . G-16
Denton (189) . . . J-15
Deshler (879). . . L-13
Deweese (80). . . K-13
Dickens J-7
Diller (287). L-15
Dix (267). I-2
Dixon (108) F-15
Dodge (700) . . . H-15
Doniphan (763) . J-12
Dorchester (615) J-15
Douglas (231) . . J-16
Du Bois (166) . . L-17
Dunbar (237) . . . J-17
Duncan (359) . . H-14
Dunning (109). . . G-9
Dwight (259). . . . I-15
Eagle (1105). . . . J-16
Eddyville (96) . . . I-10
Edgar (539) K-13
Edison (154) K-9
Elba (243) I-12
Eldorado. J-13
Elgin (735). G-13
Eli D-6
Elk City H-16
Elk Creek (112) . K-17
Elkhorn (6062) . . I-16
Ellis L-15
Ellsworth G-4
Elm Creek (894) . J-10
Elmwood (668) . J-16
Elsie (139) J-6
Elsmere F-8
Elwood (761). . . . K-9
Elyria (54) H-11
Emerald J-15
Emerson (817) . . F-15
Emmet (77) F-11
Enders K-6
Endicott (139) . . L-15
Enola G-14
Ericson G-11
Eustis (464) J-9
Ewing (433) F-12
Exeter (712) J-14
Fairbury (4262) . L-15
Fairfield (467) . . K-13
Fairmont (691) . . J-14
Falls City L-18
Farnam (223) J-8
Farwell (148) . . . I-12
Filley (174). K-16
Firth (564) K-16
Fontanelle H-16
Fordyce (182) . . E-14
Foster (63) F-13
Franklin (1026) . L-11
Fremont (25174) H-16
Friend (1174) . . . J-14
Fullerton (1378) . I-13
Funk (204) K-10
Gandy (30) H-8
Garland (247). . . J-15
Garrison I-15
Geneva (2226) . . K-14
Genoa (981) . . . H-13
Gering (7751) . . . G-1
Gibbon (1759) . . J-11
Gilead (40) L-14
Giltner (389). . . . J-13
Gladstone. L-14
Glenvil (332) . . . K-12
Goehner (186) . . J-14
Gordon (1756) . . . E-4
Gothenburg (3619) J-8
Grafton (152) . . . J-13
Grainton J-6
Grand Island (42940) J-12
Grant (1225) J-5
Greeley H-12
Greenwood (544) J-16
Gresham (270) . . I-14
Gretna (2355) . . . I-16
Gross. D-12
Guide Rock (245) L-12
Gurley (228) H-3
Hadar (312). . . . G-14
Haigler (211) L-5
Hallam (276) . . . K-15
Halsey (59) G-8
Hamlet (54) K-6
Hampton (439). . J-13
Hansen. J-12
Harbine (56). . . . L-15
Hardy (179) L-13
Harrisburg (75) . . H-1
Harrison (279) . . . E-1
Hartington (1640) E-14
Harvard (998). . . J-13
Hastings (24064) K-12
Hay Springs (652) E-3
Hayes Center (240) K-7
Hazard (66). I-11
Heartwell (80) . . K-11
Hebron (1565) . . L-14
Hemingford (993) F-3
Henderson (986) J-13
Hendley (38) L-9
Henry (162). G-1
Herman (310) . . H-16
Hershey (572). . . . I-7
Hickman (1084) . J-16
Hildreth (370) . . K-11
Holbrook (225) . . K-9
Holdrege (5636) K-10
Holland K-16
Hollinger L-9
Holmesville L-16
Holstein (229) . . K-12
Homer (590) . . . F-16
Hooper (827). . . H-16
Horace. H-11
Hordville (150) . . I-13
Hoskins (283) . . G-14
Howe K-17
Howells (632) . . H-15
Hubbard (234) . . F-16
Hubbell (73). . . . L-14
Humboldt (941) . L-17
Humphrey (786) H-14
Huntley (67). . . . L-10
Hyannis (287) . . . G-5
Imperial (1982) . . K-5
Inavale L-12
Indianola (642) . . L-8
Inglewood (382) H-16
Inland K-12
Inman (148). . . . F-12
Ithaca (168) I-16
Jackson (205) . . F-16
Jamison. D-10
Jansen (143) . . . L-15
Johnson (280) . . K-17
Johnstown E-9
Julian (63) K-17
Juniata (693) . . . K-12
Kearney (27431) J-11
Keene. K-11
Kenesaw (873). . K-12
Kennard (371) . . H-16
Keystone. I-6
Kilgore (99) D-7
Kimball (2559) . . . I-1
Kramer. K-15
La Platte I-17
La Vista D-15
Lakeside G-4
Lamar (19). K-5
Laurel (986) F-15
Lawrence (312) . K-12
Lebanon (70) L-8
Leigh (442) H-14
Lemoyne. I-5
Leshara (111) . . . I-16
Letan G-3
Lewellen (282) . . . I-4
Lewiston (86) . . K-16
Lexington (10011) J-9
Liberty (86) L-16
Lincoln (225581) J-15
Lindsay (276) . . H-13
Lindy E-13
Linwood (118). . H-15
Lisco H-3
Litchfield (280) . . I-10
Lodgepole (348) . . I-3
Loma I-15
Long Pine (341) . . E-9
Loomis (397). . . K-10
Lorenzo. I-3
Loretto. G-13
Lorton (39). J-17
Louisville (1046). I-17
Loup City I-11
Lowell J-11
Lushton (33) . . . J-13
Lyman (421) G-1
Lynch (269) E-12
Lyons (963). . . . G-16
Macon L-11
Macy (956). F-16
Madison (2367). G-14
Madrid (265) J-6
Magnet (79) F-14
Malcolm (413) . . J-15
Malmo (109). . . . I-15
Manley (191) . . . J-17
Marion L-8
Marquette (282) . I-13
Marsland F-2
Martell J-15
Martinsburg (103) E-15
Maskell (67). . . . E-15
Mason City I-10
Max L-6
Maxwell (315). . . . I-8
Maywood (331) . . J-7
McCook (7994) . . L-7
McCool Junction (385) J-14
McGrew (103) . . . G-2
McLean (38). . . . F-14
Mead (564) I-16
Meadow Grove (311) G-13
Melbeta (138) . . . G-2
Memphis (106) . . I-16
Menominee E-14
Merna (391) H-9
Merriman (118) . . D-5
Mesha. I-5
Milburn H-9
Milford (2070) . . J-15
Millard I-17
Miller J-10
Milligan (315) . . K-14
Mills D-10
Minatare (810). . . G-2
Minden (2964). . K-11
Mitchell (1831) . . G-1
Monowi (2) E-12
Monroe (307) . . H-14
Monterey G-15
Moorefield (52) . . J-8
Morrill (957) G-1
Morse Bluff (134) H-15
Mt.clare L-12
Mullen (491) G-7
Murdock (269) . . J-16
Murray (481) . . . J-17
Mynard I-17
Naper (105). . . . D-11
Naponee (132) . . L-11
Nashville . . A-16,H-17
Nebraska City . . . J-17
Nehawka (232). . J-17
Neligh. F-13
Nelson (587) . . . L-13
Nemaha (178) . . K-18
Nenzel (13) D-7
Newark. J-11
Newcastle (299). E-15
Newman Grove (797) G-13
Newport (98) . . . E-10
Nickerson (431). H-16
Niobrara (379) . . E-13
Nora (20) L-13
Norden. E-9
Norfolk (23516). G-14
Norman (49) . . . K-11
North Bend (1213) H-15
North Loup (339) H-11
North Platte (23878). I-7
Northport. H-3
O'Neill (3733). . . F-11
Oak (60). L-13
Oakdale (345) . . G-13
Oakland (1367) . G-16
Obert (49) E-15
Oconto (141) I-9
Octavia (145) . . . I-15
Odell (345). L-15
Odessa J-10
Ogallala (4930) . . . I-5
Ohiowa (142). . . K-14
Omaha (390007). I-17
Ong (67) K-13
Orchard (391) . . F-12
Ord (2269). H-11
Ordville I-3
Orleans (425). . . L-10
Osceola (921) . . . I-14
Oshkosh (887). . . H-4
Osmond (796) . . F-14
Otoe (217) J-17
Overton (646). . . J-10
Oxford (876) . . . K-10
Page (157) F-12
Palisade (386) . . . K-6
Palmer (472). . . . I-12
Palmyra (546) . . J-16
Panama (253) . . J-16
Papallion. I-17
Parks L-5
Paul J-17
Pawnee City L-17
Paxton (614). I-6
Pender (1148) . . F-15
Peru (569) K-17
Petersburg (374) G-13
Phillips J-12
Pickrell (182) . . . K-15
Pierce (1774) . . . F-14
Pilger (378) G-15
Plainview (1353) F-13
Platte Center (359) H-14
Plattsmouth (6887). I-17
Pleasant Dale (245) J-15
Pleasanton (360) J-11
Plymouth (477) . K-15
Polk (322). I-13
Ponca (1062). . . E-15
Poole J-11
Potter (390) I-2
Prague (346). . . . I-15
Preston (50). . . . L-18
Primrose (69) . . H-12
Princeton K-15
Prosser (94). . . . J-12
Purdum G-8
Raeville G-13
Ragan (46). K-10
Ralston . . . D-15,I-17
Randolph (955) . F-14
Ravenna (1341) . I-11
Raymond (186) . J-15
Red Cloud (1131) L-12
Redbird E-12
Redington H-2
Republican City . L-10
Reynolds (88) . . L-14
Richland (89). . . H-14
Ringgold H-7
Rising City I-14
Riverdale (213) . J-10
Riverton (145) . . L-11
Roca (220). J-16
Rockford K-16
Rockville (111) . . I-11
Rogers (95). . . . H-15
Rosalie (194). . . G-16
Roscoe I-6
Rose. F-10
Roseland (242) . K-12
Rosemont K-12
Royal (75) F-13
Rulo (50) L-18
Running Water . . E-13
Rushville (999) . . E-4
Ruskin (20) L-13
Salem (138). . . . L-18
Santee (302) . . . E-13
Sargent (649) . . H-10
Saronville (61) . . K-13
Schuyler (5371). H-15
Scotia (308). . . . H-11
Scribner. H-15
Seneca (51) G-7
Seward (6319) . . J-15
Shelby (690) I-14
Shelton (1140) . . J-11
Shickley (376) . . K-13
Sholes (24) F-14
Shubert (252) . . K-18
Sidney (6282) I-3
Silver Creek (441). I-14
Smithfield (68). . . K-9
Snyder (318) . . . H-15
South Bend (86) . I-16
South Sioux City. F-16
Spalding (537)
Sparks . . . . . .
Spencer (541)
Spiker . . . . . .
Sprague (146)
Springview (24
St. Edward (796) . . . . . .
St. Helena (86)
St. James. . . .
St. Libory . . .
St. Mary. . . . .
St. Paul (2218)
Stamford (202)
Stanton (1627)
Staplehurst (270) . . . . . .
Stapleton (301
Steele City . . .
Steinauer (74)
Stella (220) . .
Sterling (507)
Stockham (60)
Stockville (36)
Strang (32) . .
Stratton (396)
Stromsburg (1232). . . . .
Stuart (625) . .
Sumner (237).
Sunol . . . . . .
Superior (2055
Surprise (44)
Sutherland (11
Sutton (1447)
Swanton (106)
Swedeburg . . .
Sweetwater . . .
Syracuse (176
Table Rock (264) . . . . .
Talmage (268)

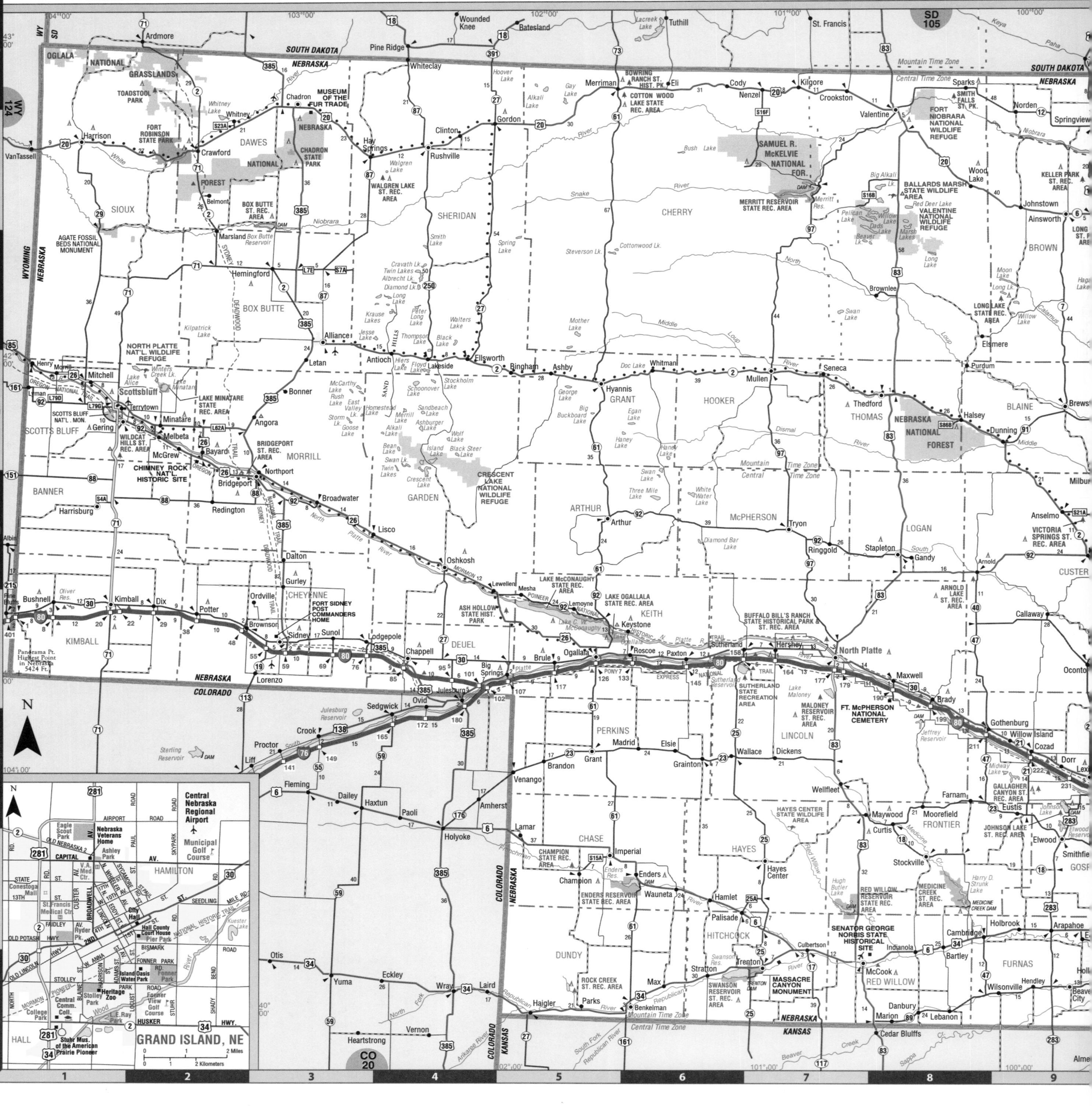

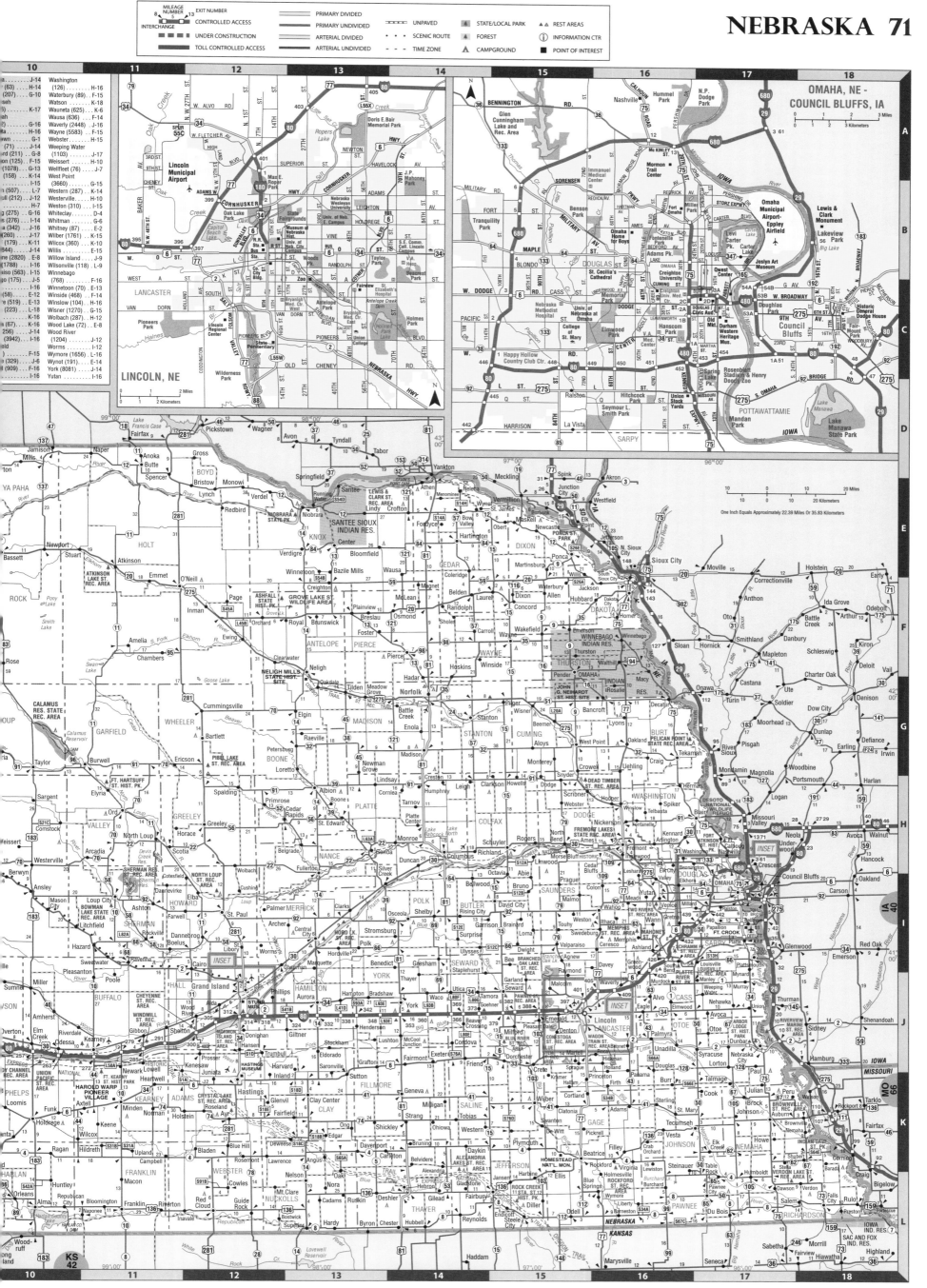

LINCOLN, NE

OMAHA, NE - COUNCIL BLUFFS, IA

	AUSTIN	CARSON CITY	LAS VEGAS	ELY	LAUGHLIN	RENO	WELLS	WINNEMUCCA
BOULDER CITY	357	0	482	278	27	43	480	423	550
CARSON CITY	176	482	0	322	456	515	363	190
LAS VEGAS	331	27	456	251	0	60	454	396	524
RENO	175	480	31	321	454	514	0	342	169

Map of Nevada with city index, highway network, and inset maps for Reno, NV; Las Vegas, NV; Las Vegas Strip, NV; and Carson City, NV.

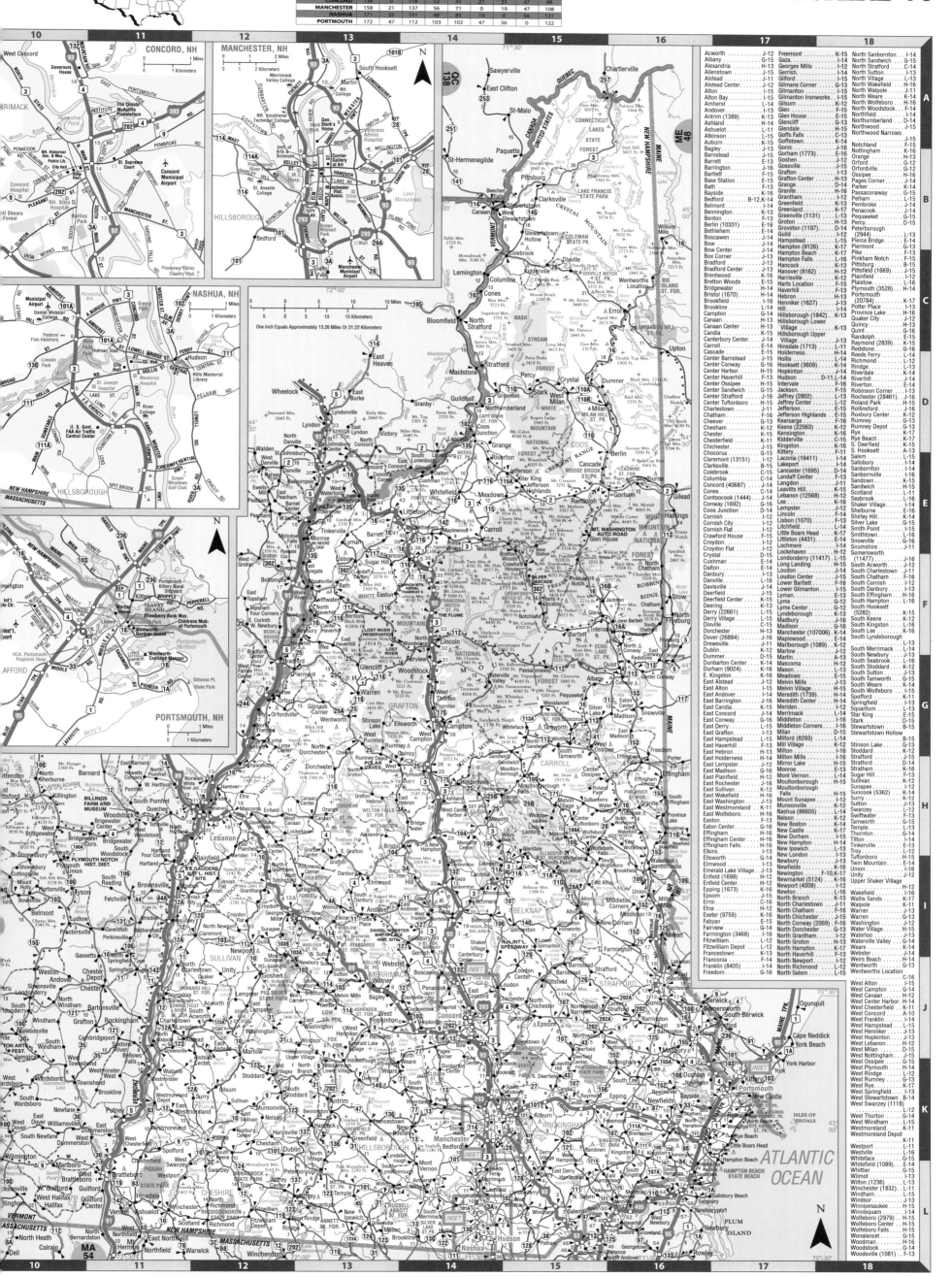

	ATLANTIC CITY	ASBURY PARK	CAMDEN	CAPEMAY	MILLVILLE	NEWARK	NEW YORK,NY	TRENTON
ATLANTIC CITY	0	77	50	49	39	112	123	83
NEW ARK	112	47	85	145	120	0	27	52
TRENTON	83	45	36	115	76	52	64	0

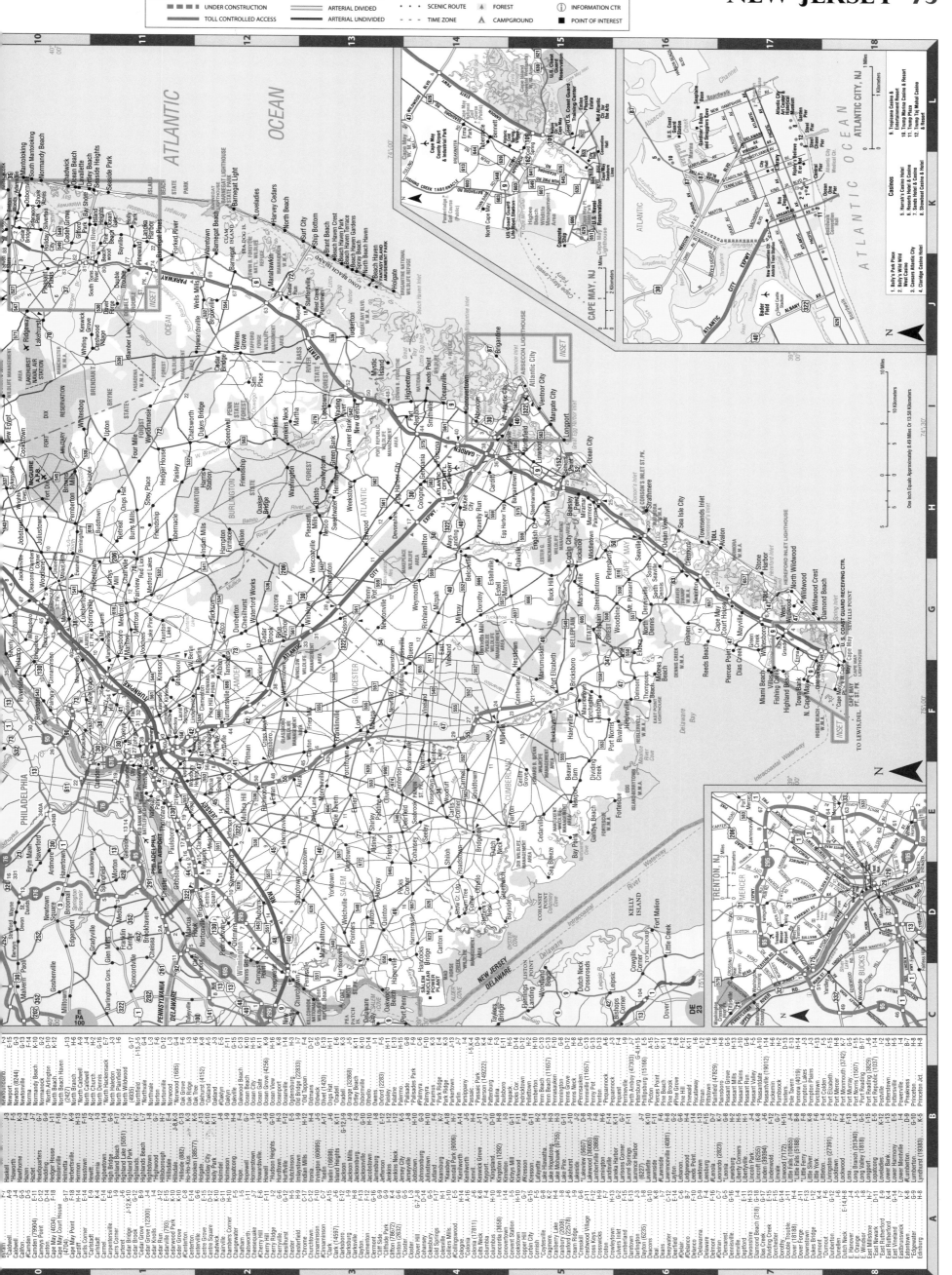

	ALBUQUERQUE	EL PASO, TX	FARMINGTON	GALLUP	LAS CRUCES	LORDSBURG	RATON	ROSWELL	SANTA FE	TUCUMCARI
ALBUQUERQUE	0	268	187	141	223	295	228	206	63	177
LAS CRUCES	223	46	419	343	0	120	452	185	286	310
ROSWELL	206	207	390	344	185	304	291	0	197	167
SANTA FE	63	331	204	201	286	358	174	197	0	168

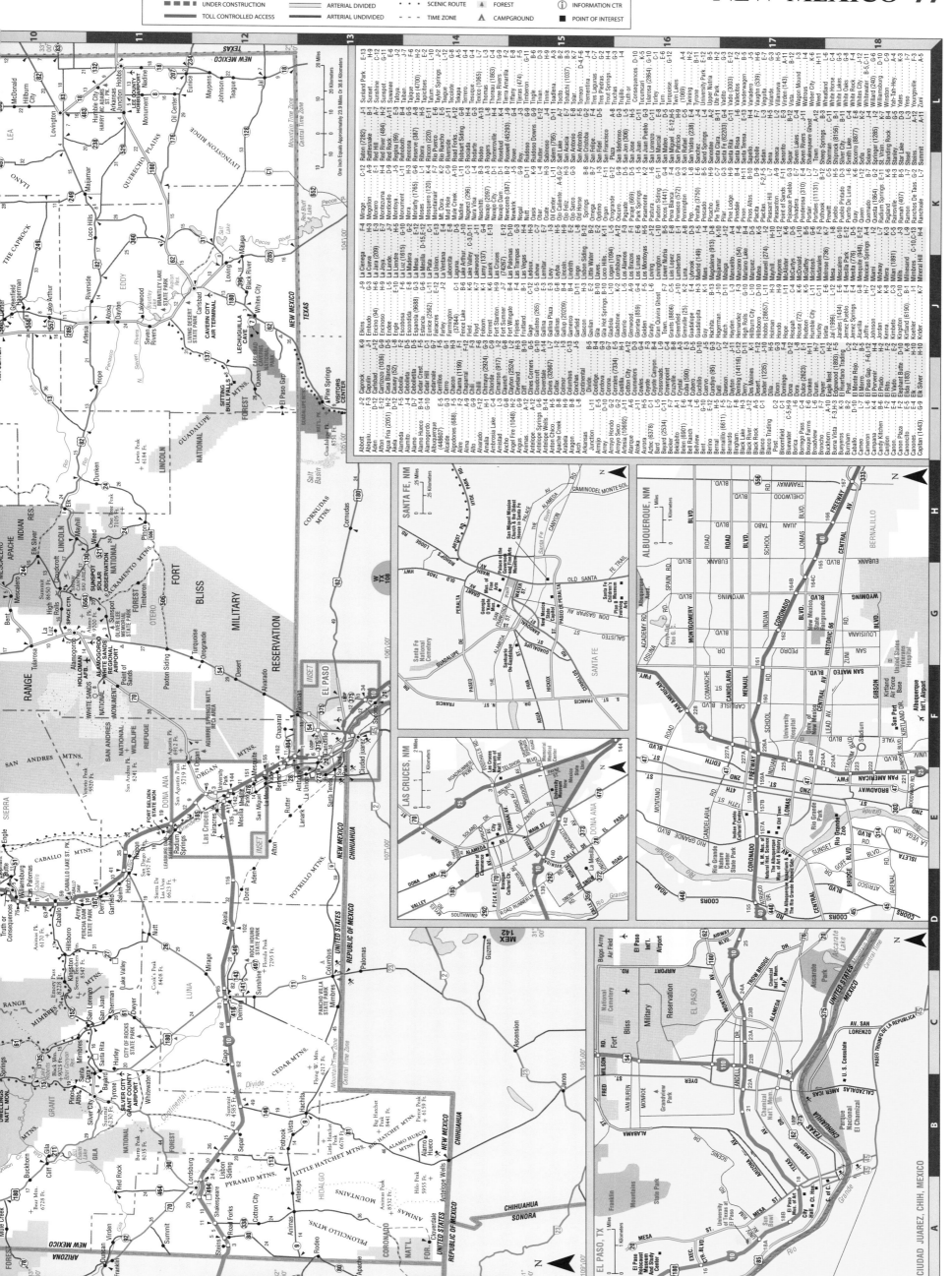

	ALBANY	BINGHAMTON	BUFFALO	CORNING	NEWBURGH	NEW YORK	NIAGARA FALLS	PLATTSBURGH	ROCHESTER	SYRACUSE	UTICA	WATERTOWN
ALBANY	0	140	291	213	91	155	304	161	228	145	96	175
BUFFALO	291	199	0	125	338	392	22	373	77	150	202	215
NEW YORK	155	195	392	267	70	0	413	317	353	266	248	337
ROCHESTER	228	162	77	101	299	353	90	310	0	87	139	152
SYRACUSE	145	75	150	301	212	266	164	228	87	0	57	71

MAP OF MANHATTAN
SHOWING MAIN AUTOMOBILE ROUTES
HOTELS AND
POINTS OF INTEREST

NEW YORK CITY 79
& Vicinity

Legend

	CONTROLLED ACCESS
	UNDER CONSTRUCTION
	TOLL CONTROLLED ACCESS
	PRIMARY DIVIDED
	PRIMARY UNDIVIDED
	ARTERIAL DIVIDED
	ARTERIAL UNDIVIDED
	UNPAVED
	SCENIC ROUTE
	TIME ZONE
	STATE/LOCAL PARK
	FOREST
	CAMPGROUND
	REST AREAS
	INFORMATION CTR
	POINT OF INTEREST

ATLANTIC OCEAN

Lower New York Bay

	ALBANY	BINGHAMTON	BUFFALO	CORNING	NEWBURGH	NIAGARA FALLS	NEW YORK	PLATTSBURGH	ROCHESTER	SYRACUSE	UTICA	WATERTOWN
ALBANY	0	140	291	213	91	155	304	161	228	145	96	175
BUFFALO	291	199	0	125	338	392	22	373	77	150	202	215
NEW YORK	155	195	392	77	101	299	353	413	317	353	266	216
ROCHESTER	228	162	77	101	310	7	310	9	0	87	139	152
SYRACUSE	145	75	150	101	212	266	164	228	87	0	57	71

Towns are keyed to maps on pages 78 thru 83.

One Inch Equals Approximately 7.85 Miles Or 12.57 Kilometers

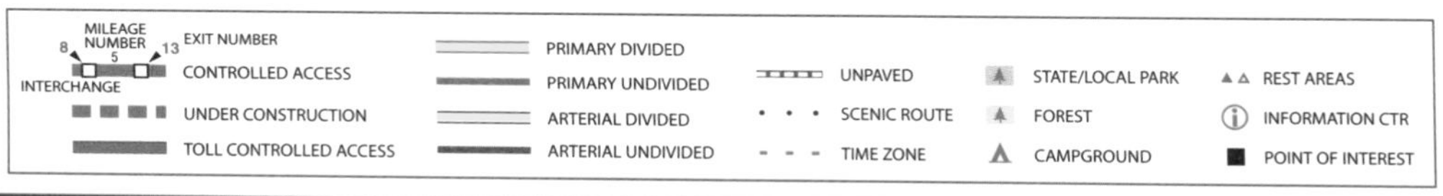

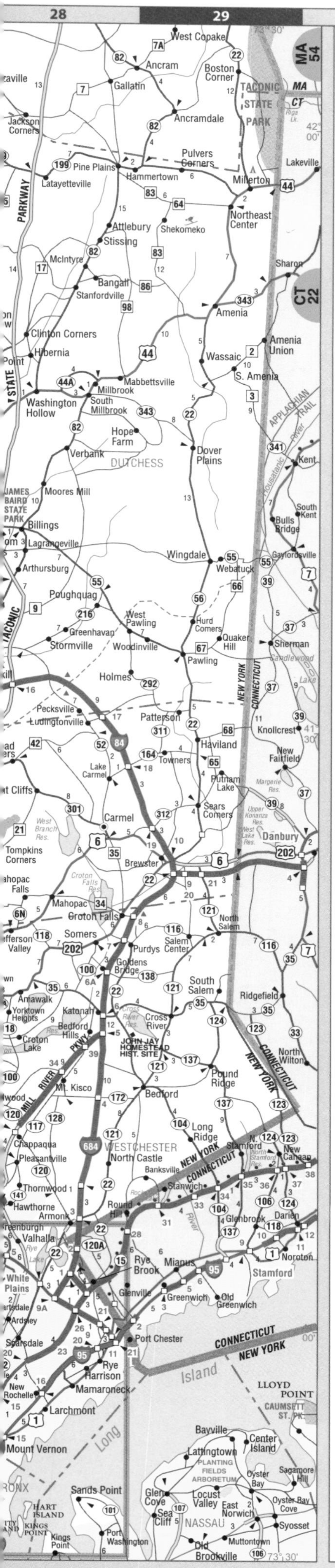

Frenchwoods	B-20
Frewsburg (1965)	L-37
Friendship (1176)	K-40
Frost Valley	B-23
Fruit Valley	G-45
Ft. Covington Ctr.	B-51
Ft. Hunter	I-51
Fullerville	D-48
Fulton (11855)	G-45
Fultonham	K-51
Fultonville	I-51
Gabriels	D-52
Gaines	G-40
Gainesville (304)	J-40
Galeville	A-42,D-25
Gallatin	A-28
Gallupville	J-51
Galway	I-52
Gang Mills (3304)	L-43
Gansevoort	H-53
Garbutt	H-41
Garden City	K-29
Gardiner (856)	D-26
Gardnertown	E-26
Garrattsville	J-49
Garrison	F-27
Garwood	A-14
Garwoods	J-41
Gasport (1248)	G-39
Gates	B-39,H-42
Genegantslet	K-47
Geneseo (7579)	I-41
Geneva (13617)	I-44
Genoa	J-45
Georgetown	J-47
German (862)	K-47
Germantown	L-52
Germonds	F-1
Gerry	K-37
Getzville	H-39
Ghent (586)	L-53
Gibson	L-43
Gibson Landing	J-43
Gifford	J-52
Gilbertsville	K-48
Gilboa	K-51
Gilmantown	G-51
Glasco (1692)	A-27
Glen	I-51
Glen Aubrey	L-46
Glen Cove (26622)	J-29
Glen Ridge	B-10
Glen Spey	E-22
Glen Wild	D-23
Glenburnie	F-54
Glendale	F-48
Glenfield	F-48
Glenford	A-26
Glenham	E-27
Glenora	J-44
Glenville	L-2
Glenwood	D-42,J-39
Gloversville (15413)	I-51
Godeffroy	E-23
Goldens Bridge	F-28
Gorham	I-43
Goshen (5676)	F-25
Gouverneur	D-48
Gowanda (2842)	J-38
Grafton	J-53
Grahamsville	B-23
Granby Center	G-45
Grand Gorge	K-50
Grand Island	A-37 H-38
Grand View	G-3
Granite	C-25
Graniteville	L-26
Grant	H-49
Grant Wood	G-9
Granville	H-54
Graphite	F-53
Grasselli	C-15
Gravesville	H-49
Gray	H-49
Great Bend (801)	E-47
Great Neck Estates (2756)	L-9
Great Neck Plaza	L-9
Great Notch	B-8
Great Valley	K-39
Greece	A-39,H-42
Green Island	A-45
Green River	L-53
Green Ville	J-4
Greenburgh	H-28,I-2
Greene (1701)	K-47
Greenfield Center	I-52
Greenfield Park	C-24
Greenhavan	D-28
Greenhurst	K-37
Greenlawn (13286)	J-30
Greenport (2048)	K-34
Greenville	K-52,F-23
Greenwich	I-53
Greenwood	L-41
Greenwood Lake	G-25
Greig	F-48
Greigsville	I-41
Griffin	G-51
Grittins Mills	I-39
Groom	J-52
Grooville	B-22
Grossinger	C-22
Groton (2470)	J-45
Groveland	J-41
Guilderland	A-43,J-52
Guilford	K-48
Guyanoga	J-43
Hadley	H-52
Hagaman	I-52
Hague	F-53
Hailesboro	D-48
Haines Falls	L-52
Halcottsville	L-50
Hale Eddy	A-19
Halfmoon	J-53
Hall	I-43
Halls Mills	B-23
Hallsport	L-41
Halsey Valley	L-45
Hamburg (10116)	I-38
Hamden	L-49
Hamilton	I-48
Hamlet	J-37
Hamlin	G-41
Hammertown	A-28
Hammond	C-48
Hammondsport	K-43
Hampton	G-54
Hampton Bays (12236)	L-34
Hancock (1189)	B-19
Hankins	C-20
Hannacroix	K-52
Hannawa Falls	C-50
Hannibal (542)	G-45
Hannibal Center	G-45
Harford	K-46
Harford Mills	K-46
Harkness	C-53
Harmon	G-27
Harpersfield	K-50
Harpursville	L-47
Harriets Town	D-52
Harriman (2252)	F-26
Harrington Park	F-5
Harris	C-22
Harrisburg	F-48,G-52
Harrison	I-28
Harrisville	D-48
Hart Lot	I-45
Hartfield	D-39
Hartford	H-54
Hartland	G-39
Hartmans Corner	A-43
Hartsdale	I-28,J-3
Hartsville	K-41
Hartwick	J-49
Hartwick Seminary	J-49
Hartwood	E-23
Harvard	A-20
Hasbrouck	C-23
Hasbrouck Heights	E-8
Haskinville	K-42
Hastings	G-46
Hastingson Hudson	I-27
Hauppauge (20100)	L-31
Haven	E-23
Haverstraw (10117)	G-27
Haviland (3710)	E-29
Hawkeye	C-53
Hawleyton	L-46
Haworth	F-5
Hawthorne	H-28,J-1
Haynersville	J-53
Hayt Cors	J-44
Hebron	H-54
Hector	J-44
Helena	B-50
Hemlock	I-42
Hempstead (56554)	K-29
Henderson	E-46
Henderson Harbor	E-46
Henrietta	H-42
Hensonville	L-51
Herkimer	I-49
Hermitage	J-40
Hermon	C-49
Herrings	E-48
Heuvelton	C-48
Hewittville	B-49
Hewlett (7060)	K-28
Hibernia	C-28
Hicksville (41260)	K-29
Higgins	K-40
Higgins Bay	G-50
High Bank	C-52
High Falls (627)	B-26
High Mount	L-50
Highland (5060)	C-27
Highland Falls	F-27
Highland Lake	E-22
Highland Mills	F-26
Highmarket	G-48
Highview	E-24
Highwood	G-7
Hillburn (881)	H-26
Hillcrest (7106)	E-1
Hillsdale	L-53,E-4
Hillside (882)	C-13
Hilton (5856)	G-41
Himrod	J-44
Hinckley	H-49
Hinmansville	H-45
Hinsdale	K-39
Hoag Corners	K-53
Hobart	K-50
Hoffmans	I-52
Hoffmeister	G-50
Hogansburg	A-50
Holbrook (27512)	L-32
Holcomb	I-42
Holcomville	F-52
Holcott Center	L-50
Holland (1261)	J-39
Holland Patent	H-48
Holley (1802)	G-41
Hollowville	L-53
Holmes	E-28
Holmesville	K-48
Holtsville (17006)	L-32
Homer	D-40,J-46
Honeoye	I-42
Honeoye Falls	I-42
Hoosick	J-54
Hoosick Falls	I-54
Hope Falls	H-51
Hope Farm	C-28
Hope Valley	H-51
Hopewell Junction (2610)	D-28
Hopkinton	C-50
Hornby	K-43
Hornell (9019)	K-41
Horseheads	L-44
Horseshoe	E-50
Hortonville	C-21
Houghton (1748)	J-40
Howard	K-42
Howells	E-24
Howes	L-47
Howes Cave	J-51
Hubbardsville	J-48
Hudson (7524)	L-52
Hudson Falls	H-53
Hudson Heights	G-10
Hudson-on-the-Lake	I-38
Hughsonville	D-27
Huguenot	F-23
Huletts Landing	G-53
Hume	J-40
Humphrey	K-39
Hunt	J-41
Hunter	L-51
Huntersland	K-51
Huntington (18403)	J-30
Huntington Station (29910)	J-30
Hunts Corners	D-21
Hurd Corners	D-29
Hurley (3561)	B-26
Hurleyville	C-23
Huron	H-44
Hyde Park	C-27
Hyndsville	J-50
Ilion	I-49
Independence	L-41
Index	J-49
Indian Falls	H-40
Indian Lake	F-51
Indian Park	G-25
Indian River	E-48
Indian Village	I-46
Ingleside	J-42
Ingreham	B-54
Inlet	F-50
Interlaken (674)	J-44
Inwood	L-28,L-14
Ionia	I-42
Ira	H-45
Ireland Corners	D-26
Irona	B-53
Irondequoit	A-40,H-42
Ironville	F-53
Irving	J-37
Irvington	H-27,H-3
Ischua	K-39
Iselin	A-17
Island Park	L-29
Islandia (3057)	L-31
Islip (20575)	L-31
Italy Hill	J-43
Ithaca (29287)	K-45
Jacks Reef	H-45
Jackson Corners	A-28
Jacksonville	J-44
Jamaica	K-28
Jamesport	K-33
Jamestown	K-37
Jamesville	C-43,I-46
Jasper	L-42
Java Center	J-39
Java Village	I-39
Jay	D-53
Jeddo	G-39
Jefferson	K-50
Jefferson Heights (1104)	L-52
Jefferson Valley	F-28
Jeffersonville	C-21
Jenksville	K-45
Jericho	B-53,J-29
Jewell	H-47
Jewett	L-51
Jewettville	I-39
Johnsburg	G-52
Johnson (15535)	F-24
Johnson City	L-46
Johnson Creek	G-39
Johnsonburg	I-40
Johnsonville	I-53
Johnstown	I-51
Jones Point	G-27
Jonesville	I-52
Jordan (1314)	H-45
Jordanville	I-49
Kanona	K-42
Katonah	G-28
Katsbaan	L-52
Kattskill Bay	G-53
Kauneonga Lake	D-22
Keasbey	A-18
Keene	D-53
Keene Valley	E-53
Keeseville	C-54
Kelloggsville	I-45
Kelly Corners	L-50
Kelsey	A-19
Kendall	G-41
Kenilworth	A-14
Kenmore	B-37
Kennedy	K-37
Kenoza Lake	C-21
Kensington (1209)	L-9
Kent	G-40
Kent Cliffs	E-28
Kenyonville	G-40
Kerhonkson	C-25
Kerley Corner	A-27
Keuka	J-43
Keuka Park	J-43
Kiamesha Lake	D-23
Kiantone	L-37
Kill Buck	K-38
Killawog	K-46
Kinderhook	K-53
King Ferry	J-44
Kings Park (16146)	K-31
Kings Point	H-7 L-9,J-28
Kingsland	D-10
Kingston (23456)	B-26
Kirk	J-47
Kirkland	I-48
Kirkville	H-46
Kirkwood	L-47
Kirschnerville	E-48
Kiryas Joel (13138)	F-25
Knapp Creek	L-39
Knowlesville	G-40
Knox	J-52
Knoxboro	I-48
Kortright	K-50
Kripplebush	B-25
Krumville	B-25
Kuckville	G-40
La Fayette	I-46
Lackawack	C-24
Lackawana	I-38
Lacona	F-46
Ladentown	G-26
Ladleton	B-23
Lafargeville	D-47
Lagrange	I-41
Lagrangeville	D-28
Lake Bluff	G-44
Lake Bonaparte	D-48
Lake Carmel (8663)	E-28
Lake Clear Junction	D-52
Lake Delta	H-48
Lake Erie Beach (4499)	I-38
Lake George	G-53
Lake Grove (10250)	K-31
Lake Hill	A-25
Lake Huntington	D-21
Lake Katrine	A-27
Lake Luzerne	H-52
Lake Minnewaska	C-25
Lake Peekskill	F-27
Lake Placid	D-52
Lake Pleasant	G-51
Lakemont	J-44
Lakeport	H-47
Lakeside	G-43
Lakeview	G-45 I-38,D-8
Lakeville	I-41
Lakewood	K-37,B-21
Lamberton	J-37
Lamont	J-40
Lamson	H-45
Lancaster (11188)	H-39
Lanesville	L-51
Langford	J-38
Lansing (3417)	K-45
Laona	J-37
Lapla	B-26
Larchmont (6485)	I-28
Lassellsville	I-50
Latayetteville	A-28
Latham	A-44
Lattingtown	J-29
Laurel (1188)	K-33
Laurens	K-49
Lavanna	I-44
Lawrence (6522)	L-28
Lawrenceville	B-50 L-43
Lawtons	J-38
Lawyersville	J-50
Le Roy (4462)	H-41
Lebanon	J-47
Lebanon Springs	K-54
Ledyard	J-44
Lee	H-48
Lee Center	H-48
Leeds (369)	L-52
Leicester (469)	I-41
Lenox	H-47
Leon	K-38
Leonardsville	J-48
Leonia	G-8
Levittown	K-29
Lewbeach	A-22
Lewis	D-53
Lewiston	D-41,G-38
Lexington	L-51
Liberty (3975)	C-22
Libertyville	C-26
Lido Beach	L-29
Lily Dale	J-37
Lima (2459)	I-42
Lime Lake	J-39
Limerick	E-46
Limestone (411)	L-39
Lincklaen	J-47
Lincoln	H-43
Linden	I-40
Lindenhurst (27819)	K-30
Lindley	L-43
Linwood	I-41
Lisbon	B-49
Lisle (302)	K-46
Litchfield	I-49
Little Britain	E-26
Little Canada	H-40
Little Falls	I-50,B-8
Little Ferry	F-8
Little France	G-46
Little Genesee	L-40
Little Italy	C-7
Little Valley	K-38
Little York	J-46,J-50
Liver Pool	H-46
Liverpool	A-41
Livingston	L-52
Livingston Manor (1355)	B-22
Livingstonville	K-51
Livonia (1373)	I-42
Livonia Center	I-42
Lloyd Harbor (3675)	I-30
Loch Muller	F-53
Loch Sheldrake	C-23
Lock Berlin	H-44
Locke	J-45
Lockport (22279)	G-39
Lockwood	L-45
Locust Valley (3521)	J-29
Lodi (338)	J-44
Lomontville	B-26
Long Beach (35462)	L-29
Long Eddy	B-20
Long Lake	E-51
Long Ridge	H-29
Loon Lake	C-52,G-52
Lordville	B-19
Lorraine	F-47
Loudonville	A-44
Louisville	B-49
Lowell	H-48
Lower South Bay	H-46
Lowes Corners	B-24
Lowman	L-44
Lowville	F-48
Ludingtonville	E-28
Ludlowville	J-45
Lycoming	G-45
Lykers	J-51
Lyn Brook	K-28
Lyndhurst	D-10
Lyndonville (862)	G-40
Lyon Mountain	B-52
Lyons (3695)	H-44
Lyons Falls	F-48
Lyonsdale	F-48
Lysander	H-45
Mabbettsville	C-28
Macdougall	I-44
Macedon (1496)	H-43
Macedon Center	H-43
Machias	J-39
Madison	I-48
Madrid	B-49
Mahopac (8478)	F-28
Mahopac Falls	F-28
Maine	L-46
Malden Bridge	K-53
Malden on Hudson	L-52
Mallory	G-46
Malone	B-51
Malta	I-53
Malta Ridge	I-53
Maltaville	I-53
Mamaroneck (18752)	I-28
Manchester (1475)	I-43
Manitou Beach	G-42
Manlius (4819)	I-46
Mannsville	F-46
Manor	L-32
Manorhaven (6138)	L-8
Manorville (11131)	K-33
Maple Grove	H-52
Maple Springs	D-39
Maple View	G-46
Maplecrest	L-51
Maplehurst	K-39
Maplewood	D-22
Marathon (1063)	K-46
Marbletown	B-26
Marcellus (1826)	I-45
Marcy	H-48
Margaretville	L-50
Mariaville	J-51
Marietta	I-45
Marilla	I-39
Marion	H-43
Markhams	J-38
Marlboro (2339)	D-27
Martindale Depot	L-53
Martinsburg	F-48
Martinsville	A-38
Martville	H-45
Maryland	K-49
Masonville	L-48
Massapequa Park (17499)	K-30
Massena	B-50
Mastens Lake	D-23
Mastic (15436)	L-32
Mastic Beach (11543)	L-32
Mattituck (4198)	K-34
Mattydale	A-42
Maybrook (3084)	E-25
Mayfield	I-51
Maynard	C-43
Mayville (1756)	D-39
Maywood	A-43,E-7
McConnellsville	H-47
McDonough	K-47
McGraw (1000)	J-46
McKeel Corners	E-27
McKeever	G-49
McKownville	B-43
McLean	J-45
McLntyre	B-28
McNab	C-40
Mead Corners	E-28
Meads Creek	K-43
Mechanicville	I-53
Mecklenburg	K-44
Meco	I-51
Medford (21985)	L-32
Medina (6415)	G-40
Medusa (376)	K-52
Mellenville	L-53
Melody Lake	D-23
Melrose	J-53
Melrose Park	I-45
Melville (14533)	J-30
Memands	B-45
Mendon	H-42
Menlo Park	A-17
Meredith	K-49
Meridale	K-49
Meridian (350)	H-45
Merrick (22764)	K-29
Merrill	B-52
Messengerville	K-46
Mexico	G-46
Middle Falls	I-53
Middle Granville	G-54
Middle Grove	I-52
Middle Hope	E-26
Middle Island (9702)	K-32
Middleburgh	K-51
Middlefield	J-50
Middleport	G-39
Middlesex	J-43
Middletown	E-24
Middleville	H-49
Mileses	B-20
Milford	J-49
Millbrook (1429)	C-28
Millburn	A-13
Miller Place (10580)	K-32
Millerton (925)	B-29
Millport (297)	K-44
Millville	G-40
Millwood	G-28
Milo	J-43
Milton (1251)	D-27
Mina	D-38
Minaville	I-51
Mineola (19234)	K-29
Minerva	F-52
Minetto (1086)	G-45
Mineville	E-53
Minisink Ford	E-21
Minoa (3348)	H-46
Model City	G-38
Modena	D-26
Moffitsville	C-53
Mohawk	I-49
Mohegan Lake	F-27
Mohonk Lake	C-26
Moira	B-51
Mombaccus	C-25
Mongaup	E-22
Mongaup Valley	D-22
Monroe (7780)	F-25
Monsey (14504)	H-26
Montauk (3851)	K-36
Montauk Beach	K-36
Montebello	H-26
Monterey	K-43
Montezuma	H-44
Montgomery	E-25
Monticello (6512)	D-22
Montour Falls	K-44
Montrose	G-27
Montvale	E-3
Moody	D-51
Mooers (440)	B-53
Mooers Forks	B-53
Moonachie	E-9
Moores Mill	C-28
Moravia (1363)	J-45
Moreland	K-44
Morganville	H-40
Moriah	E-53
Moriah Center	E-53
Moriches (2319)	L-32
Morley	C-49
Morris	K-48
Morrisonville (1702)	C-53
Morristown	C-48
Morrisville (2148)	I-47
Morton	G-41
Mottville	I-45
Mount Ivy (6536)	G-26
Mount Vernon (68381)	I-28
Mount Vision	J-49
Mountain Dale	D-23
Mountain Lodge	F-26
Mountain View	C-52 A-7
Mountainville	F-26
Mt. Hope	E-23
Mt. Kisco	G-28
Mt. Marion	A-27
Mt. Mcgregor	H-53
Mt. Morris	I-41
Mt. Tremper	A-25
Mt. Upton	K-48
Mt. Vernon	I-38
Mumford	H-41
Munnsville (437)	I-47
Murray	G-41
Muttontown	J-29
Myers	J-45
N. Chili	H-41
N. Syracuse	A-42
N. Tonawanda	H-38
N. Y. Mills	H-48
Nanticoke	K-46
Nanuet	H-26,E-2
Napanoch (1168)	C-24
Naples (1072)	J-42
Napoli	K-38
Narrowsburg	D-20
Nassau	K-53
Nassau Point	K-34
Natural Bridge	E-48
Natural Dam	D-48
Naumburg	E-48
Nedrow (2265)	I-46
Nelliston	I-50
Nelson	I-47
Nelson Corners	F-27
Nelsonville (565)	E-27
Neversink	C-23
Nevis	A-27
New Albion	K-38
New Baltimore	K-52
New Berlin	J-48
New Bremen	F-48
New Bridge	F-7
New City	H-27
New Dover	A-16
New Hackensack	D-27
New Hamburg	D-27
New Hampton	F-24
New Hartford	E-42,I-48
New Haven	G-46
New Hempstead (4767)	H-26
New Hope	I-45
New Kingston	L-50
New Lebanon	K-54
New Lebanon Center	K-54
New Lisbon	J-49
New London	H-48
New Milford	G-24,F-6
New Paltz (6034)	C-26
New Rochelle (72182)	I-28
New Russia	E-53
New Salem	J-52
New Scotland	B-43 J-52
New Suffolk	K-34
New Windsor (9077)	E-26
New Woodstock	I-47
New York Mills	D-42
Newark (9682)	H-43
Newark Valley (1071)	L-46
Newburgh (28259)	E-26
Newcomb	E-52
Neweiden	D-21
Newfane (3129)	G-39
Newfield	K-44
Newport	H-49
Newton Falls	D-49
Newtonville	A-44
Niagara on-the-Lake	C-41
Nichols (574)	L-45
Nicholville	C-50
Nile	K-40
Niles	I-45
Nimmonsburg	L-46
Nineveh	L-47
Niobe	E-39
Niskayuna (4892)	J-52
Niverville (1737)	K-53
Norfolk (1334)	B-50
Normansville	B-44
North Argyle	H-53
North Arlington	D-10
North Bangor	B-51
North Bay	H-47
North Bellport	L-32
North Blenheim	K-51
North Boston	I-38
North Branch	C-21
North Broadalbin	I-51
North Brookfield	I-48
North Caldwell	A-9
North Castle	H-28
North Chatham	K-53
North Chemung	L-44
North Chittenango	H-47
North Clymer	D-38
North Cohocton	J-42
North Collins	J-38
North Creek	F-52
North Evans	I-38
North Fair Haven	G-44
North Fenton	L-47
North Granville	G-54
North Greece	G-41
North Greenwich	L-1
North Hackensack	E-7
North Harpersfield	K-50
North Haven	K-34
North Herbon	H-54
North Highland	E-27
North Hillsdale	L-53
North Hoosick	I-54
North Hornell	K-41
North Hudson	E-53
North Java	I-40
North Lansing	J-45
North Lawrence	B-50
North Norwich	J-48
North Petersburg	J-54
North Pharsalia	J-47
North Pitcher	J-47
North Pole	D-53
North River	F-52
North Rose	H-44
North Rush	H-42
North Salem	F-29
North Sanford	L-48
North Sea (4493)	K-34
North Stockholm	B-50
North Syracuse	H-46
North Tonawanda	E-42 A-37
North Victory	H-45
North Western	H-48
North Wolcott	H-44
Northeast Center	B-29
Northport (7606)	I-30
Northumberland	I-53
Northvale	G-4
Northville	H-51,K-33
Norton Hill	K-52
Norway	H-49
Norwich (7355)	K-48
Norwood	B-50,G-4
Noyack (2696)	K-34
Nunda (1330)	J-41
Nyack (6737)	H-27
Oak Beach	L-31
Oak Hill	K-51
Oakdale (8075)	L-31
Oakfield (1805)	H-40
Oakland	J-41
Oakland Valley	E-23
Oakridge	H-46
Oaks Corners	I-43
Obernburg	C-21
Obi	L-40
Ocean Beach	L-31
Oceanside (32733)	K-29
Odessa (617)	K-44
Ogden	H-41
Ogdensburg (12364)	B-48
Ohio	H-49
Ohioville	C-26
Olcott (1156)	G-39
Old Brookville	J-29
Old Chatham	K-53
Old Forge	F-49
Old Tappan	F-4
Old Westbury	J-29
Olean (15347)	L-39
Olivebridge	B-25
Oliverea	L-50,A-24
Olmstedville	F-52
Onchiota	C-52
Oneida Castle	H-47
Oneida Valley	H-47
Oneonta (13292)	K-49
Onondaga	I-46
Onondaga Hill	B-42
Ontario	H-43
Ontario Center	H-43
Ontario on the Lake	G-43
Oppenheim	I-50
Oradell	E-6
Oramel	K-40
Oran	I-47
Orange Lake	E-26
Orangeburg	H-27,G-3
Orchard Park	I-39
Orient (709)	J-34
Oriskany	H-48
Oriskany Falls	I-48
Orleans	I-43
Orwell	F-46
Osceola	G-47
Ossian	J-41
Ossining (24010)	H-27
Oswegatchie	D-49
Oswego (17954)	G-45
Otego	K-48
Otisco	I-46
Otisville (989)	E-23
Otselic	J-47
Otter Creek	F-48
Otter Lake	G-49
Otto	J-38
Ouaquaga	L-47
Overlook	H-52
Ovid (612)	J-44
Owasco	I-45
Owego (3911)	L-45
Owls Head	B-52
Oxbow	D-48
Oxford	K-47
Oxford Depot	F-25
Oyster Bay (6826)	J-29
Oyster Bay Cove	J-29
Paines Hollow	I-49
Painted Post	L-43
Palatine Bridge	I-50
Palenville (1120)	L-52
Palermo	G-46
Palisade	G-8
Palisades	I-27,H-4
Palisades Park	F-9
Palmyra (3490)	H-43
Pamelia Four Corners	E-47
Panama (491)	D-39
Panna Center	G-41
Paradox	F-53
Paris	I-48
Parish	G-46
Parishville	C-50
Park Ridge	E-4
Parkston	B-22
Parksville	B-22
Parma	H-41
Passaic Park	D-9
Pataukunk	C-25
Patchin	I-38
Patchogue (11919)	L-32
Patterson	E-29
Pattersonville	I-52
Paul Smiths	D-52
Pavilion	I-41
Pawling (2233)	D-29
Peakville	A-20
Pearl Creek	I-41
Pearl River	H-26,E-3
Peasleeville	C-53
Pecksville	E-28
Peconic (1081)	K-34
Peekamoose	B-24
Peekskill (22441)	F-27
Pekin	D-42,G-38
Pelham Manor	J-7
Pembroke	H-39
Pendleton	H-39
Penfield	H-42
Penn Yan (5219)	J-43
Pennellville	H-46
Perkinsville	J-42
Perry (3945)	I-41
Perry Center	I-41
Perrysburg (408)	J-38
Perryville	I-47
Perth	I-51
Peru (1514)	C-53
Peruville	J-45
Peterboro	I-47
Petersburg	J-54
Petrolla	L-40
Pharsalia	J-47
Phelps (1969)	I-43
Philadelphia	D-47
Phillips Creek	K-41
Phillipsport	D-24
Philmont	L-53
Phoenicia	L-51,A-25
Phoenix (2251)	H-46
Picketts Corners	C-53
Picton	A-15
Piercefield	D-51
Piermont (2607)	G-3
Pierrepont	C-49
Pierrepont Manor	F-46
Piffard	I-41
Pike (382)	J-40
Pillar Point	E-46
Pilot Knobb	G-53
Pinckney	E-47
Pine Bush (1539)	D-25
Pine City	L-44
Pine Hill (308)	L-50
Pine Island	G-24
Pine Lake	H-50
Pine Plains	A-28
Pine Valley	K-44
Pine Woods	I-47
Pinelawn	K-30
Piseco	G-51
Pitcairn	D-49
Pitcher	J-47
Pittsfield	J-48
Pittsford	C-41,H-42
Pittstown	J-53
Plainview (25637)	K-30
Plainville	H-45
Plandome (1272)	L-9
Plattekill (1050)	D-26
Plattsburgh (18816)	C-54
Pleasant Brook	J-50
Pleasant Plains	B-27
Pleasant Valley	K-43 C-27
Pleasantdale	A-10
Pleasantville (7172)	H-28
Plessis	D-47
Plumbrook	B-50
Plutarch	C-26
Plymouth	J-47
Pocantico Hills	I-1
Poestenkil	J-53
Point Breeze	G-40
Point Lookout	L-29
Point Peninsula	E-46
Point Rock	G-48
Poland	H-49
Polkville	J-46
Pomona (2726)	G-26
Pompey	I-46
Pompey Center	I-46
Pond Eddy	E-22
Poolville	J-48
Pope Mills	C-48
Poplar Ridge	J-45
Poquott (975)	K-32
Port Byron	H-45
Port Chester	I-29
Port Dickinson	L-47
Port Ewen (3650)	B-27
Port Gibson	H-43
Port Henry	E-54
Port Jefferson (7837)	K-32
Port Jefferson Station (7527)	K-32
Port Jervis (8860)	F-23
Port Kent	C-54
Port Leyden	G-48
Port Reading	B-17
Port Washington (15215)	J-28
Portageville	J-40
Porter Corners	H-52
Porterville	I-39
Portland	C-39
Portlandville	K-49
Portville (1024)	L-39
Post Creek	K-43
Potsdam	C-50
Potter	J-43
Potter Hollow	K-51
Potters Corners	G-48
Pottersville	F-53
Poughkeepsie (29871)	C-27
Poughquag	D-28
Pound Ridge	G-29
Pratts Hollow	I-47
Prattsburg	J-43
Prattsville	L-51
Preakness	B-7
Preble	J-46
Presho	L-43
Preston	K-47
Preston Hollow	K-51
Prospect	H-49
Protection	J-39
Pulaski	G-46
Pulteney	J-43
Pultneyville	G-43
Pulvers Corners	A-29
Purdys	F-28
Putnam Lake (3855)	E-29
Putnam Station	F-54
Putnam Valley	F-27
Pyrites	C-49
Quaker Hill	D-29
Quaker Street	J-51
Queens	K-28
Queensbury	H-53
Queenston	D-41
Quogue (1018)	L-33
Rainbow Lake	C-52
Ramapo	H-26
Randall	I-51
Randallsville	J-47
Randolph (1316)	K-38
Ransomville	G-38
Rapids (1356)	H-39
Raquette Lake	F-50
Rathbone	L-42
Ravena	K-52
Rawson	K-40
Ray Brook	D-52
Raymertown	J-53
Raymondville	B-50
Reading Center	K-44
Red Creek (521)	H-44
Red Hook (1805)	A-27
Red Oaks Mill (4930)	D-27
Redfield	G-47
Redford (512)	C-53
Redwood (584)	D-47
Remsen	H-49
Rennselaer Falls	C-49
Rensselaer	B-44,J-53
Rensselaerville	K-51
Republic	K-45
Resort	H-44
Rexford	J-52
Rexville	L-41
Reynoldsville	K-44
Rhinebeck (3077)	B-27
Rhinecliff	B-27
Riceville	J-39
Richburg (448)	L-40
Richfield	I-49,C-8
Richfield Springs	I-49
Richford	K-46
Richland	G-46
Richmondville	J-50
Richville	C-48
Ridge (13380)	K-32
Ridgebury	F-24
Ridgefield	F-9
Ridgefield Park	F-8
Ridgeway	G-40
Ridgewood	G-39
Rifton (501)	C-26
Rio	E-22
Riparius	G-52
Ripley (1030)	D-38
Risingville	K-42
River Edge	F-6
River Vale	F-4
Riverhead (10513)	K-33
Riverside (594)	L-43
Riversville	L-2
Riverview	C-52
Roanoke	K-33
Rochdale	C-27
Rochelle Park	E-7
Rochester (219773)	H-42
Rock City	A-27
Rock City Falls	I-52
Rock Glen	I-40
Rock Hill (1056)	D-23
Rock Stream	K-44
Rock Tavern	E-25
Rock Valley	B-20
Rockdale	K-48
Rockefeller Lookout	H-7
Rockland	B-21
Rockland Lake	H-27
Rockleigh	G-4
Rockville Cen.	K-29
Rockwood	I-51
Rocky Point (10185)	K-32
Rodman	E-47
Rome (34950)	H-48
Romulus	I-44
Ronkonkoma (20029)	L-31
Roosevelt Beach	G-38
Rooseveltown	A-50
Roscoe (597)	B-21
Rose	H-44
Rose Hill	I-45
Roseboom	J-50
Roseland	A-10
Rosendale (1374)	B-26
Rosiere	D-46
Rossburg	J-40
Rossie	D-48
Rotterdam (20536)	J-52
Rotterdam Junction	J-52
Round Lake	I-53
Round Top	L-52
Rouses Point	B-54
Roxbury	L-50
Royalton Center	H-39
Ruby	A-26
Rural Grove	J-51
Rush	H-42
Rushford	K-40
Rushville (621)	I-43
Russell	C-49
Russell Gardens (1074)	L-9
Russia	H-49
Rutherford	D-9
Rutland	E-47
Rye (14955)	I-28
Rye Brook	H-28,L-2
S. Amenia	C-29
S. Huntington	J-30
S. Jamesport	K-33
Sabael	F-51
Sabbath Day Point	G-53
Sacandaga	H-51
Sackets Harbor	E-46
Sacketts Lake	D-22
Saddle Brook	E-7
Saddle Rock (791)	L-9
Sadom	G-52
Sag Harbor	K-34
Sagamore Hill	J-29
Sagaponack	K-34
Sailor's Haven	L-31
Saint James	K-31
Salamanca (6097)	K-38
Salem	H-54
Salem Center	F-29
Salisbury (12341)	H-50
Salisbury Center	H-50
Salisbury Mills	F-26
Salt Point	C-28
Salt Springville	I-50
Saltaire (43)	L-31
Sammonsville	I-51
Samsonville	B-25
San Remo	K-31
Sanborn	D-42,H-38
Sand Lake	J-53
Sands Point	J-28,L-8
Sandusky	J-39
Sandy Creek	F-46
Sandy Pond	F-46
Sanford	L-48
Sangerfield	I-48
Sanitaria Springs	L-47
Santa Clara	C-51
Saranac	C-53
Saranac Inn	D-51
Saranac Lake	D-52
Saratoga Springs (26186)	I-53
Sardinia	J-39
Saugerties (4955)	A-27
Sauquoit	I-48
Savannah	H-44
Savilton	D-26
Savona (822)	K-43
Sawkill	A-26
Sayville (16735)	L-31
Scarborough	H-27
Scarsdale	I-28
Schaghticoke	I-53
Schenectady (61821)	J-52
Schenevus	K-49
Schodack Center	K-53
Schodack Landing	K-52
Schoharie	J-51
Schroon Lake	F-53
Schuyler Falls	C-53
Schuyler Lake	J-49
Schuylerville	I-53
Sciba Center	G-45
Scio	K-40
Sciota	B-54
Scipio Center	I-45
Scipioville	I-45
Scotia	J-52
Scott	J-46
Scottsburg	J-41
Scottsville (2128)	H-41
Scranton	I-38
Sea Breeze	H-42
Sea Cliff (5066)	J-29
Seaford (15791)	K-30
Seager	A-23
Sears Comers	E-29
Secaucus	F-10
Seeley Creek	L-44
Selden (21861)	K-32
Selkirk	K-52
Selkirk Beach	F-46
Sempronius	J-45
Send Ridge	H-46
Seneca Castle	I-43
Seneca Falls (6861)	I-44
Seneca Hill	G-45
Seneca Point	I-42
Sennett	I-45
Setauket	K-31
Severance	F-53
Seward	J-50
Sewaren	B-17
Shady	A-25
Shandelee	B-21
Sharon	J-50
Sharon Springs	J-50
Sheds	I-47
Shekomeko	B-29
Shelby	G-40
Shelter Is. Heights	K-34
Shelter Island (1234)	K-34
Shendaken	L-51
Sherburne	J-48
Sheridan	J-37
Sherman (714)	D-38
Sherrill (3147)	I-47
Sherwood	I-45
Shinhopple	A-20
Shinnecock Hills (1749)	L-34
Shirley (25395)	L-32
Shohola	E-21
Shokan (1252)	A-25
Sholam	C-24
Shongo	L-41
Shore Oaks	G-45
Shoreham (417)	K-32
Short Tract	J-40
Shortsville (1320)	I-43
Shrub Oak (1812)	F-27
Shushan	I-54
Sidney	K-48
Sidney Center	L-48
Siloam	I-47
Silver Bay	F-53
Silver Creek	J-37
Silver Lake	I-41
Silver Springs	J-40
Sinclairville (665)	K-37
Singac	A-8
Skaneateles (2616)	I-45
Skaneateles Falls	I-45
Slate Hill	F-24
Slaterville Springs	K-45
Sleepy Hollow (9212)	H-27
Slide Mountain	A-24
Slingerlands	C-43,J-52
Sloan	B-38,H-38
Sloansville	J-51
Sloatsburg	H-25
Smith Corners	F-23
Smithboro	L-45
Smiths Basin	H-53
Smiths Mills	J-37
Smithtown	K-31
Smithville	E-46
Smithville Flats	K-47
Smyrna	J-47
Snyder	B-38
Sodus (1735)	H-43
Sodus Center	H-44
Sodus Point	G-44
Soho	C-7
Solon	J-46
Solsville	I-48
Solvay	B-41,H46
Somer Ville	D-48
Somers	F-28
Somerset	G-39
Sonora	K-43
Sonyea	J-41
Sound Beach (9807)	K-32
South Addison	L-42
South Alabama	H-40
South Apalachin	L-46
South Argyle	H-53
South Bay	H-47
South Berne	K-52
South Bradford	K-43
South Bristol	I-42
South Butler	H-44
South Byron	H-41
South Cairo	L-52
South Cambridge	I-53
South Centerville	F-23
South Colton	C-50
South Columbia	I-49
South Corinth	H-52
South Corning	L-43
South Danby	K-45
South Dansville	J-41
South Dayton	J-37
South Edmeston	J-48
South Fallsburg	C-23
South Glens Falls	H-53
South Hackensack	E-8
South Hartford	H-54
South Hartwick	J-49
South Kortright	K-50
South Lima	I-42
South Livonia	I-42
South Millbrook	C-28
South New Berlin	K-48
South Nyack	G-2
South Onondaga	I-46
South Otselic	J-47
South Plattsburgh	C-54
South Plymouth	J-47
South Ripley	D-38
South Rutland	E-47
South Salem	G-29
South Schroon	F-53
South Sodus	H-44
South Valley	J-50
South Wales	I-39
South Westerlo	K-52
South Worcester	K-50
Southampton	L-34
Southeast Owasco	J-45
Southfields	G-25
Southhold	K-34
Southport	L-44
Southwest Oswego	G-45
Southwood	C-42
Spafford	I-46
Sparkill	I-27,G-3
Sparrow Bush	F-22
Speculator	G-51
Speedsville	K-45
Speigletown	J-53
Spencer (731)	L-45
Spencerport	H-41
Spencertown	L-53
Split Rock	B-41
Sprakers	I-50
Spring Brook	I-39
Spring Glen	D-24
Spring Lake	H-44
Spring Valley (25464)	H-26
Springfield	A-13
Springfield Center	J-49
Springs (4950)	K-35
Springtown	C-26
Springville (4252)	J-39
Springwater	J-42
Sprout Brook	J-50
Spruceton	L-51
St. Bonaventure	L-39
St. Cloud	A-11
St. Davids	D-41
St. George	L-26
St. Huberts	E-53
St. Johnsburg	E-42 H-38
St. Johnsville	I-50
St. Regis Falls	C-51
St. Regis Hogansburg	A-50
St. Remy	B-26
Staatsburg (911)	B-27
Stafford	H-40
Stamford	K-50
Standish	C-52
Stanford Hgts.	J-52
Stanfordville	B-50 B-28
Stanley	I-43
Stannards (868)	L-41
Stanwix	H-48
Star Lake (860)	D-49
Starkey	J-44
Starkville	I-50
State Line	D-38
State Line Lookout	H-4
Steamburg	K-38
Stedman	D-39
Stella Niagara	D-41 G-38
Stephens Mills	K-42
Stephentown	K-54
Stephentown Center	K-54
Sterling	G-45
Sterling Forest	G-25
Sterling Valley	G-45
Stetsonville	J-48
Stilesville	L-48,A-19
Stillwater	F-49,I-53
Stissing	B-28
Stittville	H-48
Stockbridge	I-47
Stockholm Center	B-50
Stockport	L-53
Stockton	J-37
Stokes	H-48
Stone Arabia	I-50
Stone Mills	D-47
Stone Ridge	B-26
Stony Brook (13727)	K-31
Stony Creek	G-52
Stony Hollow	A-26
Stony Point (11744)	G-27
Stormville	D-28
Stottville (1355)	L-52
Stow	D-39
Stratford	H-50
Strykersville	I-39
Stuyvesant	K-52
Stuyvesant Falls	K-53
Suffern (11006)	H-26
Sugar Loaf	F-25
Sugar Town	K-39
Sullivan	I-47
Sullivanville	L-44
Summerdale	D-38
Summerhill	J-45
Summit	K-50
Summitville	D-24
Sundown	B-24
Sunmount	D-51
Sunset Bay	J-37
Surprise	K-52
Swain	J-41
Swan Lake	C-22
Swartwood	K-44
Sworm Ville	H-39
Sycaway	A-45
Sylvan Beach	H-47
Syosset (18544)	J-29
Syracuse (147306)	H-46
Taberg	H-47
Tahawus	E-52
Talcottville	G-48
Talcville	D-49
Tannersville	L-51
Tappan	I-27,G-4
Tarrytown	H-27
Taunton	B-41
Taylor	J-47
Tenafly	G-6
Terryville (10589)	K-32
Teterborp	E-8
Texas	G-46
Texas Valley	K-46
The Glen	G-52
Thendara	F-49
Theresa	D-47
Thiells (4758)	G-26
Thompson Ridge	D-25
Thompsonville	D-23
Thomson	I-53
Thornwood (5980)	H-28
Thorold	D-40
Three Mile Bay	E-46
Three Rivers	H-46
Thurman	G-52
Thurman Station	G-52
Thurston	K-42
Ticonderoga	F-54
Tillson (1709)	B-26
Tioga Center	L-45
Tivoli (1163)	A-27
Tomkins Cove	G-27
Tompkens Corners	F-28
Tonawanda (61729)	H-38
Town Line	I-39
Towners	E-29
Townsend	K-43
Treadwell	K-49
Tremley	C-15
Tremley Pt.	C-15
Trenton Falls	H-49
Triangle	K-46
Tribes Hill (1024)	I-51
Troupsburg	L-42
Trout Creek	L-48
Trout River	A-51
Troy (49170)	J-53
Trumansburg	J-44
Truxton	J-46
Tuckahoe	L-34
Tully (924)	I-46
Tunnel	L-47
Tupper Lake	D-51
Turin	F-48
Turnwood	A-22
Tuscarora	J-41
Tusten	E-21
Tuxedo Park	G-25
Tyrone	K-43
Ulster Heights	C-24
Ulster Park	B-27
Ulsterville	D-24
Unadilla	K-48
Unadilla Forks	I-48
Underwood	E-53
Union Center	L-46
Union Grove	A-22
Union Hill	H-43
Union Springs	I-44
Uniondale (23011)	K-29
Unionville	B-50,F-23
Upper Jay	D-53
Upper Lisle	K-46
Upper Montclair	B-9
Upper Montvale	E-3
Upper Nyack (1863)	G-1
Upper Red Hook	A-27
Upperville	J-47
Urbana	K-43
Utica (60651)	I-48
Vail Mills	I-51
Vails Gate (3319)	E-26
Valatie	K-53
Valcour	C-54
Valhalla	H-28,J-2
Valley Cottage	F-1
Valley Falls	I-53
Valley Stream (36368)	L-28
Valois	J-44
Van Buren Point	J-37
Van Etten (581)	L-45
Van Hornesville	I-50
Varna	K-45
Varysburg	I-40
Vauxhall	A-13
Venice Center	J-45
Verbank	C-28
Verdoy	A-44
Vermontville	D-52
Vernon	I-48
Vernon Center	I-48
Verona	H-48
Verona Beach	H-47
Verplanck (777)	G-27
Versailles	J-38
Vesper	I-46
Vestal	L-46
Vestal Center	L-46
Veteran	A-26
Victor (2433)	I-42
Victory (544)	H-45
Victory Mills	I-53
Vine Valley	I-43
Virgil	C-41,J-46
Volney	G-45
Voorheesville	J-52
W. Coxsackie	K-52
W. Hempstead	K-29
Waddington	B-49
Wadhams	D-54
Wading River (6668)	K-32
Wadsworth	I-41
Walden (6164)	D-25
Wales Center	I-39
Walker	G-41
Walker Valley	D-24
Wallace	K-42
Wallkill (2143)	D-25
Walton	L-49
Walworth	H-43
Wampsville	H-47
Wanakah	I-38
Wanakena	E-50
Wantagh (18971)	K-29
Wappingers Falls (4929)	D-27
Warners	H-45,C-16
Warnerville	J-50
Warren	I-49
Warrens Corners	G-39
Warrensburg	G-53
Warsaw (3814)	I-40
Warwick (6412)	G-24
Washington Hollow	C-28
Washington Mills	I-48
Washington Township	E-5
Washingtonville (5851)	F-25
Wassaic	C-29
Waterford	J-53
Waterloo (5111)	I-44
Watermill (1724)	L-34
Waterport	G-40
Watertown	E-47
Waterville	I-48
Watervliet	A-45,J-53
Watkins Glen	K-44
Watsessing	C-11
Watson	F-48
Watsonville	K-51
Watts Flats	E-39
Waverly (4607)	L-45
Wawarsing	C-24
Wayland (1893)	J-42
Wayne	K-43,A-7
Wayne Center	H-44
Webatuck	D-29
Webster (5216)	H-42
Webster Crossing	J-42
Weedsport	H-45
Wegatchie	D-48
Wellington	H-44
Wells	H-51
Wells Bridge	K-48
Wellsburg (631)	L-44
Wellsville (5171)	L-41
Wesley	J-38
Wesley Hills	G-26
West Almond	K-41
West Amboy	G-46
West Bainbridge	K-47
West Bangor	B-51
West Barre	H-40
West Bergen	H-41
West Berne	J-51
West Bloomfield	I-42
West Branch	G-48
West Burlington	J-49
West Carteret	C-16
West Carthage	E-48
West Chazy	B-54
West Chenango	L-46
West Clarksville	K-40
West Copake	A-29
West Danby	K-45
West Davenport	K-49
West Eaton	I-47
West Edmeston	J-48
West Elmira	L-44
West Englewood	F-7
West Exeter	J-49
West Falls	I-39
West Fulton	K-51
West Galway	I-52
West Haverstraw (10295)	G-27
West Hebron	H-54
West Henrietta	H-42
West Hurley	A-26
West Islip (28907)	L-31
West Kendall	G-41
West Kill	L-51
West Laurens	K-49
West Lebanon	K-53
West Leyden	G-48
West Martinsburg	F-48
West Milton	I-52
West Monroe	H-46
West Norwood	G-4
West Nyack	H-27,F-2
West Oneonta	K-49
West Park	C-27
West Paterson	B-8
West Pawling	D-28
West Perth	I-51
West Plattsburgh	C-53
West Point	F-27
West Potsdam	B-49
West Richmondville	J-50
West Rush	H-41
West Sand Lake	J-53
West Sayville (5003)	L-31
West Schuyler	H-49
West Seneca	C-38 I-38
West Shokan	A-25
West Sparta	J-41
West Stephentown	K-53
West Stockholm	B-50
West Valley	J-39
West Walworth	H-43
West Webster	H-42
West Windsor	L-47
West Winfield	I-49
Westbrookville	E-23
Westbury	H-44,K-29
Westdale	G-47
Westerlo	K-52
Westernville	H-48
Westfield (3481)	D-38
Westford	J-50
Westhampton	L-33
Westhampton Beach (1902)	L-33
Westmere	A-43
Westmoreland	H-48
Westons Mills	L-39
Westport	E-54
Westtown	F-23
Westvale (5166)	I-46
Westville	B-51,J-49
Westville Center	B-51
Westwood	E-5
Wethersfield Springs	I-40
Wevertown	G-52
Whallonsburg	D-54
Wheatheld	H-38
Wheatville	H-40
Wheeler	K-42
Whippleville	B-52
White Creek	I-54
White Lake	D-22
White Plains (53077)	H-28
White Sulphur Springs	C-22
Whitehall	G-54
Whitelaw	H-47
Whitesboro	D-42 H-48
Whitesville	L-41
Whitney Point (965)	K-46
Wickham Village	G-25
Willard	J-44
Willet	K-46
Williamson	H-43
Williamstown	G-47
Williamsville	B-38 H-39
Willow	A-25
Willow Grove	G-26
Willowemoc	B-23
Willsboro	D-54
Willseyville	K-45
Wilmington	D-53
Wilson (1213)	G-38
Wilton	H-53
Windham (359)	L-51
Windsor	L-47
Windsor Beach	H-42
Winebrook Hills	E-52
Winfield	A-15
Wingdale	D-29
Winnisook	A-24
Winthrop	B-50
Wiscoy	J-40
Witherbee	E-53
Wittenberg	A-25
Wolcott (1712)	H-44
Wolcottsville	H-39
Wood Ridge	E-9
Woodbourne	C-23
Woodbridge	B-17
Woodbury	J-30
Woodcliff Lake	E-4
Woodgate	G-49
Woodhull	L-42
Woodinville	D-29
Woodland	A-24
Woodlawn Beach	I-38
Woodridge (902)	C-23
Woods Mills	C-53
Woodstock	A-26
Woodsville	J-41
Woodville	F-46,J-42
Worcester	J-50
Worth	F-47
Wright	F-54
Wrights Corners	G-39
Wurtsboro	D-24
Wyandanch (10546)	K-30
Wyckoff	I-45
Wynantskill	J-53
Wyoming (513)	I-40
Yagerville	B-24
Yaphank (5025)	L-32
Yates Center	G-40
Yonkers (196086)	I-27
York	I-41
York Corners	L-41
Yorkshire (1403)	J-39
Yorktown	G-28
Yorktown Heights	G-28
Yorkville	D-43
Youngs Town	C-41
Youngstown	G-38
Youngsville	C-21
Yulan	E-21
Zena (1119)	A-26

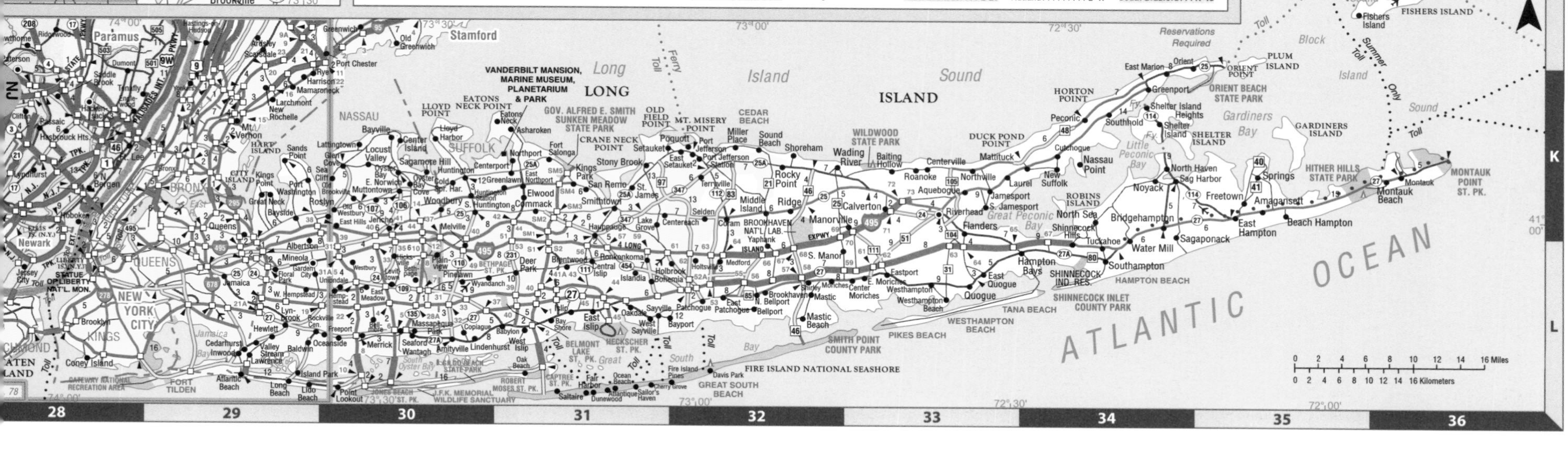

Legend:

- MILEAGE NUMBER
- EXIT NUMBER
- INTERCHANGE
- CONTROLLED ACCESS
- UNDER CONSTRUCTION
- TOLL CONTROLLED ACCESS
- PRIMARY DIVIDED
- PRIMARY UNDIVIDED
- ARTERIAL DIVIDED
- ARTERIAL UNDIVIDED
- UNPAVED
- SCENIC ROUTE
- TIME ZONE
- STATE/LOCAL PARK
- FOREST
- CAMPGROUND
- REST AREAS
- INFORMATION CTR
- POINT OF INTEREST

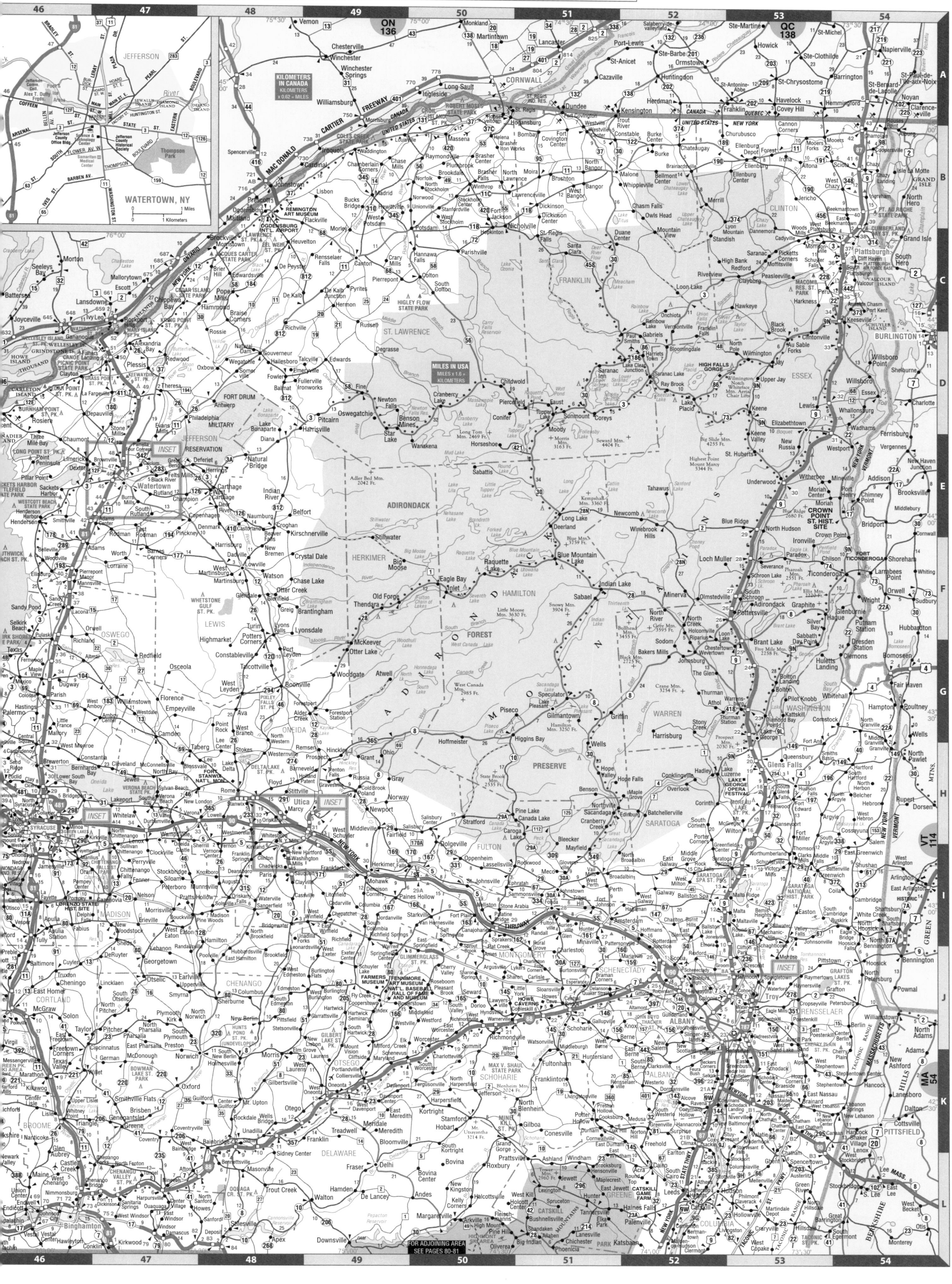

WATERTOWN, NY

KILOMETERS IN CANADA
KILOMETERS x 0.62 = MILES

MILES IN USA
MILES x 1.6 = KILOMETERS

FOR ADJOINING AREA SEE PAGES 80-81

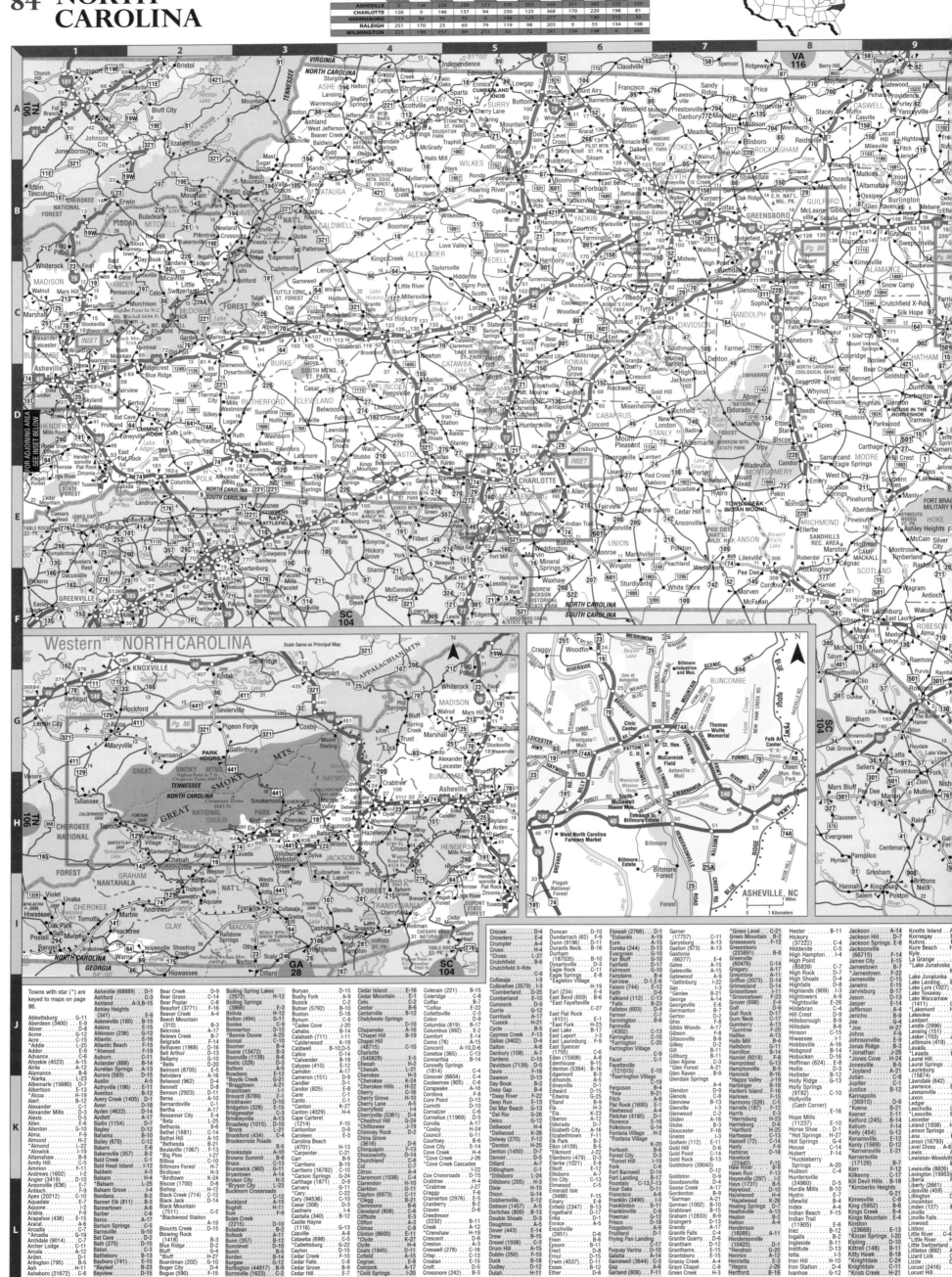

	ASHEVILLE	CHARLOTTE	DURHAM	FAYETTEVILLE	GREENSBORO	JACKSONVILLE	LUMBERTON	NAGS HEAD	RALEIGH	ROCKY MOUNT	WILMINGTON	WINSTON-SALEM
ASHEVILLE	0	126	228	250	173	370	252	450	251	355	325	150
CHARLOTTE	126	0	146	137	94	230	125	368	170	220	198	81
GREENSBORO	173	94	56	95	0	188	277	79	73	213	30	
RALEIGH	251	170	23	65	79	119	98	203	0	55	134	108
WILMINGTON	325	198	157	89	213	53	72	241	134			242

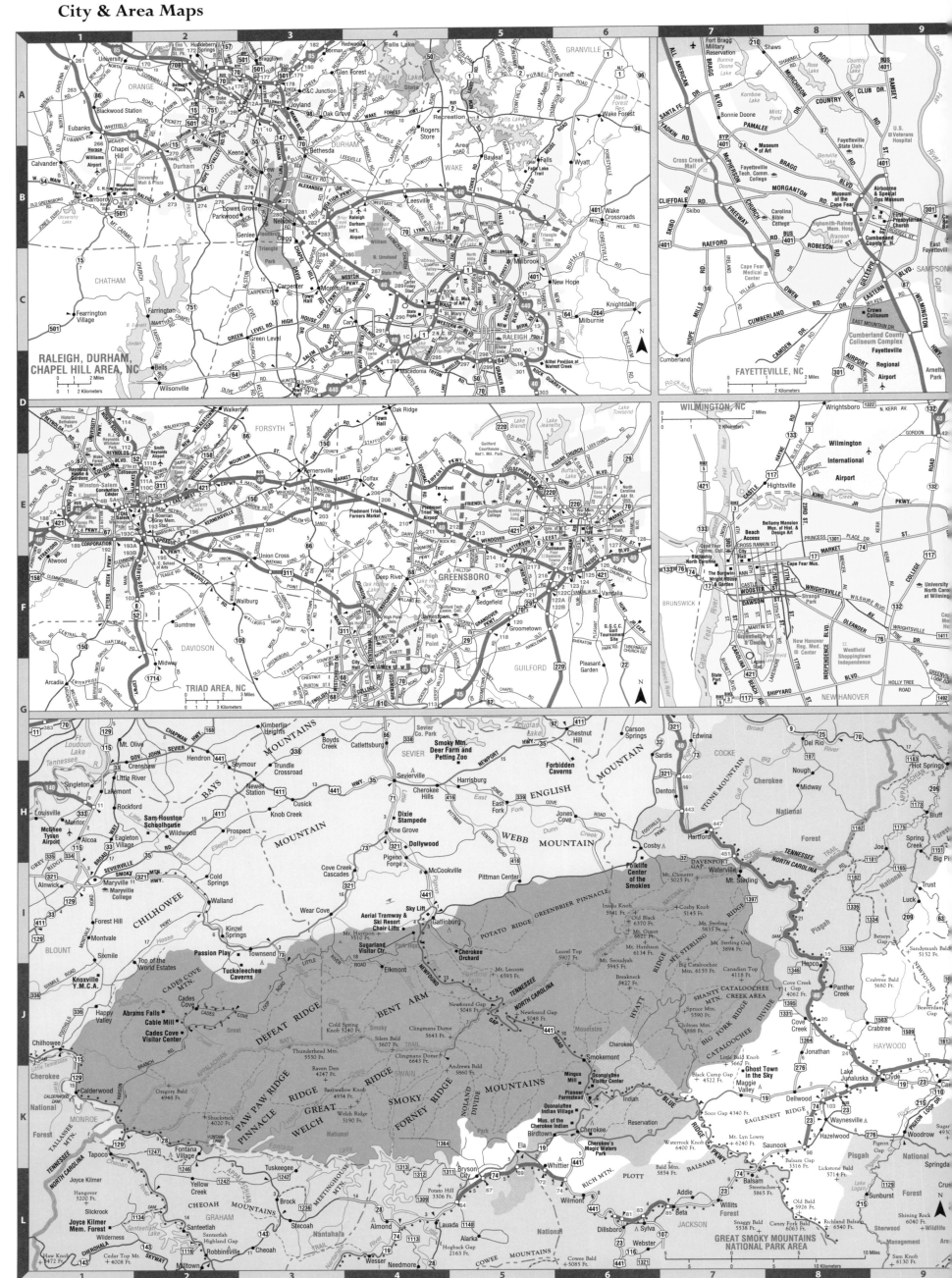

RALEIGH, DURHAM, CHAPEL HILL AREA, NC

FAYETTEVILLE, NC

WILMINGTON, NC

TRIAD AREA, NC

GREAT SMOKY MOUNTAINS NATIONAL PARK AREA

	CHURCHS FERRY	DICKINSON	GRAND FORKS	FARGO	JAMESTOWN	MINOT	WILLISTON
BISMARCK	0	180	100	198	274	105	114	234
FARGO	198	188	294	0	82	95	268	428
GRAND FORKS	274	112	369	62	0	170	216	346

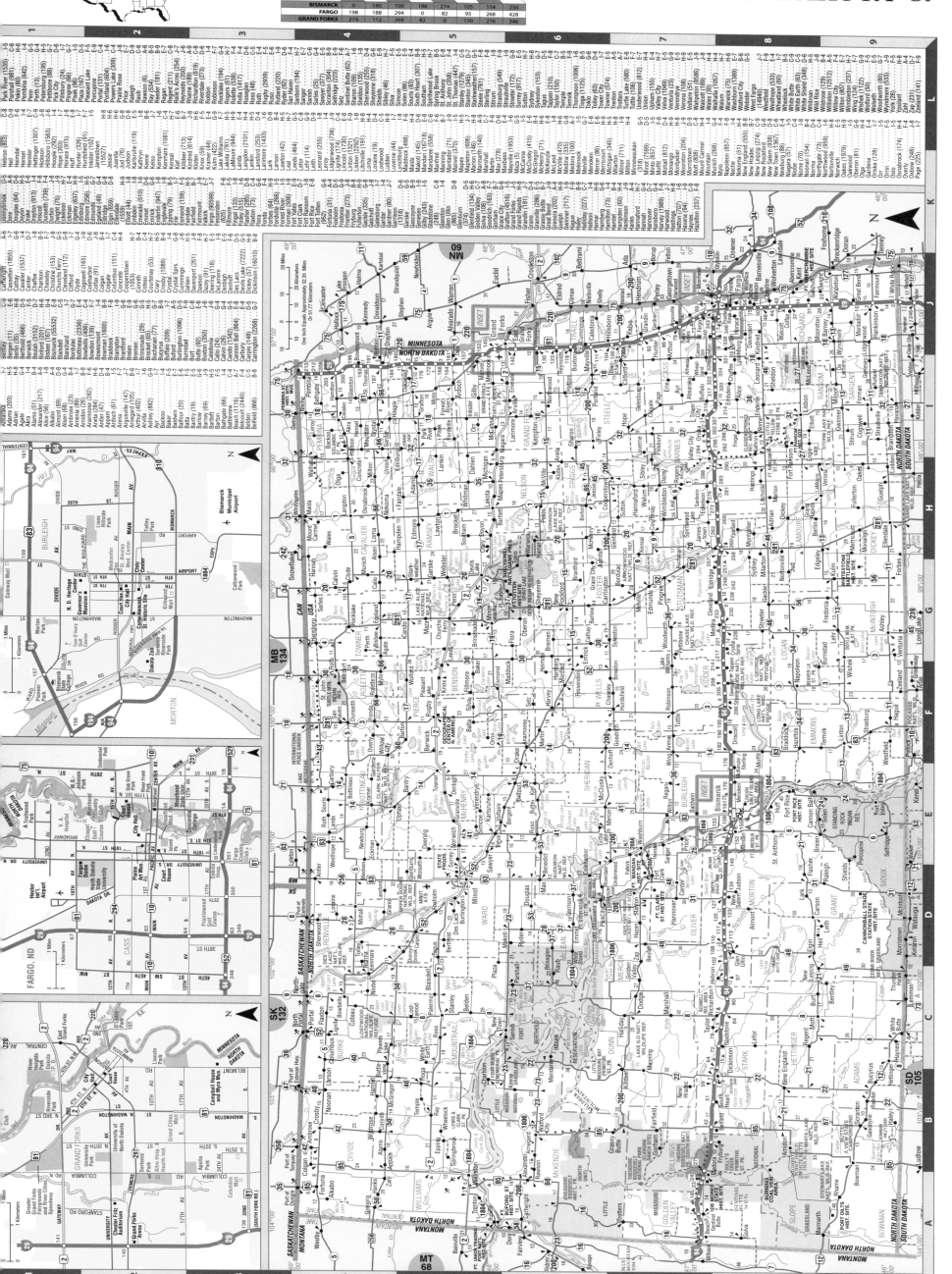

	AKRON	CAMBRIDGE	CANTON	CINCINNATI	CLEVELAND	COLUMBUS	DAYTON	LIMA	MANSFIELD	PORTSMOUTH	TOLEDO	YOUNGSTOWN
CINCINNATI	238	179	242	0	256	103	54	120	128	178	105	206	295
CLEVELAND	38	120	60	256	0	147	222	155	81	246	115	69
COLUMBUS	125	82	130	103	147	0	76	95	60	92	146	177
TOLEDO	136	188	158	208	115	146	156	82	103	231	0	173
YOUNGSTOWN	49	116	55	285	69	177	249	200	110	275	173	0

CLEVELAND, OH

Lake Erie

TOLEDO, OH

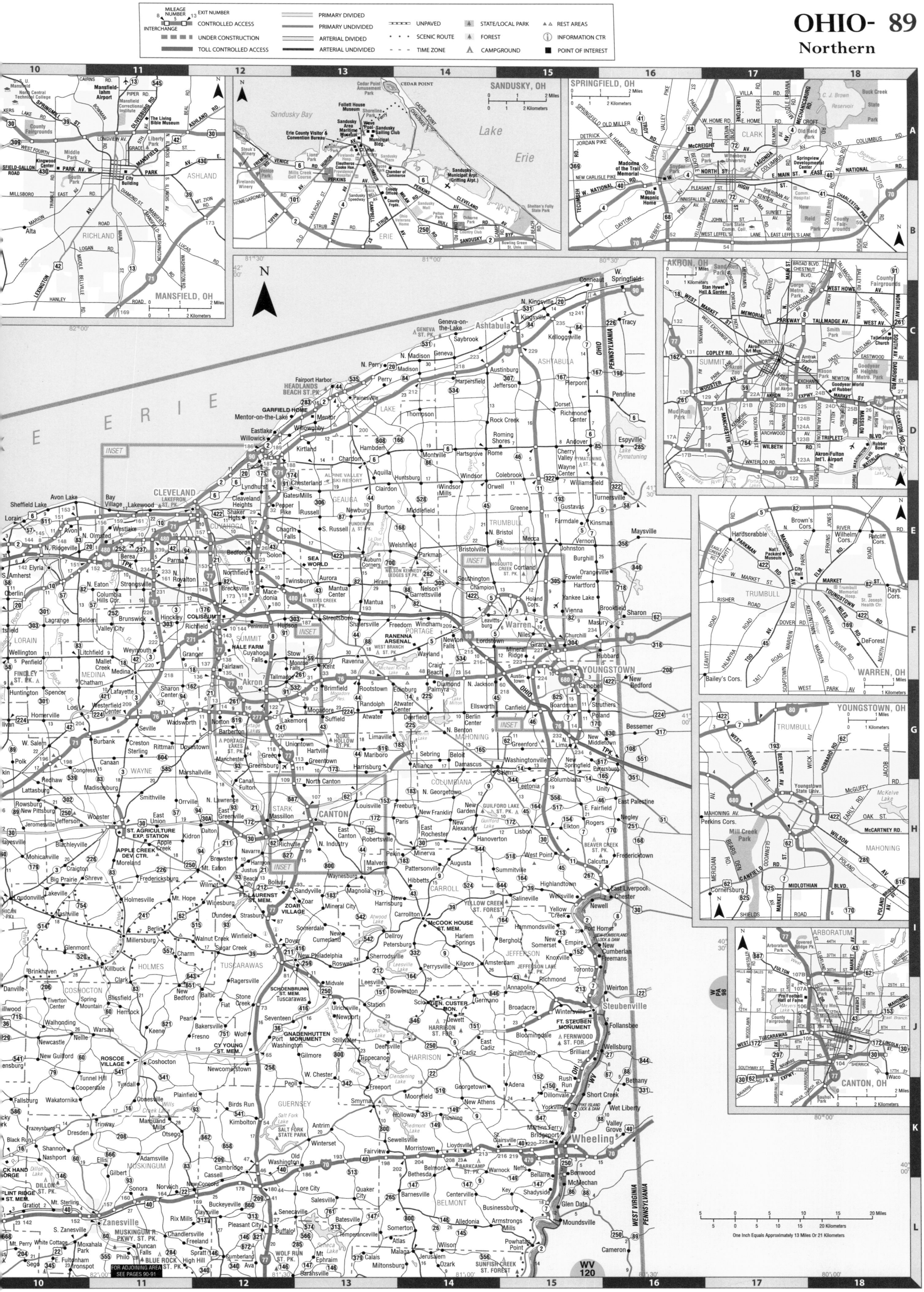
MILEAGE NUMBER
EXIT NUMBER
INTERCHANGE
CONTROLLED ACCESS
UNDER CONSTRUCTION
TOLL CONTROLLED ACCESS
PRIMARY DIVIDED
PRIMARY UNDIVIDED
ARTERIAL DIVIDED
ARTERIAL UNDIVIDED
UNPAVED
SCENIC ROUTE
TIME ZONE
STATE/LOCAL PARK
FOREST
CAMPGROUND
REST AREAS
INFORMATION CTR
POINT OF INTEREST
MANSFIELD, OH
SANDUSKY, OH
SPRINGFIELD, OH
AKRON, OH
WARREN, OH
YOUNGSTOWN, OH
CANTON, OH
LAKE ERIE
Cleveland
Akron
Canton
Youngstown
Warren
Ashtabula
Steubenville
Wheeling
Zanesville
PENNSYLVANIA
WEST VIRGINIA
FOR ADJOINING AREA SEE PAGES 90-91
WV 120
PA 98
One Inch Equals Approximately 13 Miles Or 21 Kilometers

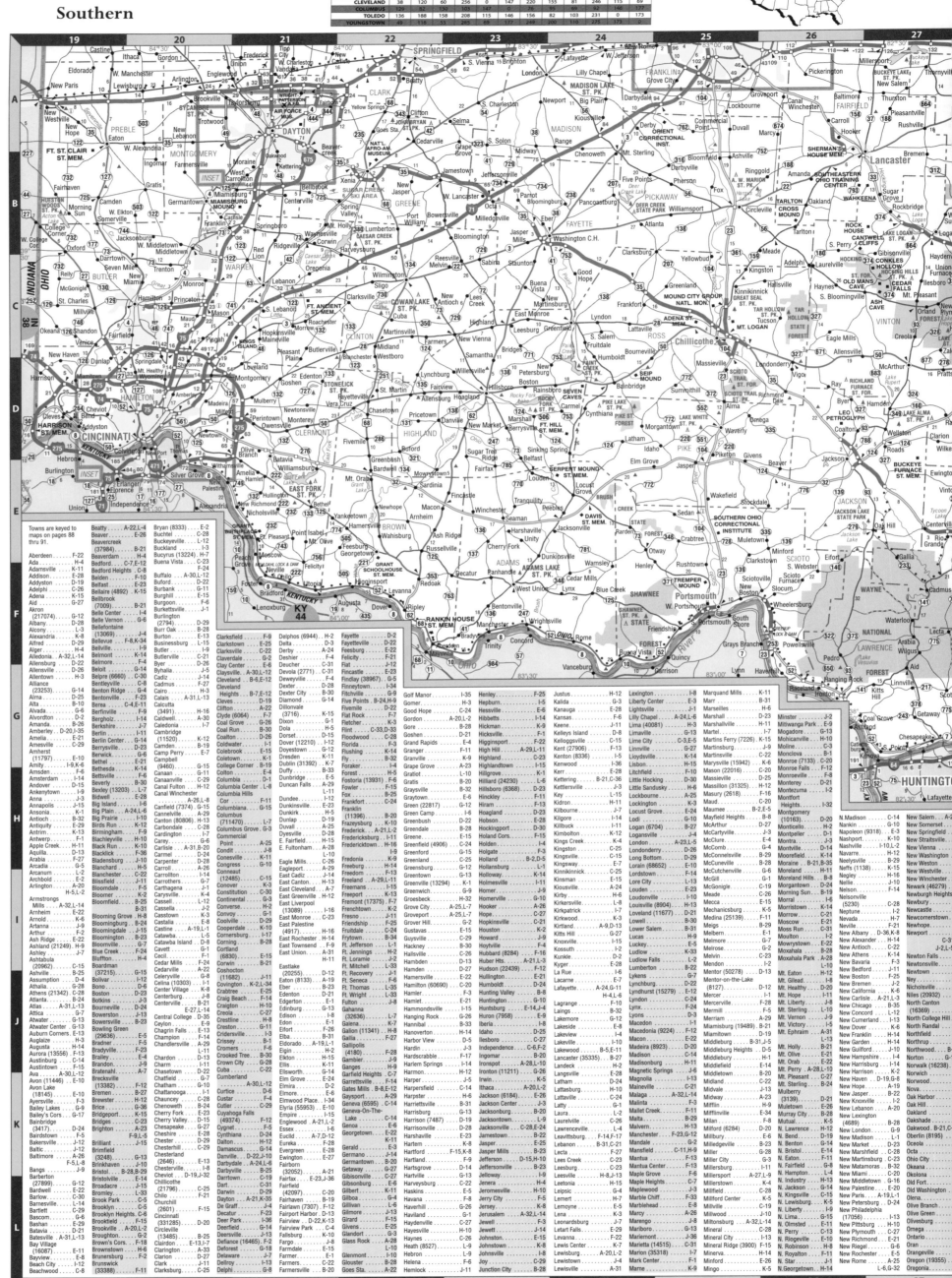

MILEAGE NUMBER — EXIT NUMBER — CONTROLLED ACCESS — INTERCHANGE — UNDER CONSTRUCTION — TOLL CONTROLLED ACCESS — PRIMARY DIVIDED — PRIMARY UNDIVIDED — ARTERIAL DIVIDED — ARTERIAL UNDIVIDED — UNPAVED — SCENIC ROUTE — TIME ZONE — STATE/LOCAL PARK — FOREST — CAMPGROUND — REST AREAS — INFORMATION CTR — POINT OF INTEREST

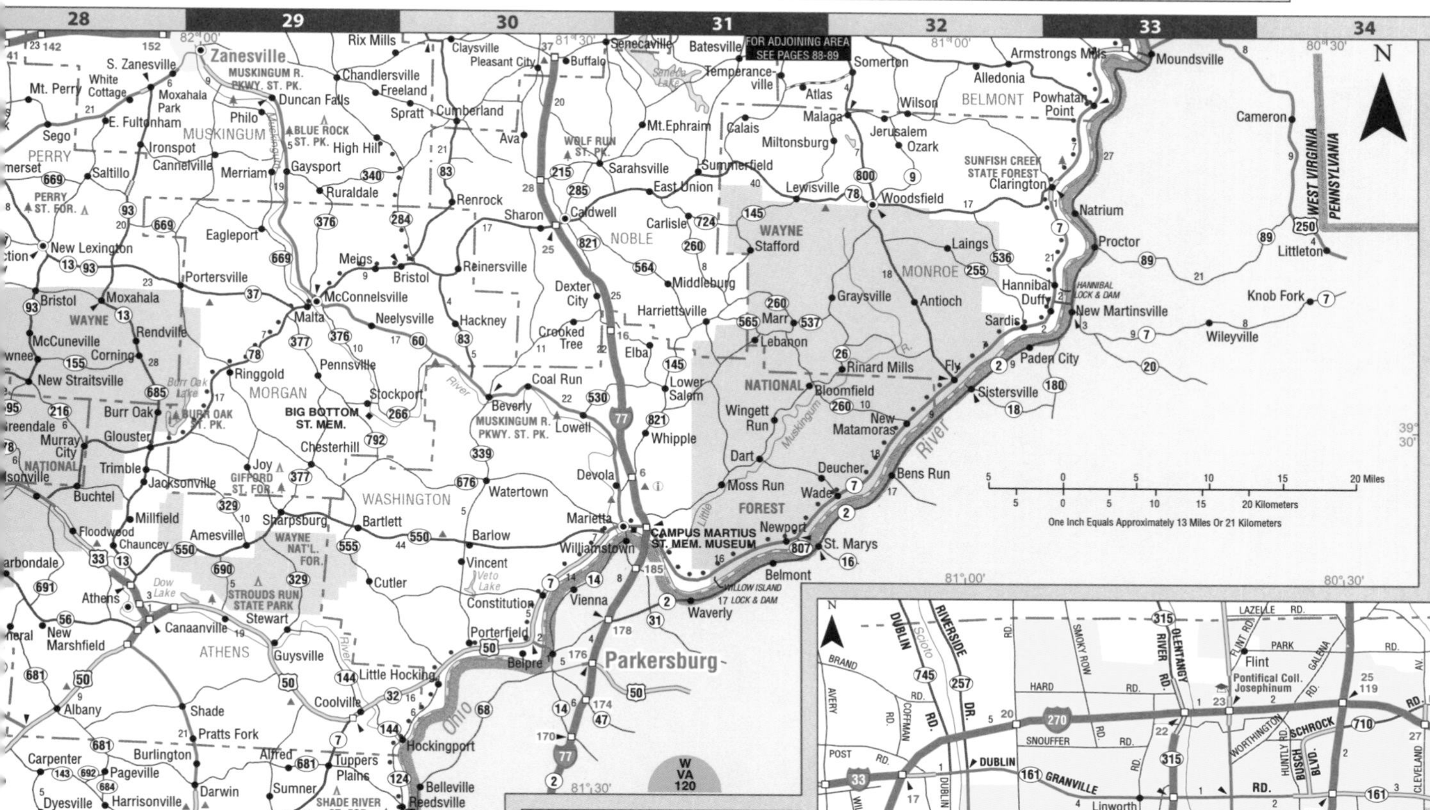

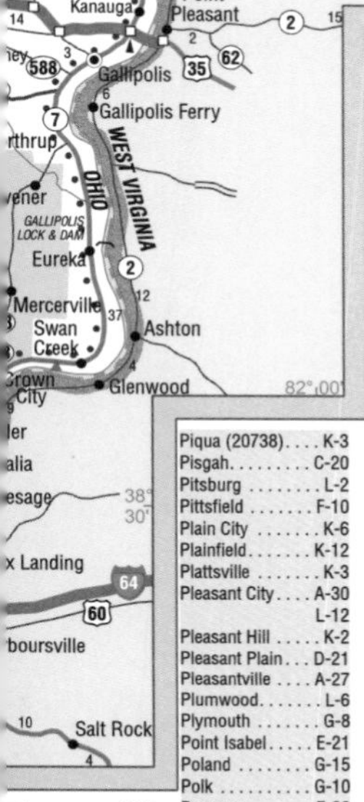

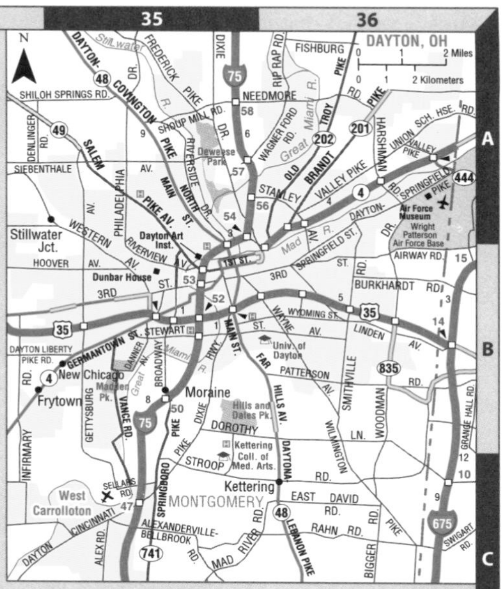

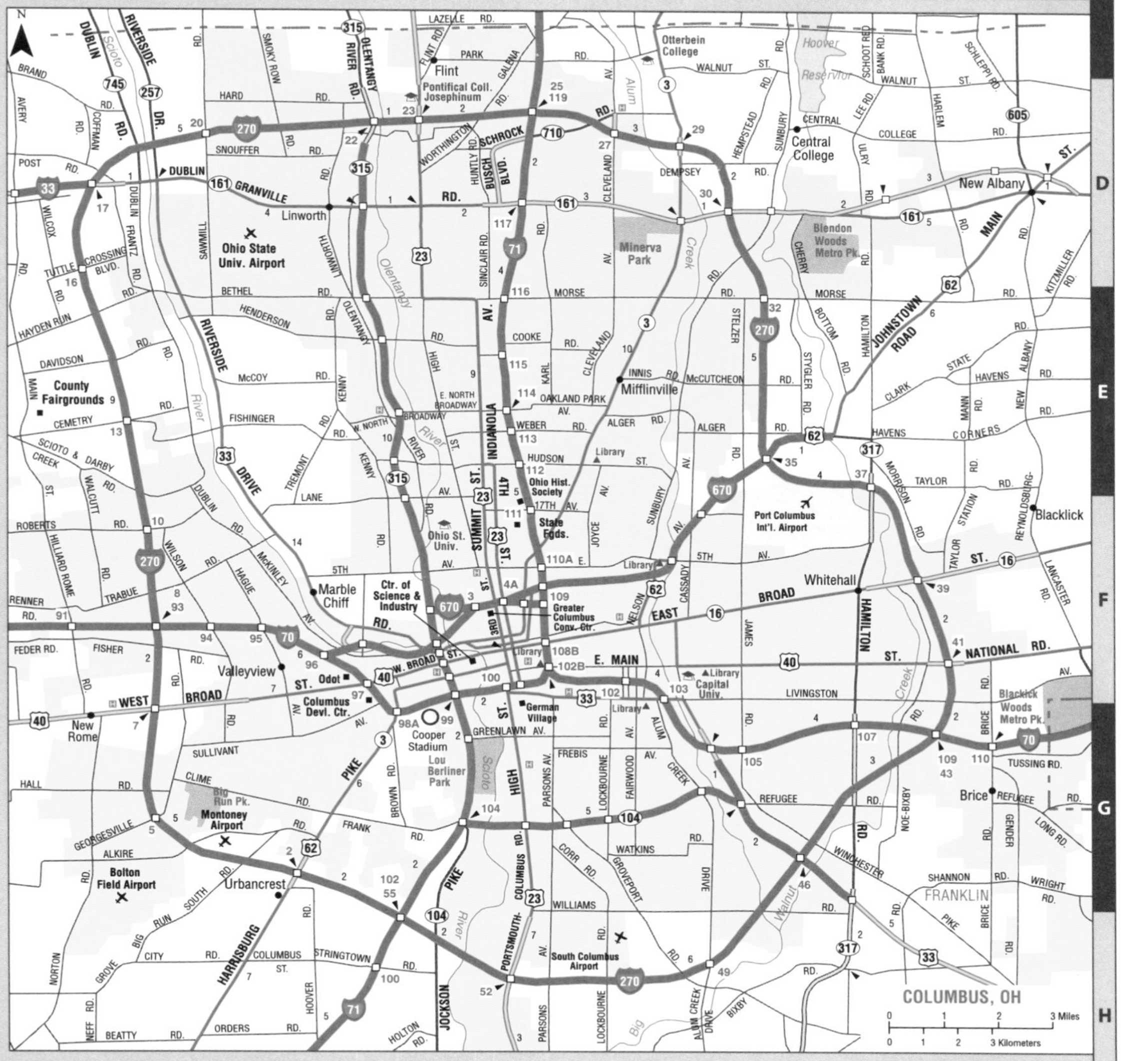

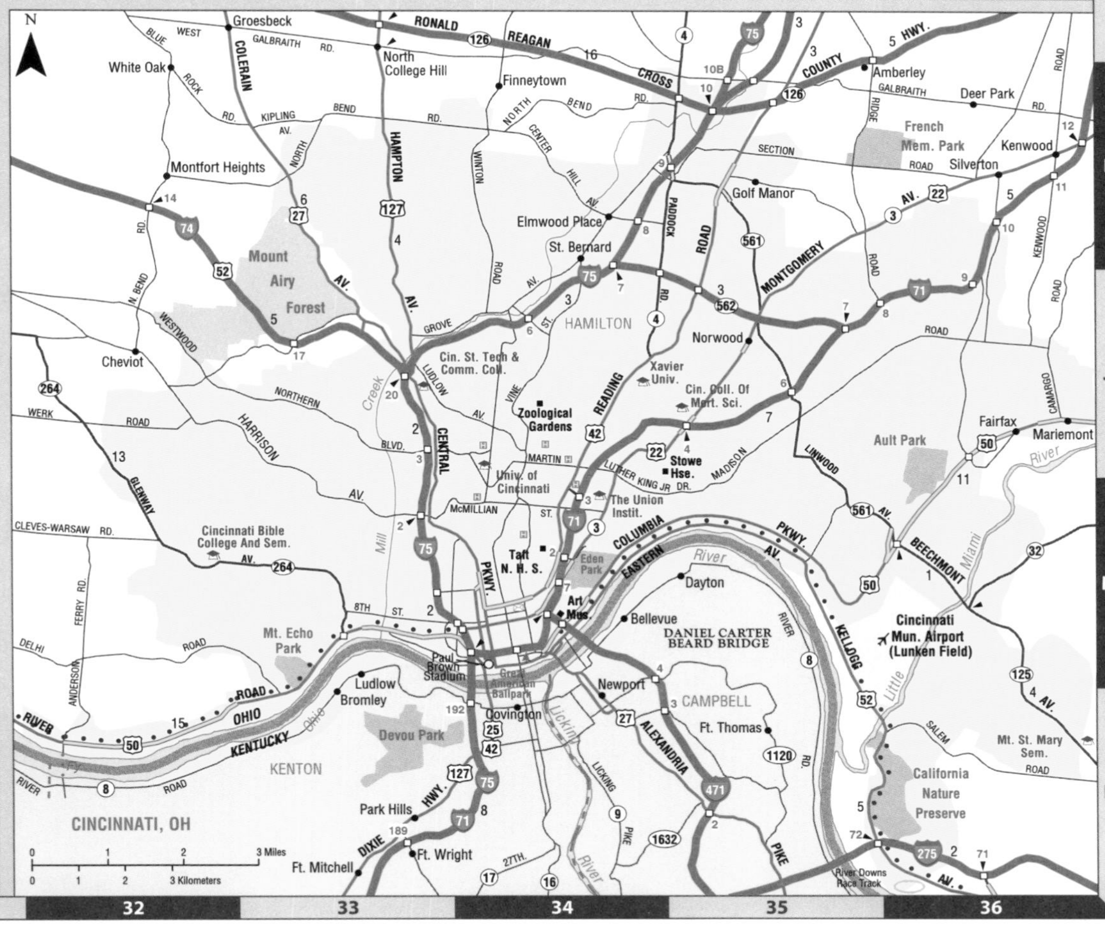

One Inch Equals Approximately 13 Miles Or 21 Kilometers

DAYTON, OH

COLUMBUS, OH

CINCINNATI, OH

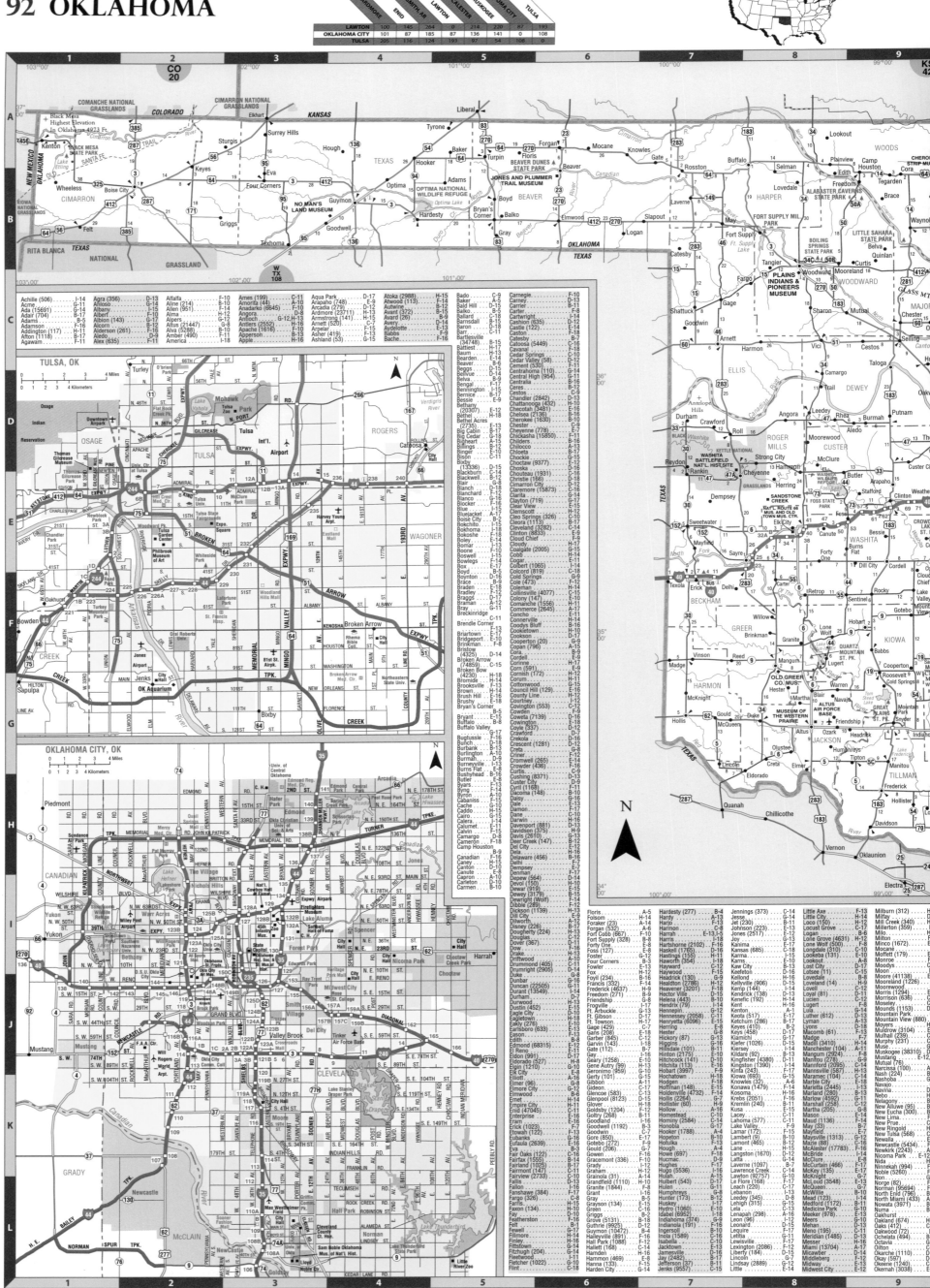

MILEAGE NUMBER — EXIT NUMBER — INTERCHANGE — CONTROLLED ACCESS — UNDER CONSTRUCTION — TOLL CONTROLLED ACCESS — PRIMARY DIVIDED — PRIMARY UNDIVIDED — ARTERIAL DIVIDED — ARTERIAL UNDIVIDED — UNPAVED — SCENIC ROUTE — TIME ZONE — STATE/LOCAL PARK — FOREST — CAMPGROUND — REST AREAS — INFORMATION CTR — POINT OF INTEREST

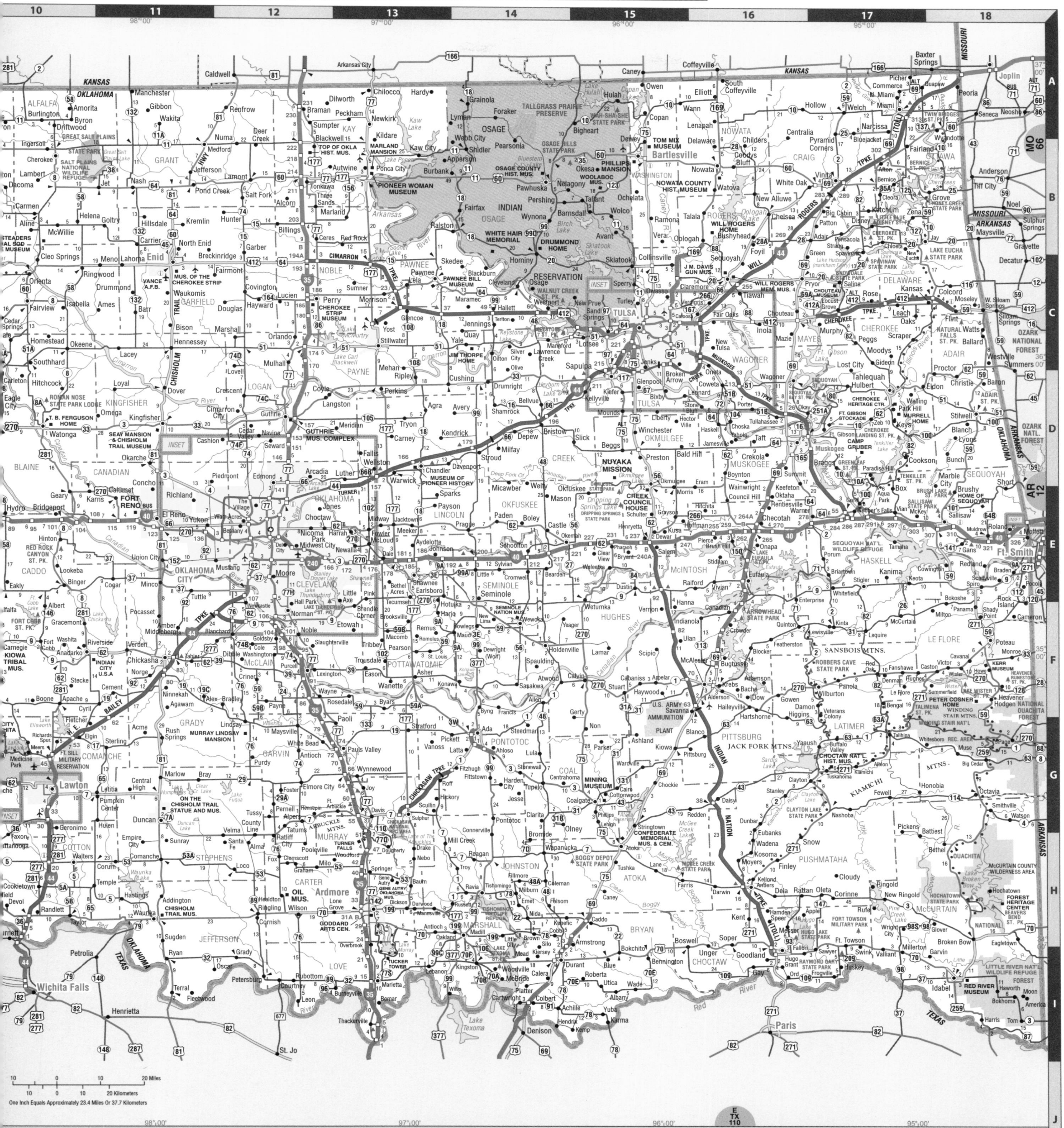

... B-15	Pensacola (71) ... B-17	Ramona (564) ... B-15	Salem (89) ... E-15	Southhard ... C-10	Talihina (1211) ... G-17	Valliant (771) ... I-17	Weleetka (1014) ... E-15
ee ... E-15	Peoria (141) ... A-18	Randlett (511) ... H-10	Salina (1422) ... C-17	Sparks (137) ... E-13	Tallant ... B-15	Vanoss ... G-13	Welling (669) ... D-17
ma City ... E-12	Perkins (2272) ... D-13	Rankin ... E-7	Sallisaw (7989) ... E-18	Spaulding (62) ... F-14	Taloga (372) ... D-9	Velma (664) ... H-12	Wellston (825) ... D-13
gee	Pernell ... G-12	Ratliff City ... H-12	Salt Fork ... B-12	Spavinaw (563) ... B-17	Tamaha (198) ... E-17	Vera (188) ... B-15	Welty ... D-14
2) ... D-15	Perry (5230) ... C-12	Rattan (241) ... H-16	Sand Springs (17451) ... C-15	Speer ... H-16	Tangier ... C-8	Verden (659) ... F-11	West Siloam Springs (877) ... C-18
... E-16	Pershing ... B-14	Ravia (459) ... H-14	Santa Fe ... H-12	Sperry (981) ... C-15	Tatums (172) ... G-12	Verdigris ... C-16	Westport (264) ... C-14
... H-17	Petersburg ... I-12	Reagan ... H-14	Sapulpa (19166) ... D-15	Spiro (2227) ... E-18	Taylor ... H-10	Vernon ... F-15	Westville (1596) ... C-18
... D-14	Pharaoh ... E-15	Red Oak (581) ... F-17	Sasakwa (150) ... F-14	Springer (577) ... H-13	Tecumseh (6098) ... E-13	Veterans Colony ... F-17	Wetumka (1451) ... F-15
... G-14	Phillips (150) ... G-15	Red Rock (293) ... B-13	Savanna (730) ... F-16	St. Louis (206) ... F-13	Tegarden ... B-9	Vian (1362) ... E-17	Wewoka (3562) ... F-14
e (680) ... G-8	Picher (1640) ... A-17	Redden ... G-15	Sawyer (274) ... I-17	Stafford ... E-9	Temple (1146) ... H-10	Vici (668) ... C-8	Wheeless ... B-1
... D-11	Pickens ... G-17	Redland ... E-18	Sayre (4114) ... E-8	Stanley ... G-16	Terlton (85) ... C-14	Victor ... F-18	White Bead ... G-12
... E-16	Pickett ... G-13	Reed ... F-7	Schoolton ... E-14	Stecke ... F-10	Terral (386) ... I-11	Vinita (6472) ... B-17	White Oak ... B-17
... C-16	Piedmont ... D-11, I-1	Remus ... F-13	Schulter (600) ... E-15	Steedman ... G-14	Texhoma (935) ... B-3	Vinson ... F-7	Whitefield (231) ... E-17
h (883) ... B-16	Pierce ... E-16	Renfrow ... A-12	Scipio ... F-15	Sterling (762) ... G-11	Texola (47) ... F-7	Vivian ... E-16	Whitesboro ... G-17
(266) ... B-4	Pink (1165) ... E-13	Rentiesville (102) ... E-16	Scraper (475) ... C-17	Stidham (23) ... E-16	Thackerville (404) ... I-13	Wade ... I-15	Wilburton (2972) ... F-17
... I-16	Pittsburg (280) ... G-15	Retrop ... F-8	Scullin ... G-13	Stigler (2731) ... E-17	The Village ... E-12	Wadena ... H-16	Willis ... I-13
... C-10	Plainview ... B-8	Reydon (177) ... E-7	Scullyville ... E-18	Stillwater (39065) ... C-13	Thomas (1238) ... D-9	Wagoner (7669) ... D-16	Willow (114) ... F-8
... C-9	Platter ... I-14	Rhea ... D-8	Seiling (875) ... C-9	Stilwell (3276) ... D-18	Three Sands ... B-12	Wainwright (197) ... D-16	Wilson (1584) ... H-12
(201) ... C-12	Pocasset (192) ... F-11	Richards Spur ... G-10	Selman ... B-8	Stone Bluff ... D-16	Tiawah ... C-16	Wakita (420) ... A-11	Winchester (424) ... D-15
(188) ... C-14	Pocola (3994) ... E-18	Richland ... E-11	Seminole (6899) ... E-14	Stonewall (465) ... G-14	Tipton (916) ... G-9	Walters (2657) ... H-10	Wister (1002) ... F-18
... I-11	Ponca City ... B-13	Ringling (1135) ... H-12	Sentinel (859) ... F-8	Strang (100) ... B-17	Tishomingo ... H-14	Wanette (402) ... F-13	Wolco ... B-15
ook ... I-13	Pond Creek (896) ... B-11	Ringold ... H-17	Sequoyah (671) ... C-16	Stratford (1474) ... G-13	Tom ... I-18	Wann (132) ... A-15	Woodford ... H-12
(18502) ... C-15	Pontotoc ... G-14	Ringwood (424) ... C-10	Seward ... D-12	Stringtown ... G-15	Tonkawa (3299) ... B-12	Wapanucka (445) ... H-14	Woodville (69) ... I-14
... A-15	Pooleville ... H-12	Ripley (444) ... D-13	Shady Point (848) ... F-18	Strong City ... D-8	Trail ... D-8	Wardville ... G-15	Woodward (11853) ... C-8
... G-8	Porter (574) ... D-16	Riverside ... F-10	Shamrock (125) ... D-14	Stroud (2758) ... D-14	Tribbey (273) ... F-13	Warner (1430) ... E-17	Wright City ... H-17
(446) ... E-14	Porum (725) ... E-17	Roberta ... I-15	Sharon (122) ... C-8	Stuart (220) ... F-15	Trousdale ... F-13	Warr Acres (9735) ... E-12	Wyandotte (363) ... A-18
... G-18	Poteau (7939) ... F-18	Rock Island (709) ... F-18	Shattuck (1274) ... C-7	Sturgis ... A-3	Troy ... H-14	Warren ... G-8	Wynnewood ... G-13
a (1362) ... F-18	Prague (2138) ... E-14	Rocky (174) ... F-9	Shawnee (28692) ... E-13	Sugden (59) ... H-11	Tryon (448) ... D-13	Warwick (235) ... D-13	Wynona (531) ... B-14
... F-17	Preston ... D-15	Roff (734) ... G-13	Shidler (520) ... B-14	Sulphur (4794) ... G-13	Tullahassee (106) ... D-16	Washington (520) ... F-12	Yahola ... D-16
549) ... G-13	Proctor ... D-18	Roland (2842) ... E-18	Short (328) ... E-18	Summerfield ... F-18	Tulsa (393049) ... C-15	Washita ... F-10	Yale (1342) ... C-14
se Hill ... D-17	Pryor ... C-16	Roll ... D-7	Silo (282) ... I-14	Summit (226) ... D-16	Tupelo (377) ... G-14	Watonga (4658) ... D-10	Yanush ... G-17
ill (3936) ... D-17	Pumpkin Center ... G-10	Romulus ... F-13	Silver City ... C-14	Sumner ... C-13	Turley (3231) ... C-15	Watova ... B-16	Yeager (67) ... F-14
... G-15	Purcell (5571) ... F-12	Roosevelt (280) ... G-9	Skedee (102) ... C-14	Sumpter ... A-12	Turpin ... A-5	Watson ... G-18	Yost ... C-13
... B-17	Purdy ... G-12	Rose ... C-17	Skiatook (5396) ... C-15	Sunray ... H-11	Tushka (345) ... H-15	Watts (316) ... C-18	Yuba ... I-15
Valley ... G-13	Putnam (46) ... D-9	Rosedale (66) ... F-13	Slapout ... B-7	Surrey Hills ... A-3	Tuskahoma ... G-17	Waukomis (1261) ... C-11	Yukon ... E-11, F-1
ska (3629) ... B-14	Pyramid Corners ... A-17	Rosston (66) ... B-7	Slaughterville ... F-12	Sweetwater ... E-7	Tussy ... G-12	Waurika (1988) ... H-11	Zeb (498) ... D-17
e (2230) ... C-13	Quapaw (984) ... A-17	Rubottom ... I-12	Slick (148) ... D-15	Swink (83) ... I-17	Tuttle (4294) ... E-11	Wayne (714) ... F-12	Zena (123) ... B-17
... F-12	Quay (47) ... C-14	Rufe ... H-17	Smithville (123) ... G-18	Sylvian ... E-14	Tyrone (880) ... A-5	Waynoka (993) ... B-9	
... E-13	Quinlan ... B-9	Rush Springs ... G-11	Snow ... H-16	Tabler ... F-11	Ulan ... F-15	Weatherford (9859) ... E-9	
n ... F-13	Quinton (1071) ... F-16	Russett ... H-13	Snyder (1509) ... G-9	Taft (349) ... D-16	Unger ... I-16	Webb City ... B-14	
nia ... B-14	Raiford ... E-16	Ryan (894) ... I-11	Soper (300) ... H-16	Tahlequah ... D-17	Union City ... E-11	Webber's Falls ... E-17	
am ... A-13	Ralston (355) ... B-14	Saddle Mountain ... F-9	South Coffeyville ... A-16	Talala (270) ... B-16	Utica ... I-15	Welch (597) ... A-17	
... C-17							

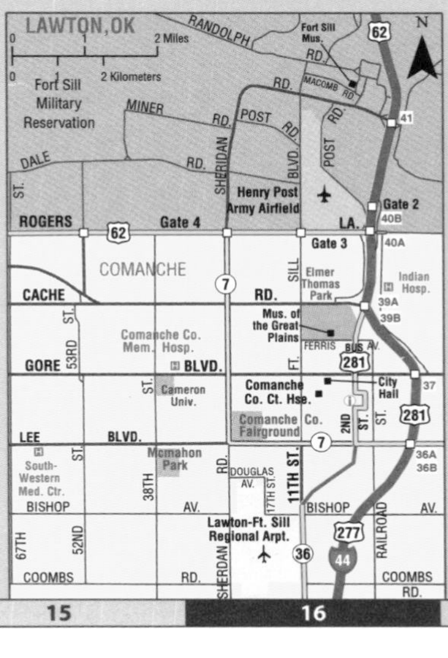

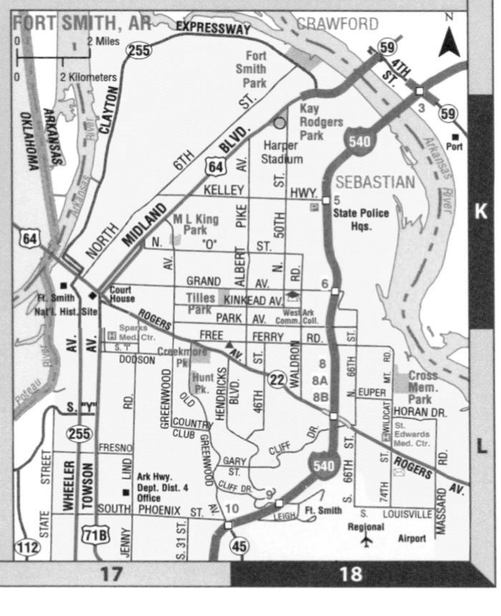

	BEND	EUGENE	GRANTS PASS	KLAMATH FALLS	MEDFORD	PENDLETON	PORTLAND	SALEM
EUGENE	130	0	139	174	168	324	113	66
PORTLAND	160	113	248	282	276	212	0	48
SALEM	133	66	200	235	229	259	48	0

Towns with star (*) are keyed to the maps on page 96.

Adair Village (536)	E-4
Adams (297)	C-13
Adel (147)	L-10
Adrian (147)	H-15
Agness	J-2
Albany (40852)	E-4
Albee	D-12
Alfalfa	G-8
Algoma	K-6
Alicel	D-1
Alkali Lake Station	J-1
Allegany	F-
Almeda	J-
Aloha (41741)	F-
Alpha	F-
Alpine	F-
Alsea	F-
Anchor	D-
Andrews	K-1
Annex	G-1
Antelope (59)	E-

One Inch Equals Approximately 24.1 Miles Or 38.7 Kilometers

PACIFIC OCEAN

MILEAGE NUMBER — EXIT NUMBER — INTERCHANGE
CONTROLLED ACCESS
UNDER CONSTRUCTION
TOLL CONTROLLED ACCESS
PRIMARY DIVIDED
PRIMARY UNDIVIDED
ARTERIAL DIVIDED
ARTERIAL UNDIVIDED
UNPAVED
SCENIC ROUTE
TIME ZONE
STATE/LOCAL PARK
FOREST
CAMPGROUND
REST AREAS
INFORMATION CTR
POINT OF INTEREST

...ate . . . K-3
...on
... C-10
... J-14
... H-2
...d (19522) . . L-4
...od . . . E-8
... A-3
... (1221) . . B-13
...ille (3003) . E-4
... F-13
...Jct. . . . F-13
... J-3
Bakeoven . . . D-8
Baker City . . . E-14
Ballston . . . D-4
Bandon (2833) . . . I-1
Banks (1286) . . . C-4
Barview (1872) . . C-3
Basque Station . . K-14
Bay City . . . C-3
Beatty . . . K-7
Beaver (145) . . . C-3
Beaver Creek . . . C-5
Beaver Marsh . . . I-6
Beaverton (76129) . . . C-5
Belknap Springs . . F-6
Bellfountain . . . F-3
Bend (52029) . . . G-7
Berlin . . . F-5
Beulah . . . G-13
Biggs . . . C-8
Birkenfeld . . . B-4
Blachly . . . F-3
Black Rock . . . D-3
Blalock . . . C-9
Blodgett . . . E-3
Blue Mtn. . . . B-13
Blue River . . . F-5
Bly . . . K-8
Boardman (2855) . . . B-10
Bonanza (415) . . . L-7
Bonneville . . . C-6
Boring . . . C-5
Bourne . . . E-13
Boyd . . . C-8
Breitenbush Hot Springs . . . E-6
Bridal Veil . . . C-6
Bridge . . . I-2
Bridgeport . . . F-14
Brighton . . . B-3
Brightwood . . . C-6
Broadbent . . . I-2
Brogan . . . G-14
Brookings (5447) . L-1
Brooks (410) . . . D-4
Brothers . . . H-9
Brownsboro . . . K-4
Brownsville (1449) . . . F-4
Buchanan . . . H-12
Buck Fork . . . I-3
Buell . . . D-3
Buena Vista . . . E-4
Bull Run . . . C-6
Burns (3064) . . . H-11
Burns Junction . . J-14
Burnt Woods . . . E-3
Butte Falls (439) . . K-5
Buxton . . . B-4
Bybee Springs . . . J-4
Cairo Jct. . . . G-15
Camas Valley . . . I-3
Camp Rilea . . . A-3
Camp Sherman . . . F-7
Canary . . . G-2
Canby (12790) . . . D-5
Cannon Beach (1588) . . . B-3
Canyon City . . . F-12
Canyonville (1293) . . . J-3
Carlton (1514) . . . C-4
Carpenterville . . . K-1
Carson . . . E-15
Cascade Locks (1115) . . . C-6
Cascadia . . . F-5
Cave Junction (1363) . . . K-2
Cayuse (59) . . . C-13
Cecil . . . C-10
Central Point (12493) . . . K-4
*Chapman Corner . . . C-4
Charleston . . . H-1
Chemult . . . I-6
Cheshire . . . F-3
Chiloquin (716) . . K-6
Chitwood . . . E-3
Christmas Valley . . I-8
*Clackamas . . . F-3
Clarno . . . E-9
Clatskanie (1528) . A-4
Clem . . . C-9
Cleveland . . . I-3
Cloverdale (242) . . C-3
Coburg (969) . . . F-4
Cochran . . . B-4
Colestin . . . L-4
Colton . . . D-5
Columbia City . . . B-5
Condon (759) . . . D-9
Coos Bay (15374) . . . H-2
Copperfield . . . E-16
Coquille (4184) . . . I-2
Cornelius (9652) . C-4
Cornucopia . . . E-15
Corvallis . . . E-4
Cottage Grove (8445) . . . G-4
Cove (594) . . . D-14
Crabtree . . . E-4
Crane . . . I-12
Crater Lake . . . J-5
Crawfordsville . . . F-4
Crescent . . . H-6
Crescent Lake . . . H-6
Creston . . . I-13
Creswell (3579) . . G-4
Crow . . . G-3
Crowley . . . I-14
Culp Creek . . . H-4
Culver (802) . . . F-7
Curtin . . . G-3
Cushman . . . G-2
Dairy . . . L-7
Dale . . . E-12
Dallas (12459) . . . D-4
Danner . . . J-15
Days Creek . . . I-3
Dayton (2119) . . . D-4
Dayville (138) . . . F-11
De Moss Springs . C-9
Deadwood . . . F-3
Dee . . . C-7
Deer Island . . . B-5
Denio . . . L-12
Denmark . . . I-1
Depoe Bay (1174) . . . E-2
Deschutes . . . G-7
Detroit (262) . . . E-6
Dexter . . . G-4
Diamond . . . J-12
Diamond Lake . . . I-6
Dilley . . . C-4
Disston . . . H-4
Divide . . . G-4
Dixonville . . . I-3
Donald (608) . . . D-4
Dora . . . I-2
Dorena . . . H-4
Drain (1021) . . . H-3
Drew . . . J-4
Drewsey . . . H-13
Dryden . . . K-3
Dufur (588) . . . C-8
Dundee (2598) . . . C-4
Dunes City . . . G-2
Durkee . . . F-15
Dutchman Burte . . . J-3
Eagle Creek . . . C-5
Eagle Point (4797) . . . K-4
Echo (650) . . . C-11
Eddyville . . . E-3
Eightmile . . . D-10
Elgin (1654) . . . C-14
Elk City . . . E-2
Elk Creek . . . L-2
Elkhead . . . H-4
Elkhorn . . . E-5
Elkton (147) . . . H-3
Elmira . . . G-3
Elsie . . . B-3
Endersby . . . C-8
Enterprise (1895) . . . C-15
Estacada (2371) . . C-5
Eugene (137893) . G-4
Fairview (7561) . . . C-5
Fall Creek . . . G-4
Falls City . . . D-3
Fields . . . L-12
Finn Rock . . . G-5
Flora . . . B-15
Florence (7263) . . . G-2
Forest Grove (17708) . . . C-4
Fort Klamath . . . J-6
Fort Rock . . . I-8
Fort Stevens . . . A-3
Fossil (469) . . . D-9
Foster . . . F-5
*Four Corners . . . D-6
Fox . . . E-11
Frenchglen . . . J-12
Friend . . . C-7
Galena . . . E-12
Gales Creek . . . C-4
Galice . . . J-3
Gardiner . . . G-2
Garibaldi (899) . . . C-3
Gaston (600) . . . C-4
Gates (471) . . . E-5
Gateway . . . E-8
Gaylord . . . I-2
Gearhart (995) . . . A-3
Gervais (2009) . . . D-4
Gibbon . . . C-13
Gilchrist . . . H-6
Gl Ranch . . . H-10
Gladstone (11438) . . . C-5
Glenada . . . G-2
Glendale (855) . . . J-3
Gleneden Beach . . D-2
Glenwood . . . B-4
Glide (1690) . . . I-4
Goble . . . B-5
Gold Beach (1897) . . . K-1
Gold Hill (1073) . . . K-4
Goldson . . . F-3
Goshen . . . G-4
Govt. Camp . . . D-7
Grand Ronde (271) . . . D-3
Granite (24) . . . E-13
Grants Pass (23003) . . . K-3
Grass Valley (171) . C-8
Gravelford . . . I-2
Greenberry . . . F-4
Greenhorn . . . E-13
Greenleaf . . . F-3
Gresham (90205) . C-5
Grizzly . . . F-8
Gunter . . . G-3
Haines (426) . . . E-14
Halfway (337) . . . E-15
Halsey (724) . . . F-4
Hamilton . . . E-11
Hamlet . . . B-3
Hampton . . . H-9
Happy Valley (4519) . . . J-12
Harbor (2622) . . . L-1
Hardman . . . D-10
Harlan . . . E-3
Harney . . . H-12
Harper . . . H-14
Harrisburg (2795) . F-4
Hauser . . . H-2
*Hayesville . . . C-6
Hebo (231) . . . C-3
Heceta Beach . . . G-2
Helix (183) . . . B-12
Heppner (1395) . . D-11
Heppner Jct. . . . B-10
Hereford . . . F-13
Hermiston (13154) . . . B-11
Hilgard . . . D-13
Hillsboro (70186) . C-4
Hines (1623) . . . H-11
Holdman . . . B-12
Holland . . . L-3
Holley . . . F-4
Homestead . . . E-16
Hood River (5831) . C-7
Horse Heaven . . . E-9
Horton . . . F-3
Hoskins . . . E-3
Hot Lake . . . D-14
Hubbard (2483) . . D-5
Huntington (515) . F-15
Idanha (232) . . . E-6
Idleyld Park . . . I-4
Illahe . . . J-2
Imbler (284) . . . C-14
Imnaha . . . C-16
Independence (6035) . . . E-4
Ione (321) . . . C-10
Ironside . . . F-14
Irrigon (1702) . . . B-11
Island City . . . D-13
Izee . . . G-11
Jacksonville (2235) . . . K-4
Jamieson . . . G-15
Jasper . . . G-4
Jefferson (2487) . . E-4
Jewell . . . B-3
John Day (1821) . F-12
Jordan Valley (239) . . . J-15
Jordon . . . E-5
Joseph (1054) . . . D-15
Junction City . . . F-4
Juntura . . . H-13
Kahneeta . . . E-8
Kamela . . . C-13
Keating . . . E-14
*Keizer . . . B-5
Keizer (32203) . . . D-4
Kellogg . . . H-3
Keno . . . L-6
Kent . . . D-8
Kerby . . . K-2
Kernville . . . D-2
Kimberly . . . E-10
Kings Valley . . . E-3
Kirk . . . J-6
Kitson Hot Springs . . . H-5
Klamath Agency . . K-6
Klamath Falls (19462) . . . L-6
Klondike . . . C-9
Knappa . . . A-3
La Grande (12327) . . . D-13
La Pine (5799) . . . H-7
Lacomb . . . E-5
Lafayette (2586) . . D-4
Lake Oswego (35278) . . . C-5
Lakecreek . . . K-4
Lakeside (1371) . . H-2
Lakeview (2474) . . L-9
Landax . . . G-5
Langell Valley . . . L-7
Langlois . . . I-1
Laurelwood . . . C-4
Lawen . . . I-12
Leaburg . . . G-5
Lebanon (12950) . E-4
Lehman Springs . D-12
Lena . . . D-11
Leona . . . H-3
Lewis . . . C-15
Lexington (263) . . C-10
Lime . . . F-15
Lincoln (7437) . . . D-4
Lincoln Beach (2078) . . . D-2
Lincoln City . . . D-2
Little Valley . . . G-14
Logdell . . . G-11
Logsden . . . E-3
London . . . H-4
Lonerock (24) . . . D-10
Long Creek (228) . E-11
Lookingglass . . . I-3
Lorane . . . G-3
Lorella . . . L-7
Lostine (263) . . . C-15
Lowell (857) . . . G-4
Lower Bridge . . . F-7
Lyons (1008) . . . E-5
Mabel . . . F-4
Madras (5078) . . . E-8
Malin (638) . . . L-7
Malloy Ranch . . . I-15
Manning . . . B-4
Manzanita (564) . . B-3
Mapleton . . . G-2
Marcola . . . F-4
Marion (274) . . . E-4
Marion Forks . . . E-6
Marquam . . . D-5
Maupin (411) . . . D-8
Maxville . . . C-14
Mayger . . . A-4
Mayville . . . D-9
McCoy . . . D-4
McCredie Springs . H-5
McDermitt . . . L-14
McKenzie Bridge . . F-6
McLeod . . . J-4
McMinnville (26499) . . . D-4
McNary . . . B-11
Meacham . . . C-13
Medford . . . K-4
Medical Springs . . E-14
Melrose . . . I-3
Merlin . . . K-3
Merrill (897) . . . L-6
Metolius (635) . . . E-8
Midland . . . L-6
Mikkalo . . . C-9
Mill City . . . E-5
Millersburg (651) . E-4
Millican . . . G-8
Millwood . . . H-3
Milo . . . J-4
Milton-Freewater (6470) . . . B-13
Milwaukie (20490) . . . C-5
Minam . . . C-14
Minerva . . . F-2
Mission (1019) . . C-12
Mist . . . B-4
Mitchell (170) . . . F-9
Modoc Point . . . K-6
Mohawk . . . F-4
Mohler . . . B-3
Molalla (5647) . . . D-5
Monitor . . . D-5
Monmouth (7741) . E-4
Monroe (607) . . . F-3
Monument (151) . E-11
Morgan . . . C-10, I-3
Moro (337) . . . C-8
Mosier (410) . . . C-7
Mt. Angel . . . D-5
Mt. Hood . . . C-7
Mt. Vernon . . . F-11
Mulino . . . D-5
Murphy . . . K-3
Myrtle Creek (3419) . . . I-3
Myrtle Point (2451) . . . I-2
Narrows . . . I-12
Nashville . . . E-3
Natron . . . G-4
Necanicum Jct. . . . B-3
Nehalem (203) . . . B-3
Neotsu . . . D-2
Nesika Beach . . . K-1
Neskowin (169) . . . D-2
Netarts (744) . . . C-2
New Bridge . . . E-15
New Pine Creek . . . L-9
New Princeton . . . I-12
Newberg (18064) . C-4
Newport (9532) . . E-2
Nimrod . . . G-5
Nonpareil . . . H-4
North Bend (9544) . . . H-2
North Fork . . . G-2
North Plains (1605) . . . C-4
North Powder (489) . . . D-14
Norway . . . I-2
Noti . . . G-3
Nye . . . C-12
Nyssa (3163) . . . H-15
O'Brien . . . L-2
*Oak Grove . . . C-6
Oakland (954) . . . H-3
Oakridge (3148) . . H-5
Oceanside (326) . . C-2
Odell (1849) . . . C-7
Olene . . . L-6
Olex . . . C-9
Olney . . . A-3
Ona . . . E-2
Ontario (10985) . G-15
Ophir . . . J-1
Oregon City . . . C-5
Orenco . . . C-4
Otis . . . D-2
Otter Rock . . . E-2
Owyhee . . . H-15
Pacific City . . . C-2
Paisley (247) . . . J-9
Paradise . . . B-15
Parkdale (266) . . C-7
Paulina . . . G-10
Payette Junction . G-16
Pedee . . . E-3
Peel . . . I-4
Pendleton (16354) . . . C-12
Perry . . . D-13
Perrydale . . . D-4
Philomath (3838) . E-3
Phoenix (4060) . . . K-4
Pilot Rock (1532) . . . C-12
Pine . . . E-15
Pine City . . . C-11
Pine Grove (162) . . D-7
Pinehurst . . . L-5
Pistol River . . . K-1
Pittsburg . . . B-4
Pleasant Hill . . . G-4
Pleasant Valley . . E-14
Plush . . . K-10
Pondosa . . . E-14
Port Orford (1153) . J-1
Portland (529121) . C-5
Post . . . G-9
Powell Butte . . . F-8
Powers (734) . . . J-2
Prairie City . . . F-12
Prescott (72) . . . A-5
Priday Ranch . . . E-8
Prineville (7356) . . F-8
Promise . . . B-14
Prospect . . . J-5
Prosper . . . I-1
Provolt . . . K-3
Quartz Mountain . . K-8
Quartzville . . . E-5
Quines Creek . . . J-3
Quinton . . . C-9
Rainbow . . . F-5
Rainier (1687) . . . A-4
Redmond (13481) . F-7
Reed . . . F-2
Reedsport (4378) . G-2
Remote . . . I-2
Reston . . . I-3
Rhododendron . . . C-6
Rice Hill . . . H-3
Richland (147) . . E-15
Richmond . . . E-10
Rickreall (57) . . . D-4
Riddle (1014) . . . I-3
Rieth . . . C-12
Riley . . . H-11
Ripplebrook . . . D-6
Ritter . . . E-11
Riverside (189) . . H-13
Riverton . . . I-1
Roaring Spring Ranch . . . K-12
Rock Creek . . . C-9
Rock Creek . . . E-13
Rockaway Beach (1267) . . . B-3
Rockville . . . I-15
Rogue River (1847) . . . K-3
Rome . . . J-14
Rose Lodge (1708) . . . D-2
Roseburg (20017) . I-3
Roy . . . C-4
Ruch . . . K-4
Rufus (268) . . . C-9
Ruggs . . . D-10
Rye Valley . . . F-15
Saginaw . . . G-4
Salem (136924) . . D-4
Sams Valley . . . K-4
Sandlake . . . C-2
Sandy (5385) . . . C-6
Scappoose (4976) . B-5
Scio (695) . . . E-4
Scotts Mills (312) . D-5
Scottsburg . . . H-2
Seal Rock . . . E-2
Seaside (5900) . . . A-3
Selma . . . K-2
Seneca (223) . . . G-12
Service Creek . . . E-10
Shady Cove (2307) . . . J-4
Shaniko (26) . . . D-8
Shaw . . . D-4
Sheaville . . . I-15
Shedd . . . F-4
Sheridan (3570) . . D-3
Sherwood (11791) . . . C-5
Siletz (1133) . . . E-2
Siltcoos . . . G-2
Silver Lake . . . I-8
Silverton (7414) . . D-5
Silvies . . . G-12
Simnasho . . . D-7
Sisters (959) . . . F-7
Sitkum . . . I-2
Sixes . . . J-1
Sodaville (290) . . . F-4
South Beach . . . E-2
Sparta . . . E-15
Sprague River . . . K-7
Spray (140) . . . E-10
Springfield (52864) . . . G-4
St. Helens (10019) . . . B-5
St. Paul (354) . . . D-4
*Stafford . . . G-1
Stanfield (1979) . B-11
Starkey . . . D-13
Stayton (6816) . . . E-5
Steamboat . . . H-4
Sublimity (2148) . . E-5
Sulphur Springs . . G-2
Summer Lake . . . J-8
Summerville (117) . . . C-14
Summit . . . E-3
Sumner . . . H-2
Sumpter (171) . . . E-13
Sunny Valley . . . J-3
Sunriver . . . G-7
Suplee . . . G-10
Susanville . . . E-12
Sutherlin (6669) . . H-3
Svensen . . . A-3
Sweet Home (8016) . . . F-5
Swisshome . . . G-2
Takilma . . . L-2
Talent (5589) . . . K-4
Tangent (933) . . . E-4
Telocaset . . . D-14
Tenmile . . . I-3
Terrebonne (1469) . F-7
The Dalles . . . C-8
Three Forks . . . K-15
Tidewater . . . F-2
Tiernan . . . G-2
Tigard (41223) . . . C-5
Tillamook (4352) . . C-3
Tiller . . . J-4
Timber . . . B-4
Trail . . . J-4
Trask . . . C-3
Tri-City . . . I-3
Triangle Lake . . . F-3
Troutdale (13777) . C-5
Troy . . . B-15
Tualatin (22791) . . C-5
Tumalo . . . G-7
Turner (1199) . . . E-4
Twickenham . . . E-9
Tyee . . . H-3
Tygh Valley (224) . D-8
Ukiah (255) . . . D-12
Umapine . . . B-13
Umatilla (4978) . . B-11
Umpqua . . . H-3
Union (1926) . . . D-14
Union Creek . . . J-5
Unity (131) . . . F-13
Upper Soda . . . F-5
Vale (1976) . . . G-15
Valley Falls . . . K-9
Valley Junction . . . D-3
Van . . . G-12
Vaughn . . . G-3
Venator . . . I-13
Veneta (2755) . . . G-3
Verboort . . . C-4
Vernonia (2228) . . B-4
Vida . . . F-5
Vinson . . . C-11
Wagontire . . . I-10
Waldo . . . L-2
Waldport (2050) . . F-2
Walker . . . G-4
Wallowa (869) . . . C-14
Walterville . . . G-4
Walton . . . G-3
Wamic (36) . . . D-7
Wapinitia . . . D-7
Warm Springs (2431) . . . E-7
Warren . . . B-5
Warrenton (4096) . A-3
Wasco (381) . . . C-9
Waterloo (239) . . . F-4
Weatherby . . . F-15
Wedderburn . . . K-1
Welches . . . C-6
Wemme . . . C-6
Wendling . . . F-4
West Linn (22261) . . . C-5
West Side . . . L-9
West Stayton . . . E-4
Westfall . . . G-14
Westfir (276) . . . G-5
Weston (717) . . . B-13
Westport . . . A-4
Wetmore . . . E-10
Wheeler (391) . . . B-3
White City . . . K-4
Whitehorse Ranch . . . L-13
Whiteson . . . D-4
Whitney . . . E-13
Wilbur . . . I-3
Wilderville . . . K-3
Wilhoit . . . D-5
Willamina (1844) . D-3
Williams . . . K-3
Willow Creek . . . G-15
Willowdale . . . E-8
Wilsonville (13991) . . . C-5
Wimer . . . K-3
Winchester . . . I-3
Winchester Bay (488) . . . G-2
Winlock . . . E-10
Winston (4613) . . . I-3
Wolf Creek . . . J-3
Wonder . . . K-3
Woodburn (20100) . . . D-4
Worden . . . L-6
Wren . . . E-3
Wrentham . . . C-8
Yachats (617) . . . F-2
Yamhill (794) . . . C-4
Yoncalla (1052) . . . H-3
Zigzag . . . C-6
Zumwalt . . . C-15

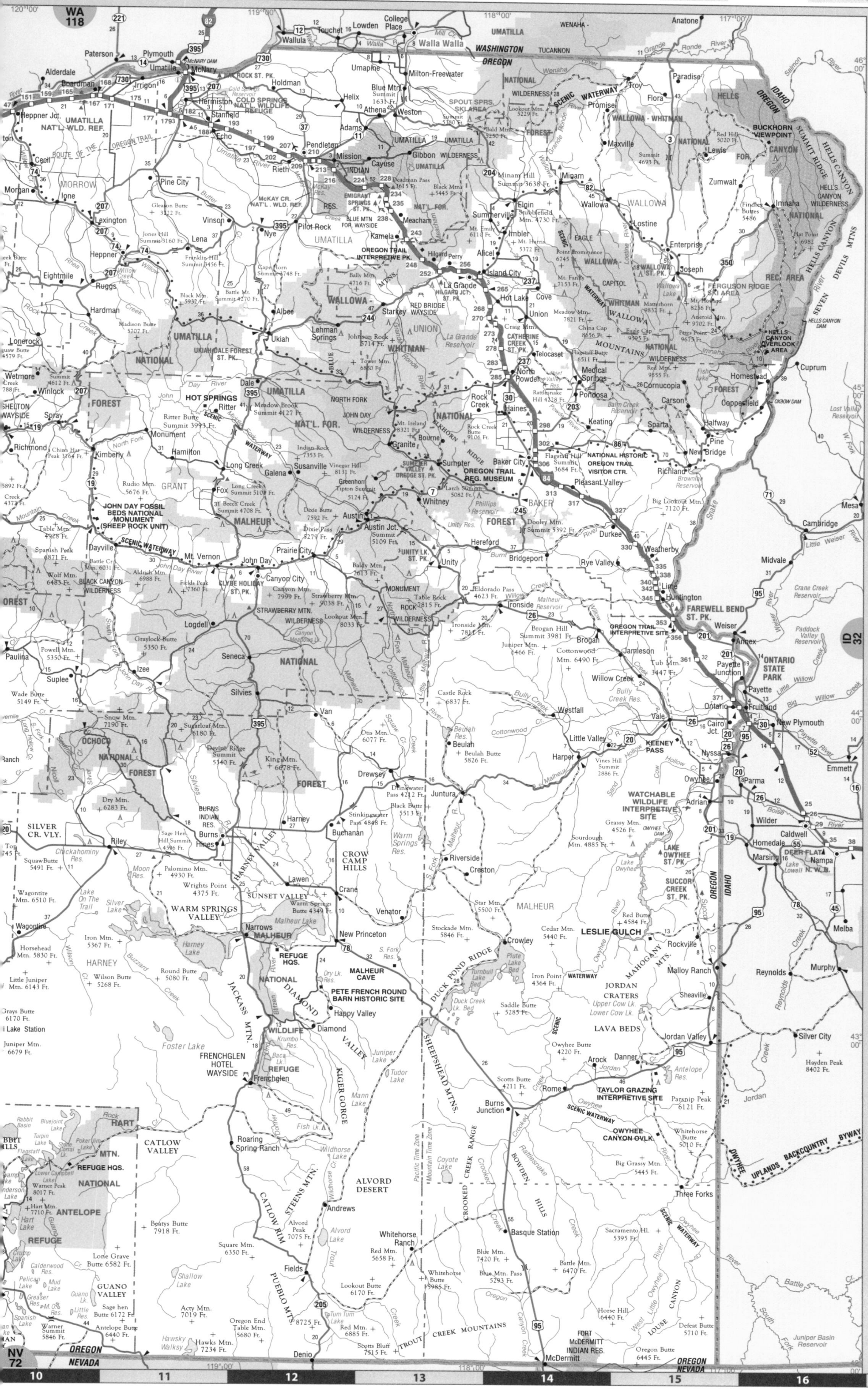

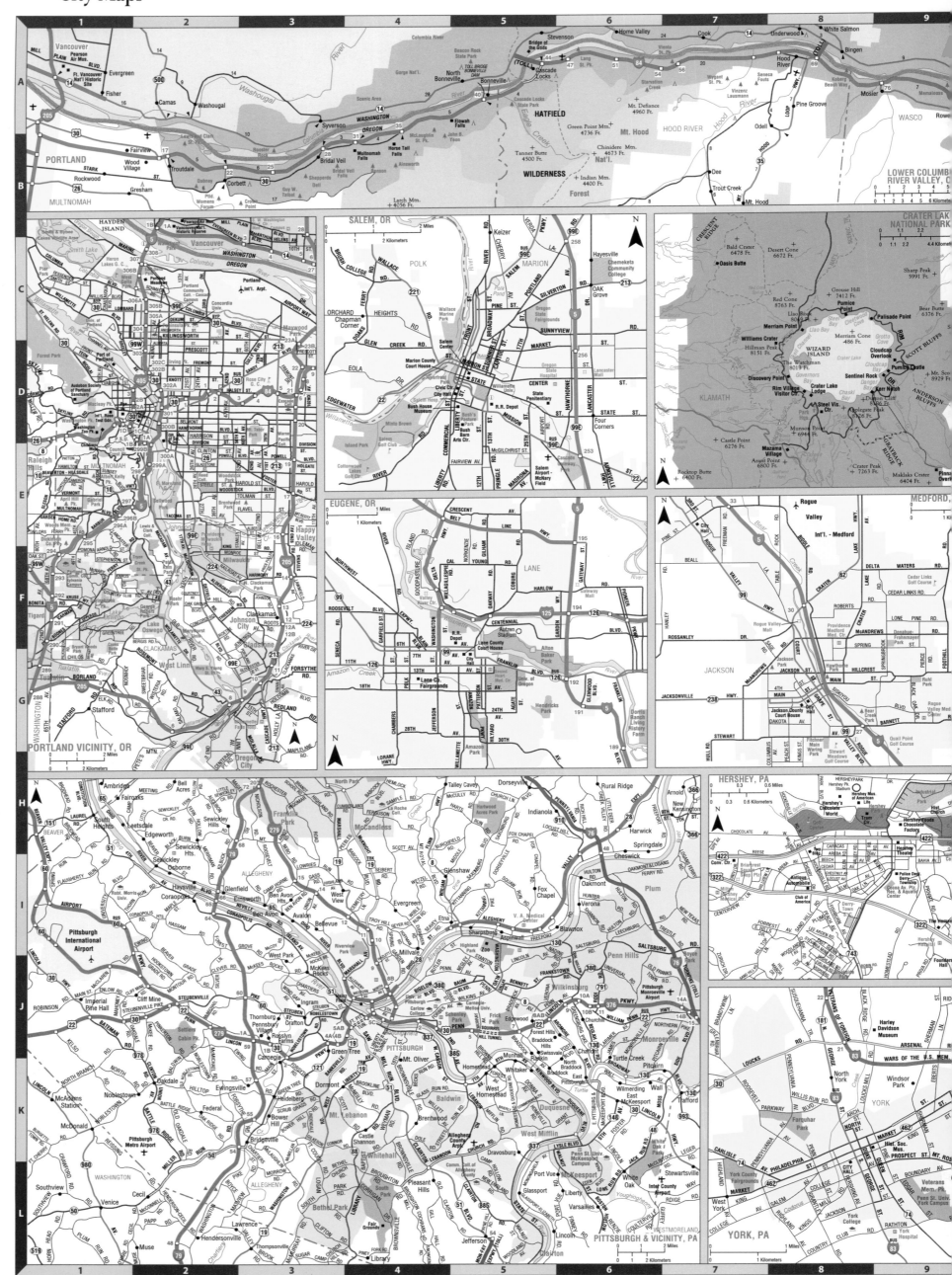

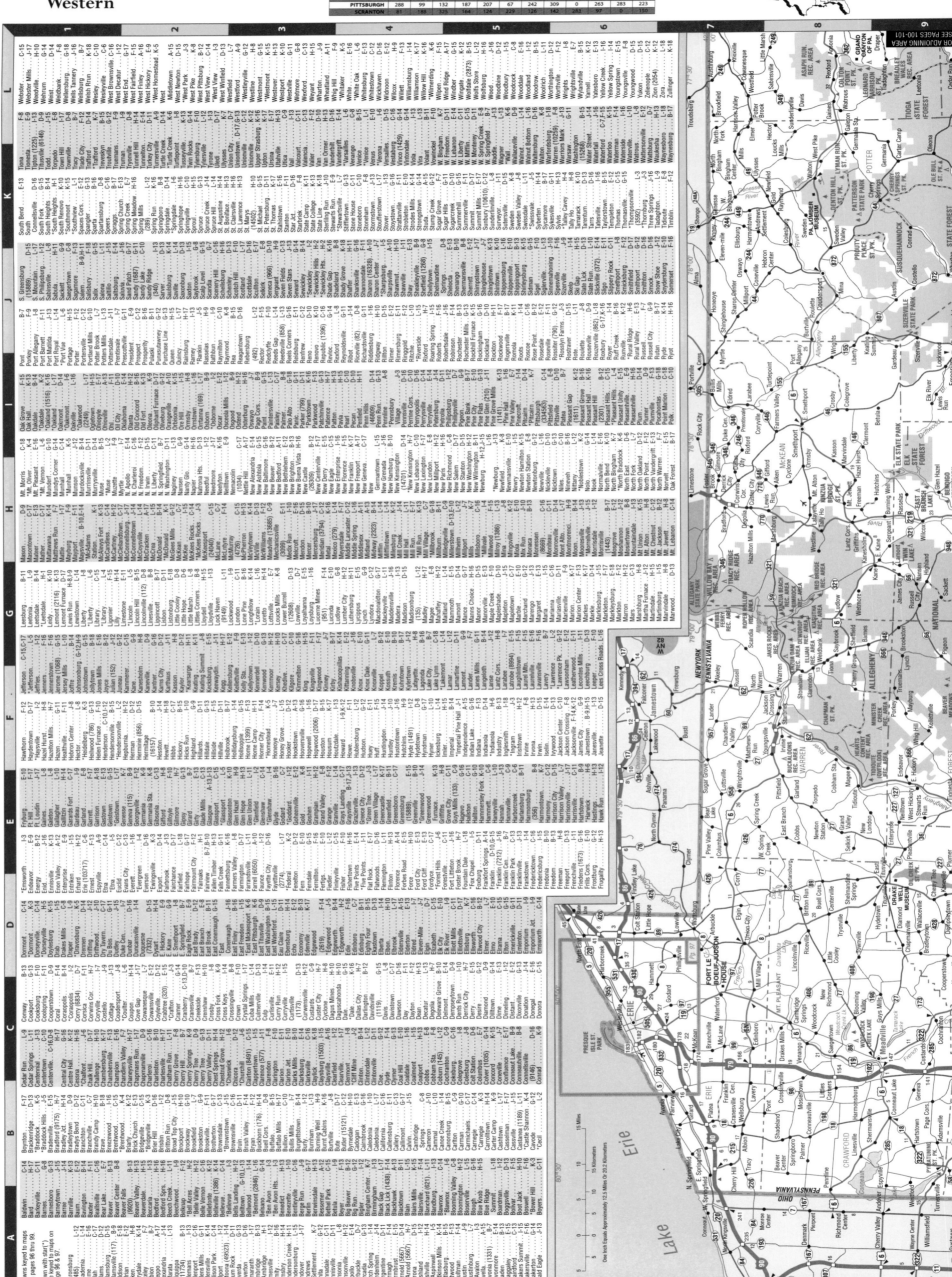

FOR ADJOINING AREA
SEE PAGES 100-101

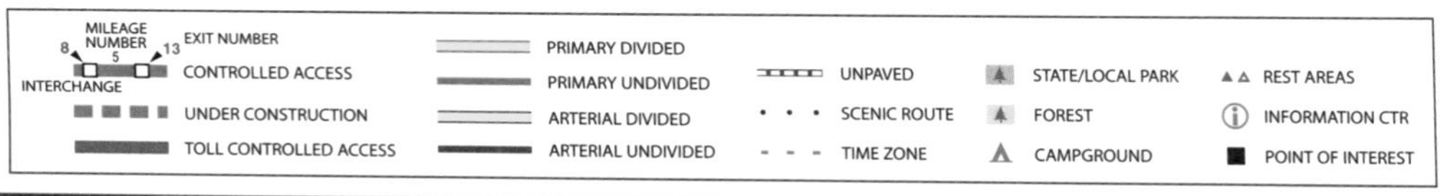
MILEAGE NUMBER
EXIT NUMBER
INTERCHANGE
CONTROLLED ACCESS
UNDER CONSTRUCTION
TOLL CONTROLLED ACCESS
PRIMARY DIVIDED
PRIMARY UNDIVIDED
ARTERIAL DIVIDED
ARTERIAL UNDIVIDED
UNPAVED
SCENIC ROUTE
TIME ZONE
STATE/LOCAL PARK
FOREST
CAMPGROUND
REST AREAS
INFORMATION CTR
POINT OF INTEREST

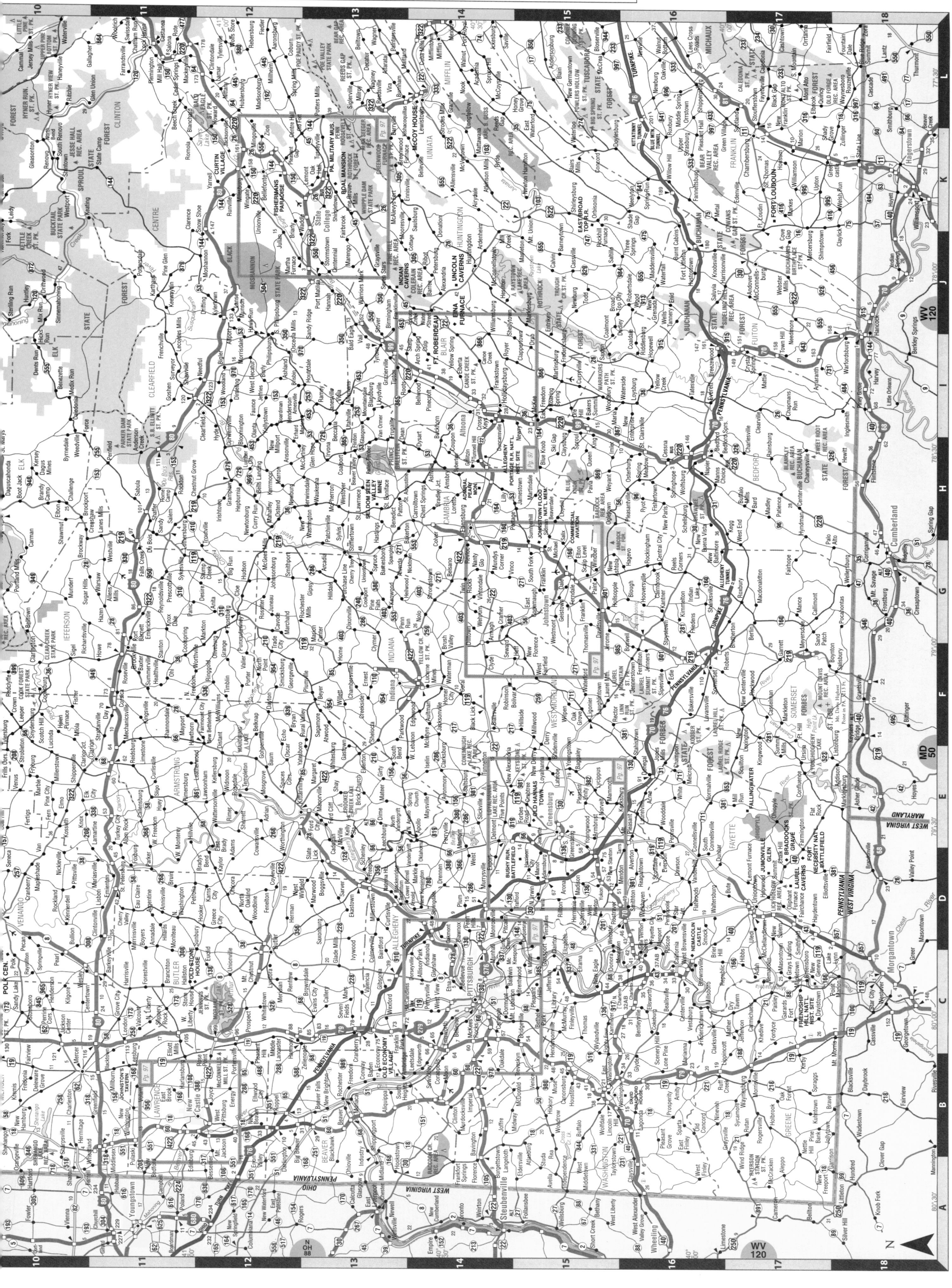
PENNSYLVANIA
OHIO
WEST VIRGINIA
MARYLAND
PITTSBURGH
Altoona
Johnstown
State College
Greensburg
Washington
Cumberland
Hagerstown
Morgantown
Wheeling
Steubenville
Youngstown
TURNPIKE

	ALLENTOWN	ALTOONA	ERIE	GETTYSBURG	HARRISBURG	JOHNSTOWN	LANCASTER	PHILADELPHIA	PITTSBURGH	READING	SCRANTON	YORK
ERIE	338	207	0	314	270	180	310	389	132	328	325	350
HARRISBURG	86	138	270	40	0	140	40	108	207	62	124	26
PHILADELPHIA	52	240	389	100	40	242	70	0	309	59	124	26
PITTSBURGH	288	99	132	187	207	67	242	309	0	283	283	223
SCRANTON	81	188	325	164	124	229	126	124	309	0	283	97	150

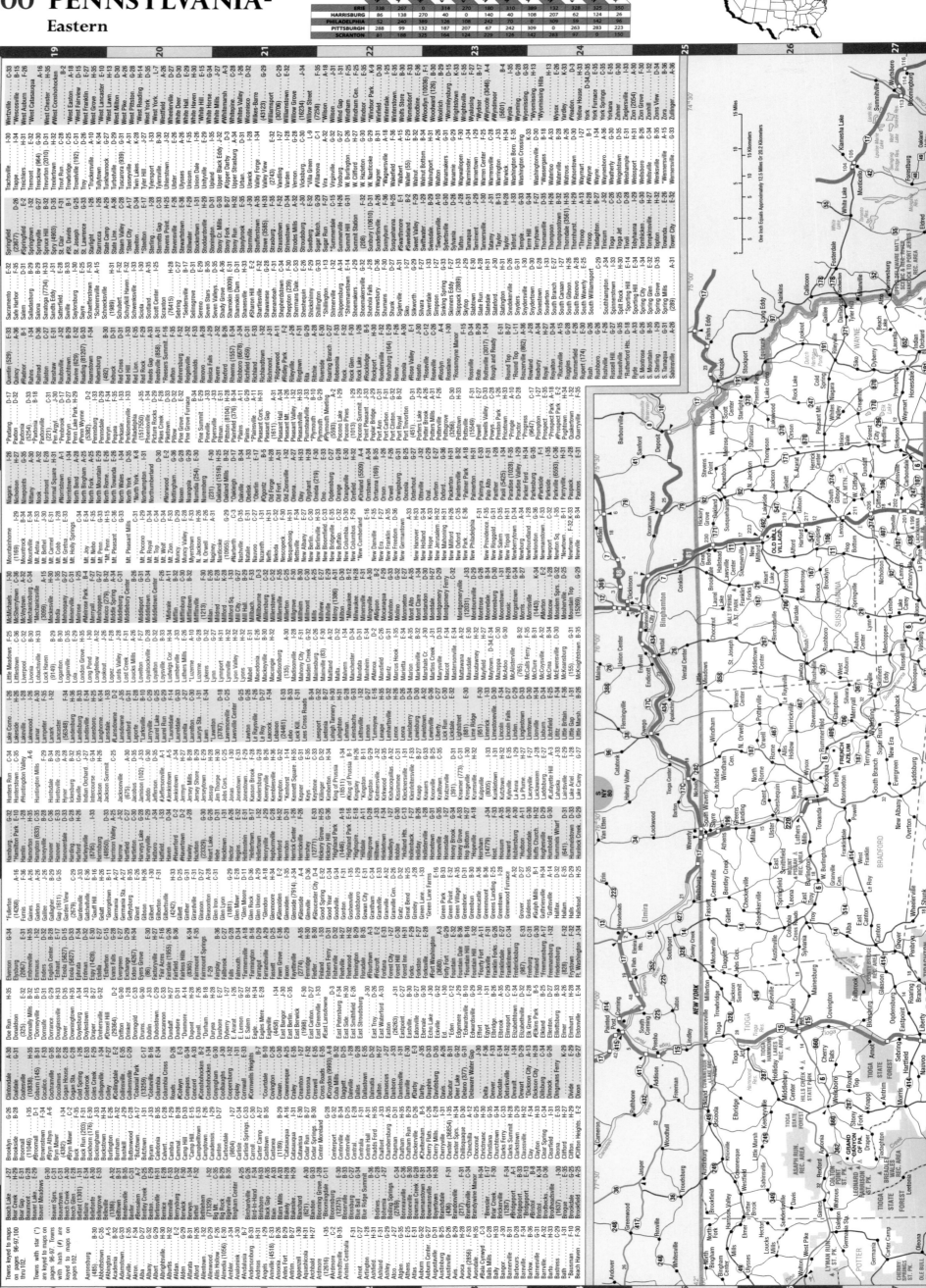

Map legend:

MILEAGE NUMBER / EXIT NUMBER	PRIMARY DIVIDED	STATE/LOCAL PARK
CONTROLLED ACCESS	PRIMARY UNDIVIDED	FOREST
INTERCHANGE	ARTERIAL DIVIDED	CAMPGROUND
UNDER CONSTRUCTION	ARTERIAL UNDIVIDED	REST AREAS
TOLL CONTROLLED ACCESS	UNPAVED	INFORMATION CTR
	SCENIC ROUTE	POINT OF INTEREST
	TIME ZONE	

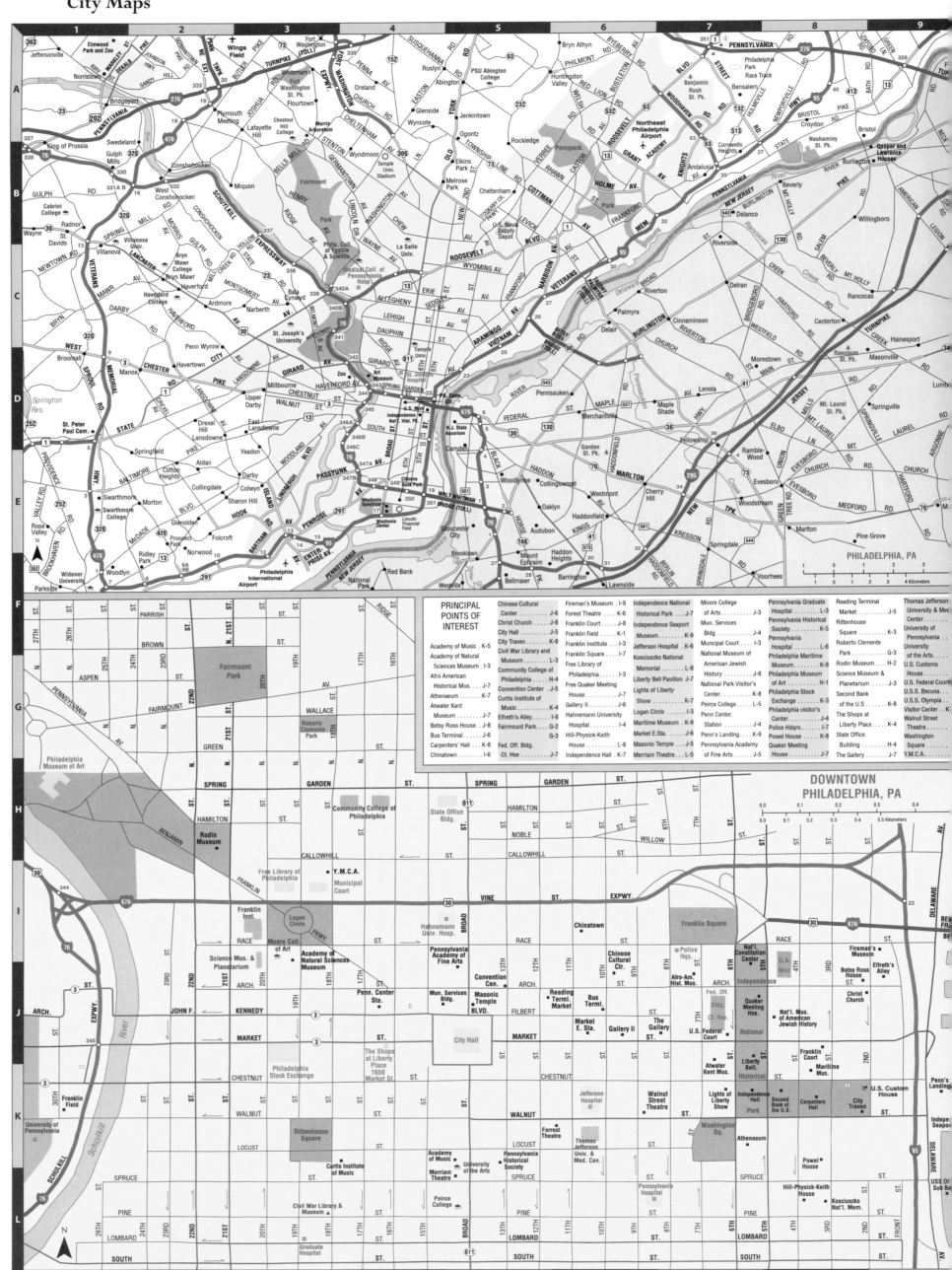

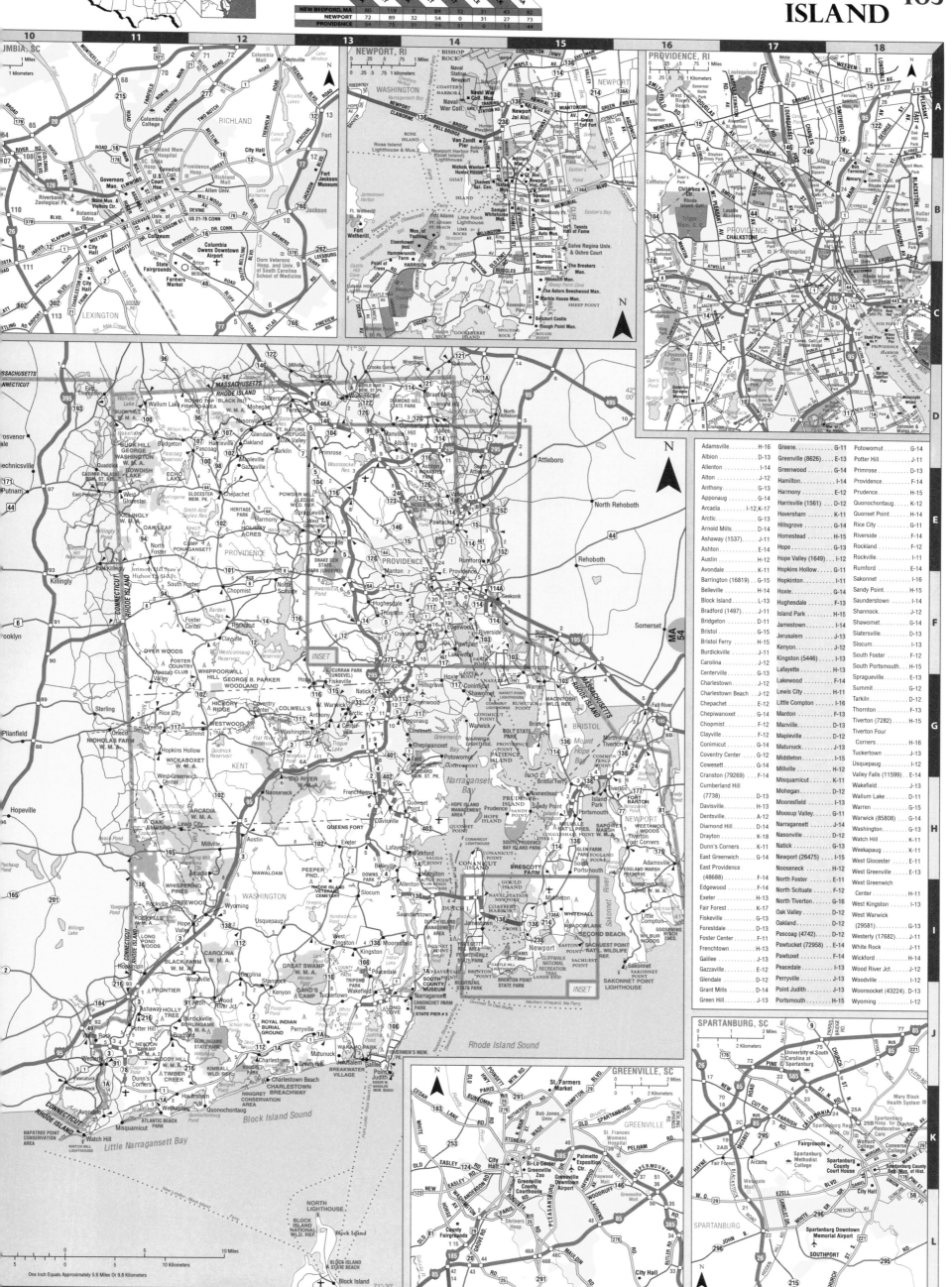

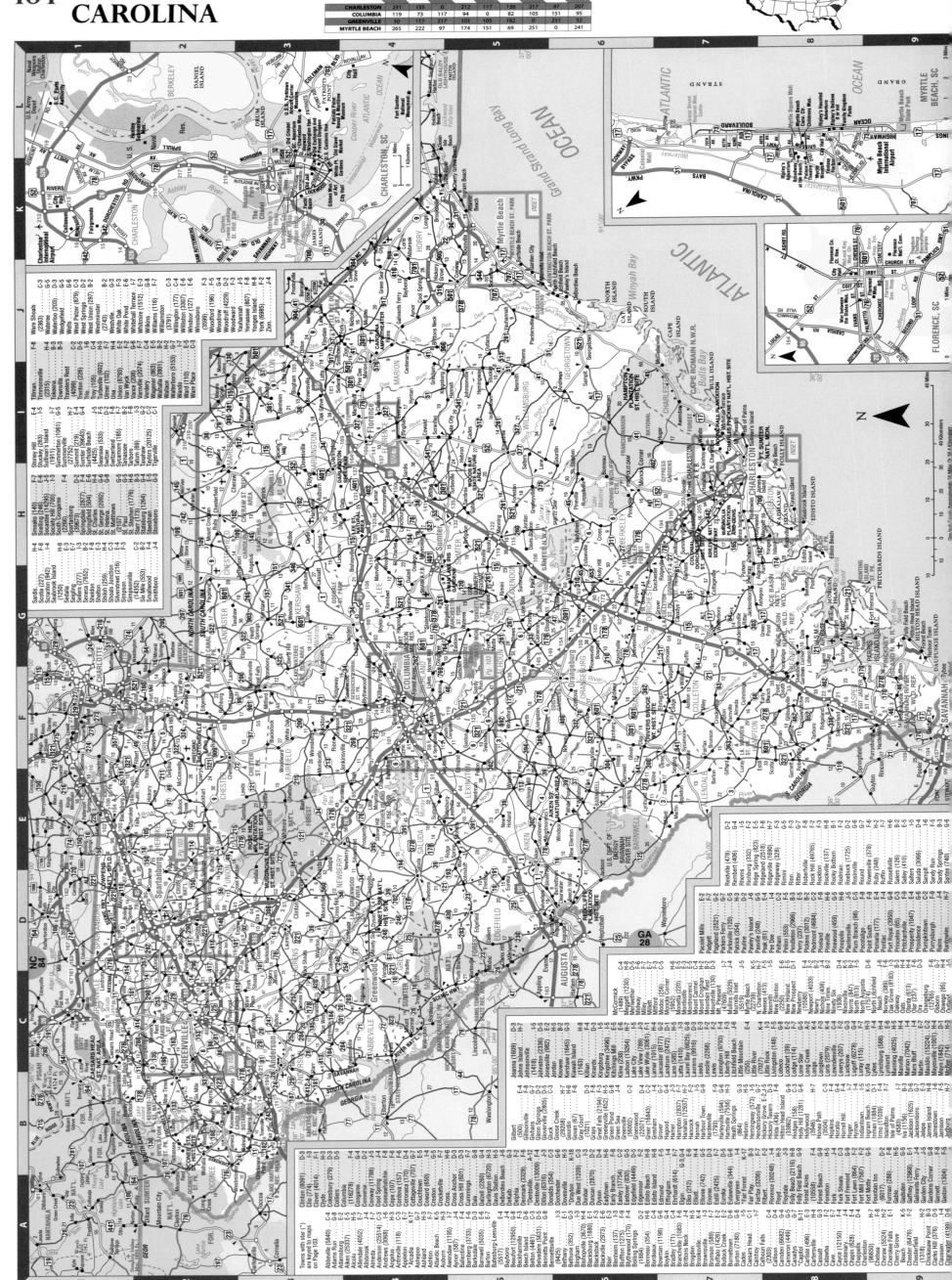

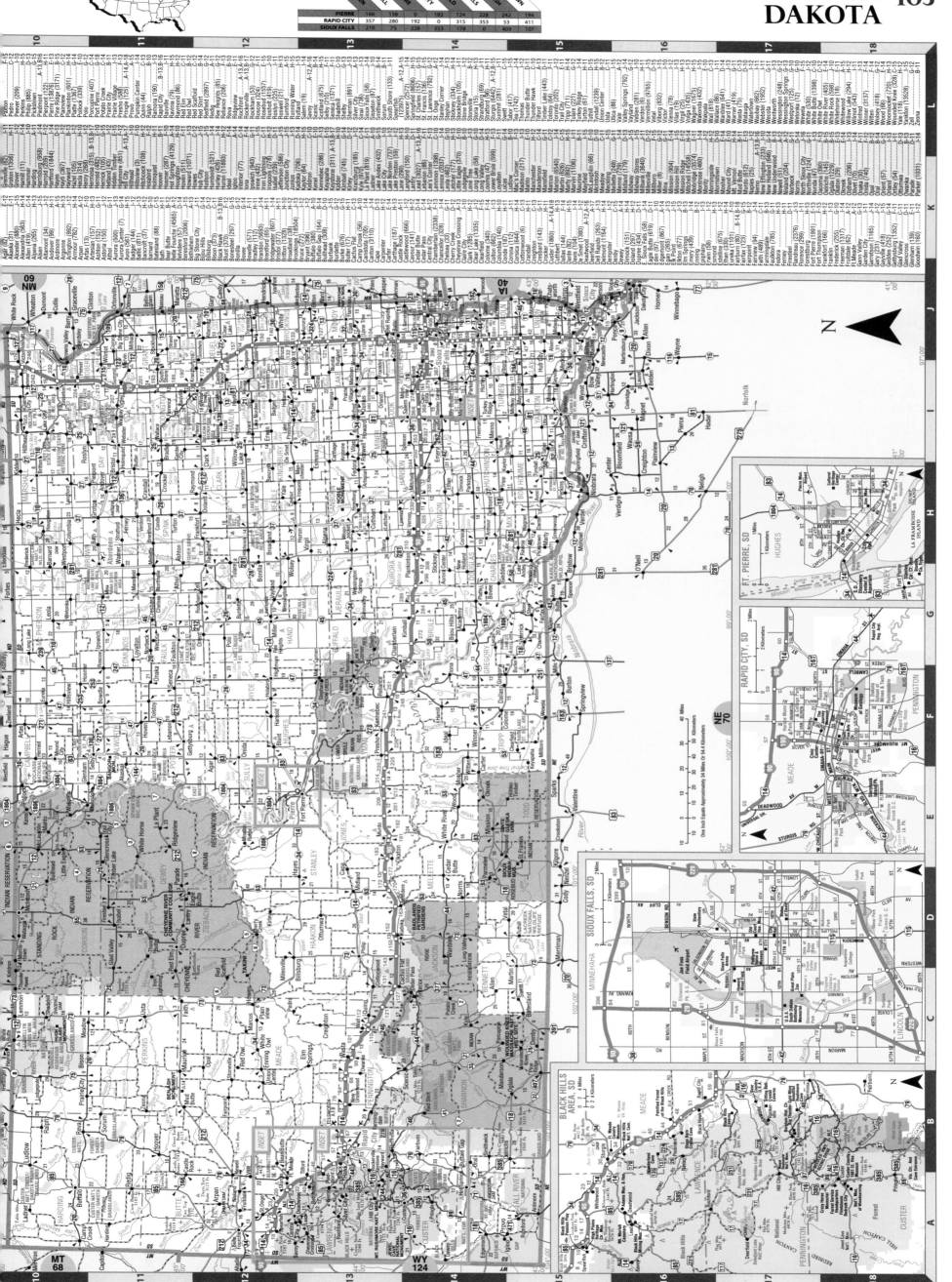

	BRISTOL	CHATTANOOGA	CLARKSVILLE	CLEVELAND	JACKSON	JOHNSON CITY	KINGSPORT	KNOXVILLE	MEMPHIS	MORRISTOWN	MURFREESBORO	NASHVILLE
BRISTOL	0	227	341	199	425	26	25	115	509	74	290	296
CHATTANOOGA	227	0	181	32	264	219	213	113	348	161	102	136
KNOXVILLE	115	113	227	85	312	107	101	0	396	49	177	182
MEMPHIS	509	348	214	377	89	501	495	396	0	443	248	216
NASHVILLE	295	135	50	164	132	287	281	181	216	229	34	0

MEMPHIS, TN

KNOXVILLE, TN

NASHVILLE, TN

CHATTANOOGA, TN

Towns with Star (*) are Keyed to maps on page 86.

Adams (566) A-9
Adamsville (1983) ... E-6
Afton ... H-16
Alamo (2392) ... C-4
*Alcoa ... H-1
Alcoa ... C-17
Alexandria (814) ... C-12
Algood (2942) ... B-13
Allardt (642) ... B-14
Allisona ... D-10
Allons ... A-13
Allred ... B-14
*Alnwick ... I-1
Alpine ... B-14
Altamont (1136) ... E-12
Alumwell ... G-15
Apison ... F-14
Ardmore (1082) ... F-9
Arp ... C-2
Arrington ... C-10
Ashland City ... B-9
Athens (13220) ... D-15
Atoka (6235) ... D-2
Atwood (1000) ... C-5
Auburntown ... C-11
Baileyton (504) ... G-16
Bairds Mill ... B-11
Bakers Crossroads ... C-13
Bakewell ... E-14
Baneberry ... H-15
Bartlett (40543) ... E-2
Bath Springs ... D-6
Baxter (1279) ... B-12
Bean Station ... B-18,G-14
Central (2717) ...
Beardstown ... D-7
Beech Bluff ... D-5
Beech Grove ... D-11
Beersheba Springs (553) ... D-12
Belfast ... E-10
Bell Buckle (391) ... D-11
Bellevue ... C-9
Bells (2171) ... D-4
Belvidere ... F-11
Benton (1138) ... E-15
Berry Hill (674) ... B-10
Bethpage ... A-11
Big Rock ... A-7
Big Sandy (518) ... B-6
Birchwood ... E-14
Blaine ... B-17
Bloomington Springs ... B-13
Blountville (2959) ... G-17
Bluewing ... C-12
Bluff City (1719) ... G-17
Bogata ... B-3
Bolivar (5802) ... E-4
Bon Aqua ... C-8
Bone Cave ... D-13
Bordeaux ... J-1
*Boyds Creek ... G-3
Braden (271) ... E-3
Bradford (1113) ... B-4
Bradyville ... D-11
Brentwood (23445) ... C-10
Briceville ... B-16
Brighton (1719) ... D-2
Bristol (24821) ... F-17
Brownsville (10748) ... D-3

Bruceton (1554) ...
Brunswick ...
Brush Creek ...
Buchanan ...
Buena Vista ...
Buffalo ...
Buffalo Valley ... B-
Bulls Gap (714) ...
Bumpus Mills ...
Burlison (453) ...
Burns (1366) ...
Burrville ...
Butler ... G-
Bybee ...
Cades Cove ...
*Cades Cove ... D-
Cagle ... D-
*Calderwood ...
Calhoun (496) ...
Camden (3828) ...
Campaign ... C-
Capleville ... F-2
Carlisle ...
*Carson Springs ...
Carthage (2251) ...
Caryville (2243) ...
Castalian Springs ...
*Catletsburg ...
Cedar Grove ...
Cedar Hill (298) ...
Celina (1379) ...
Center (257) ...
Centertown ...
Centerville (3793) ...
Central (2717) ...
Chapel Hill (943) ...
Chapmansboro ...
Charleston (630) ...
Charlotte (1153) ...
Chattanooga ... K-6,8
*Cherokee Hills ...
Cherry ...
Chestnut Hill ... D-
Chestnut Hill, C-18,
*Chestnut Hill ...
Chewalla ...
*Chilhowee ...
Christiana ...
Chuckey ...
Church Hill (5916) ...
Churchton ...
Clairfield ...
Clarkrange ...
Clarksville (103455) ...
Cleveland (37192) ...
Clevenger ... C-18,H-
Clifton (2699) ...
Clinton (9409) ...
Clover Port ...
Coalfield ...
Coalmont (948) ...
Coker Creek ...
*Cold Springs ...
College Grove ...
Collegedale ...
Collierville (31872) ...
Collinwood (1024) ...

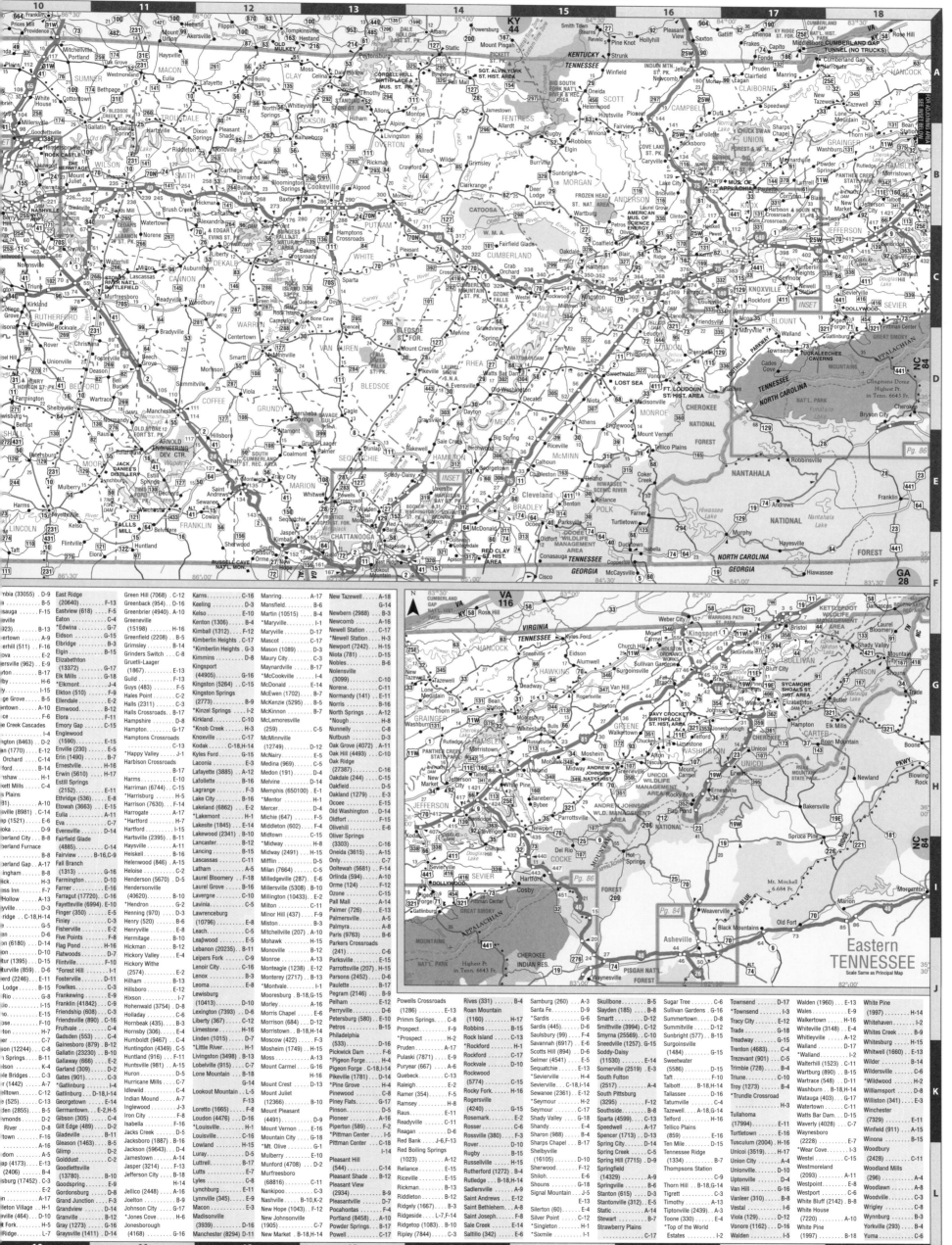

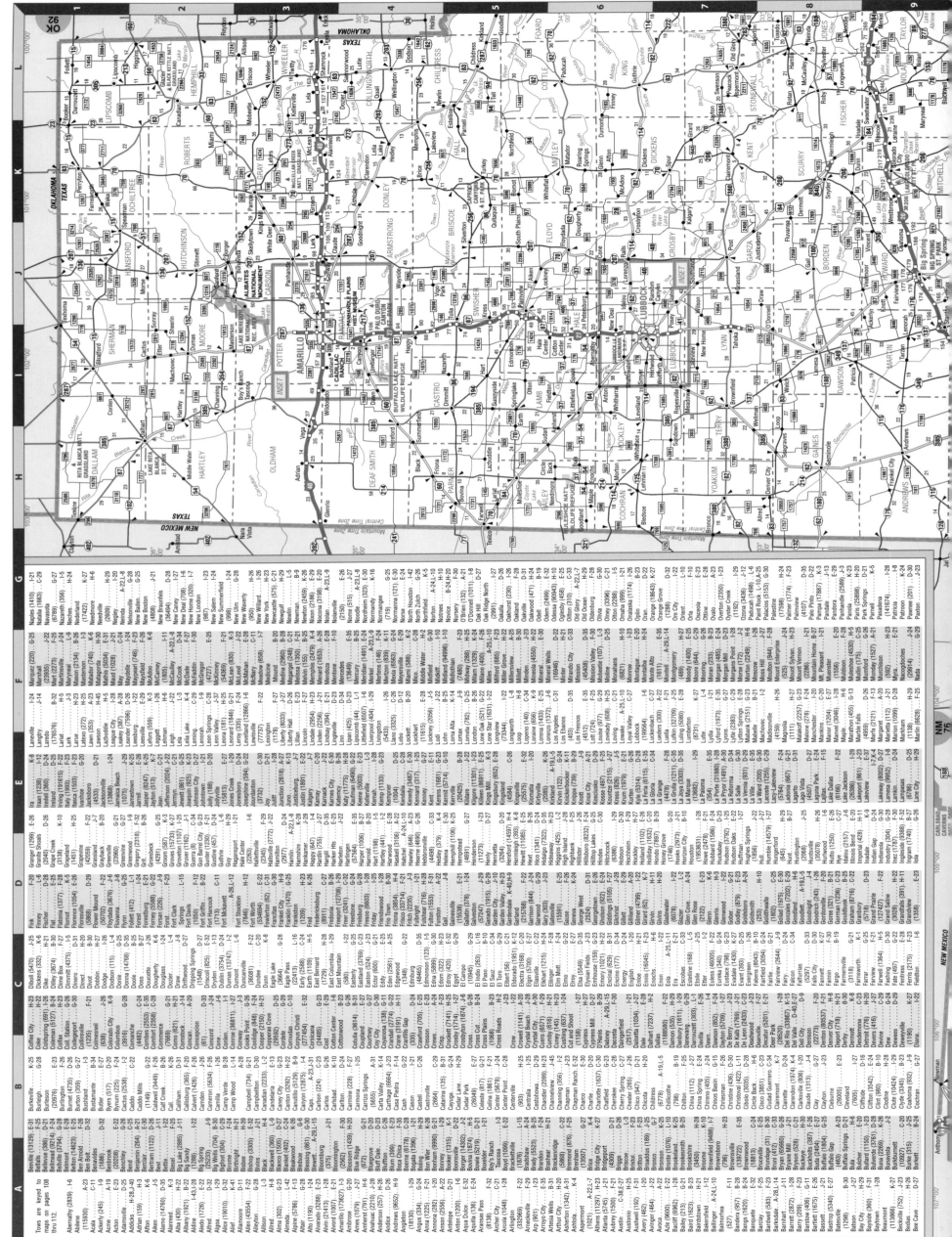

MILEAGE NUMBER · EXIT NUMBER · INTERCHANGE — CONTROLLED ACCESS
UNDER CONSTRUCTION
TOLL CONTROLLED ACCESS
PRIMARY DIVIDED
PRIMARY UNDIVIDED
ARTERIAL DIVIDED
ARTERIAL UNDIVIDED
UNPAVED
SCENIC ROUTE
TIME ZONE
STATE/LOCAL PARK
FOREST
CAMPGROUND
REST AREAS
INFORMATION CTR
POINT OF INTEREST

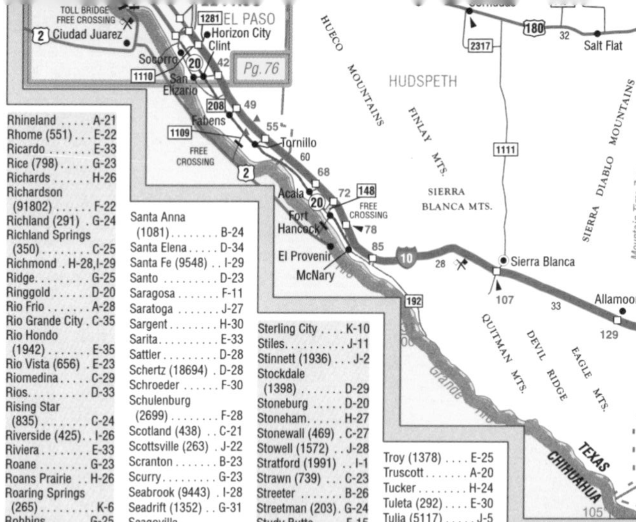

Pearland (37640) . . . I-28
Pearsall (7157) . . . B-30
Peaster . . . D-22
Pecan Gap (214) . . . H-21
Pecos (9501) . . . G-11
Peggy . . . D-30
Penelope (211) . . . F-24
Pennington . . . I-25
Penwell . . . H-10
Perrin . . . D-22
Perry . . . F-25
Perryton (7774) . . . K-1
Petersburg (1262) . . . J-6
Petrolia (782) . . . D-20
Petronila . . . G-33
Pettus . . . E-30
Petty . . . H-20
Pflugerville (16335) . . . E-27
Phalba . . . G-23
Pharr (46660) . . . D-35
Phelps . . . H-26
Pickton . . . H-22
Pierce . . . G-29
Pilot Point (3538) . . . F-21
Pine Mills . . . I-22
Pine Springs . . . D-10
Pinehurst (2274) . . . H-27
Pineland (980) . . . K-25
Pipe Creek . . . C-28
Pittsburg (4347) . . . I-22
Placedo . . . F-30
Plains (1450) . . . H-7
Plainview (22336) . . . J-5
Plano (222030) . . . F-22
Pleasant Farms . . . I-10
Pleasanton (8266) . . . D-30
Pledger . . . H-29
Plum . . . F-28
Point (792) . . . H-22
Point Blank(559) . . . I-26
Point Comfort (781) . . . G-30
Pollok . . . I-25
Ponder (507) . . . E-21
Ponta . . . I-24
Pontotoc . . . C-26
Poolville . . . D-22
Port Alto . . . G-30
Port Aransas (3370) . . . F-32
Port Arthur (57755) . . . K-27
Port Bolivar . . . J-29, L-32
Port Isabel (4865) . . . F-35
Port Lavaca (12035) . . . G-30
Port Mansfield . . . E-34
Port Neches (13601) . . . K-27
Port O'Connor . . . G-30
Porter . . . I-27
Portland (14827) . . . E-32
Posey . . . J-7
Post (3708) . . . J-7
Postoak . . . D-21
Poteet (3305) . . . C-29
Poth (1850) . . . D-29
Pottsboro (1579) . . . F-20
Pottsville . . . D-24
Powderly . . . H-20
Powell (105) . . . G-23
Poynor (314) . . . H-23
Prairie Hill . . . F-24
Prairie View (4410) . . . H-27
Premont (2772) . . . D-33
Presidio (4167) . . . E-14
Price . . . I-23
Priddy . . . C-24
Princeton (3477) . . . G-21
Pritchett . . . I-22
Proctor . . . C-24
Progreso (4851) . . . E-35
Prosper (2097) . . . F-21
Pullman . . . G-17
Purdon . . . F-24
Putnam (88) . . . B-23
Pyote (131) . . . G-10
Quail (33) . . . L-4
Quanah (3022) . . . A-19
Queen City . . . J-21
Quemado (243) . . . K-15
Quinlan (1370) . . . G-22
Quitaque (432) . . . K-5
Quitman (2030) . . . H-22
Rachal . . . D-34
Rainbow . . . E-23
Ralls (2252) . . . J-6
Ramirez . . . D-33
Rancho Viejo (1754) . . . E-35
Randado . . . C-33
Ranger (2584) . . . C-23
Rankin (800) . . . I-11
Ransom Canyon (1011) . . . J-7
Ratcliff . . . I-25
Ravenna (215) . . . G-20
Rayland . . . B-20
Raymondville (9733) . . . E-34
Raywood . . . J-27
Reagan . . . F-25
Realitos (209) . . . D-33
Red Oak (4301) . . . F-23
Red Rock . . . E-28
Red Springs . . . B-21
Redford (132) . . . E-14
Reese . . . H-23
Refugio (2941) . . . F-31
Reklaw (327) . . . I-24
Reno (2441) . . . H-20
Rhineland . . . A-21
Rhome (551) . . . E-22
Ricardo . . . E-33
Rice (798) . . . G-23
Richards . . . H-26
Richardson (91802) . . . F-22
Richland (291) . . . G-24
Richland Springs (350) . . . C-25
Richmond . . . H-28, I-29
Ridge . . . G-25
Ringgold . . . D-20
Rio Frio . . . A-28
Rio Grande City . . . C-35
Rio Hondo (1942) . . . E-35
Rio Vista (656) . . . E-23
Riomedina . . . C-29
Rios . . . D-33
Rising Star (835) . . . C-24
Riverside (425) . . . I-26
Riviera . . . E-33
Roane . . . G-23
Roans Prairie . . . H-26
Roaring Springs (265) . . . K-6
Robbins . . . G-25
Robert Lee (1171) . . . L-10
Robstown . . . E-32
Roby (673) . . . L-8
Rochelle . . . B-25
Rochester (378) . . . A-21
Rock Island . . . G-28
Rockdale (5439) . . . F-26
Rockland . . . J-25
Rockne . . . E-28
Rockport (7385) . . . F-31
Rocksprings . . . A-28, L-13
Rockwall (17976) . . . G-22
Rockwood . . . B-25
Roganville . . . K-26
Rogers (1117) . . . F-26
Roma (9617) . . . C-35
Romayor . . . J-26
Roosevelt . . . A-27, L-12
Ropesville (517) . . . I-7
Rosanky . . . E-28
Roscoe (1378) . . . K-9
Rosebud (1493) . . . F-25
Rosenberg (24043) . . . H-28
Rosevine . . . K-25
Rosharon . . . I-29
Rosser . . . G-23
Rotan (1611) . . . L-8
Round Rock (61136) . . . E-27
Round Top (77) . . . F-27
Rowena . . . A-24, L-10
Roxton (694) . . . H-21
Royalty . . . H-11
Ruidosa . . . E-13
Rule (698) . . . A-21
Runaway Bay (1104) . . . D-21
Runge (1080) . . . E-30
Rusk (5085) . . . I-24
Rye . . . J-26
Sabinal (1586) . . . B-29
Sabine Pass . . . K-28
Sacul . . . I-24
Sadler (404) . . . F-20
Sagerton . . . A-22, L-7
Saint Hedwig . . . D-29
Saint Jo . . . E-20
Salado (3475) . . . E-26
Salt Flat . . . D-10
Saltillo . . . H-21
Sam Perlita . . . E-34
Samnorwood (39) . . . L-4
San Angelo (88439) . . . L-11
San Antonio (1144646) . . . C-29
San Augustine (2475) . . . K-24
San Benito (23444) . . . E-35
San Carlos (2650) . . . D-35
San Diego (4753) . . . D-32
San Elizario (11046) . . . B-10
San Felipe . . . G-28
San Gabriel . . . F-26
San Isidro (270) . . . D-34
San Juan (26229) . . . D-35
San Manuel . . . D-34
San Marcos (34733) . . . D-28
San Patricio (318) . . . E-32
San Saba (2637) . . . C-25
San Ygnacio . . . B-33
Sand Branch . . . H-45
Sanderson (861) . . . H-13
Sandia (431) . . . E-31
Sandy Point . . . I-29
Sanford (203) . . . J-2
Santa Anna (1081) . . . B-24
Santa Elena . . . D-34
Santa Fe (9548) . . . I-29
Santo . . . D-23
Saragosa . . . F-11
Saratoga . . . J-27
Sargent . . . H-30
Sarita . . . E-33
Sattler . . . D-28
Schertz (18694) . . . D-28
Schroeder . . . F-30
Schulenburg (2699) . . . F-28
Scotland (438) . . . C-21
Scottsville (263) . . . J-22
Scranton . . . B-23
Scurry . . . G-23
Seabrook (9443) . . . I-28
Seadrift (1352) . . . G-31
Seagoville (10823) . . . F-22
Seagraves (2334) . . . H-8
Sealy (5248) . . . G-28
Sebastian (1864) . . . E-35
Sebastopol . . . I-26
Segovia . . . B-27
Seguin (22011) . . . D-28
Seminole (5910) . . . H-8
Seven Points (1145) . . . G-23
Seymour (2908) . . . B-21
Shafter . . . E-14
Shallowater (2086) . . . I-6
Shamrock (2029) . . . L-3
Shannon . . . D-21
Sheerin . . . I-2
Sheffield . . . I-12
Shelby . . . G-27
Shelbyville . . . K-24
Sheldon . . . I-45
Shenandoah (1503) . . . H-27
Shepherd (2029) . . . I-26
Sheridan . . . G-28
Sherman (35082) . . . F-20
Sherwood . . . K-11
Shiner (2070) . . . F-29
Shiro . . . H-26
Sidney . . . C-24
Sierra Blanca (533) . . . D-11
Silsbee (6393) . . . K-27
Silver . . . K-9
Silverton (771) . . . J-5
Simms . . . J-21
Simonton (718) . . . H-28
Simpsonville . . . I-22
Singleton . . . H-26
Sinton (5676) . . . E-31
Sipe Spring . . . C-24
Sisterdale . . . C-28
Sivells Bend . . . E-20
Skellytown . . . J-3
Skidmore (1013) . . . E-31
Slaton (6109) . . . J-7
Slidell . . . E-21
Slocum . . . H-24
Smiley (453) . . . E-29
Smith Point . . . J-28
Smithland . . . J-22
Smithville (3901) . . . F-27
Smyer (480) . . . I-6
Snook (568) . . . G-27
Snyder (10783) . . . K-8
Socorro (27152) . . . B-10
Somerset (1550) . . . C-29
Somerville (1704) . . . G-27
Sonora (2924) . . . K-12
Sour Lake (1667) . . . J-27
South Bend . . . C-22
South Padre Island (2422) . . . F-35
South Plains . . . J-5
Southland . . . J-7
Southmayd (992) . . . F-20
Spade (100) . . . I-6
Spanish Fort . . . E-20
Speaks . . . G-29
Spearman (3021) . . . J-1
Splendora (1275) . . . I-27
Spofford (75) . . . L-15
Spring (2062) . . . I-27
Spring Branch . . . D-28
Springlake (135) . . . I-5
Springtown . . . E-22
Spur (1088) . . . K-7
Spurger . . . K-26
St. Lawrence . . . J-10
Stafford (15681) . . . H-28
Stamford (3636) . . . A-22
Stanton (2556) . . . I-9
Staples . . . E-28
Star . . . D-25
Stephenville (14921) . . . D-23
Sterling City . . . K-10
Stiles . . . J-11
Stinnett (1936) . . . J-2
Stockdale (1398) . . . D-29
Stoneburg . . . D-20
Stoneham . . . H-27
Stonewall (469) . . . C-27
Stowell (1572) . . . J-28
Stratford (1991) . . . I-1
Strawn (739) . . . C-23
Streeter . . . B-26
Streetman (203) . . . G-24
Study Butte . . . F-15
Sudan (1039) . . . H-6
Sugar Hill . . . I-21
Sugar Land (63328) . . . H-28
Sulphur Springs (14551) . . . H-21
Summerfield . . . H-4
Sumner . . . H-20
Sundown (1505) . . . H-7
Sunnyside . . . I-5
Sunray (1950) . . . I-2
Sunset (339) . . . D-21
Surfside Beach (763) . . . I-29
Sutherland Springs . . . D-29
Sweeny (3624) . . . H-29
Sweet Home . . . F-29
Sweetwater (11415) . . . L-9
Swenson . . . L-7
Sylvester . . . L-8
Taft (3396) . . . E-31
Tahoka (2910) . . . I-7
Talco (570) . . . I-21
Talpa . . . A-24
Tankersley . . . K-11
Tarpley . . . B-28
Tarzan . . . I-9
Tatum (1175) . . . J-23
Taylor (13575) . . . E-26
Teague (4557) . . . G-24
Telegraph . . . A-27
Telephone . . . G-20
Telferner . . . F-30
Tell . . . L-5
Temple (54514) . . . E-25
Tenaha (1046) . . . J-24
Tennessee Colony . . . H-24
Tennyson . . . L-10
Terlingua . . . F-15
Terrell (13606) . . . G-22
Texarkana (34782) . . . J-21
Texas City . . . I-29
Texhoma (371) . . . I-1
Texico . . . G-5
Texline (511) . . . H-1
Texola . . . L-3
Texon . . . J-11
Thalia . . . B-20
The Colony (26531) . . . F-22
The Grove . . . E-25
The Woodlands (55649) . . . I-27
Thomaston . . . F-29
Thorndale (1278) . . . F-26
Thrall (710) . . . E-26
Three Rivers (1878) . . . D-31
Throckmorton (905) . . . B-21
Thronton . . . G-25
Tigertown . . . H-20
Tilden . . . C-31
Timpson (1094) . . . J-24
Tioga (754) . . . F-21
Tira (248) . . . H-21
Tivoli . . . F-31
Toco (89) . . . H-20
Tolar (504) . . . D-23
Tolosa . . . G-23
Tomball (9089) . . . H-27
Tool (2275) . . . G-23
Topsey . . . D-25
Tornillo . . . B-10
Tow . . . C-26
Toyah (100) . . . F-11
Toyahvale . . . F-12
Travis . . . F-25
Trawick . . . J-24
Trent . . . A-23, L-9
Trenton (662) . . . G-21
Trickham . . . B-25
Trinidad (1091) . . . G-23
Trinity (2721) . . . I-26
Troup (1949) . . . I-23
Troy (1378) . . . E-25
Truscott . . . A-20
Tucker . . . H-24
Tuleta (292) . . . E-30
Tulia (5117) . . . J-5
Turkey (494) . . . K-5
Turnersville . . . E-24
Turnertown . . . I-23
Turney . . . I-24
Tuscola (714) . . . A-23
Tuxedo . . . A-22, L-8
Twitty . . . L-3
Tye (1158) . . . A-23
Tyler (83650) . . . I-23
Tynan (301) . . . E-31
Umbarger . . . I-4
Uncertain (150) . . . J-22
Unity . . . H-20
Utley . . . E-27
Utopia (241) . . . B-28
Uvalde (14929) . . . A-29
Valentine (187) . . . E-12
Valera . . . B-24
Valley Mills (1123) . . . E-24
Valley Spring . . . C-26
Valley View (737) . . . E-21
Valley Wells . . . B-31
Van (2362) . . . H-23
Van Alstyne (2502) . . . F-21
Van Horn (2435) . . . D-11
Van Vleck (1411) . . . H-29
Vance . . . L-14
Vancourt . . . A-25, L-11
Vanderblit . . . G-30
Vanderpool . . . B-28
Vashti . . . D-21
Vealmoor . . . J-9
Vega (936) . . . H-3
Vera . . . B-21
Verhalen . . . F-11
Vernon (11660) . . . B-20
Victoria (60603) . . . F-30
Vidor (11440) . . . K-27
Vigo Park . . . J-4
Village Mills . . . J-26
Vincent . . . J-9
Violet . . . G-32
Voca . . . B-26
Voss . . . B-24
Votaw . . . J-26
Waco (113726) . . . F-25
Wadsworth . . . H-30
Waelder (947) . . . E-28
Waka . . . K-1
Wake Village (5129) . . . J-21
Wall . . . L-11
Wallis (1172) . . . H-28
Wallisville . . . J-28
Walnut Springs (755) . . . E-24
Wamba . . . J-21
Warda . . . F-27
Warren (343) . . . J-26
Washington . . . G-27
Waskom (2068) . . . K-22
Water Valley . . . K-10
Waxahachie (21426) . . . F-23
Wayside . . . J-4
Weatherford (19000) . . . D-22
Weaver . . . H-21
Webb . . . H-41
Webster (9083) . . . I-28
Weches . . . I-24
Weesatche . . . E-30
Weimar (1981) . . . F-28
Weinert (177) . . . A-21
Weir (591) . . . E-26
Welch . . . I-8
Wellington (2275) . . . L-4
Wellman (203) . . . H-7
Wells (769) . . . I-24
Weslaco (26935) . . . D-35
Wesley . . . G-27
West (2692) . . . F-24
West Columbia (4255) . . . H-29
West Orange (4111) . . . K-27
West Tawakoni (1462) . . . G-22
Westbrook (203) . . . K-9
Westfield . . . I-27
Westhoff . . . E-29
Weston (635) . . . F-21
Westover . . . B-21
Wharton (9237) . . . H-29
Wheeler (1378) . . . L-3
Wheelock . . . G-26
White Deer (1060) . . . J-3
White Oak (5624) . . . I-22
Whiteface (465) . . . H-6
Whiteflat . . . K-5
Whitehouse (5346) . . . I-23
Whitesboro (3760) . . . F-20
Whitewright (1740) . . . G-21
Whitharral . . . I-6
Whitney (1833) . . . E-24
Whitsett . . . D-30
Whitt . . . D-22
Wichita Falls (104197) . . . C-20
Wickett (455) . . . G-10
Wiergate . . . K-25
Wildorado . . . I-3
Wildwood . . . J-26
Willis (3985) . . . H-27
Willow City . . . C-27
Willow Park (2849) . . . E-22
Wills Point (3496) . . . G-22
Wilmeth . . . A-24, L-10
Wilson (532) . . . J-7
Wimberley (3797) . . . D-28
Winchell . . . B-25
Windom (245) . . . G-21
Windthorst (440) . . . C-21
Winfield (499) . . . I-21
Wingate . . . A-24, L-9
Wink (919) . . . G-10
Winnie (2914) . . . J-28
Winnsboro (3584) . . . H-22
Winona (582) . . . I-23
Winters . . . A-24, L-10
Woden . . . J-24
Wolfe City . . . G-21
Wolfforth (2554) . . . I-7
Woodcreek (1274) . . . D-27
Woodlake . . . I-25
Woodland . . . H-20
Woodsboro (1685) . . . F-31
Woodson (296) . . . B-22
Woodville (2415) . . . J-26
Woodward . . . B-30
Wortham (1082) . . . G-24
Wrightsboro . . . E-29
Wylie (15132) . . . F-22, K-31
Yancey . . . B-29
Yantis (321) . . . H-22
Yoakum (5731) . . . F-29
Yorktown . . . E-30
Zapata (4856) . . . B-34
Zavalla (647) . . . J-25
Zephyr . . . C-24

	AMARILLO	AUSTIN	BEAUMONT	CORPUS CHRISTI	DALLAS	EL PASO	FORT WORTH	HOUSTON	LAREDO	LUBBOCK	SAN ANTONIO	WICHITA FALLS
AUSTIN	545	0	254	220	199	585	190	168	242	388	81	317
DALLAS	369	199	295	417	0	649	34	243	440	355	278	141
EL PASO	447	585	849	713	649	0	618	764	603	348	560	597
HOUSTON	615	168	88	222	243	764	273	0	362	588	203	387
SAN ANTONIO	518	81	289	145	278	560	269	203	159	393	0	390

ADJOINING AREA PAGES 108-109

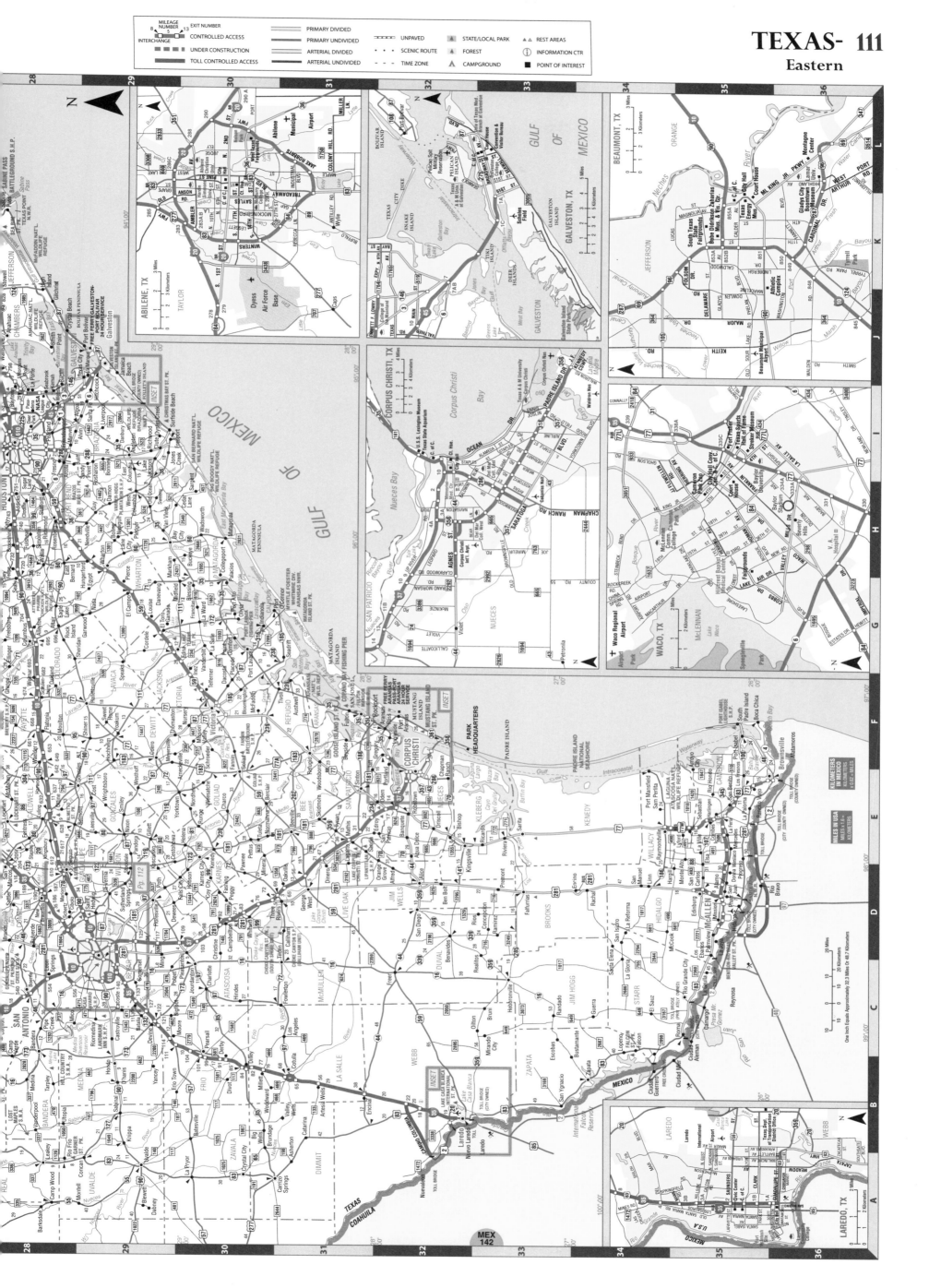

112 TEXAS & UTAH
City & Area Maps

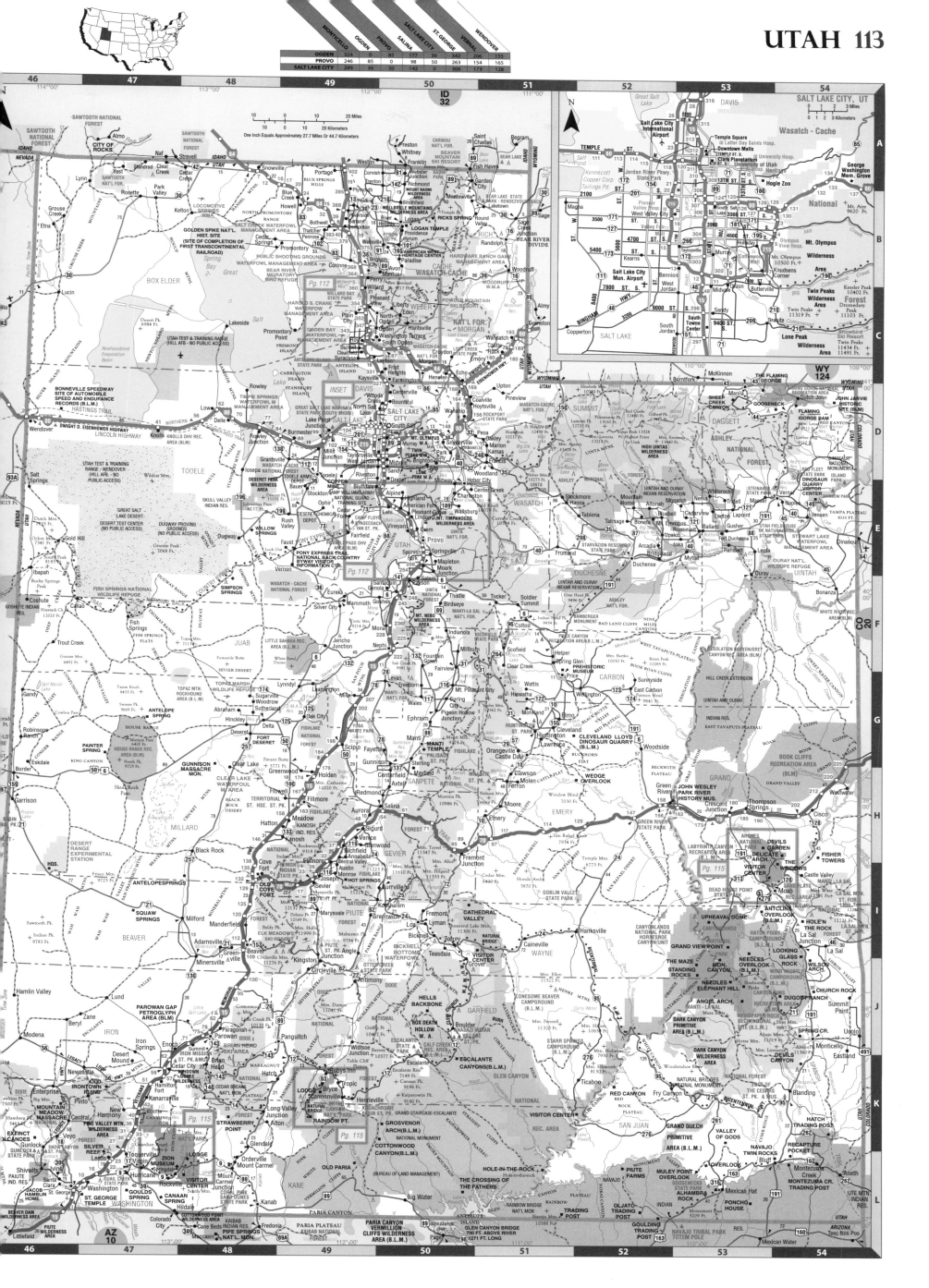

Pg. 112

Pg. 115

	BENNINGTON	BRATTLEBORO	BURLINGTON	MONTPELIER	NEWPORT	RUTLAND	ST. JOHNSBURY	WHITE RIVER JCT.
BURLINGTON	124	153	0	39	76	67	76	92
MONTPELIER	124	117	39	0	64	68	37	56
RUTLAND	56	74	67	68	128	0	106	46

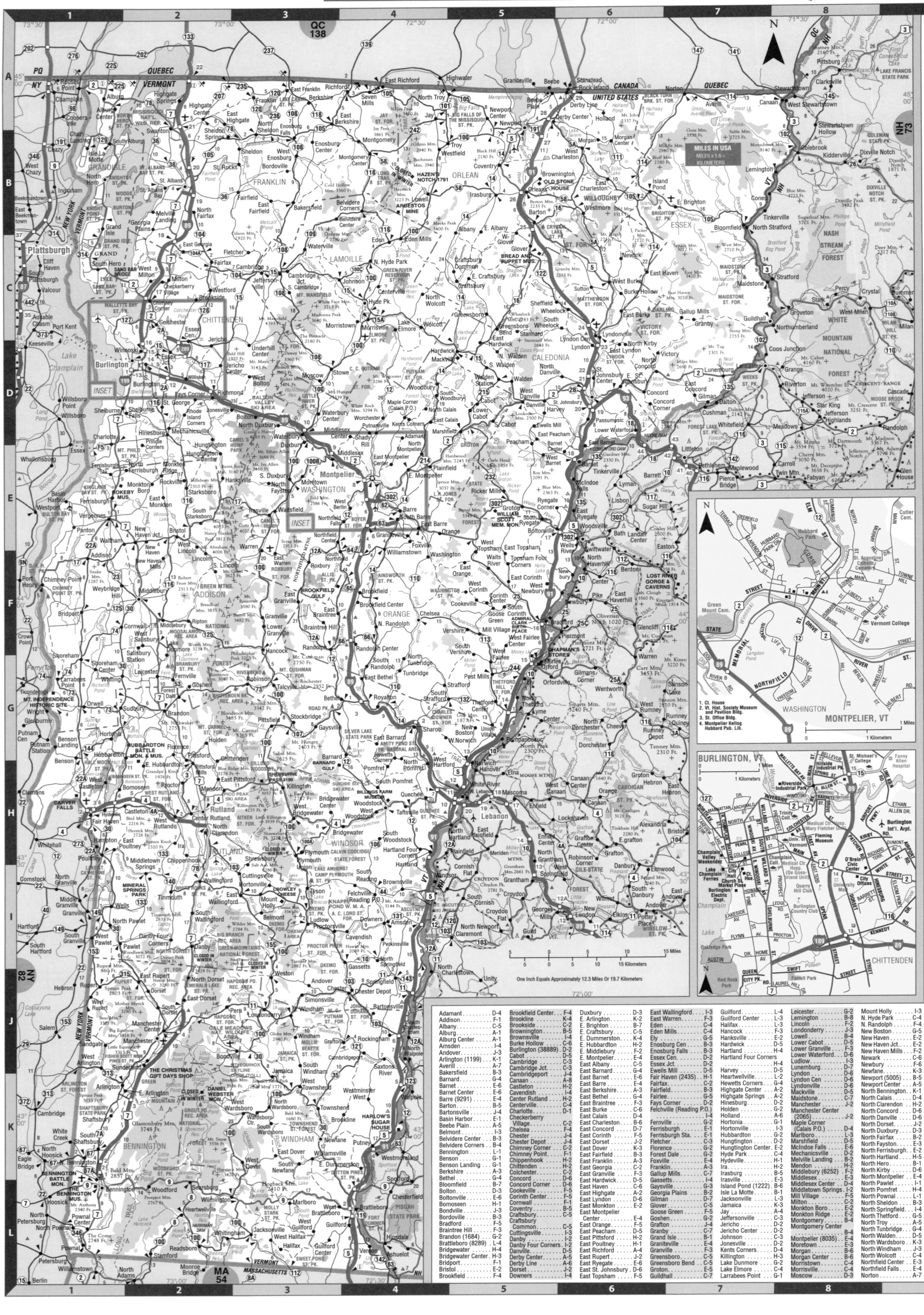
MILES IN USA
MILES x 1.6 = KILOMETERS
MONTPELIER, VT
1. Ct. House
2. Vt. Hist. Society Museum and Pavilion Bldg.
3. St. Office Bldg.
4. Montpelier Kellog Hubbard Pub. Lib.
BURLINGTON, VT
One Inch Equals Approximately 12.3 Miles Or 19.7 Kilometers

Adamant . . . D-4
Addison . . . F-1
Albany . . . C-5
Alburg . . . A-1
Alburg Center . . . A-1
Amsden . . . I-4
Andover . . . J-3
Arlington (1199) . . . K-1
Averill . . . A-7
Bakersfield . . . B-3
Barnard . . . G-4
Barnet . . . E-6
Barnet Center . . . E-6
Barre (9291) . . . E-4
Barton . . . B-5
Bartonsville . . . J-4
Basin Harbor . . . E-1
Beebe Plain . . . A-5
Belmont . . . I-3
Belvidere Center . . . B-3
Belvidere Corners . . . B-4
Bennington . . . L-1
Benson . . . G-1
Benson Landing . . . G-1
Berkshire . . . A-3
Bethel . . . G-4
Bloomfield . . . B-7
Bolton . . . D-3
Boltonville . . . E-6
Bomoseen . . . H-1
Bondville . . . J-3
Bordoville . . . B-3
Bradford . . . F-5
Braintree Hill . . . F-3
Brandon (1684) . . . G-2
Brattleboro (8289) . . . L-4
Bridgewater . . . H-4
Bridgewater Center . . . H-3
Bridport . . . F-1
Bristol . . . E-2
Brookfield . . . F-4
Brookfield Center . . . F-4
Brookline . . . K-4
Brookside . . . C-2
Brownington . . . B-5
Brownsville . . . I-4
Burke Hollow . . . C-6
Burlington (38889) . . . D-2
Cabot . . . D-5
Cambridge . . . C-3
Cambridge Jct. . . . C-3
Cambridgeport . . . J-4
Canaan . . . A-8
Castleton . . . H-2
Cavendish . . . I-4
Center Rutland . . . H-2
Centerville . . . C-4
Charlotte . . . D-1
Checkerberry Village . . . C-2
Chelsea . . . F-4
Chester . . . J-4
Chester Depot . . . J-4
Chimney Corner . . . C-2
Chimney Point . . . F-1
Chippenhook . . . H-2
Chittenden . . . H-2
Colchester . . . C-2
Concord . . . D-6
Concord Corner . . . D-6
Cookeville . . . F-5
Corinth Center . . . F-5
Cornwall . . . F-1
Coventry . . . B-5
Craftsbury . . . C-5
Craftsbury Common . . . C-5
Cuttingsville . . . I-3
Danby . . . I-2
Danby Four Corners . . . I-2
Danville . . . D-5
Derby Center . . . A-5
Derby Line . . . A-6
Dorset . . . J-2
Downers . . . I-4
Duxbury . . . D-3
E. Arlington . . . K-2
E. Brighton . . . B-7
E. Craftsbury . . . C-5
E. Dummerston . . . K-4
E. Hubbardton . . . H-2
E. Middlebury . . . F-2
E. Montpelier . . . E-4
East Albany . . . C-5
East Barnard . . . G-4
East Barnet . . . E-6
East Barre . . . E-4
East Berkshire . . . A-3
East Bethel . . . G-4
East Braintree . . . F-3
East Burke . . . C-6
East Calais . . . D-4
East Charleston . . . B-6
East Concord . . . D-7
East Corinth . . . F-5
East Dorset . . . J-2
East Dover . . . K-3
East Fairfield . . . B-3
East Franklin . . . A-3
East Georgia . . . C-2
East Granville . . . F-3
East Hardwick . . . D-5
East Haven . . . C-6
East Highgate . . . A-2
East Lyndon . . . D-6
East Monkton . . . E-2
East Montpelier Center . . . E-4
East Orange . . . F-5
East Peacham . . . D-5
East Pittsford . . . H-2
East Poultney . . . H-1
East Richford . . . A-4
East Rupert . . . J-2
East Ryegate . . . E-6
East St. Johnsbury . . . D-6
East Topsham . . . F-5
East Wallingford . . . I-3
East Warren . . . F-3
Eden . . . C-4
Eden Mills . . . C-4
Ely . . . G-5
Enosburg Cen . . . B-3
Enosburg Falls . . . B-3
Essex Cen. . . . D-2
Essex Jct. . . . D-2
Ewells Mill . . . D-5
Fair Haven (2435) . . . H-1
Fairfax . . . C-2
Fairfield . . . B-3
Fairlee . . . G-5
Fays Corner . . . D-2
Felchville (Reading P.O.) . . . I-4
Fernville . . . G-2
Ferrisburgh . . . E-1
Ferrisburgh Sta. . . . E-1
Fletcher . . . C-3
Florence . . . G-2
Forest Dale . . . G-2
Foxville . . . E-4
Franklin . . . A-3
Gallup Mills . . . C-7
Gassetts . . . I-4
Gaysville . . . G-3
Georgia Plains . . . B-2
Gilman . . . D-7
Glover . . . C-5
Goose Green . . . F-5
Goshen . . . G-2
Grafton . . . J-4
Granby . . . C-7
Grand Isle . . . B-1
Graniteville . . . E-4
Granville . . . F-3
Greensboro . . . C-5
Greensboro Bend . . . C-5
Groton . . . E-5
Guildhall . . . C-7
Guilford . . . L-4
Guilford Center . . . L-3
Halifax . . . L-3
Hancock . . . F-3
Hanksville . . . E-2
Hardwick . . . D-5
Hartland . . . H-4
Hartland Four Corners . . . H-4
Harvey . . . D-5
Heartwellville . . . L-2
Hewetts Corners . . . G-4
Highgate Center . . . A-2
Highgate Springs . . . A-2
Hinesburg . . . D-2
Holden . . . G-2
Holland . . . A-6
Hortonia . . . G-1
Hortonville . . . I-3
Hubbardton . . . G-2
Hungtington . . . D-2
Hungtington Center . . . E-2
Hyde Park . . . C-4
Hydeville . . . H-1
Ira . . . H-2
Irasburg . . . B-5
Irasville . . . E-3
Island Pond (1222) . . . B-6
Isle La Motte . . . B-1
Jacksonville . . . L-3
Jamaica . . . K-3
Jay . . . A-4
Jeffersonville . . . C-3
Jericho . . . D-2
Jericho Center . . . D-2
Johnson . . . C-3
Jonesville . . . D-2
Kents Corners . . . D-4
Killington . . . H-3
Lake Dunmore . . . G-2
Lake Elmore . . . C-4
Larrabees Point . . . G-1
Leicester . . . G-2
Lemington . . . B-8
Lincoln . . . F-2
Londonderry . . . J-3
Lowell . . . B-4
Lower Cabot . . . D-5
Lower Granville . . . F-3
Lower Waterford . . . D-6
Ludlow . . . I-3
Lunemburg . . . D-7
Lyndon . . . D-6
Lyndon Cen . . . D-6
Lyndonville . . . D-6
Mackville . . . D-5
Maidstone . . . C-7
Manchester . . . J-2
Manchester Center (2065) . . . J-2
Maple Corner (Calais P.O.) . . . D-4
Marlboro . . . L-3
Marshfield . . . D-5
McIndoe Falls . . . E-6
Mechanicsville . . . D-2
Melville Landing . . . B-2
Mendon . . . H-2
Middlebury (6252) . . . F-2
Middlesex . . . E-3
Middlesex Center . . . D-4
Middletown Springs . . . I-2
Mill Village . . . F-5
Milton . . . C-2
Monkton Boro . . . E-2
Monkton Ridge . . . E-2
Montgomery . . . B-4
Montgomery Center . . . B-4
Montpelier (8035) . . . E-4
Moretown . . . E-3
Morgan . . . B-6
Morgan Center . . . B-6
Morristown . . . C-4
Morrisville . . . C-4
Moscow . . . D-3
Mount Holly . . . I-3
N. Hyde Park . . . C-4
N. Randolph . . . F-4
New Boston . . . G-5
New Haven . . . E-2
New Haven Jct. . . . E-2
New Haven Mills . . . F-2
Newark . . . C-6
Newbury . . . F-6
Newfane . . . K-3
Newport (5005) . . . B-5
Newport Center . . . A-5
North Bennington . . . K-1
North Calais . . . D-4
North Clarendon . . . H-2
North Concord . . . D-6
North Danville . . . D-6
North Dorset . . . J-2
North Duxbury . . . D-3
North Fairfax . . . B-2
North Fayston . . . E-3
North Ferrisburgh . . . E-2
North Hartland . . . H-5
North Hero . . . B-1
North Kirby . . . D-6
North Montpelier . . . E-4
North Pawlet . . . I-1
North Pomfret . . . H-4
North Pownal . . . L-1
North Sheldon . . . B-3
North Springfield . . . I-4
North Thetford . . . G-5
North Troy . . . A-5
North Tunbridge . . . G-4
North Walden . . . D-5
North Wardsboro . . . K-3
North Windham . . . J-3
North Wolcott . . . C-4
Northfield Center . . . E-3
Northfield Falls . . . E-4
Norton . . . A-7
Norwich
Orange
Orleans
Orwell
Panton
Passumpsic
Pawlet
Peacham
Perkinsville
Peru
Pittsfield
Pittsford
Pittsford Mills
Plainfield
Plymouth
Plymouth Union
Pomfret
Pompanoosuc
Post Mills
Poultney
Pownal
Pownal Center
Prindle Corners
Proctor
Proctorsville
Putnamville
Putney
Quechee
Randolph
Randolph Center
Readsboro
Rhode Island Corners
Richford
Richmond
Ricker Mills
Ripton
Robinson
Rockingham
Rockville
Roxbury
Royalton
Rupert
Rutland (17292)
Ryegate Corner
S. Burlington
Salisbury Station
Sandgate
Saxtons River
Searsburg
Seven Mills
Shady Rill
Shaftsbury
Sharon
Sheffield
Shelburne
Shelburne Falls
Sheldon
Sheldon Springs
Shoreham
Shoreham Cente
Shrewsbury
Simonsville
South Alburg
South Barre
South Cabot
South Cambridge
South Corinth
South Dorset
South Duxbury
South Hero
South Lincoln
South Newbury
South Newfane
South Northfield
South Pomfret
South Randolph
South Reading
South Ryegate
South Shaftsbury (772)
South Starksboro
South Strafford
South Vershire
South Walden
South Wallingfor
South Wardsboro
South Wheelock
South Windham
South Woodbury
South Woodstoc
Springfield
St. Albans
St. Albans Bay
St. George
St. Johnsbury
St. Johnsbury Center
St. Rocks
Stamford
Stannard
Starksboro
Stockbridge
Stowe
Strafford
Sudbury
Sunderland
Sutton
Swanton
Taftsville
Talcville
Thetford Center
Tinmouth
Topsham Four Corners
Townshend
Troy
Tunbridge
Tyson
Underhill Center
Union Village
Vergennes
Vernon
Vershire
Victory
W. Glover
W. Norwich
Waits River
Waitsfield
Walden
Walden Station
Wallingford
Waltham
Wardsboro Cent
Warren
Washington
Waterbury
Waterbury Cente
Waterville
Wells
Wells River
West Arlington
West Barnet
West Berlin
West Bolton
West Brattleboro (3222)
West Bridgewate
West Burke
West Castleton
West Charleston
West Corinth
West Danville
West Dover
West Enosburg
West Fairlee
West Fairlee Cen
West Guilford
West Halifax
West Hartford
West Lincoln
West Milton
West Newbury
West Pawlet
West Rupert
West Rutland
West Salisbury
West Topsham
West Townshend
West Wardsboro
West Woodstock
Westfield
Westford
Westminster We
Westmore
Weston
Weybridge Hill
Wheelock
White River
Whiting
Whitingham
Williamstown
Williamsville
Williston
Wilmington
Windham
Windsor
Winooski (6651) . . . H-
Wolcott
Woodbury
Woodford
Woodstock
Worchester

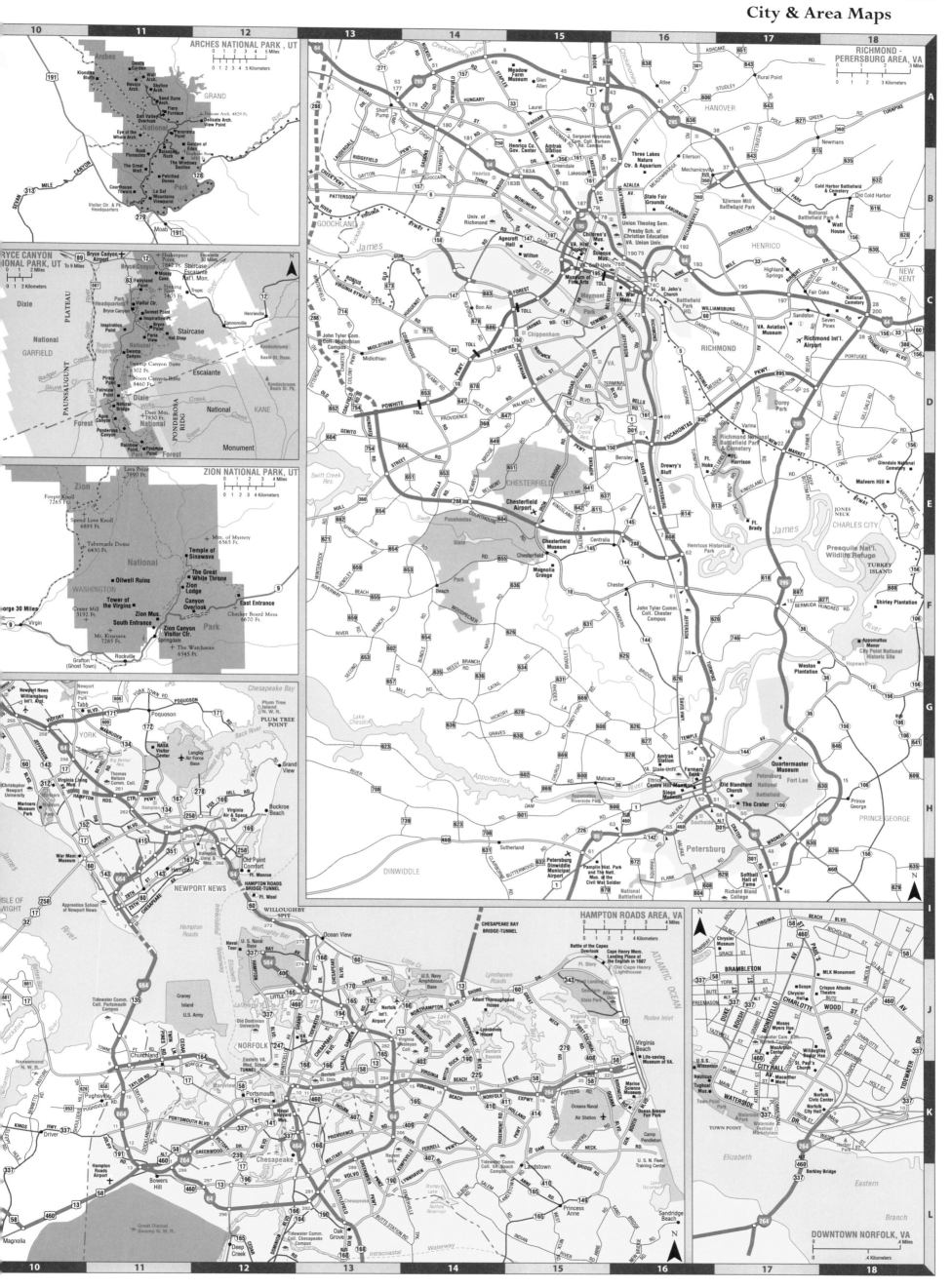

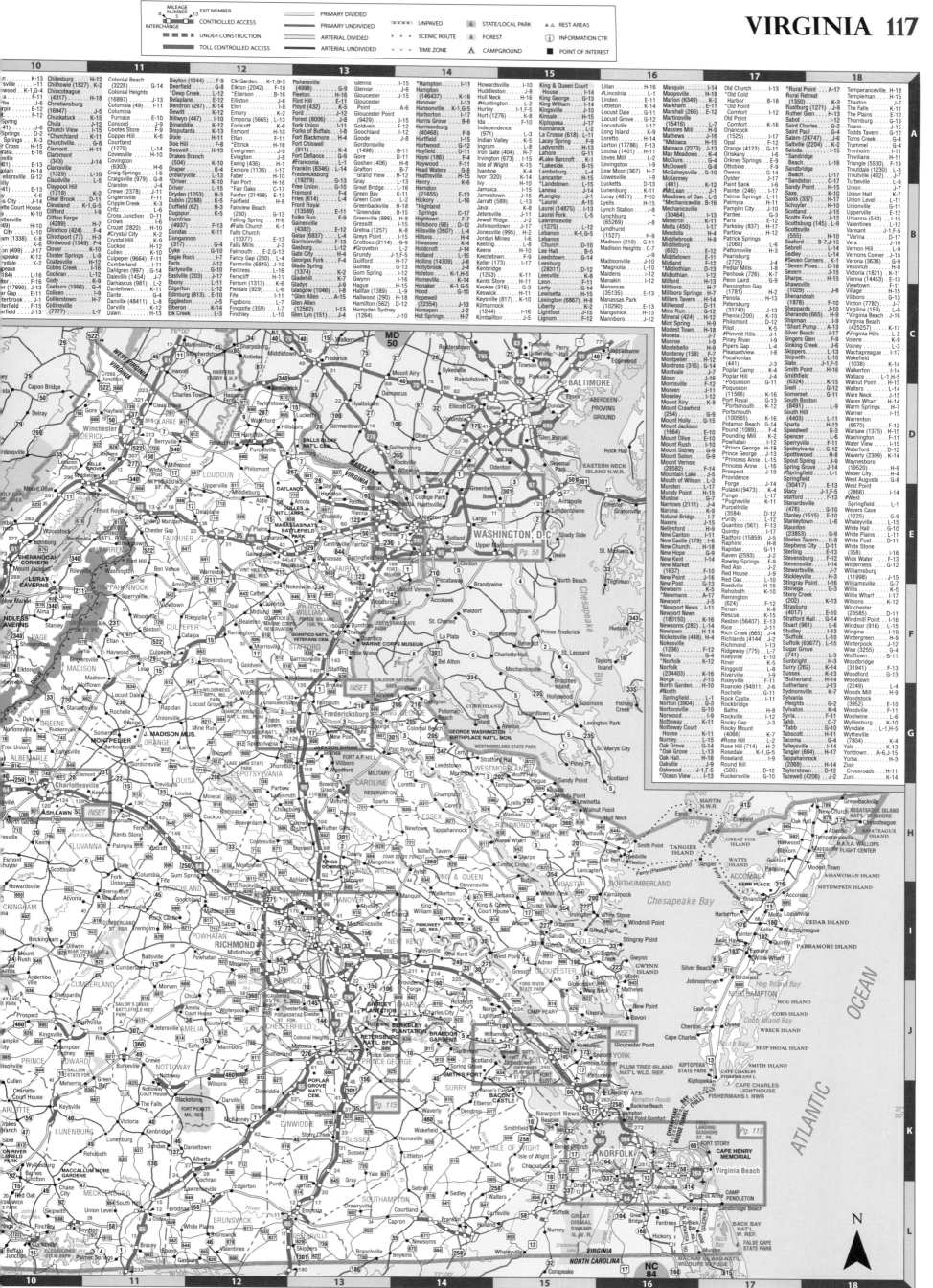

	ABERDEEN	BELLINGHAM	ELLENSBURG	KELSO	OLYMPIA	OMAK	PASCO	PORT ANGELES	SEATTLE	SPOKANE	TACOMA	YAKIMA
OLYMPIA	48	151	145	67	0	277	264	118	62	320	32	181
SEATTLE	110	90	104	127	62	235	223	82	0	279	35	140
SPOKANE	369	364	178	386	320	144	138	362	279	0	293	210
TACOMA	80	124	118	96	32	250	237	109	35	293	0	154
YAKIMA	229	224	38	170	181	200	86	222	140	210	154	0

Towns are keyed to maps on pages 118 thru 120

Arlington (11713) E-9	Blyn (162) F-7	Chinook (457) J-5	Colville (4988) D-16	Cumberland H-9	Diamond Lake F-18	Edison (133) D-8	Federal Way (83259) H-3
Arctic I-6	Boistfort J-7	Cinebar J-8	Colville Indian Agency	Cunningham I-15	Disautel E-14	Edmonds F-2,G-1
Ashford (267) I-9	Bonney Lake (9687) H-8	Clallam Bay E-5	. . . . F-14	Curlew C-15	Discovery Bay F-7	Edwall G-16
Acme (263) D-9	Bossburg D-16	Clarkston (7337) J-18	Conconully (185) D-13	Curtis J-7	Dixie (220) I-17	Elbe (21) I-8	Ferry C-15
Addy E-17	Bothell (30150) F-2	Clayton F-17	Concrete (790) D-9	Cusick (212) E-18	Dockton H-2	Eldon G-7	Fife H-3
Adna I-7	Boundary C-17	Cle Elum H-11	Connell (2956) J-15	Custer (299) C-8	Dodge J-17	Electric City F-14	Fircrest H-2
Agnew E-7	Bow D-8	Clear Lake (942) E-9	Conway D-8	Cowiche I-11	Doe Bay D-7	Elk (3120) E-18	Ford F-17
Airway Heights (4500) G-17	Boyds D-16	Clearview F-4	Cook L-9	Coyle G-7	Doty J-7	Elk (3120) E-18	Forks (3120) F-5
Albion (616) I-18	Bainbridge Island G-1,G-8,H-1	Clearwater G-5	Copalis Beach (489) H-5	Cusick (212) E-18	Douglas G-13	Ellisforde D-14	Fort Steilacoom . . . .
Alder I-8	Bangor G-7	Cliffdell I-11	Copalis Crossing H-5	Dalkena E-18	Dryden G-12	Elma (3049) H-6	Freeland (1313) F-3
Alderdale L-13	Barring (233) F-10	Clinton (868) F-3	Copiah (242)	Danville C-15	Du Pont H-2	Elmer City E-7	Freeman G-18
Alderton L-3	Basin City J-14	Clipper D-9	Cosmopolis (1595) H-6	Darrington (1136) D-10	Dungeness E-7	Eltopia J-14	Friday Harbor (1989) D-7
Algar (89) D-8	Battle Ground L-8	Cloverland J-18	Cougar K-8	Davenport (1730) G-16	Dusty J-17	Endicott (621) I-17	Fruitland E-17
Allen D-8	Batum H-15	Clyde J-15	Coulee City G-14	Dayton H-7,J-16	Duvall (4616) F-3	Entiat (957) G-12	Galvin I-7
Allyn G-7	Bay Center I-6	Colbert F-17	Coulee Dam (1044) F-14	Deer Meadows F-16	Eatonville (2012) H-8		Garfield (641) I-18
Almira (302) G-15	Bay City H-5	Colbert F-17	Coupeville (1723) E-8	Deer Harbor D-7			Galvin I-7
Aloha H-5	Beaux Arts H-2	Coles Corner G-11	Covington H-3	Deer Park (3017) F-17			Gardiner E-7
Altoona J-6	Beaver (Tyree) E-5	Colfax (2844) I-17	Cowiche I-11	Deming (210) D-9			Gig Harbor (6465) H-2
Amanda Park G-5	Belfair G-7	College Place (7818) K-16	Creston (232) G-15	Desert Aire (1124) I-13			Gilmer E-3
Amboy (2085) K-8	Bellevue G-9,H-3	Colton (386) J-18	Crystal Mountain I-10	Diablo D-11			Glacier (90) C-9
Anacortes (14557) D-8	Bellingham (67171) D-8						Glenoma J-9
Antantum A-1	Belmont H-18						Glenwood K-10
Anatone K-18	Beverly I-13						Gold Bar (2014) F-10
Antantum J-11	Bickleton (113) K-12						Goldendale (3760) L-11
Appleton L-10	Big Lake (1153) D-9						Goose Prairie I-10
Arden E-16	Birch Bay C-8						Graham (8739) H-8
Ardenvoir G-12	Black Diamond (4961) H-9						
Ariel K-8	Blaine (3770) H-9						
	Carlisle H-5						
	Carlton E-12						

Legend

- MILEAGE NUMBER
- EXIT NUMBER
- INTERCHANGE
- CONTROLLED ACCESS
- UNDER CONSTRUCTION
- TOLL CONTROLLED ACCESS
- PRIMARY DIVIDED
- PRIMARY UNDIVIDED
- ARTERIAL DIVIDED
- ARTERIAL UNDIVIDED
- UNPAVED
- SCENIC ROUTE
- TIME ZONE
- STATE/LOCAL PARK
- FOREST
- CAMPGROUND
- REST AREAS
- INFORMATION CTR
- POINT OF INTEREST

Place Index

Place	Grid
Hoquiam (9097)	H-5
Humptulips (216)	H-5
Hunts Point	I-8
Husum	F-16
Ilwaco (950)	J-5
Inchelium (389)	E-17
Index (157)	F-10
Irby	H-14
Irondale	F-8
Issaquah (11212)	G-9
Joyce	E-6
Kahlotus (214)	I-15
Kalaloch	G-5
Kalama (1783)	K-7
Kamilche	H-7
Kapowsin	I-8
Keller	F-15
Kelso (11895)	K-7
Kendall (158)	C-9
Kennewick (54693)	J-14
Kent (79524)	G-8
Kettle Falls	D-16
Key Center	G-7
Keyport	G-8
Keystone	F-7
Kid Valley	J-8
Kingston (1611)	F-8
Kiona	K-14
Kirkland	G-8
Kittitas (1105)	I-12
Klickitat (417)	I-17
Klipsan Beach	J-5
Krupp (Marlin P.O.)	H-14
La Center (1654)	K-7
La Conner (761)	E-8
La Crosse (380)	I-16
La Grand	F-4
La Push	F-4
Lacey (31226)	H-7
Lake Forest Park	F-3
Lake Stevens	F-8
Lakebay	H-7
Lakeview Park	H-14
Lamona	H-15
Lamont (106)	H-16
Lancaster	I-17
Langley (959)	F-8
Latah (151)	H-18
Laurel	C-8
Laurier	C-16
Leavenworth (2074)	G-11
Lebam (176)	J-6
Lexington	K-7
Liberty	H-11
Lilliwaup	G-7
Lincoln	F-16
Littell	I-7
Littlerock	H-7
Long Beach (1283)	J-5
Longbranch	H-7
Longmire	I-9
Longview (34660)	K-7
Loomis	D-13
Loon Lake	E-17
Lopez	D-7
Lowden	K-15
Lucerne	E-12
Lummi Island	D-8
Lyle (530)	L-16
Lyman (309)	E-8
Lynden (9020)	C-8
Lynnwood	F-8
Manchester	H-1
Mansfield (319)	F-13
Manson	F-12
Maple Beach	C-7
Maple Falls (277)	C-9
Marblemount (251)	D-10
Marcus (117)	D-16
Marietta	D-8
Markham (95)	I-5
Marshall	H-17
Marysville (25315)	F-8
Matlock	H-7
Mattawa (2609)	I-13
Maytown	H-7
Mazama	D-12
McCleary (1454)	H-6
McKenna	H-8
McMurry	E-8
Medical Lake	G-17
Medina	G-8
Meadow Glade	L-8
Mercer Island (22036)	G-8
Mesa (425)	J-14
Metaline (162)	D-17
Metaline Falls (223)	D-17
Methow	F-13
Mica	H-18
Midland	L-2
Miles	F-16
Millwood (1649)	G-18
Mineral	I-8
Mineral Springs	H-11
Moclips (615)	H-5
Mohler	H-14
Molson	C-14
Monitor	G-11
Monroe (13795)	F-9
Monse	E-13
Montesano (3312)	H-6
Morton (1045)	I-8
Moses Lake (14953)	H-14
Mossyrock (486)	J-8
Mount Vernon (26232)	E-8
Moxee (821)	J-12
Mukilteo (18019)	F-8
Murdock	L-16
Naches (643)	I-11
Nahcotta	J-5
Napavine (1361)	J-7
Naselle (377)	J-5
Neah Bay (794)	E-4
Neilton (345)	G-5
Nemah	J-5
Nespelem (212)	E-14
Newhalem	D-10
Newport (1921)	E-18
Nighthawk	C-13
Nisqually	H-8
North Bend (4746)	G-9
North Bonneville (593)	L-9
North Cove	I-5
Northport (336)	C-17
Nugents Corner	C-9
Oak Harbor (19795)	E-8
Oakesdale (420)	H-18
Ocean City	H-5
Ocean Park (1459)	J-5
Ocean Shores (3836)	H-5
Odessa (957)	H-15
Ohanapecosh	I-10
Okanogan (2484)	E-13
Olalla	J-1
Olga	D-7
Olympia (42514)	H-7
Omak (4721)	E-13
Opportunity (25065)	G-18
Orcas	D-7
Orient	D-16
Orin	E-16
Orondo	G-12
Oroville (1653)	C-14
Orting (3760)	H-8
Oso (246)	E-9
Outlook (5847)	J-13
Oyehut	H-5
Oysterville	J-5
Pacific Beach	H-5
Packwood	J-9
Palisades	G-13
Palouse (1011)	H-18
Paradise	I-9
Park Rapids	D-17
Parker	J-12
Pasco (32066)	K-14
Pataha	J-17
Pateros (643)	E-13
Paterson	K-13
Pe Ell (657)	J-6
Piedmont	E-6
Plain	G-11
Plaza	H-17
Plymouth	K-14
Point Roberts	C-7
Pomeroy (1517)	J-17
Port Angeles (18397)	E-6
Port Gamble	F-8
Port Ludlow (1968)	F-8
Port Orchard (7693)	G-8
Port Townsend	E-8
Portage	J-1
Porter	H-6
Porcupine Bay	F-16
Potlatch	G-7
Poulsbo (6813)	F-8
Prescott (351)	K-16
Prosser (4838)	K-14
Pullman (24675)	I-18
Puyallup (33011)	H-8
Queets	G-5
Quilcene (591)	F-7
Quinault	G-5
Quincy (5044)	H-13
Rainier (1492)	I-8
Ralston	I-15
Randle	J-9
Raymond (2975)	I-6
Reardan (608)	G-16
Redmond	G-4, G-9
Redondo	K-2
Renton (50052)	G-8
Republic (954)	D-15
Rice	E-16
Richland (38708)	K-14
Ridgefield (2147)	L-7
Rimrock	I-10
Ritzville (1736)	H-15
Riverside (348)	E-14
Riverton Heights	J-2
Robe	F-9
Roche Harbor	D-7
Rochester (1829)	I-7
Rock Island (863)	H-12
Rockford (413)	G-18
Rockport (102)	E-10
Ronald (265)	H-11
Roosevelt (79)	L-12
Rosalia (648)	H-17
Rosburg	J-6
Roy (260)	H-8
Royal City	I-13
Ruston	J-1
Ryderwood	J-7
S. Wenatchee	H-7
Salkum	J-8
Sappho	E-5
Satus (746)	K-12
Sawyer	J-12
Schawana	I-13
Sea Tac	G-8, J-2
Seabeck	G-7
Seattle	J-5
Seaview	J-5
Sedro Woolley	D-9
Sekiu	E-5
Selah (6310)	J-12
Sequim (4334)	E-7
Seven Bays	F-16
Sheffler	J-15
Shelton (8442)	H-7
Shoreline	F-2
Silver Creek	J-8
Silverdale (15816)	G-8
Silverton	F-10
Skamania	L-9
Skamokawa	J-6
Skykomish (214)	G-10
Snohomish (8494)	F-9
Snoqualmie (1631)	G-9
Snoqualmie Pass	G-10
Soap Lake (1733)	H-14
South Bend (1807)	I-5
South Cle Elum	H-11
South Colby	I-1
Southworth	G-8, I-1
Spangle (240)	G-17
Spokane	G-18
Sprague (490)	H-16
Springdale (283)	F-17
Stanwood (3923)	E-8
Starbuck (130)	J-16
Startup (817)	F-9
Stehekin	E-11
Steilacoom (6049)	H-8
Stella	K-7
Steptoe	H-17
Stevenson	L-9
Sultan (3344)	F-9
Sumas (969)	C-9
Summit	L-2
Sumner	H-8
Sunnyside (13905)	J-12
Sunrise	I-9
Tahlequah	K-1
Taholah (824)	G-5
Tahuya	G-7
Tampico	J-11
Teanaway	H-11
Tekoa (826)	H-18
Tenino (1447)	I-7
Thornton	H-17
Thorp (273)	H-11
Thrashers Corner	F-3
Tieton (1154)	I-11
Tiger	D-17
Tokeland (194)	I-5
Toledo (653)	J-8
Tonasket (994)	D-14
Tono	I-7
Toppenish (8946)	J-12
Touchet (396)	K-15
Toutle	J-7
Trout Lake	K-10
Tukwila	I-3
Tumtum	F-17
Tumwater	H-7
Twisp (938)	E-12
Tyler	G-17
Union (35)	G-7
Union Gap	E-20, J-12
Uniontown	J-18
Usk	E-18
Utsalady	E-8
Vader (590)	J-7
Valley	E-17
Van Horn	D-10
Van Zandt	D-9
Vancouver (70)	L-8
Vantage	I-12
Vashon	G-8, I-1
Vashon Center	J-1
Verlot (170)	F-9
Wahkiacus	I-17
Wahluke	I-12
Waitsburg	K-16
Walla Walla (29686)	K-16
Wallula (197)	K-15
Wapato (4582)	J-12
Warden (2544)	I-14
Washougal (8595)	L-8
Washtucna (260)	I-16
Waterville	G-12
Wauconda	D-14
Waukon	G-17
Waverly (121)	H-18
Wellpinit	F-16
Wenatchee (27856)	G-11
West Richland	J-14
Westport (2137)	I-5
Wheeler	H-14
White Center	I-2
White Pass	J-10
White Salmon (2193)	L-10
White Swan (3033)	J-11
Wickersham	D-9
Wilbur (914)	G-15
Wiley City	J-11
Willapa (194)	I-6
Willard	L-7
Wilson Creek (227)	G-14
Winchester	H-13
Winlock (1166)	J-7
Winthrop (349)	E-12
Wishram (324)	L-11
Withrow	G-13
Woodinville	F-4
Woodland (3780)	K-7
Woodway	F-2
Yacolt (1055)	L-8
Yakima (71845)	J-12
Yale	K-8
Yarrow Point	H-3
Yelm (3289)	H-8
Zillah (2198)	J-12

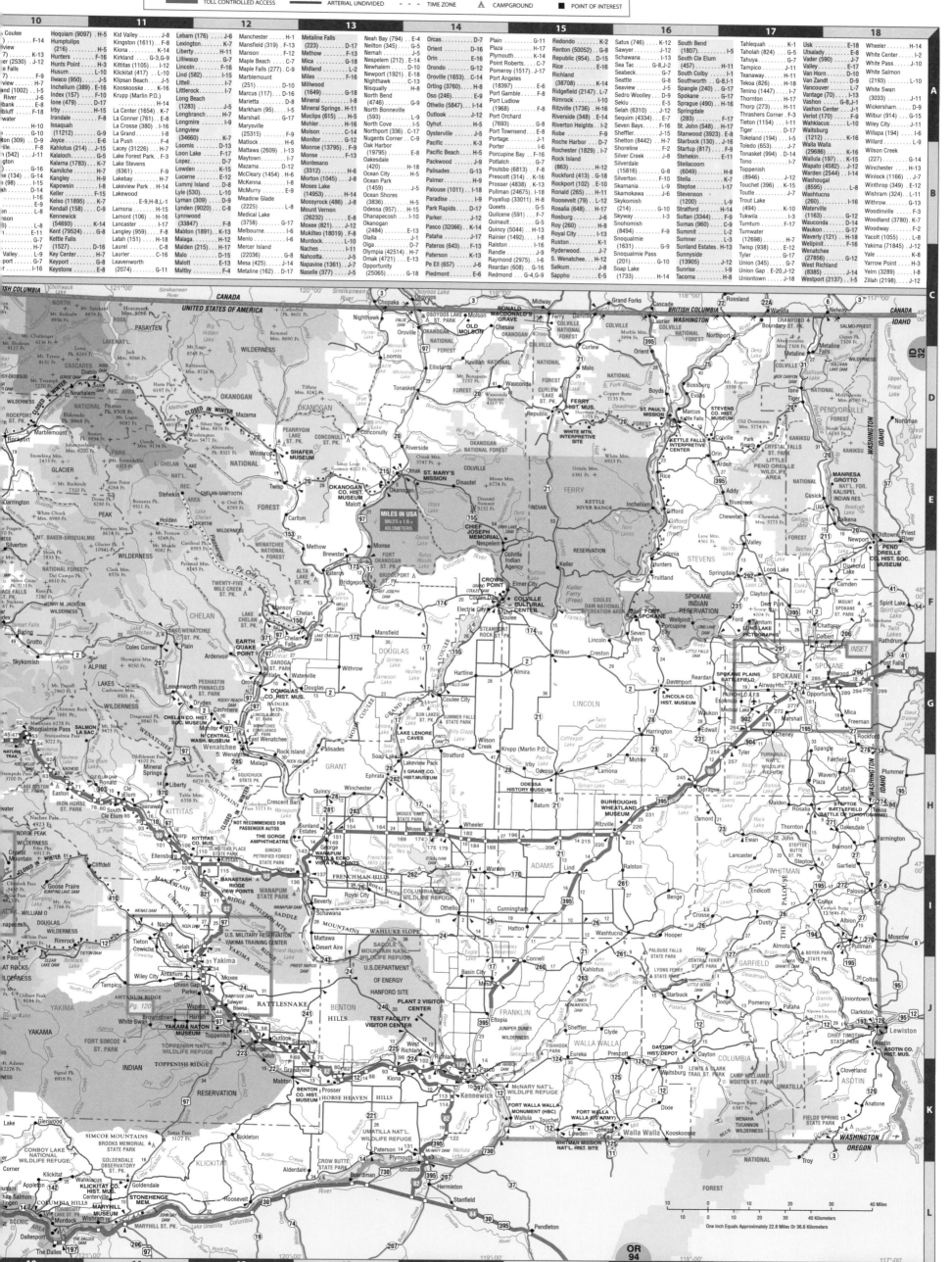

WEST VIRGINIA & WASHINGTON
City & Area Maps

	CHARLESTON	BECKLEY	CLARKSBURG	FAIRMONT	HUNTINGTON	MORGANTOWN	PARKERSBURG	SUTTON	WHEELING	WHITE SULPHUR SPRINGS
CHARLESTON	62	0	125	142	52	158	70	182	125
HUNTINGTON	113	52	174	191	0	208	93	117	216	176
PARKERSBURG	135	78	74	93	112	0	103	201
WHEELING	243	182	85	71	216	71	106	160	0	264

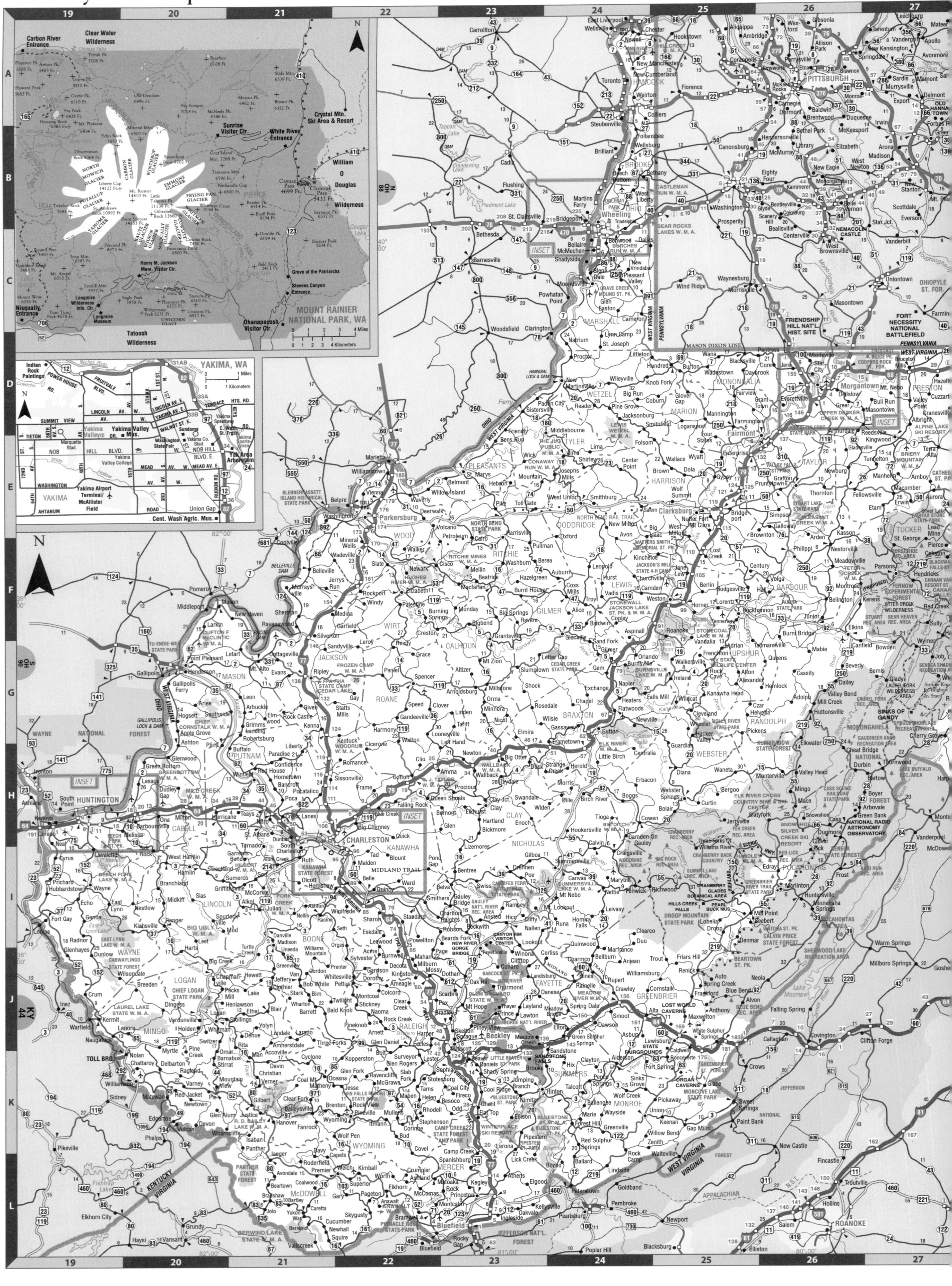

MOUNT RAINIER NATIONAL PARK, WA

YAKIMA, WA

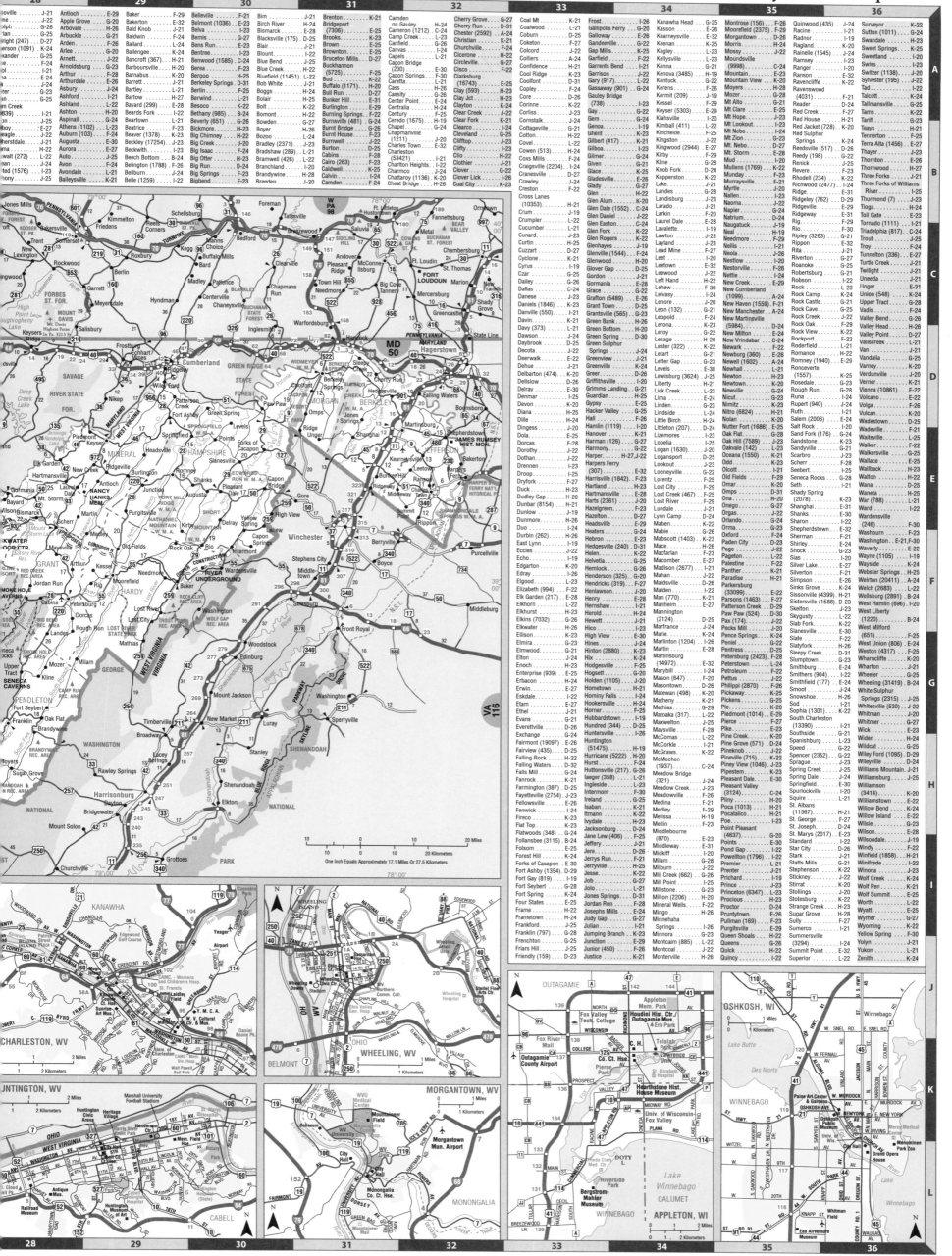

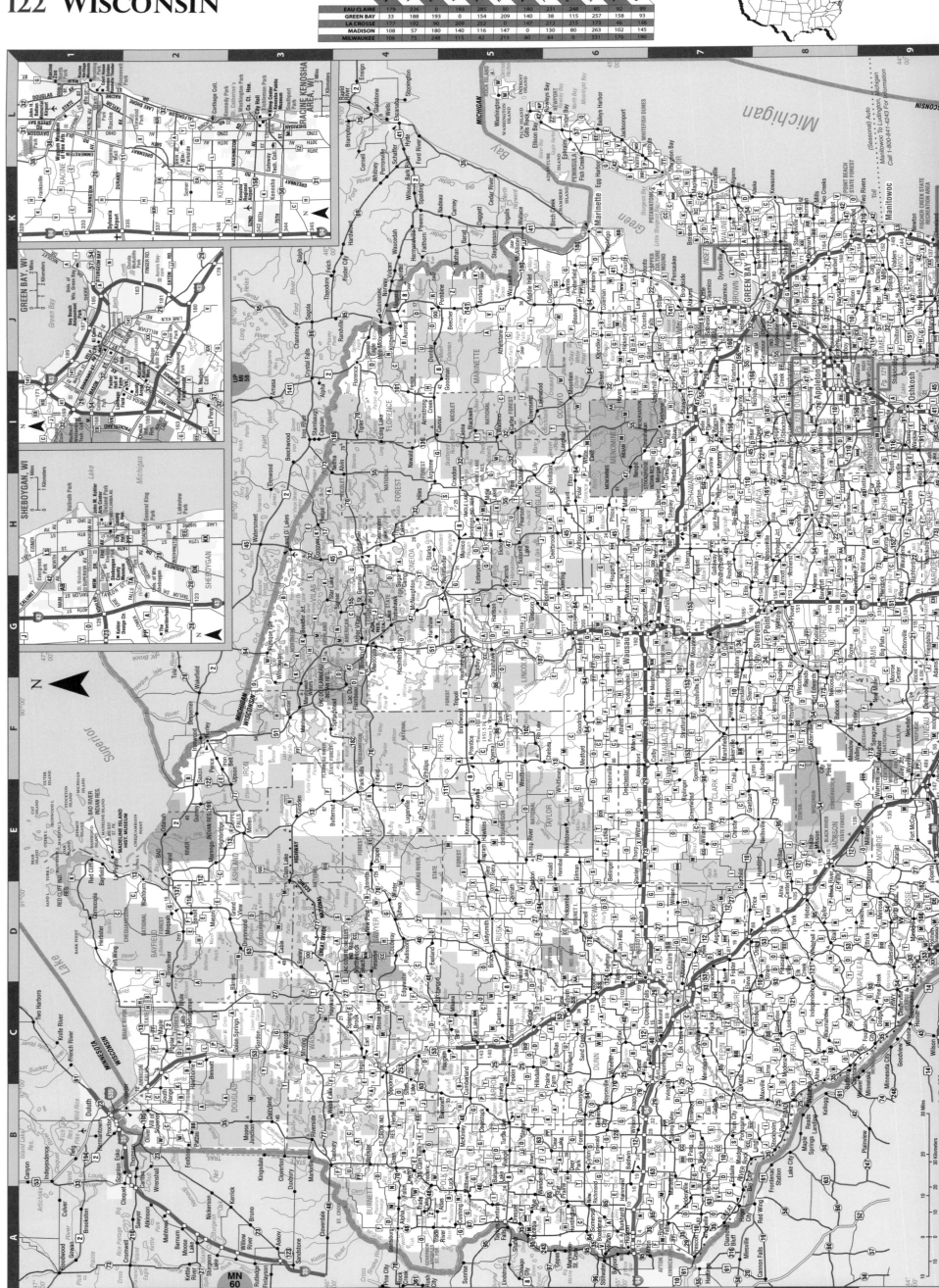

	APPLETON	BELOIT	EAU CLAIRE	GREEN BAY	LA CROSSE	MADISON	MANITOWOC	MILWAUKEE	SPOONER	TOMAH	WAUSAU
EAU CLAIRE	179	226	0	193	285	90	180	231	248	85	82	99
GREEN BAY	33	188	193	0	154	209	140	38	115	257	158	93
LA CROSSE	177	192	90	209	252	0	147	212	215	173	45	148
MADISON	108	57	180	140	116	147	0	130	80	263	102	145
MILWAUKEE	106	75	248	115	42	215	80	84	0	331	170	190

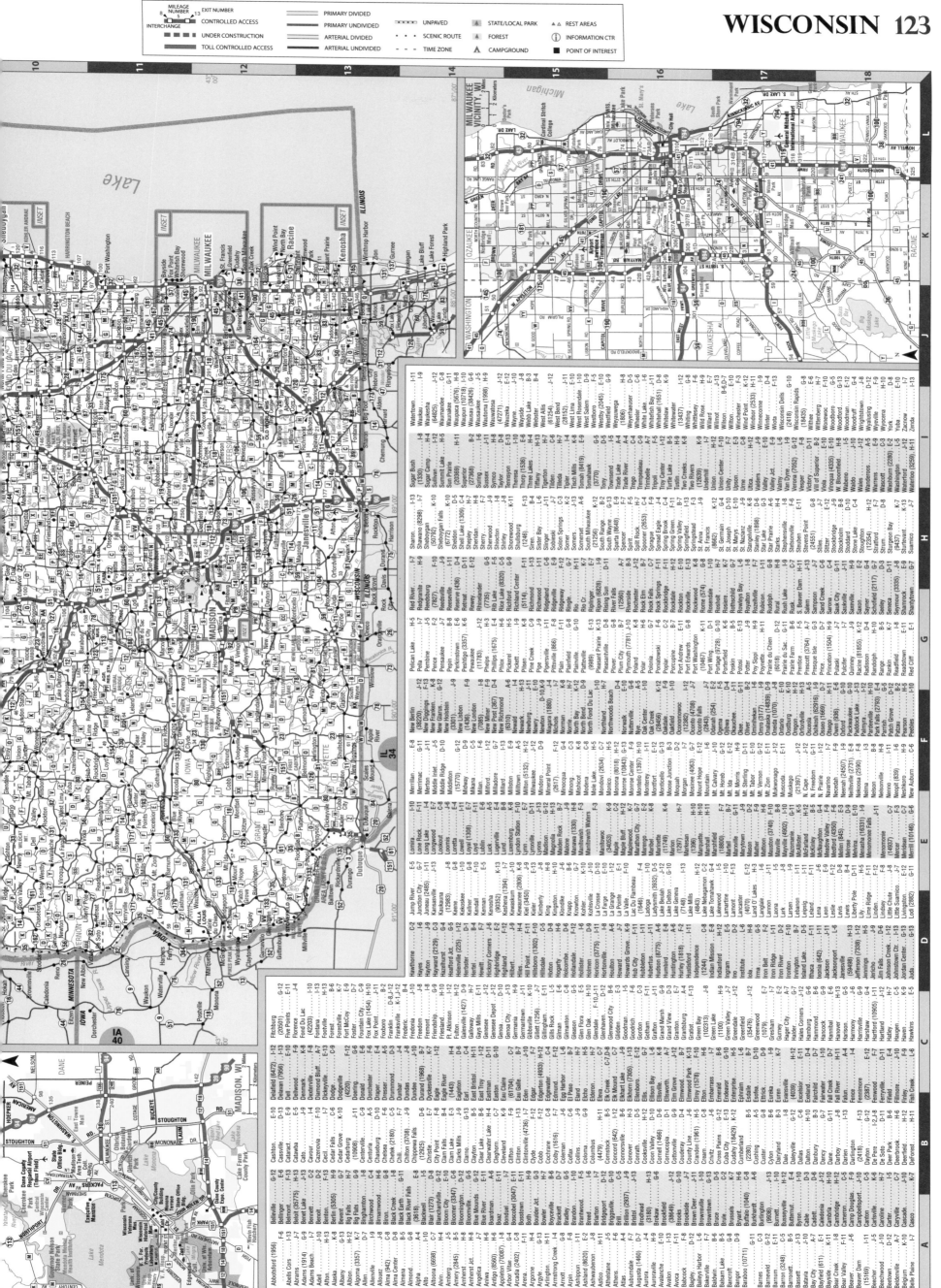

	BUFFALO	CASPER	CHEYENNE	GILLETTE	LITTLE AMERICA	MORAN JCT.	RAWLINS	SHERIDAN
CASPER	116	0	180	129	265	252	122	151
CHEYENNE	294	180	0	244	291	401	148	329
SHERIDAN	35	151	329	102	413	340	270	0

CASPER, WY.

CHEYENNE, WY.

Yellowstone and Grand Teton National Parks, WY

Legend

MILEAGE NUMBER / EXIT NUMBER	
CONTROLLED ACCESS	PRIMARY DIVIDED
INTERCHANGE	PRIMARY UNDIVIDED
UNDER CONSTRUCTION	ARTERIAL DIVIDED
TOLL CONTROLLED ACCESS	ARTERIAL UNDIVIDED
UNPAVED	STATE/LOCAL PARK
SCENIC ROUTE	FOREST
TIME ZONE	CAMPGROUND
REST AREAS	
INFORMATION CTR	
POINT OF INTEREST	

ROAD DISTANCES IN KILOMETERS

From	distances (km) →
CALGARY, AB	4805 309 4436 4891 3630 3443 1475 3880 760 4333 6175 625 2668 2008 3347 916 993 2246 3169 1329 1746
CHARLOTTETOWN, PE	4792 372 257 1187 1369 6218 957 4050 322 1425 4259 2138 2798 1715 5714 6051 6731 2158 3469 6227
EDMONTON, AB	4422 4875 3615 3426 1435 3866 790 4319 6161 533 2652 1992 3331 1215 1292 1944 3150 1313 1443
FREDERICTON, NB	455 816 999 5848 587 3680 113 1738 3888 1768 2430 1344 5343 5680 6361 1787 3097 5855
HALIFAX, NS	1002 1192 6305 978 4088 320 1475 4295 1960 2621 1530 5854 5849 6769 1953 3506 6050
MONTREAL, QC	193 5243 261 2875 706 2555 3081 962 1622 537 4537 4803 5553 883 2291 5049
OTTAWA, ON	4854 444 2689 896 2766 2895 774 1435 444 4348 4426 5361 790 2103 4862
PRINCE RUPERT, BC	5297 2216 5747 7587 1960 4080 3419 4760 954 976 928 4578 2740 2204
QUEBEC, QC	3126 700 2325 3332 1213 1872 788 4788 5125 5802 1134 2542 5300
REGINA, SK	3578 5420 255 1916 1253 2592 1664 1742 2726 2302 574 2224
SAINT JOHN, NB	1689 3784 1665 2325 1240 5241 5702 6256 1739 2996 5757
ST. JOHN'S, NF	5623 3506 4166 3082 7059 7156 8098 3525 4837 7594
SASKATOON, SK	2121 1464 2798 1529 1606 2470 2618 780 1968
SAULT-STE.-MARIE, ON	661 680 3575 3654 4590 570 1330 4088
THUNDER BAY, ON	1339 2916 3295 3929 1230 669 3427
TORONTO, ON	4328 4394 5267 364 2010 4767
VANCOUVER, BC	148 2415 3950 2239 2275
VICTORIA, BC	1905 3905 2315 2652
WHITEHORSE, YUKON	5089 3250 2475
WINDSOR, ON	1842 4586
WINNIPEG, MB	2750
YELLOWKNIFE, NT	

One Inch Equals Approximately 259 Kilometers Or 160 Miles

	CRANBROOK	DAWSON CREEK	HOPE	KAMLOOPS	NANAIMO	OSOYOOS	PRINCE GEORGE	PRINCE RUPERT	VANCOUVER	VICTORIA
KAMLOOPS	383	582	117	0	260	188	329	782	213	262
PRINCE GEORGE	711	255	391	329	536	480	0	460	489	538
VANCOUVER	595	742	98	213	51	248	489	942	0	72
VICTORIA	574	792	148	262	73	298	538	636	72	0

FOR ADJOINING AREA SEE PAGE 9

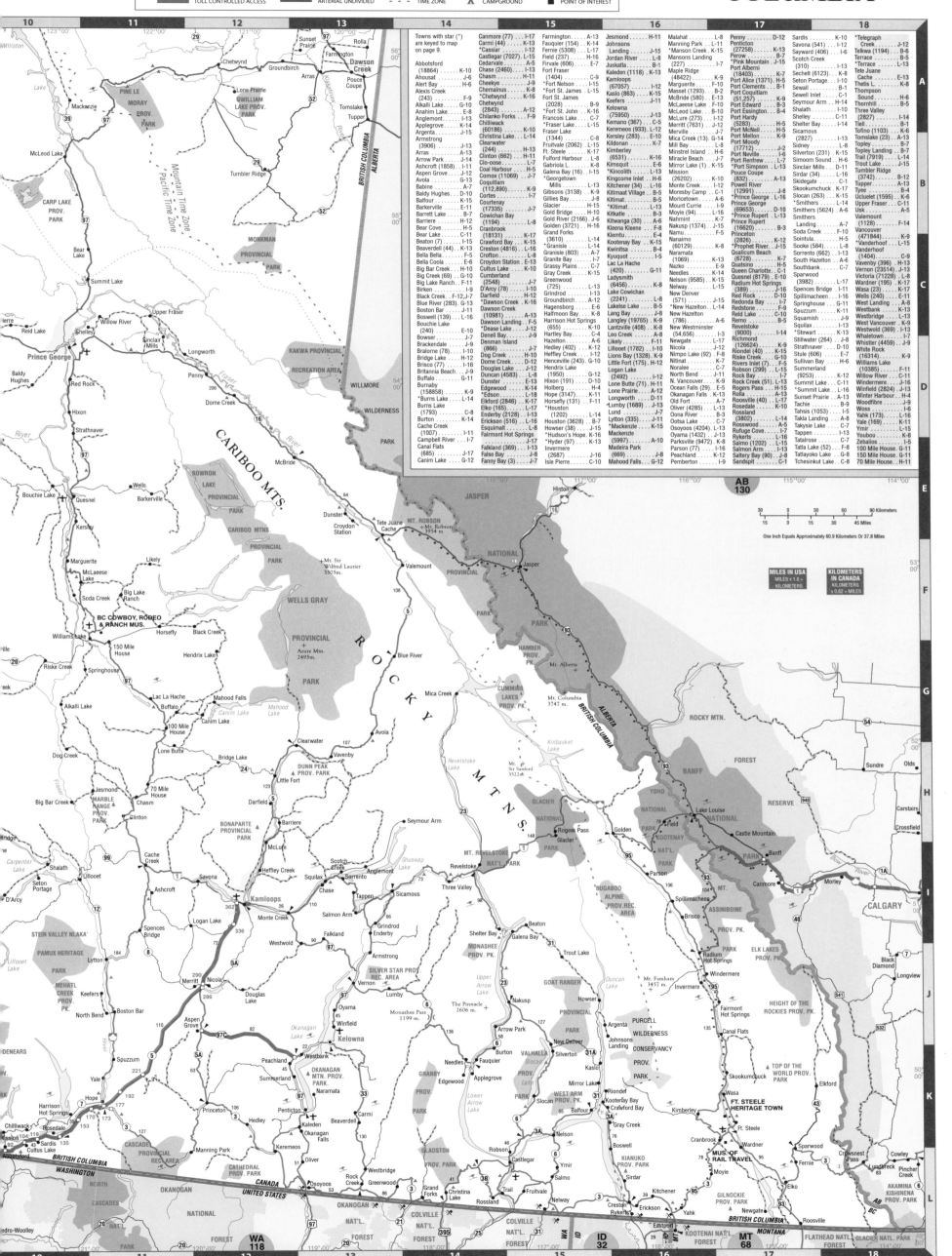

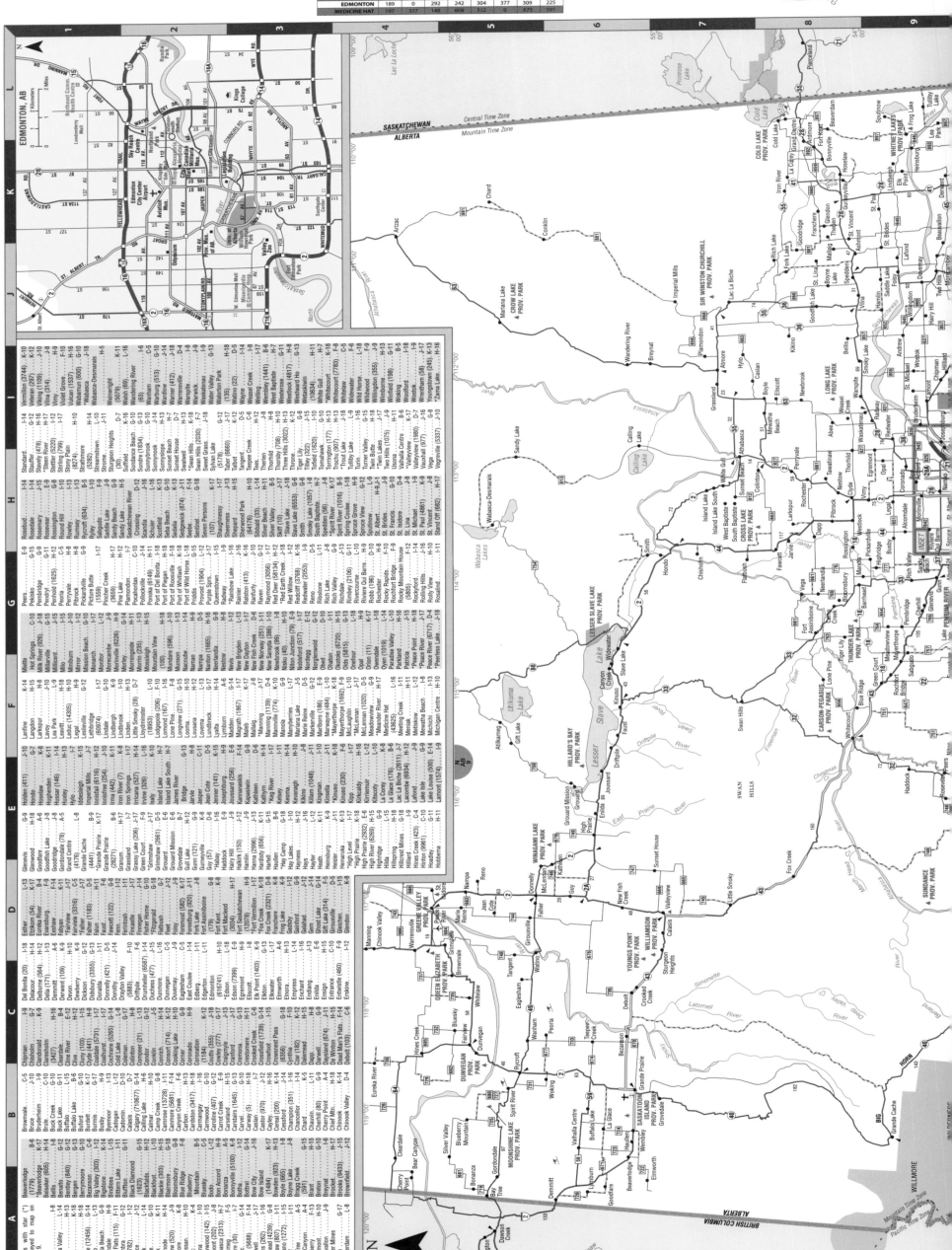

Legend

MILEAGE NUMBER EXIT NUMBER
CONTROLLED ACCESS
INTERCHANGE
UNDER CONSTRUCTION
TOLL CONTROLLED ACCESS

PRIMARY DIVIDED
PRIMARY UNDIVIDED
ARTERIAL DIVIDED
ARTERIAL UNDIVIDED

UNPAVED
SCENIC ROUTE
TIME ZONE

STATE/LOCAL PARK
FOREST
CAMPGROUND

REST AREAS
INFORMATION CTR
POINT OF INTEREST

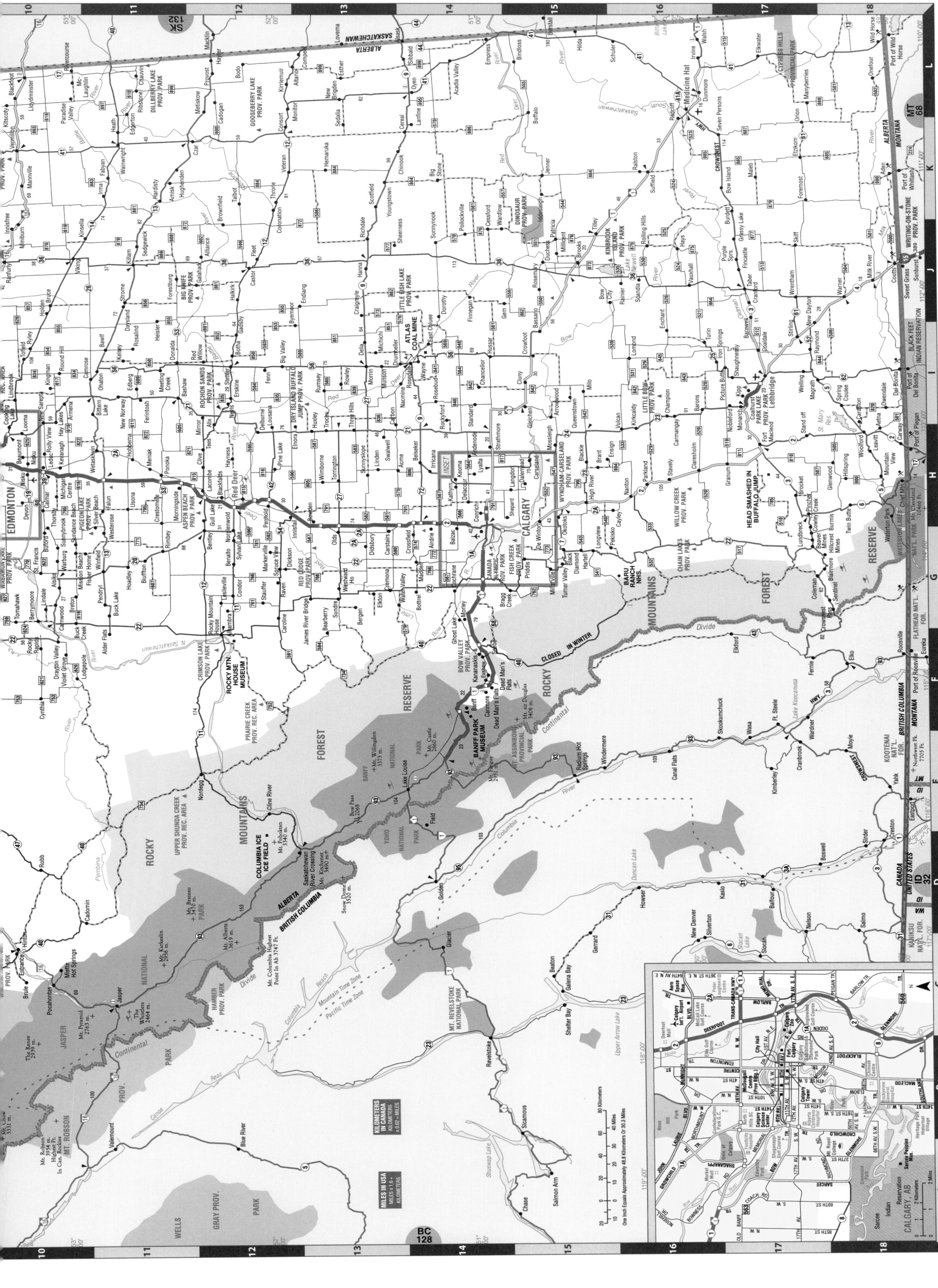

Major features and place names

SASKATCHEWAN
ALBERTA
MONTANA
BRITISH COLUMBIA
UNITED STATES / CANADA
MT / ID / WA

EDMONTON
CALGARY
Red Deer
Medicine Hat
Lethbridge
Lloydminster
Jasper
Banff
Lake Louise

DINOSAUR PROV. PARK
WRITING-ON-STONE PROV. PARK
CYPRESS HILLS PROVINCIAL PARK
DILLBERRY LAKE PROV. PARK
GOOSEBERRY LAKE PROV. PARK
BIG KNIFE PROV. PARK
ROCHON SANDS PROV. PARK
DRY ISLAND BUFFALO JUMP PROV. PARK
LITTLE FISH LAKE PROV. PARK
ATLAS COAL MINE
ASPEN BEACH PROV. PARK
PIGEON LAKE PROV. PARK
RED LODGE PROV. PARK
CRIMSON LAKE PROV. PARK
ROCKY MTN. HOUSE MUSEUM
KINBROOK ISLAND PROV. PARK
LITTLE BOW PROV. PARK
WYNDHAM-CARSELAND PROV. PARK
FISH CREEK PROV. PARK
CANADA OLYMPIC PARK
HEAD SMASHED IN BUFFALO JUMP
CHAIN LAKES PROV. PARK
WILLOW CREEK PROV. PARK
BAR U RANCH NHS.

ROCKY MOUNTAINS
ROCKY MOUNTAIN FOREST RESERVE
CONTINENTAL DIVIDE
COLUMBIA ICE FIELD
BANFF NATIONAL PARK
JASPER NATIONAL PARK
YOHO NATIONAL PARK
MT. REVELSTOKE NATIONAL PARK
KOOTENAY NAT'L. PARK
MT. ASSINIBOINE PROVINCIAL PARK
HAMBER PROV. PARK
MT. ROBSON PROV. PARK
WELLS GRAY PROV. PARK
KANANASKIS
BANFF PARK MUSEUM
CLOSED IN WINTER

Mt. Columbia Highest Point in AB 3747 Ft.
Mt. Robson 3954 m. Highest Pt. in Can. Rockies
Mt. Alberta 3619 m.
Mt. Pobokton 3340 m.
Mt. Kitchener 3490 m.
Mt. Willingdon 3373 m.
Mt. Castle 2860 m.
Mt. Forget 2957 m.
Mt. Assiniboine 3618 m.
Mt. Pyramid 2763 m.
Mt. Chown 3331 m.
The Whistlers 2464 m.
Mt. Kerkeslin 2956 m.
Snow Dome 3520 m.
Bow Pass 2068

MIEETTE HOT SPRINGS
RADIUM HOT SPRINGS
Saskatchewan River Crossing

MOUNTAIN TIME ZONE
PACIFIC TIME ZONE

KILOMETERS IN CANADA
KILOMETERS x 1.6 = MILES
MILES IN USA
MILES x 1.6 = KILOMETERS
One Inch Equals Approximately 48.8 Kilometers Or 30.3 Miles

Calgary inset

CALGARY, AB
Calgary Int'l. Airport
Calgary Zoo
Calgary Tower
City Hall
Fort Calgary
TRANS-CANADA HWY.
DEERFOOT TR.
BARLOW TR.
GLENMORE TR.
MACLEOD TR.
CROWCHILD TR.
SARCEE TR.
BLACKFOOT TR.
Sarcee Indian Reservation
Heritage Park
Glenmore Res.

BLACK FEET INDIAN RESERVATION
BLOOD INDIAN RESERVE
KANISKU NAT'L. FOR.
FLATHEAD NAT'L. FOR.
WATERTON LAKES NAT'L. PARK

BC 128
SK 132
MT 68

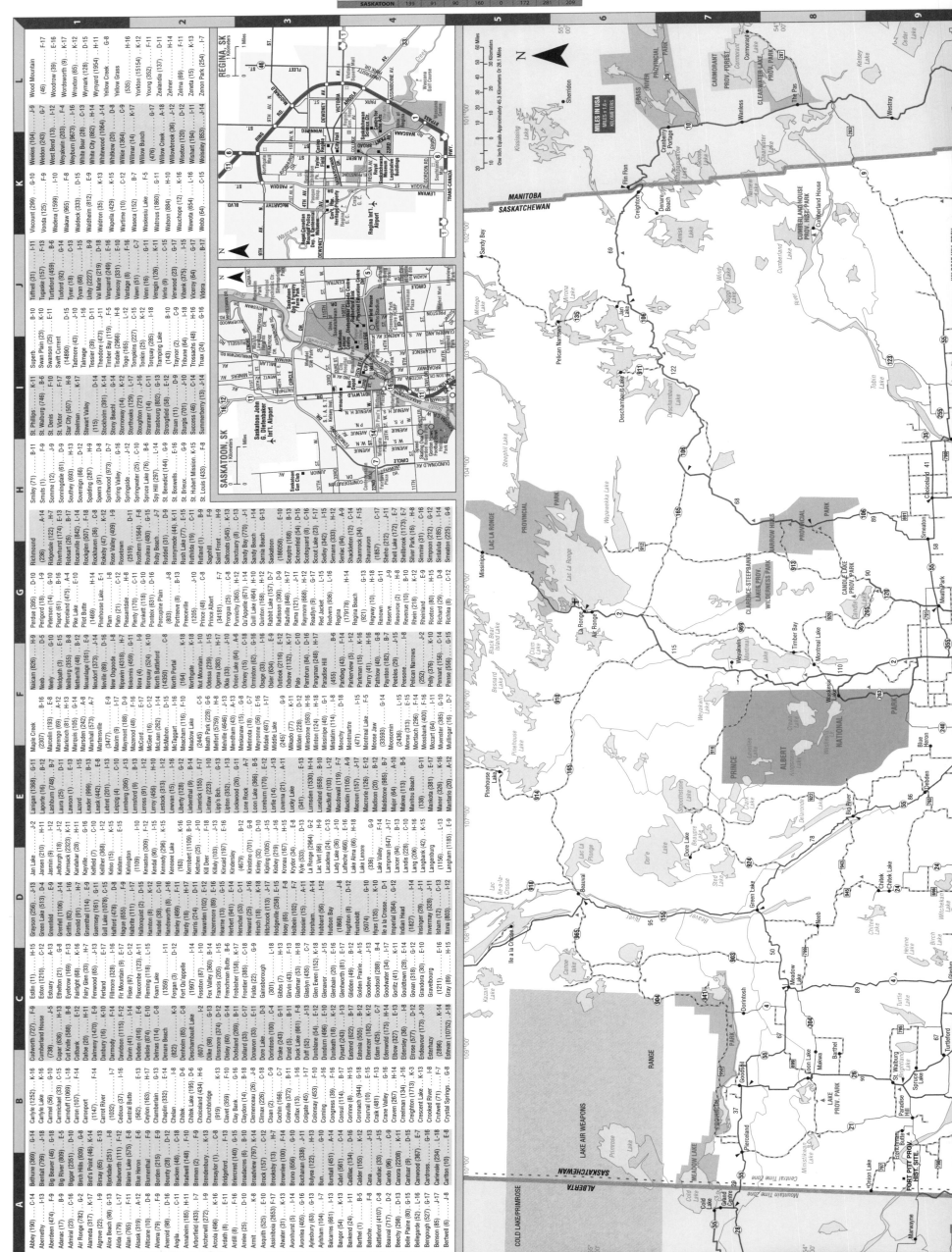

MILEAGE NUMBER 8 5 13 EXIT NUMBER
INTERCHANGE CONTROLLED ACCESS
UNDER CONSTRUCTION
TOLL CONTROLLED ACCESS
PRIMARY DIVIDED
PRIMARY UNDIVIDED
ARTERIAL DIVIDED
ARTERIAL UNDIVIDED
UNPAVED
SCENIC ROUTE
TIME ZONE
STATE/LOCAL PARK
FOREST
CAMPGROUND
REST AREAS
INFORMATION CTR
POINT OF INTEREST

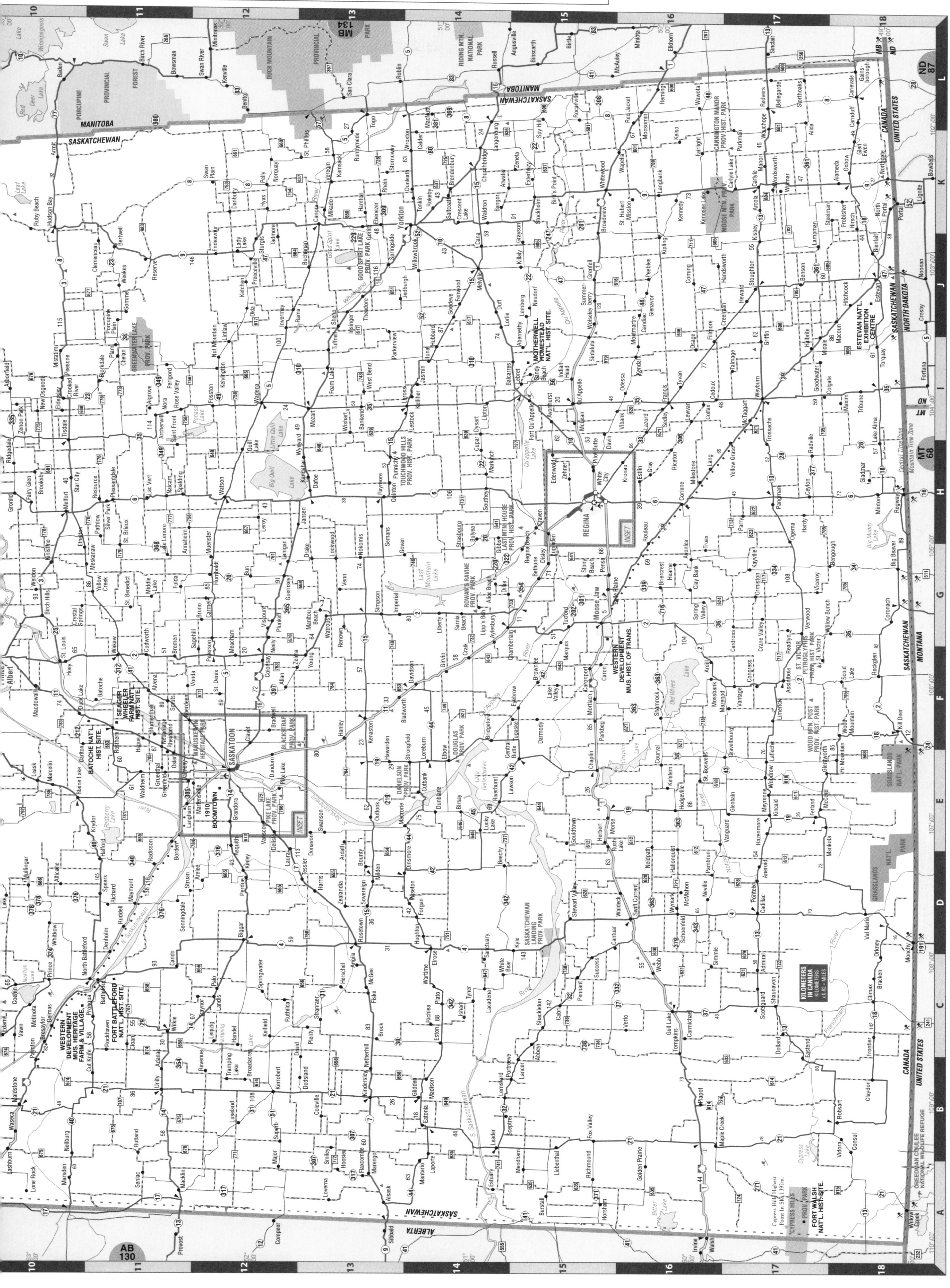

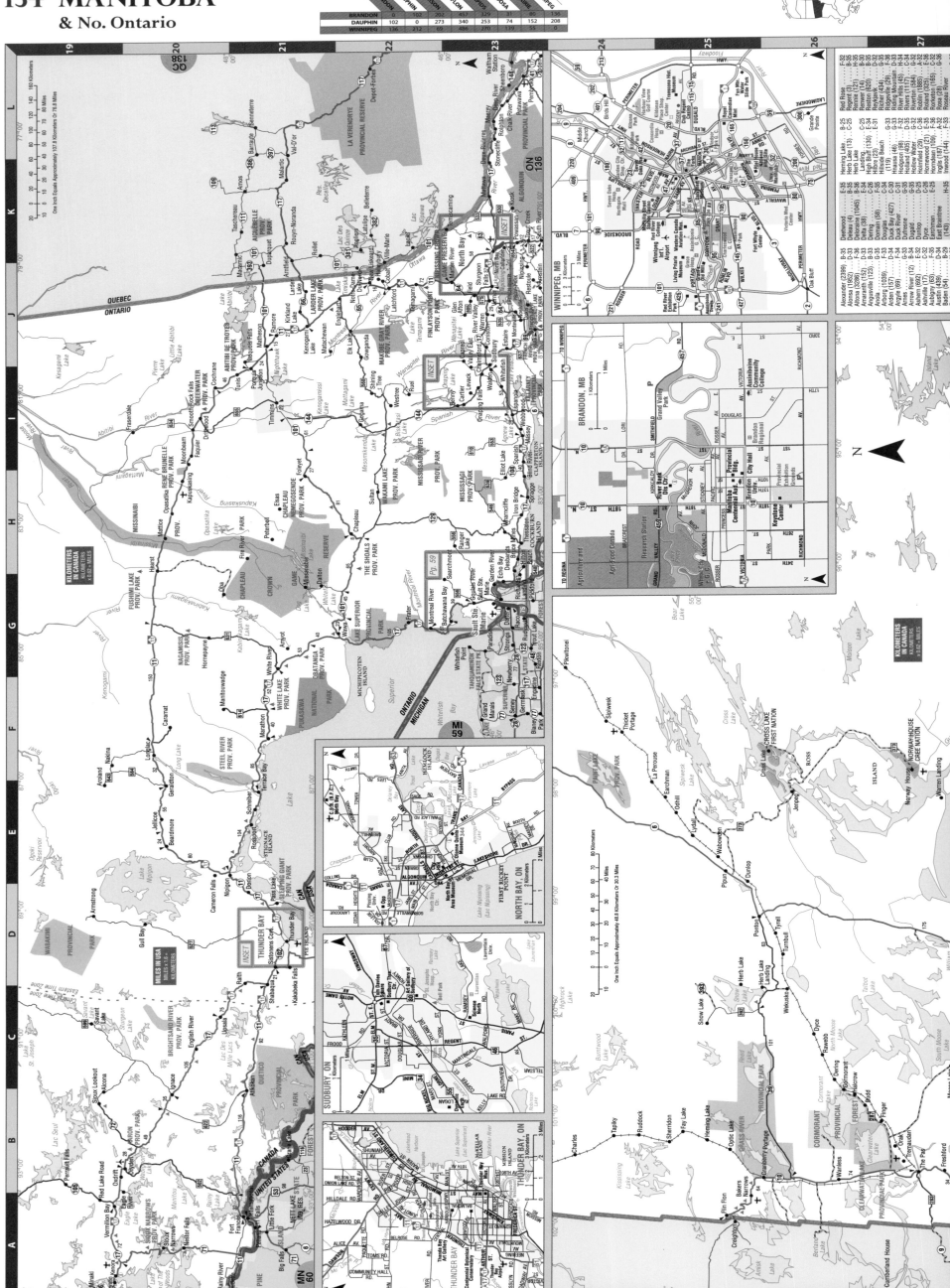

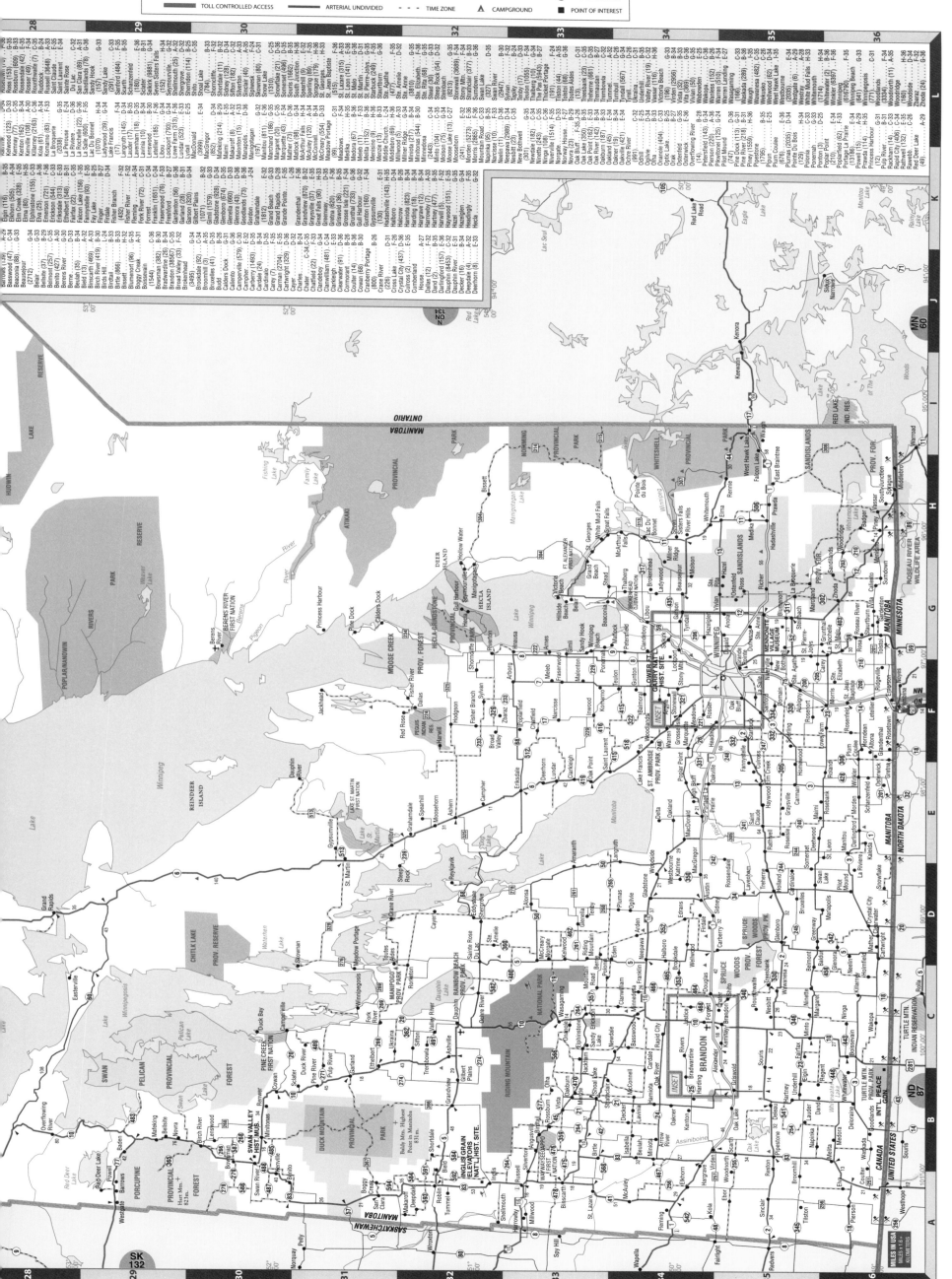

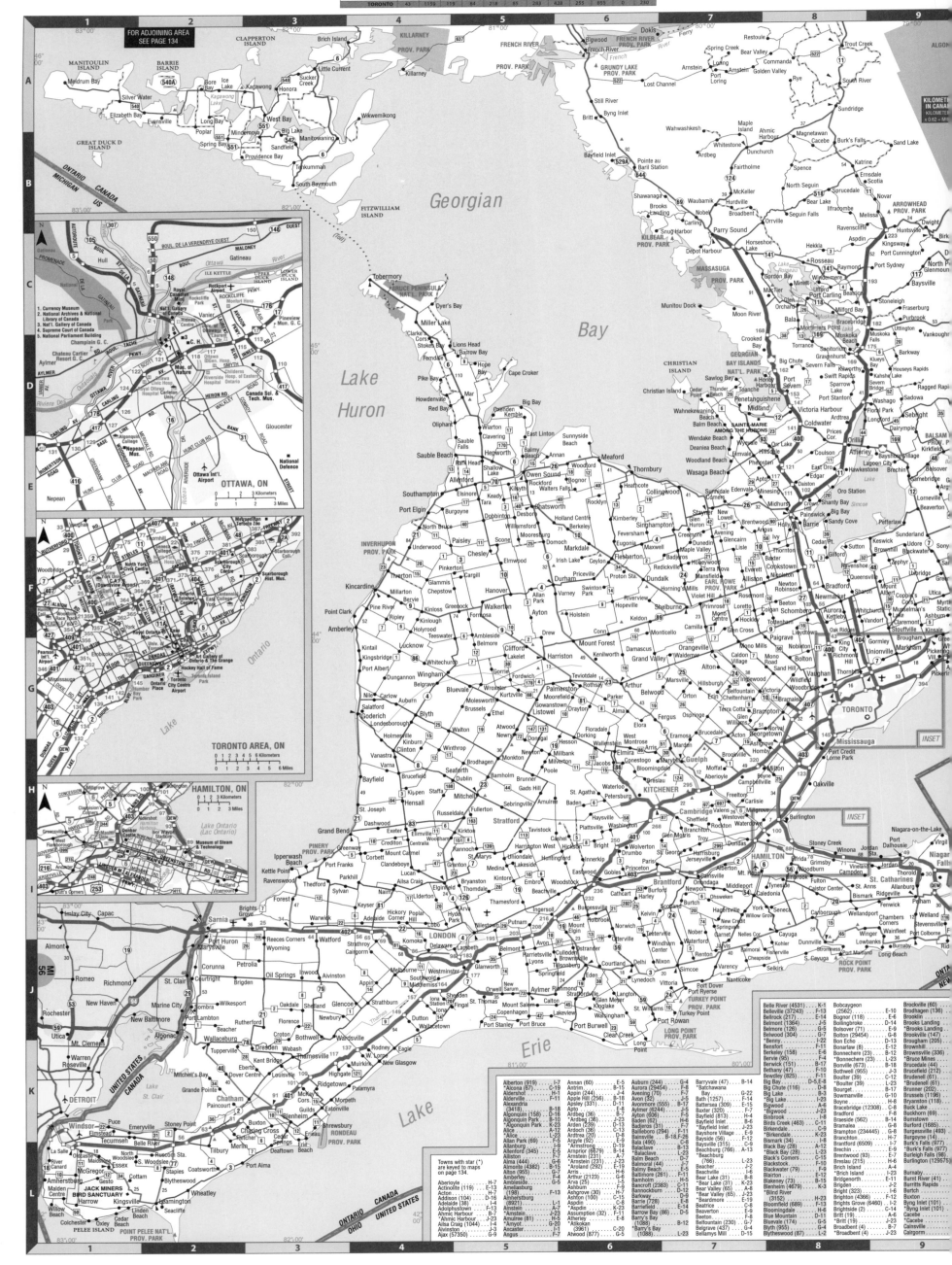

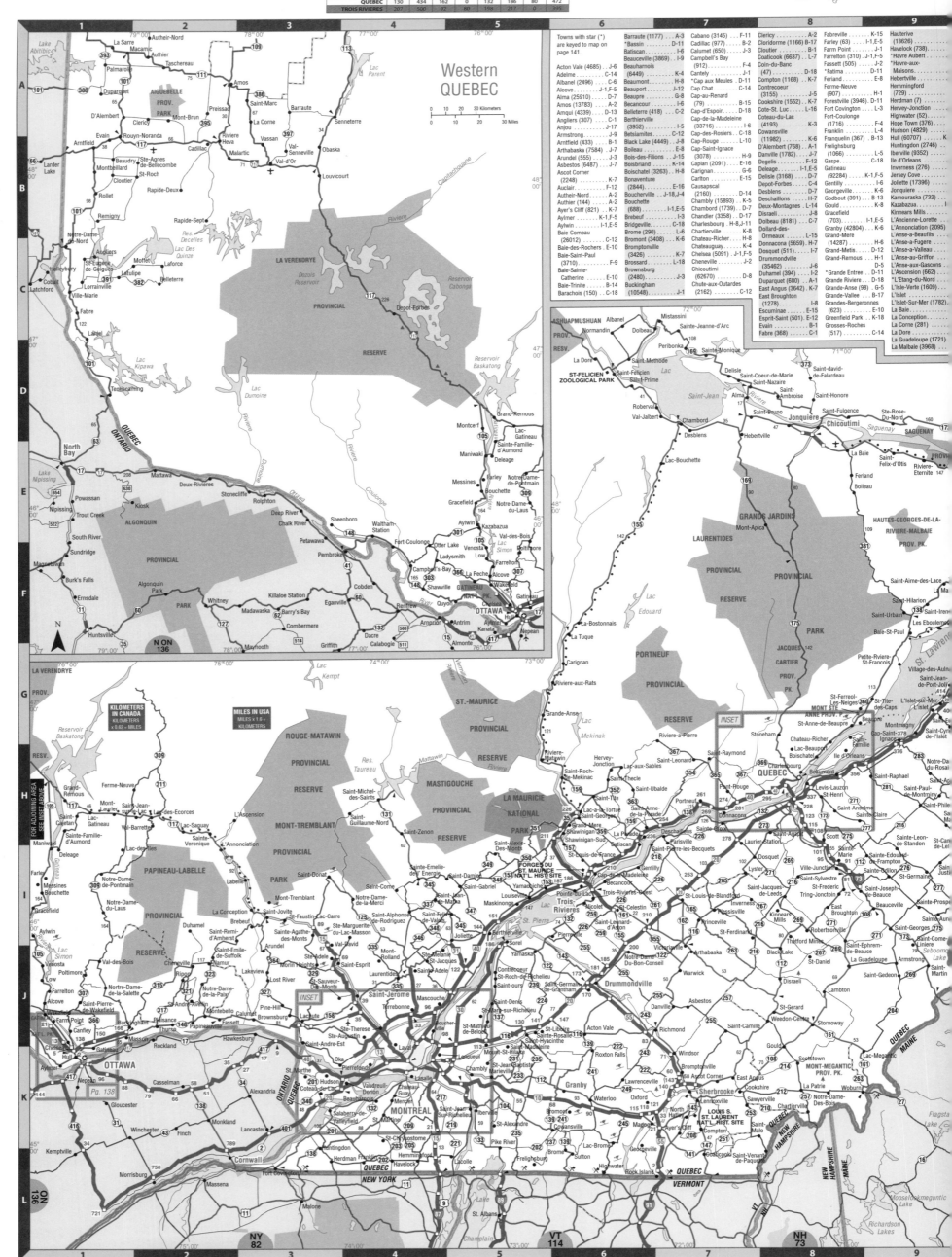

	CAMPBELLTON, NB	PORT AUX BASQUES, NF	CHARLOTTETOWN, PE	FREDERICTON, NB	HALIFAX, NS	MONCTON, NB	NEW GLASGOW, NS	PORT HASTINGS, NS	SAINT JOHN, NB	ST. JOHN'S, NF	SYDNEY, NS	YARMOUTH, NS
CHARLOTTETOWN, PE	278	428	0	216	203	103	159	225	198	985	326	382
FREDERICTON, NB	246	523	216	0	273	114	254	320	68	1079	421	184
HALIFAX, NS	346	369	203	273	0	160	100	166	255	925	267	192
SAINT JOHN, NB	278	505	198	68	255	96	236	302	0	1062	404	120
ST. JOHN'S, NF	1153	557	985	1079	925	967	827	762	1062	0	683	1105

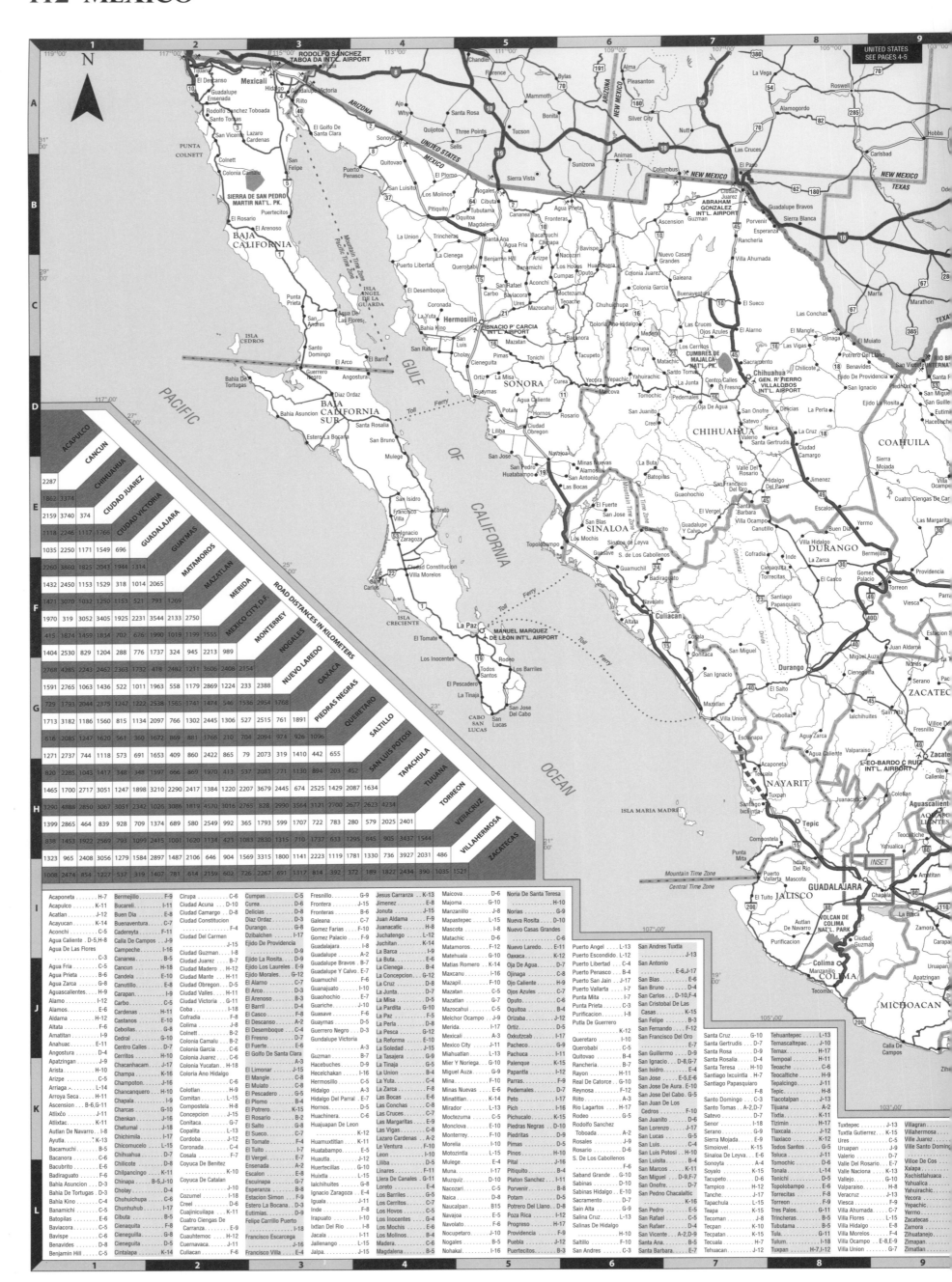

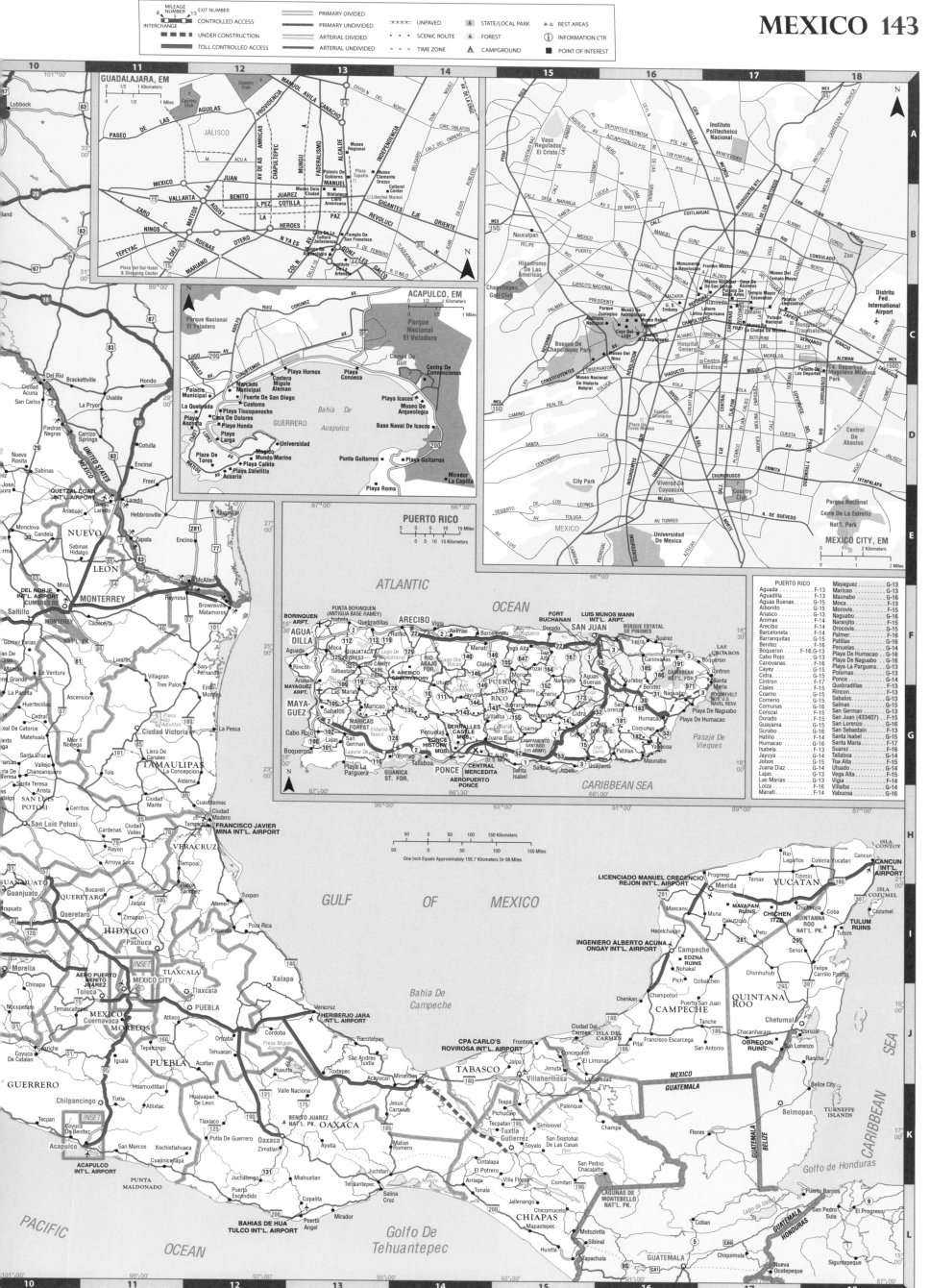

ALABAMA 6
Autauga J6
Baldwin B14
Barbour J10
Bibb D7
Blount H4
Bullock H10
Butler E11
Calhoun G4
Chambers H7
Cherokee H4
Chilton E7
Choctaw B10
Clarke C11
Clay G6
Cleburne H4
Coffee G12
Colbert C2
Conecuh F13
Crenshaw H12
Cullman E3
Dale H12
Dallas D8
De Kalb H3
Elmore G7
Escambia D13
Etowah G4
Fayette B5
Franklin B2
Geneva G13
Greene B7
Hale C8
Henry J11
Houston J12
Jackson F2
Jefferson E5
Lamar B4
Lauderdale C2
Lawrence D2
Lee H8
Limestone D2
Lowndes E9
Macon H9
Madison E2
Marengo C9
Marion B3
Marshall F3
Mobile A13
Monroe C11
Montgomery F8
Morgan E3
Perry C8
Pickens B6
Pike G11
Randolph H6
Russell J9
Shelby F6
St. Clair F4
Sumter B8
Talladega G5
Tallapoosa G7
Tuscaloosa C6
Walker D4
Washington A12
Wilcox D10
Winston D3

ALASKA 8
Aleutians East K6
Aleutians West L3
Anchorage H4
Bethel E5
Bristol Bay K6
Denali H4
Dillingham F5
Fairbanks North Star J3
Haines J5
Juneau K6
Kenai Peninsula H5
Ketchikan Gateway L12
Kodiak Island G6
Lake And Peninsula J8
Matanuska Susitna G4
Nome D3
North Slope F1
Northwest Arctic B4
Prince Of Wales-Outer Ketchikan L11
Sitka K6
Skagway-Hoonah-Angoon J5
Southeast Fairbanks J3
Valdez Cordova H4
Wade Hampton E2
Wrangell-Petersburg K6
Yakutat J9
Yukon - Koyukuk G3

ARIZONA 10
Apache K6
Cochise K12
Coconino E4
Gila G8
Graham J11
Greenlee K9
La Paz A9
Maricopa E9
Mohave B5
Navajo H4
Pima F13
Pinal G10
Santa Cruz E6
Yavapai E6
Yuma C11

ARKANSAS 12
Arkansas H14
Ashley H17
Baxter F8
Benton A5
Boone C6
Bradley G17
Calhoun F17
Carroll C6
Chicot H18
Clark E15
Clay K5
Cleburne G11
Cleveland G16
Columbia E17
Conway E12
Craighead K9
Crawford A11
Crittenden K11
Cross J11
Dallas F16
Desha H16
Drew H17
Faulkner F12
Franklin B10
Fulton G7
Garland D13
Grant F15
Greene K8
Hempstead D16
Hot Spring E14
Howard B15
Independence G10
Izard G8
Jackson H10
Jefferson G14
Johnson C10
Lafayette D18
Lawrence H8
Lee J13
Lincoln H16
Little River A16
Logan C12
Lonoke G13
Madison C9
Marion E7
Miller C18
Mississippi K9
Monroe H13
Montgomery C14
Nevada D16
Newton D8
Ouachita E17
Perry D13
Phillips J14
Pike C15
Poinsett J9
Polk A14
Pope D11
Prairie G13
Pulaski F13
Randolph J6
Saline E14
Scott A13
Searcy E9
Sebastian A12
Sevier A15
Sharp H7
St. Francis J12
Stone F9
Union F18
Van Buren E10
Washington A8
White G11
Woodruff H12
Yell C12

CALIFORNIA 14
Alameda K5
Alpine H4
Amador G3
Butte E2
Calaveras G3
Colusa E2
Contra Costa K4
Del Norte A8
El Dorado G2
Fresno C20
Glenn E1
Humboldt B9
Imperial L34
Inyo E29
Kern E29
Kings D27
Lake G4
Lassen F2
Los Angeles H30
Madera E8
Marin A26
Mariposa A26
Mendocino C13
Merced A25
Modoc G1
Mono A27
Monterey B14
Napa H4
Nevada H3
Orange J30
Placer G2
Plumas F2
Riverside J33
Sacramento F3
San Benito B25
San Bernardino G13
San Diego L32
San Francisco A24
San Joaquin K5
San Luis Obispo E26
San Mateo K6
Santa Barbara D23
Santa Clara A25
Santa Cruz A23
Shasta H1
Sierra H2
Siskiyou F1
Solano I5
Sonoma H3
Stanislaus A24
Sutter F3
Tehama E1
Trinity C4
Tulare C26
Tuolumne G27
Ventura G27
Yolo F3
Yuba G6

COLORADO 20
Adams E14
Alamosa D13
Arapahoe F13
Archuleta J3
Baca K17
Bent I15
Boulder E12
Chaffee H11
Cheyenne L6
Clear Creek F12
Conejos J13
Costilla J12
Crowley I15
Custer H14
Delta H2
Denver F13
Dolores J6
Douglas G13
Eagle F9
El Paso H13
Elbert F14
Fremont H11
Garfield F7
Gilpin E10
Grand E10
Gunnison D2
Hinsdale J3
Huerfano J13
Jackson I10
Jefferson F11
Kiowa K14
Kit Carson H9
La Plata J4
Lake G10
Larimer E12
Las Animas K15
Lincoln G7
Logan G12
Mesa G7
Mineral J2
Moffat C5
Montezuma K6
Montrose H3
Morgan G5
Otero J15
Ouray J2
Park G12
Phillips G17
Pitkin C5
Prowers K16
Pueblo I14
Rio Blanco D6
Rio Grande J10
Routt D8
Saguache I10
San Juan J6
San Miguel J6
Sedgwick G17
Summit F18
Teller G12
Washington G16
Weld D13
Yuma H7

CONNECTICUT 22
Fairfield D6
Hartford H2
Litchfield E2
Middlesex H5
New Haven H5
New London K4
Tolland J2
Windham K2

DELAWARE 23
Kent H6
New Castle A3
Sussex I4

FLORIDA 24
Alachua F3
Baker F3
Bay D3
Bradford F3
Brevard I6
Broward I16
Calhoun E16
Charlotte H4
Citrus F4
Clay G3
Collier I9
Columbia F3
Desoto H10
Dixie D6
Duval G4
Escambia A15
Flagler G4
Franklin B10
Gadsden E4
Gilchrist E4
Glades F14
Gulf E17
Hamilton E2
Hardee F6
Hendry F6
Hernando F4
Highlands H5
Hillsborough D15
Holmes D15
Indian River B15
Jackson E15
Jefferson E3
Lafayette D5
Lake H2
Lee H11
Leon A2
Levy C4
Liberty E16
Madison E2
Manatee C2
Marion F4
Martin A5
Miami - Dade K9
Monroe J10
Nassau G3
Okaloosa B4
Okeechobee F13
Orange H4
Osceola K11
Palm Beach K13
Pasco F14
Pinellas F8
Polk A14
Putnam F3
Santa Rosa B16
Sarasota G12
Seminole I6
St. Johns H3
St. Lucie G14
Sumter D2
Suwannee E4
Taylor C5
Union F15
Volusia I5
Wakulla B2
Walton E16

GEORGIA 28
Appling J13
Atkinson H12
Bacon H4
Baker E14
Baldwin F10
Banks H6
Barrow D6
Bartow B4
Ben Hill F12
Berrien F6
Bibb E9
Bleckley F10
Brantley J13
Brooks E17
Bryan K11
Bulloch J10
Burke H7

HAWAII 30
Hawaii H14
Honolulu C5
Kalawao D12
Kauai A1
Maui C5

IDAHO 32
Ada B15
Adams A13
Bannock J18
Bear Lake J18
Benewah B4
Bingham H15
Blaine F15
Boise C14
Bonner B2
Bonneville J14
Boundary B1
Butte G14
Camas E15
Canyon A15
Caribou J16
Cassia F18
Clark H13
Clearwater C6
Custer F12
Elmore D16
Franklin J18
Fremont J12
Gem B14
Gooding E16
Idaho C10
Jefferson J14
Jerome F16
Kootenai B3
Latah B5
Lemhi F11
Lewis C7
Lincoln F16
Madison J13
Minidoka G17
Nez Perce A6
Oneida H18
Owyhee C17
Payette A14
Power H17
Shoshone C4
Teton K13
Twin Falls F17
Valley C12
Washington A13

ILLINOIS 34
Adams A9
Alexander B17
Bond D12
Boone J2
Brown B9
Bureau G4
Calhoun B11
Carroll F2
Cass C9
Champaign K8
Christian E10
Clark K11
Clay H13
Clinton D13
Coles J10
Cook H3
Crawford K12
Cumberland J11
De Kalb J3
De Witt H8
Douglas J9
Du Page H3
Edgar K9
Edwards J14
Effingham H12
Fayette F12
Ford H7
Franklin F16
Fulton E7
Gallatin H17
Greene C11
Grundy G4
Hamilton H15
Hancock B7
Hardin H17
Henderson B6
Henry E4
Iroquois J7
Jackson E16
Jasper J12
Jefferson G14
Jersey C11
Jo Daviess E1
Johnson G17
Kane H3
Kankakee J5
Kendall H4
Knox D6
La Salle G5
Lake J2
Lawrence K13
Lee G3
Livingston H6
Logan E8
Macon F9
Macoupin D11
Madison C12
Marion F13
Marshall F6
Mason D8
Massac G17
McDonough C7
McHenry H2
McLean G8
Menard D9
Mercer C4
Monroe C14
Montgomery E11
Morgan C10
Moultrie H10
Ogle G2
Peoria E7
Perry E15
Piatt H9
Pike B10
Pope H17
Pulaski G17
Putnam F5
Randolph C15
Richland H13
Rock Island C3
Saline G16
Sangamon D9
Schuyler C8
Scott C10
Shelby G11
St. Clair C13
Stark E5
Stephenson H1
Tazewell E7
Union D16
Vermilion K8
Wabash K14
Warren C6
Washington E14
Wayne H14
White J15
Whiteside F3
Will H4
Williamson F16
Winnebago H1
Woodford F7

INDIANA 38
Adams I5
Allen I3
Bartholomew G10
Benton C6
Blackford H5
Boone E7
Brown F10
Carroll E5
Cass E4
Clark G13
Clay C11
Clinton E6
Crawford F13
Daviess C12
Dearborn J10
Decatur H10
De Kalb I2
Delaware H6
Dubois D13
Elkhart G1
Fayette I9
Floyd F13
Fountain C7
Franklin J9
Fulton F3
Gibson B13
Grant G5
Greene C11
Hamilton F6
Hancock G7
Harrison F14
Hendricks F7
Henry H7
Howard F5
Huntington H4
Jackson G11
Jasper D3
Jay I5
Jefferson H12
Jennings H11
Johnson F9
Knox B12
Kosciusko G2
Lagrange H1
Lake C1
La Porte E1
Lawrence E11
Madison G6
Marion F7
Marshall F2
Martin D12
Miami F4
Monroe E10
Montgomery D7
Morgan E9
Newton C3
Noble H2
Ohio J10
Orange E12
Owen D9
Parke C8
Perry E15
Pike C13
Porter D1
Posey A14
Pulaski E3
Putnam D8
Randolph I6
Ripley H10
Rush H8
Scott G12
Shelby G8
Spencer C15
St. Joseph F1
Starke E2
Steuben I1
Sullivan B11
Switzerland J11
Tippecanoe D6
Tipton F5
Union J8
Vanderburgh B14
Vermillion B8
Vigo B10
Wabash G4
Warren C7
Warrick C14
Washington F12
Wayne I8
Wells H4
White E4
Whitley H3

IOWA 40
Adair D11
Adams D12
Allamakee J1
Appanoose G14
Audubon C10
Benton H9
Black Hawk H7
Boone E8
Bremer H6
Buchanan I8
Buena Vista D6
Butler G6
Calhoun E7
Carroll D8
Cass C11
Cedar J10
Cerro Gordo G5
Cherokee C6
Chickasaw H5
Clarke E12
Clay D5
Clayton J6
Clinton K9
Crawford C8

KANSAS 42
Allen J13
Anderson J12
Atchison J7
Barber D9
Barton E7
Bourbon J13
Brown I6
Butler H10
Chase H10
Chautauqua H13
Cherokee K14
Cheyenne A5
Clark C10
Clay G6
Cloud G5
Coffey I11
Comanche D10
Cowley H12
Crawford K13
Decatur C5
Dickinson G8
Doniphan J6
Douglas J9
Edwards D9
Elk I12
Ellis D7
Ellsworth F7
Finney C8
Ford C9
Franklin J11
Geary H7
Gove C6
Graham D6
Grant A9
Gray C9
Greeley A7
Greenwood I11
Hamilton A8
Harper F12
Harvey G10
Haskell B9
Hodgeman D8
Jackson I8
Jefferson I8
Jewell F5
Johnson J9
Kearny A8
Kingman F11
Kiowa D10
Labette J13
Lane C7
Leavenworth J8
Lincoln F6
Linn J11
Logan B6
Lyon I10
Marion H9
Marshall H6
McPherson G9
Meade B10
Miami J10
Mitchell F5
Montgomery I13
Morris H9
Morton A11
Nemaha H6
Neosho J13
Ness D7
Norton C5
Osage I10
Osborne E6
Ottawa G7
Pawnee D8
Phillips D5
Pottawatomie H7
Pratt E10
Rawlins B5
Reno F10
Republic G5
Rice F9
Riley H7
Rooks D6
Rush D7
Russell E7
Saline G8
Scott B7
Sedgwick G11
Seward B10
Shawnee I9
Sheridan C6
Sherman A6
Smith E5
Stafford E9
Stanton A9
Stevens A10
Sumner G12
Thomas B6
Trego D7
Wabaunsee H8
Wallace A7
Washington G6
Wichita B7
Wilson I12
Woodson I12
Wyandotte J9

KENTUCKY 44
Adair F11
Allen E12
Anderson H6
Ballard B10
Barren E11
Bath K7
Bell K13
Boone H3
Bourbon I6
Boyd L6
Boyle G8

LOUISIANA 46
Acadia E13
Allen D11
Ascension G11
Assumption G12
Avoyelles E10
Beauregard C11
Bienville C6
Bossier B5
Caddo A5
Calcasieu C13
Caldwell E7
Cameron C14
Catahoula E8
Claiborne D4
Concordia F9
De Soto A7
East Baton Rouge G11
East Carroll G3
East Feliciana G10
Evangeline D11
Franklin F7
Grant D8
Iberia F13
Iberville G11
Jackson D6
Jefferson I12
Jefferson Davis D13
La Fourche H13
La Salle E9
Lafayette E12
Lincoln D5
Livingston H11
Madison G6
Morehouse F4
Natchitoches C8
Orleans I12
Ouachita E6
Plaquemines J14
Pointe Coupee F10
Rapides D9
Red River B7
Richland F6
Sabine A8
St. Bernard J12
St. Charles H12
St. Helena G10
St. James H12
St. John The Baptist H12
St. Landry E11
St. Martin F12
St. Mary G13
St. Tammany I11
Tangipahoa H10
Tensas G7
Terrebonne G14
Union E4
Vermilion E14
Vernon C10
Washington I10
Webster B5
West Baton Rouge G11
West Carroll G3
West Feliciana F10
Winn D8

MAINE 48
Androscoggin C13
Aroostook E3
Cumberland B14
Franklin B10
Hancock I12
Kennebec D12
Knox D14
Lincoln D14
Oxford A11
Penobscot F9
Piscataquis F8
Sagadahoc C14
Somerset C8
Waldo E12
Washington I10
York A15

MARYLAND 50
Allegany B2
Anne Arundel I6
Baltimore I4
Calvert I8
Caroline L7
Carroll G3
Cecil K3
Charles G8
Dorchester K9

MASSACHUSETTS 54
Barnstable L6
Berkshire A3
Bristol I6
Dukes K8
Essex K2
Franklin D2
Hampden D4
Hampshire D3
Middlesex I3
Nantucket L8
Norfolk J4
Plymouth K5
Suffolk K3
Worcester F3

MICHIGAN 56
Alcona I10
Alger D5
Allegan E15

MINNESOTA 60
Aitkin E6
Anoka G14
Becker B9
Beltrami D7
Benton F13
Big Stone B13
Blue Earth F17
Brown E16
Carlton H6
Carver F15
Cass D10
Chippewa C14
Chisago H13
Clay A9
Clearwater D7
Cook I2
Cottonwood C17
Crow Wing E10
Dakota G15
Dodge H18
Douglas C11
Faribault F18
Fillmore I18
Freeborn G18
Goodhue H16
Grant B11
Hennepin F14
Houston J18
Hubbard C9
Isanti G13
Itasca E6
Jackson D18
Kanabec G12
Kandiyohi D14
Kittson A2
Koochiching E4
Lac Qui Parle B14
Lake H4
Lake Of The Woods D2
Le Sueur F16
Lincoln B16
Lyon C16
Mahnomen C8
Marshall B4
Martin E18
McLeod E15
Meeker E14
Mille Lacs G12
Morrison E11
Mower H18
Murray C17
Nicollet F16
Nobles C18
Norman B8
Olmsted H17
Otter Tail B10
Pennington B5
Pine H11
Pipestone B17
Polk B7
Pope C12
Ramsey G14
Red Lake B6
Redwood D16
Renville D15
Rice G16
Rock B18
Roseau B2
Scott F15
Sherburne F13
Sibley E16
St. Louis G5
Stearns E12
Steele G17
Stevens C12
Swift C13
Todd D11
Traverse B12
Wabasha I16
Wadena C10
Waseca G17
Washington H14
Watonwan E17
Wilkin A11
Winona I17
Wright F14
Yellow Medicine B15

MISSISSIPPI 64
Adams D12
Alcorn G2
Amite D16
Attala E7
Benton F2
Bolivar C5
Calhoun F5
Carroll E6
Chickasaw G5
Choctaw F6
Claiborne C11
Clarke H9
Clay G6
Coahoma C4
Copiah D11
Covington F12
De Soto C2
Forrest F13
Franklin C14
George I13
Greene I12
Grenada E5
Hancock F16
Harrison G16
Hinds D9
Holmes E8
Humphreys D7
Issaquena C9
Itawamba H3
Jackson H16
Jasper G10
Jefferson C12
Jefferson Davis E12
Jones G11
Kemper H8
Lafayette F3
Lamar E14
Lauderdale H9
Lawrence E12
Leake F8
Lee G3
Leflore D6
Lincoln D13
Lowndes H6
Madison E9
Marion E14
Marshall E2
Monroe H4
Montgomery E6
Neshoba G8
Newton G9
Noxubee H7
Oktibbeha G6
Panola D3
Pearl River E15
Perry G13
Pike D15
Pontotoc G4
Prentiss G3
Quitman D3
Rankin E10
Scott F9
Sharkey C8
Simpson E11
Smith F10
Stone G14
Sunflower D6
Tallahatchie D4
Tate D2
Tippah F2
Tishomingo H2
Tunica C2
Union F3
Walthall E15
Warren C10
Washington C6
Wayne H11
Webster F6
Wilkinson C16
Winston G7
Yalobusha E4
Yazoo D8

MISSOURI 66
Adair B11
Andrew C9
Atchison D12
Audrain H12
Barry B20
Barton B17
Bates B15
Benton G10
Bollinger L19
Boone G11
Buchanan B10
Butler K21
Caldwell E10
Callaway H12
Camden H13
Cape Girardeau L19
Carroll F10
Carter K19
Cass C14
Cedar C17
Chariton F10
Christian D20
Clark I7
Clay C11
Clinton D10
Cole G13
Cooper G12
Crawford I15
Dade C18
Dallas D16
Daviess E9
De Kalb D9
Dent I16
Douglas F19
Dunklin L23
Franklin K13
Gasconade I13
Gentry D8
Greene D19
Grundy F9
Harrison F7
Henry E13
Hickory E15
Holt C7
Howard G11
Howell H20
Iron K17
Jackson C13
Jasper B18
Jefferson L14
Johnson E12
Knox I9
Laclede E16
Lafayette E11
Lawrence C19
Lewis I9
Lincoln K11
Linn G9
Livingston F9

MONTANA 68
Beaverhead D14
Big Horn C11
Blaine I5
Broadwater E12
Carbon B14
Carter H17
Cascade E9
Chouteau F7
Custer H12
Daniels I2
Dawson H9
Deer Lodge C12
Fallon I13
Fergus G9
Flathead C4
Gallatin E13
Garfield F9
Glacier D2
Golden Valley F11
Granite C11
Hill F4
Jefferson D12
Judith Basin F9
Lake C7
Lewis And Clark D9
Liberty E4
Lincoln A2
Madison D13
McCone H8
Meagher F11
Mineral A9
Missoula B9
Musselshell G11
Park E14
Petroleum G9
Phillips G4
Pondera D5
Powder River H14
Powell C11
Prairie H11
Ravalli B11
Richland I8
Roosevelt I4
Rosebud G12
Sanders A6
Sheridan I2
Silver Bow C12
Stillwater F13
Sweet Grass F13
Teton D7
Toole D3
Treasure G12
Valley H4
Wheatland F11
Wibaux I10
Yellowstone G13

NEBRASKA 70
Adams G12
Antelope H6
Arthur H5
Banner H1
Blaine H8
Boone H8
Box Butte D3
Boyd D12
Brown G4
Buffalo H10
Burt J8
Butler I10
Cass K10
Cedar I5
Chase E6
Cherry F4
Cheyenne I3
Clay K13
Colfax I9
Cuming I8
Custer H9
Dakota I6
Dawes D2
Dawson I10
Deuel F5
Dixon J5
Dodge I9
Douglas J9
Dundy E7
Fillmore K13
Franklin H13
Frontier J8
Furnas J8
Gage K12
Garden F4
Garfield H7
Gosper H11
Grant G5
Greeley H9
Hall H11
Hamilton I11
Harlan H12
Hayes F6
Hitchcock J8
Holt I6
Hooker G5
Howard I10
Jefferson J13
Johnson K11
Kearney H12
Keith F5
Keya Paha H4
Kimball I1
Knox I5
Lancaster J11
Lincoln G8
Logan H8
Loup H7
Madison I7
McPherson G7
Merrick I10
Morrill E3
Nance I9
Nemaha K11
Nuckolls H13
Otoe K10
Pawnee K12
Perkins F6
Phelps H11
Pierce I5
Platte I9
Polk I10
Red Willow J8
Richardson K12
Rock H6
Saline J12
Sarpy J9
Saunders I9
Scotts Bluff D3
Seward J11
Sheridan D2
Sherman H10
Sioux A1
Stanton I7
Thayer J13
Thomas H6
Thurston I6
Valley H9
Washington J9
Wayne I6
Webster H13
Wheeler H7
York I12

NEVADA 72
Churchill C7
Clark K12
Douglas A8
Elko I3
Esmeralda D11
Eureka G5
Humboldt D3
Lander E4
Lincoln J8
Lyon B7
Mineral C9
Nye H8
Pershing C4
Storey A7
Washoe A4
White Pine J5

NEW HAMPSHIRE 73
Belknap H5
Carroll H4
Cheshire I7
Coos F2
Grafton G4
Hillsborough I8
Merrimack H5
Rockingham I6
Strafford I5
Sullivan G6

NEW JERSEY 74
Atlantic H13
Bergen H2
Burlington H11
Camden F11
Cape May H15
Cumberland F14
Essex D53
Gloucester F12
Hudson K5
Hunterdon B8
Mercer C10
Middlesex J8
Monmouth L7
Morris C6
Ocean J11
Passaic C5
Salem D13
Somerset I8
Sussex C2
Union K6
Warren A7

NEW MEXICO 76
Bernalillo D8
Catron B10
Chaves I10
Cibola B6
Colfax I2
Curry J7
Debaca H8
Dona Ana E13
Eddy I12
Grant B12
Guadalupe G6
Harding I4
Hidalgo A13
Lea K12
Lincoln G10
Los Alamos D4
Luna D13
McKinley A4
Mora H4
Otero F12
Quay I5
Rio Arriba D2
Roosevelt J8
Sandoval C5
San Juan B2
San Miguel H5
Santa Fe E5
Sierra C11
Socorro D9
Taos F2
Torrance E8
Union J2
Valencia D8

NEW YORK 80
Albany K7
Allegany E8
Bronx C2
Broome I9
Cattaraugus D9
Cayuga H6
Chautauqua A9
Chemung F9
Chenango J8
Clinton L1
Columbia K9
Cortland H7
Delaware J9
Dutchess D29
Erie B7
Essex D53
Franklin J1
Fulton J5

NORTH CAROLINA 84
Alamance C4
Alexander C9
Alleghany B9
Anson E7
Ashe A8
Avery B9
Beaufort D15
Bertie C5
Bladen E11
Brunswick H1
Buncombe C1
Burke C8
Cabarrus D5
Caldwell C9
Camden A9
Carteret C18
Caswell A4
Catawba C9
Chatham C5
Cherokee B5
Chowan B15
Clay B6
Cleveland B10
Columbus G1
Craven F16
Cumberland E10
Currituck A8
Dare C17
Davidson C5
Davie C4
Duplin F12
Durham C4
Edgecombe D13
Forsyth B7
Franklin B11
Gaston B6
Gates C5
Graham A5
Granville A5
Greene E14
Guilford B6
Halifax C12
Harnett D8
Haywood C1
Henderson C2
Hertford B5
Hoke C8
Hyde C16
Iredell C4
Jackson B6
Johnston D7
Jones F16
Lee D6
Lenoir E14
Lincoln C8
Macon A11
Madison C9
Martin E10
McDowell C5
Mecklenburg B8
Mitchell B8
Montgomery B20
Moore D8
Nash C11
New Hanover F14
Northampton A14
Onslow F4
Orange C5
Pamlico F17
Pasquotank A9
Pender F13
Perquimans B16
Person A9
Pitt D15
Polk D1
Randolph C6
Richmond C8
Robeson F9
Rockingham A3
Rowan C5
Rutherford D3
Sampson E9
Scotland C9
Stanly C6
Stokes A5
Surry A9
Swain A7
Transylvania B2
Tyrrell B16
Union B8
Vance A10
Wake C11
Warren A13
Washington B16
Watauga A8
Wayne E9
Wilkes A8
Wilson D12
Yadkin B4
Yancey B9

NORTH DAKOTA 87
Adams E4
Barnes I9
Benson I6
Billings C7
Bottineau E2
Bowman B5
Burke E1
Burleigh F7
Cass I8
Cavalier H3
Dickey H5
Divide C1
Dunn D7
Eddy I7
Emmons F5
Foster H7
Golden Valley A6
Grand Forks J6
Grant E5
Griggs I8

OHIO 88
Adams F23
Allen B9
Ashland F9
Ashtabula C29
Athens H22
Auglaize A32
Belmont J17
Brown E22
Butler A18
Carroll I11
Champaign C16
Clark C17
Clermont E21
Clinton D19
Columbiana J11
Coshocton H13
Crawford E10
Cuyahoga H6
Darke A15

OKLAHOMA 92
Adair C18
Alfalfa A10
Atoka B4
Beaver B6
Beckham D7
Blaine A11
Bryan A15
Caddo B15
Canadian D11
Carter H2
Cherokee C17
Choctaw L18
Cimarron B1
Cleveland E12
Coal L6
Comanche E15
Cotton H16
Craig H13
Creek H3
Custer D8
Delaware C17
Dewey D8
Ellis C6
Garfield C11
Garvin G1
Grady E13
Grant B11
Greer D8
Harmon C9
Harper C6
Haskell C16
Hughes K4
Jackson C9
Jefferson E15
Johnston L2
Kay A11
Kingfisher C11
Kiowa D16
Latimer C16
Le Flore K13
Lincoln F12
Logan D11
Love J2
Major B10
Marshall K3
Mayes C17
McClain E13
McCurtain L14
McIntosh L5
Murray G1
Muskogee C15
Noble A11
Nowata H13
Okfuskee I4
Oklahoma E11

OREGON 94
Baker F14
Benton F4
Clackamas G5
Clatsop B1
Columbia D2
Coos A9
Crook G7
Curry A11
Deschutes G7
Douglas C9
Gilliam H3
Grant F10
Harney H12
Hood River H4
Jackson C12
Jefferson G6
Josephine B12
Klamath F12
Lake F11
Lane E6
Lincoln D4
Linn F5
Malheur I12
Marion F4
Morrow H3
Multnomah F3
Polk E4
Sherman H4
Tillamook C3
Umatilla I3
Union H12
Wallowa I13
Wasco H5
Washington E3
Wheeler G7
Yamhill E4

PENNSYLVANIA 98
Adams G14
Allegheny C13
Armstrong D11
Beaver B12
Bedford F13
Berks L12
Blair F11
Bradford H3
Bucks N11
Butler C11
Cambria E12
Cameron F7
Carbon K8
Centre G8
Chester L14
Clarion D9
Clearfield F9
Clinton G7
Columbia I8
Crawford B7
Cumberland I12
Dauphin J11
Delaware L14
Elk E7
Erie B5
Fayette C15
Forest D8
Franklin G14
Fulton F14
Greene B16
Huntingdon G11
Indiana D11
Jefferson E9
Juniata H11
Lackawanna L6
Lancaster K13
Lawrence B11
Lebanon K11
Lehigh L10
Luzerne K7
Lycoming G6
McKean F6
Mercer B9
Mifflin G10
Monroe M8
Montgomery M12
Montour I8
Northampton M9
Northumberland I9
Perry H11
Philadelphia N13
Pike N6
Potter G5
Schuylkill J9
Snyder H10
Somerset D14
Sullivan I6
Susquehanna K4
Tioga G4
Union H9
Venango C8
Warren E6
Washington B14
Wayne N5
Westmoreland D13
Wyoming J5
York I14

RHODE ISLAND 103
Bristol G12
Kent C9
Newport E16
Providence B12
Washington B13

SOUTH CAROLINA 104
Abbeville B5
Aiken E5
Allendale E7
Anderson A5
Bamberg F6
Barnwell E6
Beaufort E9
Berkeley H7
Calhoun F5
Charleston H8/7
Cherokee D2
Chester E2
Chesterfield G2
Clarendon G5
Colleton F8
Darlington H3
Dillon I3
Dorchester G6
Edgefield D5
Fairfield E3
Florence H4
Georgetown I6
Greenville B3
Greenwood B5
Hampton E8
Horry J5
Jasper D8
Kershaw F3
Lancaster F2
Laurens B4
Lee G4
Lexington E4
Marion I4
Marlboro I2
McCormick C6
Newberry D4
Oconee A4
Orangeburg F6
Pickens A3
Richland F4
Saluda D5
Spartanburg C2
Sumter G4
Union D3
Williamsburg H5
York E1

SOUTH DAKOTA 105
Aurora H10
Beadle H8
Bennett E11
Bon Homme I11
Brookings J7
Brown H3
Brule G10
Buffalo G9
Butte A5
Campbell F3
Charles Mix H11
Clark I6
Clay J12
Codington I6
Corson D4
Custer A9
Davison H10
Day I4
Deuel J6
Dewey D6
Douglas H11
Edmunds G4
Fall River A11
Faulk G6
Grant J5
Gregory G12
Haakon D8
Hamlin J6
Hand H7
Hanson H10
Harding B2
Hughes F7
Hutchinson I11
Hyde G7
Jackson D9
Jerauld H9
Jones E9
Kingsbury I7
Lake J8
Lawrence A6
Lincoln J11
Lyman F9
Marshall I3
McCook I10
McPherson G3
Meade B6
Mellette E10
Miner I8
Minnehaha J9
Moody J8
Pennington B8
Perkins C3
Potter F6
Roberts J3

TENNESSEE 106
Anderson B7
Bedford K23
Benton B7
Bledsoe A24
Blount F10
Bradley C24
Campbell D7
Cannon J22
Carroll B8
Carter A6
Cheatham H20
Chester A10
Claiborne E6
Clay A20
Cocke G9
Coffee K24
Crockett G25
Cumberland A22
Davidson I21
Decatur B9
De Kalb J22
Dickson H21
Dyer F24
Fayette D10
Fentress A21
Franklin K24
Gibson G25
Giles I24
Grainger F7
Greene G7
Grundy K24
Hamblen F7
Hamilton B24
Hancock F6
Hardeman B10
Hardin B10
Hawkins G6
Haywood F25
Henderson A9
Henry B7
Hickman I23
Houston G20
Humphreys H21
Jackson A20
Jefferson F8
Johnson A5
Knox E8
Lake E24
Lauderdale E25
Lawrence I24
Lewis I23
Lincoln J25
Loudon D9
Macon A20
Madison A9
Marion L24
Marshall I23
Maury I23
McMinn C24
McNairy A10
Meigs C24
Monroe D9
Montgomery G20
Moore J24
Morgan B22
Obion F24
Overton A21
Perry I23
Pickett A20
Polk C25
Putnam A21
Rhea A24
Roane C23
Robertson H20
Rutherford J22
Scott A22
Sequatchie L24
Sevier F9
Shelby D10
Smith A20
Stewart G20
Sullivan A5
Sumner I20
Tipton D25
Trousdale B20
Unicoi A6
Union E7
Van Buren A23
Warren A23
Washington A6
Wayne I24
Weakley B7
White A22
Williamson I22
Wilson J21

TEXAS 108
Anderson H24
Andrews H9
Angelina F31
Aransas C21
Archer D2
Armstrong I4
Atascosa S6
Austin G28
Bailey H5
Bandera B28
Bastrop B27
Baylor B21
Bee E26
Bell C26
Bexar C29
Blanco E27
Borden H12
Bosque C24
Bowie K23
Brazoria E26
Brazos F27
Brewster G13
Briscoe I5
Brooks D33
Brown C24
Burleson F27
Burnet D26
Caldwell E28
Calhoun F26
Callahan G21
Cameron C35
Camp I23
Carson J3
Cass J23
Castro H5
Chambers G29
Cherokee H25
Childress I6
Clay D2
Cochran H7
Coke G21
Coleman A24
Collin G21
Collingsworth I4
Colorado G28
Comal D28
Comanche C23
Concho L11
Cooke F20
Coryell C25
Cottle L5
Crane J11
Crockett J13
Crosby J7
Culberson E11
Dallam J1
Dallas F22
Dawson H10
Deaf Smith H4
Delta H21
Denton F21
De Witt E25
Dickens L6
Dimmit C32
Donley J4
Duval D28
Eastland G22
Ector H10
Edwards A30
Ellis F23
El Paso A9
Erath C23
Falls D26
Fannin G20
Fayette F28
Floyd J6
Foard A21
Fort Bend G28
Franklin I22
Freestone G25
Frio C30
Gaines H8
Galveston G29
Garza J7
Gillespie C27
Glasscock H11
Goliad E26
Gonzales E27
Gray J3
Grayson G20
Gregg I24
Grimes F28
Guadalupe D28
Hale I6
Hall I5
Hamilton C24
Hansford J2
Hardeman B21
Hardin G30
Harris G28
Harrison J24
Hartley J2
Haskell B22
Hays E28
Hemphill J2
Henderson H24
Hidalgo C34
Hill C24
Hockley H7
Hood F22
Hopkins I22
Houston F29
Howard H11
Hudspeth E9
Hunt H21
Hutchinson J2
Irion K11
Jack E21
Jackson F26
Jasper F30
Jeff Davis E12
Jefferson G30
Jim Hogg D32
Jim Wells D32
Johnson F22
Jones B23
Karnes D26
Kaufman G22
Kendall C28
Kenedy D33
Kent H12
Kerr B28
Kimble A29
King B51
Kinney A31
Kleberg D32
Knox B21
Lamar H20
Lamb H6
Lampasas C26
La Salle C31
Lavaca F27
Lee E27
Leon G26
Liberty F29
Limestone F25
Lipscomb K1
Live Oak D27
Llano D26
Loving H9
Lubbock J6
Lynn H7
Madison F27
Marion I23
Martin H11
Mason B27
Matagorda H30
Maverick A32
McCulloch L11
McLennan D25
McMullen D30
Medina C29
Menard L12
Midland H11
Milam E27
Mills C25
Mitchell H11
Montague E20
Montgomery G28
Moore J2
Morris I23
Motley L5
Nacogdoches H31
Navarro G24
Newton G31
Nolan G20
Nueces E32
Ochiltree J1
Oldham H3
Orange G31
Palo Pinto E22
Panola J24
Parker F22
Parmer G5
Pecos H12
Polk F30
Potter J3
Presidio E13
Rains H22
Randall I4
Reagan K11
Real A30
Red River I20
Reeves H11
Refugio E26
Roberts J2
Robertson E26
Rockwall G21
Runnels A23
Rusk I24
Sabine H31
San Augustine H31
San Jacinto F29
San Patricio E31
San Saba L11
Schleicher K12
Scurry H11
Shackelford B22
Shelby H31
Sherman J1
Smith H23
Somervell F22
Starr C33
Stephens F22
Sterling K11
Stonewall H12
Sutton K12
Swisher I5
Tarrant F21
Taylor G21
Terrell G13
Terry H7
Throckmorton B21
Titus I22
Tom Green L11
Travis E27
Trinity F29
Tyler G30
Upshur I23
Upton J11
Uvalde B30
Val Verde K13
Van Zandt H23
Victoria F26
Walker F28
Waller G28
Ward H10
Washington F28
Webb C32
Wharton G28
Wheeler K3
Wichita D21
Wilbarger A21
Willacy C34
Williamson D27
Wilson D29
Winkler H9
Wise F21
Wood I22
Yoakum H7
Young E21
Zapata B33
Zavala B30

UTAH 112
Beaver J4
Box Elder B50
Cache J7
Carbon J2
Daggett L8
Davis H9
Duchesne K2
Emery J2
Garfield I6
Grand L3
Iron I5
Juab H2
Kane J6
Millard H4
Morgan I8
Piute I4
Rich J7
Salt Lake H49
San Juan L6
Sanpete H50
Sevier I5
Summit J48
Tooele E48
Uintah L2
Utah H1
Wasatch J1
Washington I6
Wayne J4
Weber H8

VERMONT 114
Addison B6
Bennington A11
Caledonia E4
Chittenden B4
Essex F3
Franklin B2
Grand Isle A2
Lamoille C3
Orange D6
Orleans D1
Rutland A8
Washington C4
Windham C12
Windsor C9

VIRGINIA 116
Accomack M17
Albemarle I8
Alleghany E10
Amelia I11
Amherst G9
Appomattox G10
Arlington A3
Augusta F8
Bath E8
Bedford F10
Bland B12
Botetourt E11
Brunswick H13
Buchanan K3
Buckingham H9
Campbell F11
Caroline J8
Carroll B13
Charles City K10
Charlotte G12
Chesterfield I11
Clarke H5
Craig D11
Culpeper I7
Cumberland H10
Dickenson J3
Dinwiddie I12
Essex K9
Fairfax J6
Fauquier I6
Floyd C12
Fluvanna H9
Franklin D12
Frederick G4
Giles C11
Gloucester L10
Goochland H10
Grayson A13
Greene H8
Greensville H14
Halifax F13
Hanover J9
Henrico I10
Henry D13
Highland E7
Isle Of Wight K12
James City L10
King And Queen K9
King George J7
King William K9
Lancaster L8
Lee J4
Loudoun I5
Louisa I9
Lunenburg H12
Madison H7
Mathews L10
Mecklenburg G14
Middlesex L9
Montgomery C11
Nelson G9
New Kent K10
Northampton M17
Northumberland L8
Nottoway H11
Orange H8
Page G6
Patrick C13
Pittsylvania E13
Powhatan I10
Prince Edward H11
Prince George J11
Prince William I6
Pulaski B11
Rappahannock H7
Richmond L8
Roanoke D11
Rockbridge F9
Rockingham G7
Russell J3

WASHINGTON 118
Adams I7
Asotin L8
Benton H9
Chelan F6
Clallam B4
Clark D12
Columbia K9
Cowlitz D11
Douglas G6
Ferry I3
Franklin I8
Garfield L8
Grant H7
Grays Harbor B8
Island D5
Jefferson C6
King E7
Kitsap D6
Kittitas F8
Klickitat F10
Lewis C10
Lincoln I5
Mason C7
Okanogan G3
Pacific B10
Pend Oreille L2
Pierce E8
San Juan C4
Skagit E4
Skamania E10
Snohomish E6
Spokane L5
Stevens K3
Thurston C8
Wahkiakum B11
Walla Walla J9
Whatcom E2
Whitman K7
Yakima F9

WEST VIRGINIA 120
Barbour F26
Berkeley D31
Boone B31
Braxton E24
Brooke G20
Cabell A30
Calhoun E23
Clay C27
Doddridge E22
Fayette D28
Gilmer E24
Grant F28
Greenbrier D25
Hampshire F30
Hancock H20
Hardy F29
Harrison E24
Jackson B25
Jefferson H22
Kanawha B28
Lewis E24
Lincoln A30
Logan A25
Marion E25
Marshall G21
Mason A24
McDowell C27
Mercer C27
Mineral F27
Mingo J6
Monongalia D25
Monroe D27
Morgan D30
Nicholas C23
Ohio G21
Pendleton F28
Pleasants D22
Pocahontas E25
Preston F24
Putnam A27
Raleigh C26
Randolph F25
Ritchie D23
Roane C24
Summers D27
Taylor E25
Tucker F27
Tyler E20
Upshur E23
Wayne J6
Webster E24
Wetzel F20
Wirt D22
Wood D22
Wyoming B26

WISCONSIN 122
Adams G9
Ashland E2
Barron B5
Bayfield D2
Brown K7
Buffalo C8
Burnett A4
Chippewa D6
Clark E7
Columbia H10
Crawford E12
Dane G11
Dodge I10
Door A6
Douglas C1
Dunn C6
Eau Claire D7
Florence I4
Fond Du Lac I9
Forest H4
Grant E13
Green G12
Green Lake H9
Iowa F11
Iron G3
Jackson E8
Jefferson I11
Juneau F9
Kenosha J13
Kewaunee L6
La Crosse D9
Lafayette F12
Langlade I5
Lincoln G5
Manitowoc L7
Marathon G6
Marinette J4
Marquette H9
Menominee I5
Milwaukee K12
Monroe E9
Oconto J5
Oneida H4
Outagamie J7
Ozaukee K10
Pepin C7
Pierce B7
Polk A5
Portage G8
Price F4
Racine J12
Richland F11
Rock H12
Rusk D5
Sauk F10
Sawyer D4
Shawano I6
Sheboygan K9
St. Croix B6
Taylor F5
Trempealeau D8
Vernon E10
Vilas H3
Walworth I12
Washburn C4
Washington J10
Waukesha I11
Waupaca H7
Waushara H8
Winnebago I8
Wood F8

WYOMING 124
Albany I15
Big Horn E4
Campbell H6
Carbon G14
Converse I9
Crook J4
Fremont E11
Goshen K11
Hot Springs E7
Johnson G6
Laramie K14
Lincoln B11
Natrona G9
Niobrara K8
Park C4
Platte J11
Sheridan G3
Sublette B10
Sweetwater D13
Teton A7
Uinta A14
Washakie F6
Weston J6

Acadia National Park Maine

PARK INFORMATION

Coast of Maine
Established January 19, 1929
47,390 acres

Acadia National Park
PO Box 177
Eagle Lake Road
Bar Harbor, ME 04609-0177
207/288-3338
www.nps.gov/acad

Visitor Centers
Winter Visitor Center is open year-round except January 1, Thanksgiving Day, and December 24 and 25. Hulls Cove Visitor Center is closed November 1 through April.

Entrance Fees
$20/vehicle for seven days or $5/individual for seven days.

Accommodations
Blackwoods Campground accepts reservations (800/365-CAMP) and is open year-round. Seawall Campground is first-come, first-served and is open from mid-May through mid-September. Camping on Isle au Haut requires a special use permit (207/288-3338) and is available from mid-May through mid-October.

The same pristine Maine coast that inspired maritime artist Winslow Homer can be seen in the sweeping landscapes of Acadia National Park, a 47,390-acre park located about 45 miles southeast of Bangor. Visitors can spend a morning among the tidal pools, gazing in wonder at the colorful sponges, sea anemone, starfish, and periwinkles, or they can go for an extended hike among the Canadian-like forests of white spruce and paper birch, red maple, and quaking aspen near the summit of Cadillac Mountain. At 1,530 feet, Cadillac Mountain is the highest point on the Atlantic Coast of the Americas north of Brazil. From its often breezy summit, hikers can take in a panoramic view of this wonderland of granite islands and tranquil sea.

For people looking for more solitude, Acadia offers several smaller outer islands, including Isle au Haut, about 15 miles southwest of the primary island in the park (Mount Desert). Acadia is also known for its wildlife, which includes a profusion of coastal birdlife, such as great blue herons and gulls, warblers and juncos, ospreys and eagles, guillemots and terns. Master wildlife photographer Eliot Porter was known to spend hours stalking the birds of Acadia. Marine mammals include harbor and gray seals, porpoises, and finback whales.

Atlantic coast

Badlands National Park South Dakota

PARK INFORMATION

Southwestern South Dakota
Established November 10, 1978
242,756 acres

Badlands National Park
25216 Ben Reifel Road
PO Box 6
Interior, SD 57750
605/433-5361
www.nps.gov/badl

Visitor Centers
Ben Reifel Visitor Center is open daily, except January 1, Thanksgiving Day, and December 25. White River Visitor Center is open only during the summer months.

Entrance Fees
$10/vehicle for seven days or $5/individual for seven days.

Accommodations
Cedar Pass Campground and Sage Creek Campground are open all year and operate on a first-come, first-served basis. Cedar Pass Lodge (605/433-5460) is open from mid-April through mid-October.

Located about one hour south of Rapid City, South Dakota, on the old homeland of the Sioux, the Badlands is a unique national park that comprises about 242,756 acres and features both high northern prairie wildlife and outstanding geological features. Without the big crowds of some of the other western parks, the Badlands is a good place to experience the solitude of nature.

Visitors will discover perpetually active prairie dog colonies and quietly grazing herds of bison, golden eagles soaring overhead, and scattered bands of mule deer and pronghorn antelope. One of the rarest and most endangered mammals in the world is the black-footed ferret, which can occasionally be seen on the park grasslands, where it lives and feeds on the prairie dogs.

Elsewhere in the park there are brightly colored ridges (the sedimentary bands of color range from gray and blue to yellow and pink) and sandy tablelands. Landscape photography in these scenic areas is best pursued at sunrise or sunset when the warm orange and red light adds to the brilliance of the natural earth tones and blue shadows that begin to artfully form among the contours of the earth. The park is best visited in the spring when the prairie wildflowers (evening primrose, mariposa lily, wild rose, and scarlet globemallow) are at their peak or in the fall when the summer sun has bleached the prairie grasses and the cloudless blue sky goes on forever. Such scenic wonder is a fabulous experience for all visitors who love the great outdoors.

Rock formation

Arches National Park Utah

PARK INFORMATION

Southeastern Utah
Established November 12, 1971
76,519 acres

Arches National Park
PO Box 907
Moab, UT 84532-0907
435/719-2299
www.nps.gov/arch

Visitor Center
The visitor center is open daily,
except December 25.

Entrance Fees
$10/vehicle for seven days or
$5/individual for seven days.

Accommodations
The Devils Garden Camp-
ground is open year-round.
Reservations are available
(877/444-6777).

Arch formation

Arches National Park, located a few miles north of Moab, Utah, contains the world's largest concentration of natural stone arches. There are hundreds of them, and they come in every shape and color imaginable, from the world-famous Delicate Arch, silhouetted magnificently against the nearby La Sal Mountains, to the colossal Landscape Arch. Another noted feature that is easily accessible via the park road is "Park Avenue," where vertical slabs or fins of red Entrada sandstone tower over the surrounding painted desert like New York sky-scrapers.

Close by Park Avenue is Courthouse Towers, where some of the best hiking in the park is found. Visitors often spot such high-desert fauna as mule deer and coyotes at sunrise and sunset. The Win-dows section of the park provides yet another set of fantastic vistas. The lovely rock scenery has been fea-tured in such classic films as Steven Spielberg's *Indiana Jones and the Last Crusade* (Double Arch) and the com-edy *City Slickers* (North Window).

Of course, no trip to Arches would be complete without a walk through Devils Garden, an intricately eroded region of red and orange sandstone in which hikers can view such features as Fin Canyon and Tunnel Arch. Grateful is the way most people feel on visiting the Arches. Grateful that the park is here in America and not in some far-off corner of a distant continent.

Big Bend National Park Texas

PARK INFORMATION

Southwestern Texas
Established June 12, 1944
801,163 acres

Big Bend National Park
PO Box 129
Big Bend National Park, TX
  79834
432/477-2251
www.nps.gov/bibe

Visitor Centers
Chisos Basin Visitor Center and
Persimmon Gap Visitor Center
are open daily year-round. Panther Junction Visitor Center is
open daily, except December 25.
Castolon Visitor Center and Rio
Grande Village Visitor Center are
open November through April.

Entrance Fees
$15/vehicle for seven days or
$5/individual for seven days.

Accommodations
Camping is available year-
round. Reservations are sometimes available (877/444-6777).
Chisos Mountains Lodge
(432/477-2291) is open year-
round.

It is fitting that one of the largest national parks east of the Rocky Mountains should be located in Texas, the second-largest state. Big Bend National Park protects more than 800,000 acres of desert lowlands and moun-tains, all nestled in a bend of the Rio Grande.

The Chisos Mountains, a spectacular self-contained massif, serve as a natural geographic anchor for Big Bend National Park. The centrally located mountains are a complicated geological wonderland of volcanic plugs, igneous crags, forested buttes, jagged outcrops, wild dry pastures, and bone-dry streams. Old horse paths and game trails crisscross the range. On some of those trails you may see bear tracks. The panoramic view from the south rim of the Chisos Mountains, looking out over thousands of square miles in northern Mexico, is one of the finest in the national park system.

The other splendid part of the park is the region around

Texas foothills

the Rio Grande, which forms the southern border of Big Bend National Park for 118 miles. Canyon walls in this area range from 1,200 to 1,600 feet. Down along the river the thick subtropical vegetation forms a veritable jungle. Three great canyons can be found along the Rio Grande: Santa Elena, Mar-iscal, and Boquillas. It is always possible, along these junglelike stretches, for visi-tors to see some of the rarest wild felines in the United States—the ocelot, the jaguarundi, and the jaguar.

Biscayne National Park Florida

PARK INFORMATION

Southern Florida
Established June 28, 1980
172,924 acres

Biscayne National Park
9700 SW 328 Street
Homestead, FL 33033-5634
305/230-7275
www.nps.gov/bisc

Visitor Center
Dante Fascell Visitor Center is open year-round except December 25.

Entrance Fees
Admission is free.

Accommodations
Boca Chita Key Campground and Elliott Key Campground are open year-round.

Biscayne National Park is a place of wonders. Located just a few miles from the crowded streets of Miami, Florida, this park includes over 172,000 acres and protects a unique assemblage of coral reefs, off-shore islands, and associated aquatic environments in the upper Florida Keys.

This park was created by Congress after intense pressure from environmentalists, sports enthusiasts, and other concerned citizens who wanted to save the bay from the threat of developers.

Visitors may snorkel, scuba dive, kayak, or take boat tours among the subtropical waters and reefs. For the most part, the water is shallow—less than ten feet between the keys and the mainland and increasing to 30 feet out among the reefs. Nourished by the sun and the gently moving, warm-water currents, the reef systems are incredibly rich. Swimmers and divers can behold the exotic beauty of the reefs—the crenelated surface of the brain coral, the widely branching elkhorn coral, and the bright colors of the fire coral—and the multitudes of small and large fish, which include everything from schools of neon-bright hamlets to slow-moving solitary parrot fish. Other fauna include rays, sharks, barracudas, and moray eels.

For those unable to get into the water, tours in glass-bottom boats are conducted daily if surface winds are not too severe and bottom sediments are not too roiled. On these tours, visitors can float above rich green beds of sea grasses, which shelter such fascinating life-forms as sea urchins, sponges, sea worms, sea feathers, and sea whips, or they can head out farther into the magical fairy world of the coral reefs, where angel fish drift gently on the wave surge and the bright colors and unusual forms seem like something from a child's dream. One thing is certain—visit the legendary reefs of Biscayne once, and you will be sure to return.

Cape Florida Lighthouse

Bryce Canyon National Park Utah

PARK INFORMATION

Southwestern Utah
Established September 15, 1928
35,835 acres

Bryce Canyon National Park
PO Box 170001
Bryce Canyon, UT 84717-0001
435/834-5322
www.nps.gov/brca

Visitor Center
The visitor center is open daily except January 1, Thanksgiving Day, and December 25.

Entrance Fees
$10/vehicle for seven days or $5/individual for seven days.

Accommodations
North Campground is open year-round. Some reservations are available (877/444-6777). Sunset Campground is open from mid-April to mid-October and operates on a first-come, first-served basis. Bryce Canyon Lodge (888/297-2757) is open from April to October.

Hoodoos: That's the evocative word used to describe the eerie orange and red pinnacle formations of eroded sandstone that make Bryce Canyon National Park, located in southwestern Utah, famous around the world. Each year, one million or so pilgrims journey to Bryce Canyon, many arriving on tour buses from nearby Las Vegas.

Nowhere else in the world can you see so many oddly shaped and brightly colored rock pillars. The distinctive hoodoos are scattered over the countryside in sharp warriorlike ridges, solitary hermit spires, or closely clustered familial groups. From the coliseumlike overlooks, commanding vistas can be had of the remarkable eroded landscape that makes up the scenery in Bryce Canyon National Park.

Many people choose to visit the park in the winter months when snowdrifts make the hoodoos look even more striking (and the crowds are diminished). The pink, yellow, orange, and red rocks provide a spectacular contrast with the white snow, green pines, and blue sky. Cross-country skiing is a favorite pastime at that season of the year. Best of all, in any season, are the fantastic trails of Bryce Canyon, including the Riggs Spring Loop, which drops deeply into the rock spire country, and the Wall Street Trail, where photographers often come to take photos of the Douglas firs, which tower distinctly upward from the steep canyon bottom.

Hoodoos

Black Canyon of the Gunnison National Park Colorado

PARK INFORMATION

Western Colorado
Established October 21, 1999
32,950 acres

Black Canyon of the Gunnison National Park
102 Elk Creek
Gunnison, CO 81230
970/641-2337
www.nps.gov/blca

Visitor Center
The South Rim Visitor Center is open year-round except January 1, Thanksgiving Day, and December 25.

Entrance Fees
$8/vehicle for seven days or $4/individual for seven days (persons 16 years old and younger are free).

Accommodations
South Rim campgrounds are available year-round. Some reservations are available (877/444-6777). North Rim campgrounds are available from mid-May to mid-October and operate on a first-come, first-served basis.

The Gunnison River commences high in the central Rockies of Colorado. For nearly 100 miles it flows through a rolling sage-and-aspen-covered country before entering one of the most spectacular gorges in North America—the Black Canyon. Here the melted snow of the distant peaks cuts through half a mile of dark-colored gneisses and schists. These formations are among the oldest rocks on the planet (some of the rocks date back more than 1.7 billion years).

Visitors to Black Canyon of the Gunnison National Park can view the steep bluffs from viewpoints on the North Rim, which is accessible from Hotchkiss, or on the South Rim, which is reached via Montrose. Such vista points as Chasm View and Dragon Point offer panoramas every bit as remarkable as anything at the much more crowded Grand Canyon.

The gorge is a favorite among kayakers and hikers as well as wildlife enthusiasts, for it offers excellent habitat for such species as bighorn sheep, mule deer, and elk. Bird-watchers often spot raptors—golden eagles, bald eagles, and red-tailed hawks, in addition to common upland species—ravens, pinyon jays, black-billed magpies, and violet-green swallows.

Although small in terms of acreage, Black Canyon offers a concentrated experience of one of the most remarkable creations of nature in the Rocky Mountains. The park is particularly beautiful in the autumn when the color of the Gambel oak turns a warm rust red and the aspen are as bright as gold.

Black Canyon

Canyonlands National Park Utah

PARK INFORMATION

Southeastern Utah
Established September 12, 1964
337,598 acres

Canyonlands National Park
2282 SW Resource Boulevard
Moab, UT 84532
435/719-2313
www.nps.gov/cany

Visitor Centers
The Island in the Sky Visitor Center and The Needles District Visitor Center are open daily except December 25. The Hans Flat Ranger Station in The Maze District is open daily except December 25.

Entrance Fees
$10/vehicle for seven days or $5/individual for seven days.

Accommodations
Willow Flat Campground in the Island in the Sky District and Squaw Flat Campground in the Needles District are open year-round and operate on a first-come, first-served basis.

Two great rivers in the West are the Green River and the Colorado River, which make their confluence in Canyonlands National Park. Because it is less crowded than the Grand Canyon or Arches, Canyonlands National Park has become one of the most popular parks on the Colorado Plateau. In fact, Canyonlands is a hiker's paradise, with hundreds of miles of excellent trails into the slickrock backcountry.

The park is conveniently divided into three regions—The Island in the Sky, The Needles, and The Maze. The Island in the Sky lies north of the Green/Colorado confluence; The Needles consists of the country south of the Colorado River; and The Maze (the wildest and most remote area of the park) is found west of the Green and the Colorado. Only those with a four-wheel-drive vehicle, plenty of drinking water, and a good pair of hiking boots can enter The Maze. Prior to the park's formation in 1964, most of the country in The Maze had been essentially unexplored. Today, however, many "desert rats" are familiar with the features of this starkly beautiful "Land of Standing Rocks."

Most visitors to Canyonlands National Park tour The Island in the Sky district, which features such spectacular overlooks as Grand Point View and Green River, and The Needles, where the trails lead to such wonderful spots as Chesler Park, Peekaboo Spring, Horse Canyon, Butler Flat, and the Devil's Kitchen. Hundreds of prehistoric Native American sites are in Canyonlands, including some awesome examples of rock art (especially in The Maze region).

Colorado River

Capitol Reef National Park Utah

PARK INFORMATION

Southern Utah
Established December 18, 1971
241,904 acres

Capitol Reef National Park
HC 70 Box 15
Torrey, UT 84775-9602
435/425-3791
www.nps.gov/care

Visitor Center
The visitor center is open daily except December 25.

Entrance Fees
$5/vehicle for seven days.

Accommodations
Cathedral Valley Campground, Cedar Mesa Campground, and Fruita Campground are open year-round.

Canyon mesa

Capitol Reef does not have any "reefs," per se, except in the sense of upthrust rocky ramparts that resemble tropical coral reefs in their varied colors. It is also renowned for its enormous light-colored domes that resemble the dome of the U.S. Capitol and for its intricate mazes of red cliffs, pinnacles, and canyons.

Capitol Reef National Park is located in south central Utah among many other of the legendary "slickrock" parks. Its chief feature is the Waterpocket Fold, an immense doubling up of sedimentary rock layers along a 100-mile front in the painted desert. Breached in many places by streams and erosion, the up-folding rocks present a striking spectacle of nature in the Southwest.

One of the most wonderful parts of the canyon is along the Fremont River. In this deep-cut passage, the early Mormons settled and planted extensive groves of fruit trees, including apple and peach. The park headquarters and visitor center are found here, along with a fine camp-

ground. At sunrise and sunset scattered bands of mule deer are often seen feeding in this area, as well as the occasional coyote and gray fox.

Another marvelous area is located in Cathedral Valley to the north of the Fremont River Canyon. In fact, Ansel Adams took one of his most memorable photographs (of the Temple of the Sun rock formation) at this site. The backcountry of Capitol Reef National Park is a rugged realm, and careful preparations should be made before undertaking any major trips. Most importantly, sufficient water must be taken in this vast desert region.

Channel Islands National Park California

PARK INFORMATION

Off the Southern California coast
Established March, 5, 1980
249,561 acres

Channel Islands National Park
1901 Spinnaker Drive
Ventura, CA 93001
805/658-5730
www.nps.gov/chis

Visitor Center
Robert J. Lagomarsino Visitor Center is open daily except Thanksgiving Day and December 25.

Entrance Fees
Admission is free.

Accommodations
Campsites are available year-round on all five islands. Reservations are available (800/365-CAMP).

Arch Rock

Only 90 minutes by boat from the coast of California is Arch Rock, a 40-foot high arch and the gateway to the Channel Islands. The national park comprises the five northernmost islands of this eight-island chain jutting

from the Pacific along the Santa Barbara coast.

The islands were inhabited as early as 11,000–30,000 years ago. How people arrived there still remains a mystery. Today the fire pits with the bones of small

mammals that the people cooked can still be found in the outlying islands.

Archaeological remains are not the only treasures on the islands. On tidepool walks visitors may see starfish, sponges, periwinkles, crabs,

and limpets. While snorkeling or scuba diving, the seaweed may seem like a multihued carpet on the sea floor, with sea anemones nesting together in small colonies that resemble wildflower beds. Boat-in backcountry campers will observe a variety of wildlife depending on the time of year. In the spring, double-crested cormorants, brown pelicans, pigeon guillemots, surfbirds, and oyster catchers prowl along the coast. In June, hulking sea lions give birth to their young while vying for space on the rocks with the bulbous-snouted northern elephant seals. In December, 20-ton gray whales migrate south from their summer feeding grounds up north in places like Glacier Bay National Parks. Higher up in the mountains, the sand dunes are anchored by the abundant vegetation, such as tree sunflowers that burst into a rich golden hue in the autumn months. Many people believe the best time of year to visit Channel Islands National Park is in the fall.

Carlsbad Caverns National Park New Mexico

Stalactites

Carlsbad Caverns, known locally to southern New Mexicans as the "Bat Caves," are one of the largest natural caverns in the Western Hemisphere. Within the 46,766 acres of Carlsbad Caverns National Park are more than 84 major caves, featuring such unusual formations as the Giant Dome, an enormous pedestal of coral reeflike mineral projections, and the King's Palace, which is distinguished by a multitude of hanging stone draperies.

Visitors enter the park (the greatest depth of which is 1,034 feet!) either by walking into the natural entrance or by riding the elevator. Once in the caverns, people either take the ranger-guided tours or go off on one of the self-guided trails, which include such spectacles as the magnificent Big Room.

In 1986 an extensive series of new caverns were discovered, many of the corridors of which lead off for many miles beyond what was originally known as the Carlsbad Cav-

erns. Above the surface, the park protects a rugged region of the Chihuahuan Desert, the largest desert in North America. Fauna includes such species as mule deer, coyotes, mountain lions, and ringtails. Flora includes the agave, or century plant, prickly pear cactus, and ocotillo. Although summers are hot, winters are quite mild. As with all caverns, the air beneath the earth remains in the comfortable 50s year-round.

Congaree National Park South Carolina

One of the newest national parks, Congaree is a primal forest on the river of the same name that's a true sanctuary for plant and animal life. The park contains the largest contiguous tract of old-growth floodplain hardwood forest in the United States. The soaring trees here are some of the tallest in the eastern part of the country; together they make up one of the highest forest canopies in the whole world. Types of trees run the gamut from cedar to cypress to pine; there are 75 species in all. Because of the endangered nature of Congaree's woodlands, the park has also been designated an International Biosphere Reserve.

The park draws recreational visitors in the form of boaters, hikers, anglers, and campers. While the park has several well-developed trails, the canoe is the vehicle of choice for those who want to see Congaree's pristine heart; administration has marked several canoe trails that vary in length and difficulty. Cedar Creek is the body of water of choice here, as there is no vehicle access to Congaree River.

Beyond the numerous recreational opportunities, many visitors come to the park to try to catch a fleeting glimpse of Congaree's abundant wildlife, highlighted by about 175 bird species. On that long list are eight woodpecker species perfectly adapted to this dense forest, including the endangered red-cockaded woodpecker. The park's mammal checklist includes such creatures as river otters, mule deer, opossums, bobcats, flying squirrel, and wild boar.

Old-growth forest

Crater Lake National Park Oregon

PARK INFORMATION

Southwestern Oregon
Established May 22, 1902
183,224 acres

Crater Lake National Park
PO Box 7
Crater Lake, OR 97604
541/594-3100
www.nps.gov/crla

Visitor Centers
Steel Visitor Center is open daily except December 25. Rim Village Visitor Center is open from early June through late September.

Entrance Fees
$10 for seven days.

Accommodations
Mazama Campground is open from mid-June to early October. Lost Creek Campground is open from mid-July to early October. Crater Lake Lodge (541/830-8700) is open from mid-May to mid-October. Mazama Village Motor Inn (541/830-8700) is open from early June to early October.

One would have to search long and hard to find a blue as intense as the blue of Crater Lake. This phenomenon occurs in part because the freshwater lake is incredibly deep—almost 2,000 feet! The purity, tranquility, and hauntingly translucent color of Crater Lake has long attracted artists, photographers, and nature aficionados.

Crater Lake

A rim road completely encircles the six-mile-wide crater far above the surface of the water, and a small village on the rim completes the picture. Despite the modest developments, visitors can still have those peaceful moments of solitude with the lake on hiking trails that wander among the thick quiet forests of spruce and fir before turning suddenly toward the steep rim.

Crater Lake National Park is well known for its deep snows (some years, they are more than 50 feet). Those same prodigious drifts nourish the wildflower displays that linger long into September, and, some years, even into early October. These include monkeyflower, spreading phlox, paintbrush, aster, lupine, and penstemon, among many others. The forests provide a sanctuary for such native fauna as deer, elk, coyotes, black bears, bobcats, and assorted bird life (from common jays to bald and golden eagles). It is hard to believe, among all the harmony and gentle birdsong that surround Crater Lake today, that at one time it was the scene of one of nature's most violent events: a volcanic eruption.

Death Valley National Park California

PARK INFORMATION

East central California
Established October 31, 1994
3,372,402 acres

Death Valley National Park
PO Box 579
Death Valley, CA 92328
760/786-3200
www.nps.gov/deva

Visitor Centers
Beatty Information Center, Furnace Creek Visitor Center and Museum, and Scotty's Castle Visitor Center and Museum are open daily.

Entrance Fees
$10/vehicle for seven days or $5/individual for seven days.

Accommodations
Five campgrounds are open year-round. Five more campgrounds are open on a more limited basis. Some reservations are available (800/365-CAMP). Lodging is available year-round at Furnace Creek Ranch (760/786-2345), Panamint Springs Resort (775/482-7680), and Stovepipe Wells Village (760/786-2387). Furnace Creek Inn (760/786-2345) is open from mid-October to mid-May.

A brutally rugged but delicately beautiful land of extremes, Death Valley National Park owns the distinction of having the lowest elevation in the Western Hemisphere (282 feet below sea level near Badwater), as well as the record for the highest temperature (134 degrees Fahrenheit). The park is a place of radical geography, for it also protects Telescope Peak, with an elevation of 11,049 feet. At the higher elevations, desert fir, spruce, and quaking aspen are found in abundance in stark contrast to the plantless desert floor of the valley.

Death Valley is the largest U.S. national park outside of Alaska. Its landscape encompasses numerous ecosystems and destinations of interest, including salt and alkaline flats that stretch for miles, broad regions of sand dunes, winding ancient canyons, multicolored rock cliffs and ridges, and historical sites. Although the average annual rainfall is less than two inches, Pacific storms occasionally roar in and cause flash floods that wash out roads, trails, and campgrounds. On most days of the year, however, Death Valley is a sunny paradise where one can experience great solitude and tranquility. In the wintertime, it is a haven for "snowbirds," who park their recreational vehicles and stay for weeks, sometimes months.

Because of its unique climate and geography, Death Valley is a realm unlike any other, except perhaps the Dead Sea region of Israel (which is even farther below sea level). Death Valley is a place where life has been largely stripped away, and the original surface of the earth can be seen, naked and bare, in its pure and elementary shapes. Line, form, and color reign here—not humans, beasts, or nature.

There are rocks in Death Valley formed when life first trafficked in the tides of the moon, and mountain ranges that will still be standing into the far distant future. Death Valley will forever be the domain of the sun, sand, wind, and rock.

Sand dunes

Cuyahoga Valley National Park Ohio

PARK INFORMATION

Northeastern Ohio
Established October 11, 2000
32,861 acres

Cuyahoga Valley National Park
15610 Vaughn Road
Brecksville, OH 44141
216/524-1497, 440/546-5991
www.nps.gov/cuva

Visitor Centers
Canal Visitor Center is open daily. Happy Days Visitor Center is open Wednesday through Sunday year-round. The Hunt Farm Visitor Information Center is open daily from June to August and on weekends from September to May. All visitor centers are closed on January 1, Thanksgiving Day, and December 25.

Entrance Fees
Admission is free.

Accommodations
Camping is not allowed in the park. Cuyahoga Valley HI-Stanford Hostel (330/467-8711) and the Inn at Brandywine Falls (330/467-1812) are open year-round.

In the backyard of Cleveland and Akron is Cuyahoga Valley National Park, centered on the historically and ecologically significant Cuyahoga River. While the river runs directly into the suburbs of both cities from the Cuyahoga Valley, the park is a world away. The only national park in the state of Ohio, Cuyahoga Valley has remnants of the old Ohio & Erie Canal, a scenic railroad, golf courses, ski resorts, a music center, and entire towns.

At the center of all of the activity is the twisty Cuyahoga—"crooked river" in the regional Native American tongue—which winds its way through floodplains, valleys, and ravines on its 22-mile journey through the park. Nearly 200 miles of streams feed the river. The ecology here is diverse, the intermingling of two distinct geographic regions—the Appalachian Plateau and the bordering Central Lowlands—as well as some of the only remaining wetlands environments in Ohio.

The valley's 1,200 wetlands acres help support a diverse wildlife population, with white-tailed deer being the park's most visible resident. Cuyahoga supports nearly 200 species of birds, as well as numerous invertebrates, fish, amphibians, mammals, and reptiles. Beavers, coyotes, turtles, and wild turkeys are just a few of the park's wild denizens. The rich soil of the Cuyahoga Valley supports a mosaic of flora, more than 900 plant species in all. There are forests rich in oak, hickory, and maple. Today the Park Service authorizes a number of sustainable agricultural operations within the boundaries of Cuyahoga Valley National Park, including a vineyard and an herb farm.

Brandywine Falls

Dry Tortugas National Park Florida

PARK INFORMATION

Off Florida's southwestern coast
Established October 26, 1992
64,701 acres

Dry Tortugas National Park
PO Box 6208
Key West, FL 33041
305/242-7700
www.nps.gov/drto

Visitor Center
The visitor center is open year-round.

Entrance Fees
$5/adult for seven days.

Accommodations
Garden Key Campground operates on a first-come, first-served basis.

Seventy miles west of Key West, Florida, is one of the hidden jewels of the national park system: Dry Tortugas National Park. The centerpiece of this unusual park is Fort Jefferson, the largest brick and masonry structure in the Western Hemisphere and the biggest fort still standing from the 19th century.

From the standpoint of natural history, the park is important to the region in that it protects seven coral islands—the Dry Tortugas, the most pristine coral reef in the continental United States. These reefs include substantial beds of turtle grass, as well as hard corals—brain, elkhorn, and fan. Such fish as angelfish, butterfly fish, hamlets, tarpon, and snapper are found here. In fact, the celebrated author and sports enthusiast Ernest Hemingway once fished for Atlantic marlin in these cerulean-blue and jade-green seas.

Sea turtles also breed on the sandy beaches of the park, and seabirds include pelicans, gulls, terns, frigate birds, and tropic birds. In addition, the park holds a number of sunken shipwrecks, some dating back several centuries. Needless to say, the park is a favorite of divers and snorkelers, as well as beachcombers. Who says you have to travel to Micronesia to see a pristine reef? Just a short boat ride from the easily accessible islands of Key West will bring you to a reef system just as spectacular.

Fort Jefferson

Denali National Park Alaska

PARK INFORMATION

Central Alaska
Established December 2, 1980
6,075,030 acres

Denali National Park
PO Box 9
Denali Park, AK 99755-0009
907/683-2294
www.nps.gov/dena

Visitor Center
The visitor center is open daily from May to August. Talkeetna Ranger Station and Murie Science and Learning Center are open year-round.

Entrance Fees
$20/family for seven days or $10/individual for seven days.

Accommodations
Riley Creek Campground is open year-round. Savage River Campground, Sanctuary River Campground, and Teklanika River Campground are open from May to September, depending on the weather. Wonder Lake Campground is open from June to September, depending on the weather. Reservations are available (800/622-7275).

A cold wind rattled through the tundra valley, letting everyone know this was the rooftop of the world. Suddenly there was the sound of hooves, of lungs breathing hard, of animals grunting from exertion. On the hill across the river there was one caribou, then three, then a dozen, then 50, and then still more. In a continual mass the caribou moved steadily down the hill and toward the river. When they reached it, the herd did not pause but jumped in and began swimming across until the river seemed not a river of water but a river of caribou.

It is scenes like this—of vast herds of migratory animals living in absolute freedom and natural abundance—that make Denali National Park such a unique wildlife sanctuary in the modern world. One of the largest national parks anywhere in the world, Denali stretches more than 100 miles along the Alaska range and protects an area approximately the size of the state of Massachusetts.

Near the center of the park is Mount McKinley, also known by its native Athabascan name of Denali, "The High One." At 20,320 feet, it is the highest mountain in North America and one of the tallest freestanding mountains in the world (18,000 feet from base to summit). Down the flanks of Denali flow deep glaciers of ice, which give rise to the rivers that shape the surrounding landscape and support the legendary wildlife of the region.

Most visitors concentrate their wildlife viewing activities along the 90-mile gravel road that bisects the northern range of the park. Along the way to Wonder Lake, the park road crosses five river valleys and climbs four mountain passes. Views are magnificent, and wildlife—grizzly and black bears, wolves, caribou, moose, and sheep—are frequently in view.

Toklat River

Everglades National Park Florida

PARK INFORMATION

Southern Florida
Established December 6, 1947
1,508,537 acres

Everglades National Park
40001 State Road 9336
Homestead, FL 33034-6733
305/242-7700
www.nps.gov/ever

Visitor Centers
Five visitor centers are open year-round.

Entrance Fees
$10/vehicle for seven days or $5/individual for seven days.

Accommodations
Flamingo Campground and Long Pine Key Campground are open year-round. Reservations are available (800/365-CAMP). Backcountry camping is also available. Flamingo Lodge, Marina, and Outpost Resort (800/600-3813) are open year-round.

Imagine a place where migratory birds flock in such huge numbers as to evoke a scene from the Book of Genesis and alligators carry sleeping water turtles on their backs, where Caribbean manatees float gently among sleepy backwaters and windy seas of saw grass go on forever, and you have Everglades National Park, one of the most unique ecosystems on the planet.

The park—more than 1.5 million acres—was established in 1947, largely through the efforts of now-forgotten conservation leaders such as native Floridian Marjorie Stoneman Douglas (author of *The Everglades: River of the Grass*). The park occupies a sizable portion of south Florida, west of Miami and south of Alligator Alley, and it includes such singular habitats as mangrove and cypress swamps, freshwater lakes and swamps, subtropical hardwood hummocks, saw grass prairie, and marine islands. It is so alive that you can almost feel the pulse of nature. The park serves as one of the last refuges for the Florida panther, which is among the most critically endangered mammals on the planet. Although it may seem incongruous, the Everglades also support a small population of black bear. Fauna that visitors more commonly see includes white-tailed deer, raccoons, herons, egrets, and bald eagles.

The best time to visit the park is mid-December through mid-April when the bugs are less prevalent. At that time of the year, people can escape the crowds by boating on the interior backwaters or by kayaking among the coastal islands.

Freshwater pool

Gates of the Arctic National Park Alaska

PARK INFORMATION

Northern Alaska
Established December 2, 1980
8,472,506 acres

**Gates of the Arctic
National Park**
Bettles Ranger Station
PO Box 26030
Bettles, AK 99726
907/692-5494
www.nps.gov/gaar

Visitor Center
Bettles Ranger Station/Visitor
Center is open year-round, but
hours vary depending on the
season.

Entrance Fees
Admission is free.

Accommodations
There are no established
campgrounds. Backcountry
camping is available.

The Dalton Highway connects Fairbanks, Alaska, with the Arctic Ocean to the north. Only five miles west of this road is Gates of the Arctic National Park, an immense wilderness sanctuary. Yet for the foreseeable future this road is as close as you can get by car to this nearly 8.5-million-acre national park. For the most part, travel into the spectacular park is limited to light aircraft launched from such remote bush villages as Coldfoot, Bettles, or Prospect Creek. Popular wilderness entry points include beautiful Anaktuvuk Pass, remote Wild Lake, and the headwaters of various wild rivers (all totaled, there are six national wild rivers in the park—Alatna, John, Kobuk, Noatak, North Fork Koyukuk, and Tinayguk).

Other than the actual Gates of the Arctic between Frigid Crags and Boreal Mountain, the chief attraction in the park is the Arrigetch Peaks, which are reached via a float plane trip to Circle Lake, west of Bettles. These smooth and steep granite peaks lure many mountain and rock climbers. To the north are lovely mountain lakes, a scattering of diminutive cottonwoods, and a vast wilderness of pale-green tundra, which turns all shades of red, yellow, and orange in the fall. This is the same area that famed conservationist Bob Marshall explored during the 1920s (the Bob Marshall Wilderness in Montana is named for him). Walk in this magnificent setting, and you will be convinced that you are really in one of those "end of the world" places.

Permafrost

Glacier National Park Montana

PARK INFORMATION

Northwestern Montana
Established May 11, 1910
1,013,572 acres

Glacier National Park
PO Box 128
West Glacier, MT 59936
406/888-7800
www.nps.gov/glac

Visitor Centers
Apgar Visitor Center is open
year-round (weekends only
November to March). St. Mary
Visitor Center is open May
through mid-October. Logan
Pass Visitor Center is open
early June through mid-
October.

Entrance Fees
$20/vehicle for seven days or
$5/individual for seven days.

Accommodations
There are 13 campgrounds in
the park variously open from
late spring to early fall. Some
reservations are available
(800/365-CAMP), but most
operate on a first-come, first-
served basis. The park also has
eight lodges and hotels that are
variously open from early May
to late September.

Without a doubt, Glacier National Park is one of the most spectacular parks in North America. Some have gone so far as to call Glacier National Park "Little Switzerland" for its tall spires, deep valleys, and plunging canyons. The park is renowned for its lovely mountain lakes—Grinnel, St. Mary's, Two Medicine, and McDonald—its cascading waterfalls (especially around Logan Pass), and its wilderness trails—Avalanche Basin, Sperry Glacier, the Garden Wall, and Swiftcurrent Valley.

Visitors often spot small family bands of the elusive mountain goat near the trail to Hidden Lake on Logan Pass. Grizzly bears are frequently observed on the 14-mile trail along the Garden Wall, especially in the autumn when the huckleberries are thick at higher elevations. Black bears are sometimes spotted in the avalanche slides near the park roads. Shiras moose are commonly seen in the river and stream meadows at lower elevations. The high

St. Mary's Lake

country of Glacier is well known for its spring and summer wildflower displays, including bear grass (not a grass but a lily) with its tall stalk and gigantic cream-colored flower heads, avalanche lilies, purple gentians, larkspur, and Jones columbine.

No trip to Glacier is complete without a drive up and over the Going-to-the-Sun Road, arguably the most beautiful drive in the entire national park system, with its vast expanses of tundra, falling cataracts, soaring peaks, and scenic valleys. On the eastern side of the park are such striking peaks as Mount Siyeh, Mount Logan, and Reynolds Mountain. Drivers on the western side of the highway are treated to magnificent views of Lake McDonald, the largest lake in the park.

Glacier Bay National Park Alaska

PARK INFORMATION

Southeastern Alaska
Established December 2, 1980
3,283,246 acres

Glacier Bay National Park and Preserve
PO Box 140
Gustavus, AK 99826-0140
907/697-2230
www.nps.gov/glba

Visitor Centers
The visitor center is open daily from late May to early September.

Entrance Fees
Admission is free.

Accommodations
Bartlett Cove campground (907/697-2627) is open from May through September. Four lodges are open variously from mid-May through mid-September.

Glacier

When John Muir first visited Glacier Bay on his 1879 Alaskan trip, he called the place "a wonderland" and "one of the sublimest spectacles of nature."

Glacier Bay is, indeed, just that. Surrounded by towering mountains—some of the tallest in Alaska—and presenting 16 massive tidewater glaciers to the sea, Glacier Bay is also one of the most important wildlife habitats in Alaska, with everything from marine mammals, such as humpback whales, minke whales, killer whales, por-

poises, seals, and river otters, to large land mammals, such as Yukon moose, Alaskan black and brown bears, wolves, and black-tail deer. More than 200 bird species are found in the area, including large colonies of seabirds, and the fishing (halibut, Dolly Varden, and salmon) is among the best in Alaska. Hikers also enjoy some of the best berry picking, specifically blueberries and salmonberries, on the planet.

Most visitors begin their adventures in Glacier Bay from Bartlett Cove, located in the extreme southeastern corner of the park. From there they can hitch rides on park tour boats and go 40 or 50 miles to the north to fabled regions such as Muir Glacier, where John Muir built his cabin more than a century ago. When the sun breaks through the clouds, the icebergs are struck with light, and faraway a thousand birds turn in one graceful movement on the wind. Glacier Bay is truly a place of pure epiphany and revelation.

Great Sand Dunes National Park Colorado

PARK INFORMATION

Southern Colorado
Established November 22, 2000
84,670 acres

Great Sand Dunes National Park and Preserve
11500 Highway 150
Mosca, CO 81146-9798
719/378-6300
www.nps.gov/grsa

Visitor Center
The visitor center is open daily except January 1 and December 25.

Entrance Fees
$3/individual for seven days; individuals 16 years old and younger are free.

Accommodations
Pinyon Flats campground is open year-round and operates on a first-come, first-served basis.

In the shadow of the Sangre de Cristo ("Blood of Christ") mountains in southwestern Colorado, this national park is home to the tallest dunes in North America, mountains of sand measuring 750 feet in height in the San Luis Valley. The dunes come in two varieties: reversing dunes, the largest and the product of wind blowing predominately in opposite directions; and star dunes, shaped by winds blowing in all directions.

The dunes are the product of competing elements: wind and water. Winds of more than 13 miles per hour from the southwest and northeast shake loose available sand, blowing it into one of three deposits in the valley: the cementlike sabkha, the outer sand sheet, and the inner dunefield (home of the biggest dunes). Medrano and Sand creeks also carry sand from the dunefield's north and east borders, transporting it back to where the wind can blow it into the heart of the dunes. All in all, the dunes

Mount Herard

contain nearly 5 billion cubic meters of sand.

Hiking in the dunes is well worth the effort because of the amazing views, with the summit of High Dune offering the best panorama. For visitors with more time to spend, there are also plenty of hiking trails in the surrounding wilderness. Photography, camping, and building sand

castles are also popular activities in the park.

Above the dunes, the park and preserve also include a parcel of alpine tundra, complete with a number of lakes, and six peaks over 13,000 feet in elevation. The forests here, populated by spruce, pine, aspen, and cottonwood, are bordered by grasslands and wetlands,

making good habitat for a wide variety of life.

The park's animal residents include mule deer, elk, coyotes, and bald eagles; bison graze on the adjacent grassland. A number of insect species found in the dunes, such as the Great Sand Dunes tiger beetle and the giant sand treader camel cricket, live nowhere else on Earth.

Grand Canyon National Park Arizona

The true magnificence of the Grand Canyon takes all visitors by surprise. You approach from the south across a gently rising plateau, or from the north across higher and wilder country. Nothing in the topography on either side gives you a hint of what is soon to unfold.

Suddenly you are there, standing on the rim of one of the most sublime and profound spectacles on this planet. The chasm is so vast and so deep that on first sight it looks as though the earth has opened to allow us to glimpse the secrets that lie at its greatest depths.

In the Grand Canyon, the Colorado River has cut through the accumulated layers of the earth's surface to reach what Norman Maclean dubbed "the basement of time." A billion years of history can be seen at a glance, from the Precambrian bedrock at the distant river's edge to fossilized sand dunes only a million years old at the rim.

People lived in the canyon centuries ago, but the first Europeans to explore the area were 13 members of Coronado's expedition. They arrived around 1540. One wrote a letter of disgust because his expedition had encountered an unbridgeable barrier to further exploration.

Canyon at sunrise

In the 1850s, the U.S. Army sent a surveying party into the area, and in 1869, John Wesley Powell, a one-armed major, became the first modern explorer in the canyon's history. Powell set out with a small party in four boats to explore as much of the length of the Colorado River and the canyon as he could. It was an exciting journey that cost the major two of his boats. But he proved that the canyon could be explored. Accounts of his bold river run were widely published, leading to in-creased public interest in the Southwest. By the 1880s, a prospector named John Hance, who was known for his quick wit and tall tales, had begun leading sightseeing parties into the canyon.

For modern travelers, there are actually two Grand Canyons to be visited—the South Rim and the North Rim. Although these two areas are less than a dozen miles apart as the crow flies, they are distinctly different. The North Rim, a thousand feet higher than the South Rim and more remote from major interstates and towns, is less crowded. The South Rim, with an elevation of 7,000 feet and direct access from Interstate 40 and Flagstaff, can be congested, especially during the tourist season. Roughly nine out of ten park visitors go to the South Rim, partly because the views there are thought to be better than those at the North Rim.

For those who want a different perspective, three spectacular trails lead down into the canyon from both the North Rim and the South Rim. The popular Bright Angel Trail winds eight miles from the South Rim down to the Phantom Ranch, a lodge and campground that is clustered among a glen of Fremont cottonwoods on the canyon floor.

An alternative is the famous muleback ride through the natural wonders of the canyon. The mules depart from the South Rim for both day trips and overnight pack trips to Phantom Ranch, where guests can stay in rustic cabins and dormitories. Plan up to 23 months ahead—available spots fill quickly!

While reservations are required months in advance, rafting trips down the Colorado are another means of getting deep into the Grand Canyon. These expeditions vary in length from about three days by motorized raft to 18 days or more by non-motorized dories, which are similar to those used by John Wesley Powell, whose journals are still used as guides by modern river runners.

Grandview

Grand Teton National Park Wyoming

PARK INFORMATION

Northwest Wyoming
Established February 26, 1929
309,995 acres

Grand Teton National Park
PO Drawer 170
Moose, WY 83012-0170
307/739-3300
www.nps.gov/grte

Visitor Centers
Moose Visitor Center is open daily except December 25. Colter Bay Visitor Center is open from early May to early December. Jenny Lake Visitor Center is open from early June to late September. Flagg Ranch Information Station is open from early June to early September.

Entrance Fees
$20/vehicle for seven days; $15/individual on motorcycle for seven days; $10/individual on foot or bicycle for seven days. Fee is valid for Grand Teton and Yellowstone national parks.

Accommodations
Six campgrounds are available at various times from early May to mid-October. They mostly operate on a first-come, first-served basis, but reservations can sometimes be available (800/443-2311). Lodging at Dornan's Spur Ranch Cabins (307/733-2522) is available year-round. Seven other lodges or ranches offer lodging variously from early May to mid-October.

Balsamroot field

The summit of Grand Teton is 13,770 feet above sea level, and the mountain shoots a mile and a half straight up into the Wyoming sky without intervening foothills. Flanked by stunning spires, pinnacles, and buttes, the steepness is breathtaking.

Grand Teton National Park encompasses the 6,300-foot-high valley called Jackson Hole, with Yellowstone to the north and the Tetons to the west. The Grand Teton massif, which includes five consort peaks (Middle and South Tetons, Mount Owen, Teewinot, and Nez Perce), dominates the central part of the range. To the north, Mount Moran is a stark granite hulk 12,605 feet high. It rises in splendid isolation from the shore of Jackson Lake, the largest of six jewel-like lakes strung along the base of the mountains.

The Snake River flows peacefully from Jackson Lake. The 30-mile-long stretch that traverses the park is braided into several channels that run through a forested, serpentine trough. Rafting down the Snake provides a unique perspective on some of America's most spectacular scenery. Wildlife flourishes in the river's valley. Bald eagles nest in dead trees alongside the stream, as do the great ospreys that cruise above the river casting their sharp eyes about for the native cutthroat trout that is their favorite meal. Moose, otters, and beavers also frequent these waters.

Plant life ranges from open grass and sage communities at the lower elevations to sub-alpine forests of lodgepole pine, Engelmann spruce, and Douglas fir. The Tetons are famous for summertime wildflower displays. Common flowers include wild rose, Indian paintbrush, blue columbine, and yellow balsamroot.

The fierce geology of the Tetons accounts for almost everything unusual about the region: the afternoon thunderstorms that can turn suddenly nasty, the deep canyons that shelter bears and deer, the broad river basin that provides grazing for moose and a refuge for elk, and the long and bitter winters. A walk into any of the canyons between the mountains reveals this geology firsthand.

The granite on the summits of some of the peaks is more than three billion years old, which makes it some of the oldest rock in North America. But the mountains themselves are the youngest of the Rocky Mountains. Only 12 million years old, they are mere adolescents compared with the rest of the 60-million-year-old range.

Because of their relative youth, the Tetons are more rugged than the rest of the Rockies. The eastern side of the mountains is more abrupt and dramatic than the somewhat gentler western side. The first people came to Jackson Hole around 8,500 years ago. In 1807, John Colter, a member of the Lewis and Clark expedition, wandered alone into the Yellowstone-Jackson Hole area and brought back incredible tales of exploding geysers and impenetrable mountains.

Today, winter is increasingly popular at the park, with numerous opportunities for snowshoeing, cross-country skiing, and wildlife viewing on the adjacent National Elk Wildlife Refuge.

Regardless, most visitors still come in summer, when the hiking trails are free of snow. Just north of Grand Teton, a deep slice in the mountains called Cascade Canyon gives visitors a good feel for some of the geological wonders of the park. The hike starts on the west side of Jenny Lake. In the lower part of the canyon, rushing water, here and there in the form of cascading falls, seems to be constantly at work, eating away at the granite walls.

Mount Moran overlooking Leigh Lake

Great Basin National Park Nevada

Wheeler Peak

For decades before the Great Basin became a national park in 1986, the Snake Range of Nevada was known for its soaring peaks (13 over 11,000 feet), bristlecone pine groves, and extensive natural caverns. The range is part of the extensive system of fault-block mountains—over 100—that sharply wrinkle the otherwise flattened landscape of the Great Basin Desert.

While the surrounding lowlands of sagebrush and creosote receive only about ten inches of annual precipitation, the high country of Snake Range receives three times that, resulting in grassy meadows, thick forests, and lingering snowfields. Scientists estimate that some of the bristlecone pines in the range are more than 4,000 years old. Prior to the establishment of the park, one tree that was cut down revealed from its annual growth rings that it had lived for 4,844 years. That tree began its life a long time ago—before Sargon of Akkad, Hammurabi, Ramses, Moses, or any other well-known individuals from early human history. Touch one of those primeval trees, and you are touching something exceedingly ancient from a human perspective.

Most visitors to the park come to see either the soaring granitic spires of Wheeler Peak (13,063 feet) or the well-known Lehman Caves. These extensive caverns are something to see, with fantastic displays of stalactites, stalagmites, sculpted stone columns, rock curtains, and even mushroomlike rock formations.

Guadalupe Mountains National Park Texas

Guadalupe Mountains National Park encom-passes the four highest points in Texas (up to 8,749 feet) and is located in the extreme western point of the Lone Star State, near the historic border town of El Paso. This park is a national park of extremes, from the Chihua-huan Desert at lower ele-vations, which includes such plant species as New Mexico agave and prickly pear cactus, to the thick forests of pon-derosa pine, limber pine, and Douglas fir that darkly cover the higher peaks.

El Capitan

Guadalupe Mountains National Park includes more than 80 miles of rugged and scenic trails that wind in and out of canyons, ascend rocky crags, and wander through quiet forests, where hum-mingbirds dart by and mule deer graze. Some side canyons within the park shelter excep-tional fragments of original ecosystems, as well as exposed sections of the formi-dable Capitan Reef and its associated rock segments.

The park is also well known for its mountain and desert bird life. It was to the Guadalupe Mountains that landscape photographer Ansel Adams came in the summer of 1947. While in the park, he made his celebrated image of majestic El Capitan (Spanish for "The Chief"), which rises to 8,085 feet in a squarelike mass from the desert floor. The Guadalupe Mountains today are much as Adams found them half a century ago—a little-visited desert mountain range that is pure inspiration at certain times of the day and year.

PARK INFORMATION

Border of eastern Tennessee and western North Carolina
Established June 15, 1934
521,752 acres

Great Smoky Mountains National Park
107 Park Headquarters Road
Gatlinburg, TN 37738
865/436-1200
www.nps.gov/grsm

Visitor Centers
Cades Cove Visitor Center, Oconaluftee Visitor Center, and Sugarlands Visitor Center are open year-round.

Entrance Fees
Admission is free.

Accommodations
Cades Cove Campground and Smokemont Campground are open year-round (reservations available at 800/365-CAMP). Backcountry camping is also available year-round. Nine other campgrounds are available at various times from mid-March through November.

Great Smoky Mountains National Park North Carolina / Tennessee

Newfound Gap Road

Straddling the border between North Carolina and Tennessee, the Great Smoky Mountains preserve one of the finest deciduous forests left on Earth. These ancient mountains are, in fact, among the oldest on the planet. The Smokies are also the highest range east of the Black Hills.

In the mountains' shadows, the great forest looks like a remnant of an ancient time when the world was covered with trees—a time of constant showers, fog, and endless mist. The forest floor is thick with spongy green moss and colorful wood sorrel, and everywhere there are waterfalls cascading into nooks of rivers and streams. During the summer, a cacophony of sounds finds your ears: the chatter of red squirrels and the calls of wrens and other birds.

Ridge upon rounded ridge, the Great Smoky Mountains rise beyond the horizon. These behemoths are considerably older than the rough, craggy mountains of the western states. About 10,000 years ago, when glaciers advanced from the north during the last Pleistocene ice age, the mountains were already millions of years old. The glaciers cooled the cli-

mate of the entire region. Lured by the cold, northern evergreens and other plants extended their range south.

Later, as the glaciers receded, these forests also withdrew, remaining only on the heights of the Smokies where conditions were cool and moist. Throughout the park signs advise visitors to see "the world as it once was." Because the great glaciers were stopped in their southward journey by these

mountains, which include 25 peaks above 6,000 feet, the Great Smokies today harbor a unique blend of northern and southern animals and plants.

The park is truly a vestige of an age lost in the mists of time. It supports an abundance of wildlife, including white-tailed deer, black bear, opossum, and an amazing diversity of bird life. At the higher altitudes, hikers can hear the pervasive drumming of ruffed grouse and the

characteristic thumping of the woodpecker. Down lower, the songs of vireo and warbler fill the air. In all, more than 200 bird species inhabit the park.

Part of the Appalachian system, the Great Smokies are remarkable for their wild and luxuriant vegetation. More than 100 species of trees and more than 1,300 kinds of flowering plants grow here. The incredible tangle of trees and brush throughout the park is responsible for the "smoke" that gives the mountains their name. Water and hydrocarbons are exuded in great profusion by the close-packed array of air-breathing leaves, producing the filmy haze that never leaves this place during warm weather.

The park, which covers 800 square miles in the heart of these mountains, has so many types of eastern forest vegetation that it has been designated an International Biosphere Reserve. About half of this large lush forest is virgin growth that dates back to well before Colonial times.

Although this is our most popular national park—it normally sees more than twice as many visitors as runner-up Grand Canyon—it is not necessarily the most crowded. Over 900 miles of trails provide good back-country access.

A good start in terms of getting off the beaten path, the Appalachian Trail, the world's longest continuous walking route, almost perfectly bisects the park from southwest to northeast.

Little Pigeon River

Haleakala National Park Hawaii

PARK INFORMATION

Island of Maui
Established August 1, 1916
29,094 acres

Haleakala National Park
PO Box 369
Makawao, Maui, HI 96768
808/572-4400
www.nps.gov/hale

Visitor Centers
Haleakala Visitor Center,
Kipahulu Visitor Center, and
Park Headquarters Visitor
Center are open year-round.

Entrance Fees
$20/vehicle for seven days or
$10/individual for seven days.

Accommodations
Hosmer Grove Campground
and Kipahulu Campground are
available year-round and
operate on a first-come, first-
served basis. Backcountry
camping is also available all
year. Reservations for three
wilderness cabins are available
through a mail-in monthly
lottery.

Haleakala Crater

When the Promethean-like native god Maui captured the sun in a great mountain's summit basin on Hawaii's Maui island, the mountain came to be known as Haleakala, or "House of the Sun." This enormous volcano extends 33 miles in one direction and 24 miles in the other. Although Haleakala has been dormant since 1790, cinder cones and lava sculptures create fantastic shapes that stand as vivid reminders of its dramatic past. Nevertheless, earthquakes rumble deep beneath the surface (the crater descends nearly 2,720 feet below the volcano rim). Ancient stone formations that are relics of prehistoric religious ceremonies can still be found.

As visitors ascend the auto route to the 10,000-foot summit, which is almost two miles above the level of the sea, they will notice the vegetation gradually change from tropical to subalpine. The view down to the other major attraction of the park, lovely Kipahulu valley, is breathtaking, as the landscape drops thousands of feet in a vast sweeping curve to the seacoast. In the valley you will find trails lined with tree ferns and gigantic waterfalls, as well as mango and guava trees. High on the mountain, 47 species of honeycreepers dart among the mamane, a yellow flowering brush, and the rare silversword (a plant that grows only on this island).

As with the other Hawaiian Islands, all flora and fauna arrived here by swimming, flying, or floating on debris. This has made the park a mecca for conservation biologists, who, increasingly, are seeing many of the world's great ecosystems, from Yellowstone to the Serengeti, slowly becoming island-habitats like Haleakala.

Hawai'i Volcanoes National Park Hawaii

PARK INFORMATION

Island of Hawai'i
Established August 1, 1916
323,431 acres

Hawai'i Volcanoes National Park
PO Box 52
Hawai'i National Park, HI 96718-0052
808/985-6000
www.nps.gov/havo

Visitor Center
Kilauea Visitor Center is open daily.

Entrance Fees
$10/vehicle for seven days or
$5/individual for seven days.

Accommodations
Namakani Paio and
Kulanaokuaiki campgrounds are
available year-round and
operate on a first-come, first-
served basis. A hotel, Volcano
House (808/967-7321), is
available year-round.

Kilauea Volcano

A volcanic eruption begins with a deep trainlike rumble that is often more strongly felt than heard. There are slow rumbling quakes and cracking snaplike sounds that portend the beginning of one of nature's most colossal displays of destructive power. Along the Pacific Ring of Fire, a region containing most of the world's 500 or so active volcanoes, none surpass the visual grandeur or the uncontained energy of Hawai'i Volcanoes.

Kilauea Volcano, of which Mark Twain wrote so eloquently in his 1871 travel narrative *Roughing It,* is by far the most frequently visited, primarily because of its easy accessibility. In fact, it is often called "the drive-in volcano." The view from the 11-mile-long Crater Rim Drive around the summit caldera is astonishing. The caldera is two miles wide, three miles long, and surrounded by cliffs that are more than 400 feet high. Inside the volcano, 2,000-degree lava bursts from fresh cracks on a near-continual basis, lighting the sky for miles around at night and burning the air with the pungent scent of sulfur. Nearby, incongruously, are thick forests of tree fern and coconut palm, as well as extensive lava deserts. Drive along the southeast coast to see historic Polynesian villages and native religious sites.

A visit to Hawai'i Volcanoes National Park can be compared to a visit to the distant past of our own planet, when the landscape was just beginning to form and life had, at best, a tenuous hold.

Hot Springs National Park Arkansas

PARK INFORMATION

Southern Arkansas
Established March 4, 1921
5,550 acres

Hot Springs National Park
PO Box 1860
Hot Springs, AR 71902
501/624-2701
www.nps.gov/hosp

Visitor Center
The visitor center is open daily except January 1, Thanksgiving Day, and December 25.

Entrance Fees
Admission is free.

Accommodations
Gulpha Gorge Campground is open year-round and operates on a first-come, first-served basis.

In 1832, the Hot Springs of Arkansas became one of the first natural areas to be set aside for the purposes of preservation in the history of American conservation when President Andrew Jackson afforded it federal protection. The singular area was later established as a national park in 1921, shortly after World War I.

Hot Springs Mountain, from which water flows at 143 degrees Fahrenheit, rises above the heart of the park. This park includes a total of 47 hot springs, as well as some of the finest hardwood forests to be found in the Ouachita Mountains of central Arkansas. It offers more than 24 miles of wonderful hiking and bridle trails that wander through woods of oak, hickory, flowering dogwood, eastern redbud, southern magnolia, and shortleaf pine. Local bird-watchers have counted nearly 150 bird species in the hills and valleys of this unique national park. Indeed, it is nationally known as a bird-watcher's paradise.

Hot Springs National Park is a place to come if your body is sore and you want to enjoy the rejuvenative waters, or as a natural refuge where you can hike peacefully among the squirrels, rabbits, deer, foxes, warbling vireos, and warblers. Hot water springs have been cherished since the beginning of civilization, from the Roman baths of Pompeii to the ancient thermal springs of England's Bath. At Hot Springs National Park, visitors can know the simple pleasure of resting in water that has been gently warmed in the bosom of the earth.

Hot springs

Isle Royale National Park Michigan

PARK INFORMATION

Northern Michigan
Established April 3, 1940
571,790 acres

Isle Royale National Park
800 East Lakeshore Drive
Houghton, MI 49931-1895
906/482-0984
www.nps.gov/isro

Visitor Centers
Houghton Visitor Center is open year-round Monday-Friday (and Saturday during the summer). Rock Harbor Visitor Center and Windigo Visitor Center are open from mid-June through August.

Entrance Fees
$4/person for each day.

Accommodations
More than 35 campgrounds are available from mid-April through October on a first-come, first-served basis. Rock Harbor Lodge (270/773-2191) is open from late May to mid-September.

Isle Royale National Park protects the largest island in Lake Superior, which measures about 40 miles from one end to the other. It is a wilderness paradise protecting paper birches, balsam fir, wild orchids, violets, mallards, mergansers, loons, herons, wolves, moose, deer, and bobcats.

In ages past, Canadian and American Indians would canoe to this remote island of woods, lakes, streams, and ponds to dig for copper from which they made tools, jewelry, and cookware. Visitors today can look forward to kayaking among the fjordlike coves, picking raspberries and blueberries, hiking on more than 160 miles of trails, or listening to the distant howls of northern gray wolves on moon-filled autumn nights.

Separated from mainland Michigan, which claims it, by 56 miles of rough water (and from the shores of Minnesota by only 20 miles), Isle Royale is pure wilderness, with no roads and almost no development. Access is provided either by seaplane or ferry. The island's isolation has helped to keep it pristine, looking much as it did more than two centuries ago when European explorers first stepped on its shores.

This is the only place in the United States outside of Alaska and the Greater Yellowstone Ecosystem where wolves roam free. Moose, the wolf's main prey, also inhabit the island. Most everyone agrees that autumn is the best time to visit the park, with the sugar maples and yellow birch aflame in color, the wild berries thick underfoot, and the moose appearing in the ridges to the valleys.

Isle Royale coastline

Joshua Tree National Park California

Joshua trees

In 1844, Western explorer John C. Frémont, while traveling through the Mojave Desert, encountered an odd-looking plant, which he called "the most repulsive tree in the vegetable kingdom." A few years later the Mormons passed through a grove of these plants, and in contrast to Frémont's response, they thought the uplifted branches evoked the arms of Joshua beckoning them toward the promised land. Thus the name was born.

The Joshua tree, a member of the lily family, is actually an oversized yucca. The "trees" cover the highlands of Joshua Tree National Park, which was designated a national park in 1994 (the area had been a national monument since 1936). Visitors continue to find the park's symbol and namesake to be either grotesque or exquisite.

The first impression is of top-heaviness. At the end of each stout branch are heavy daggerlike leaves. In early spring, after a wet winter, the branch tips visibly droop with heavy, ivory blossom clusters. These flowers attract everything from butterflies and birds to legions of landscape photographers and artists.

Joshua Tree, located within a short drive from Palm Springs, California, has become increasingly popular in recent years. Bird-watchers find the area particularly attractive in the spring; rock climbers test themselves among the giant boulderlike formations of quartz monzonite; and hikers enjoy such wonderful trails as the four-mile path to Lost Palms Oasis, where the rare California Fan Palm can be seen. In the end, Joshua Tree is one of the most interesting parks on the West Coast, and certainly one of the best introductions to the quiet splendor of the Mojave Desert.

Kenai Fjords National Park Alaska

Holgate Glacier

Stretching more than 100 miles from Seward, Alaska, very nearly to Point Graham, Kenai Fjords National Park is distinguished by its many rocky narrow inlets or fjords, much like the fabled coasts of Norway and Sweden. In these deep, cold fjords live an amazing profusion of sea mammals, including sea otters, sea lions, harbor seals, Pacific dolphins, harbor porpoises, orcas, and humpback and gray whales. On the rugged cliffs above the water, enormous colonies of sea birds, most notably horned puffin, can be seen.

Many Alaskans believe this to be their most beautiful park, containing as it does the immense Kenai Mountains, which run for 75 miles through the park, as well as wonderfully diverse maritime landscapes. But the park's best feature may be that the immense wilderness is easily accessible from the road system south of Anchorage, with sea trips departing daily from the docks at Seward near the park visitor center.

The park, not surprisingly, has become a sort of mecca for sea kayakers, most of whom hitch rides on tour boats and are then picked up at predetermined locations many days or weeks later. Elsewhere, hikers enjoy long invigorating treks through the coastal rain forest, which includes such species as western and mountain hemlocks and Sitka spruce, as well as jaunts up the trail to Exit Glacier near Seward.

Katmai National Park Alaska

PARK INFORMATION

Southern Alaska
Established December 2, 1980
4,725,188 acres

Katmai National Park and Preserve Headquarters
PO Box 7, #1 King Salmon Mall
King Salmon, AK 99613
907/246-3305
www.nps.gov/katm

Visitor Centers
King Salmon Visitor Center is open year-round. Brooks Camp Visitor Center is open from June to mid-September.

Entrance Fees
Admission is free.

Accommodations
Brooks Camp Campground (800/365-CAMP) and Brooks Lodge (800/544-0551) are open from June through mid-September.

The Valley of Ten Thousand Smokes

On June 6, 1912, following a week of severe earthquakes, the Novarupta Volcano south of Iliamna Lake in southwestern Alaska exploded as if a nuclear missile had struck the area. In what was one of the three most powerful volcanic explosions ever recorded, the entire top of the mountain was violently blown off. Scientists estimate that the total volume of displaced material was more than seven cubic miles—two times the amount expelled by the 1883 Krakatoa explosion in Indonesia. A nearby river valley was buried in 700 feet of solid debris. This event is estimated to have had ten times the force of the 1980 eruption of Washington state's Mount St. Helens.

Four years later, exploring the still-smoldering area for the National Geographic Society, Robert Griggs discovered the primary scene of destruction, an area now referred to as the Valley of Ten Thousand Smokes. Many people have been to Yellowstone and seen Old Faithful—imagine a valley with hundreds of geysers, some shooting as high as 1,000 feet into the air (ten times the height of Old Faithful). That is the sight that greeted these early explorers.

Today the Valley of Ten Thousand Smokes forms the centerpiece of Katmai National Park, which is also famous for the immense congregations of Alaskan brown bears—up to 60 at one time—that gather on the Brooks Falls each summer to feed on sea-run salmon. Visitors fly into the Brooks Camp from Anchorage or Homer, via the bush village of King Salmon, and then view the bears from specially constructed bear observation facilities right on the river.

Kobuk Valley National Park Alaska

PARK INFORMATION

Northern Alaska
Established December 2, 1980
1,750,700 acres

Kobuk Valley National Park
PO Box 1029
Kotzebue, AK 99752
907/442-3890
www.nps.gov/kova

Visitor Center
Headquarters is open Monday-Friday.

Entrance Fees
Admission is free.

Accommodations
The park offers no developed campgrounds. Backcountry camping is available.

In 1980, just as he was leaving office, President Jimmy Carter signed the bill that established this 1.7-million-acre area as Kobuk Valley National Park. This park is one of the loveliest in Alaska, replete with clear running streams and rivers, the northernmost sand dune field in the Western Hemisphere, ancient archaeological sites, and all of the diverse fauna and flora typical of a vast province of the Brooks Range. These include such wildlife as barren-ground caribou and Yukon moose and such plant species as white spruce and paper birch.

The Kobuk River is the main artery for transportation in the park, which lies entirely above the Arctic Circle and has no roads. One of the most fascinating sites is known as Onion Portage. Located near the Kobuk River, archaeologists have studied the site since 1940. Scientists have found chiseled stone spearheads and tools, ancient hearthbeds, Siberian-style pit houses, and other

Mountain wilderness

artifacts. Data suggests that native people have been using this game-rich area for at least 12,000 years.

The two other major attractions of this park are the 25-square-mile Kobuk Sand Dunes, some of which rise more than 150 feet in height, and the Salmon River, which was classified as a national wild and scenic river.

Lake Clark National Park Alaska

PARK INFORMATION

Southwestern Alaska
Established December 2, 1980
4,030,025 acres

Lake Clark National Park
Field Headquarters
1 Park Place
Port Alsworth, AK 99653
907/781-2218
www.nps.gov/lacl

Visitor Center
Port Alsworth Visitor Center is open daily May-October and by request November-April.

Entrance Fees
Information not available. Some user fees may apply.

Accommodations
The park offers no developed campgrounds. Backcountry camping is available. Private lodging in the park is also available.

The name of Dick Proenneke, a pioneering homesteader, will forever be associated with Lake Clark National Park, located in southwestern Alaska across the Cook Inlet from the Kenai Peninsula. Proenneke arrived in 1967, fell in love with the area's rugged wilderness, eventually found some good land, and built a sturdy cabin from hand-felled logs. His Thoreau-like experiment in independent living inspired a memoir, *One Man's Wilderness: An Alaskan Odyssey,* now considered a classic of Alaskan literature and a must-read for anyone contemplating a visit to this park.

Tanalian Mountain

It is no longer possible to homestead at Lake Clark, but it is still feasible to stay a few days, weeks, or months and enjoy the tremendous solitude of the place. At 4 million acres, Lake Clark is approximately 13 times the size of Grand Teton National Park. In Lake Clark visitors will find everything from coastal rain forests to alpine tundra, from active volcanoes to serene fjords, from high mountain lakes to saltwater estuaries. The wildlife is just as diverse, ranging from beluga whales to Alaskan brown and black bears, from river otters to bald and golden eagles.

The Newhalen River is famous for its fantastic runs of red salmon, as is the Iliamna River for its rainbow trout. Lake Clark and nearby Lake Iliamna support the world's largest runs of sockeye salmon. If you can visit only one place in Alaska and wish to avoid the crowds of the Kenai Peninsula or Denali National Park, Lake Clark will be the place for you.

Mammoth Cave National Park Kentucky

PARK INFORMATION

Southern Kentucky
Established July 1, 1941
52,830 acres

Mammoth Cave National Park
PO Box 7
Mammoth Cave, KY 42259
270/758-2180
www.nps.gov/maca

Visitor Center
The visitor center is open daily except December 25.

Entrance Fees
Admission to the park is free. Cave tours are available for adults from $4 to $46 (children $2.50-$18). Reservations are recommended (800/967-2283).

Accommodations
Houchins Ferry Campground is open year-round. Headquarters Campground and Maple Springs Group Campground are open from March through November. Reservations are available (800/365-CAMP).

The very names are enchanting—flowstones, travertine, scallopes, flutes, and domepits. Gypsum flowers and dissolved carbonates. Sinkholes and disappearing springs. Vertical shafts, tubular passages, and open caverns. Even the basic field rocks of the southern Kentucky cave country have a certain natural poetry to them—limestone, dolomite, sandstone, and shale.

Truly, Mammoth Cave is a place of beauty and wonder, mystery and paradox. In room after subterranean room there is an incredibly rich array of exotic forms: tapered stalactites and stalagmites, thick hanging draperies, lacy crystals, slender columns, and fluted shields. Hikers find themselves wandering through a sprawling realm of underground lakes and canyons, waterfalls and streams, and narrow side corridors and vaulted ballrooms. It is a weird landscape, a sometimes grand and occasionally grotesque place, a buried lost geological world that seems alternately to have come from a Walt Disney fairy tale or the off-kilter imagination of Edgar Allen Poe.

All of these extraordinary features can be found in Mammoth Cave National Park. Located about 50 miles northeast of Bowling Green, Kentucky, Mammoth Cave contains one of the world's largest and most diverse known systems of underground caverns. The haunting beauty of the place—the mysterious sinkholes, the subterranean waterfalls, and the delicate gypsum cave formations—will stay with you forever.

Limestone stalactites

Lassen Volcanic National Park California

PARK INFORMATION

Northeastern California
Established August 9, 1916
106,372 acres

Lassen Volcanic National Park
PO Box 100
Mineral, CA 96063
530/595-4444
www.nps.gov/lavo

Visitor Centers
Headquarters Information Desk is open Monday-Friday year-round; daily from late June to early September. Loomis Museum, Information, and Bookstore is open Fridays, Saturdays, and Sundays from late May to late September; daily from late June to early September.

Entrance Fees
$10/vehicle for seven days or $5/individual for seven days.

Accommodations
Several campgrounds are available from late spring through early fall (until closed by snow). Some reservations are available at 877/444-6777. Drakesbad Guest Ranch (530/529-1512) is open from early June through early October.

In 1914, Lassen Peak, about one hour east of Redding, California, began a period of sustained eruptions that continued for seven years. Eventually more than 106,372 acres of this decimated landscape were designated as the Lassen Volcanic National Park. Some of the landscape is still geologically active, with boiling water, hot streams, fumaroles, sulfur vents, and steam holes.

Lassen Peak is a craggy massif that rises to the considerable height of 10,457 feet. Most of the park has been reclaimed by nature and presents a familiar northern California scene—aspen, firs, pines, willows, alders, poplar, shrubs, and wildflowers. Resident fauna ranges from black-tailed deer to mountain lions. Yet throughout the park, cinder crags and magma canyons continue to offer proof of former violence, while gurgling thermal features suggest the possibility of a fiery future.

As is also true of a large portion of northern California, the park is covered with deep snow for much of the year, which has had the effect of producing several beautiful lakes. The park is a favorite with snowshoers and cross-country skiers. Many hikers first encounter this park on their trek down the Pacific Coast Trail, which passes through the park's wilderness backcountry.

Snowscape

Mount Rainier National Park Washington

PARK INFORMATION

Central Washington
Established March 2, 1899
235,625 acres

Mount Rainier National Park
Tahoma Woods, Star Route
Ashford, WA 98304-9751
360/569-2211
www.nps.gov/mora

Visitor Centers
Longmire Museum is open daily. Jackson Visitor Center–Paradise is open daily from mid-April through mid-October, weekends only mid-October through mid-April. Other visitor centers are open seasonally.

Entrance Fees
$10/vehicle for seven days or $5/individual for seven days.

Accommodations
Sunshine Point Campground is open year-round and operates on a first-come, first-served basis. Five other campgrounds are open variously from mid-May through mid-October. Reservations are available at 800/365-CAMP. National Park Inn (360/569-2275) is open year-round. Paradise Inn (360/569-2275) is open for the summer season.

Mount Rainier

Highest of the great peaks of the Cascade Range is Mount Rainier, a gigantic mountain that is covered with 26 active glaciers, more than any other peak in the lower 48 states. The mountain is a mecca for climbers around the world, and quite often it claims a life or two.

Even though the mountain is its most prominent feature, the nearly quarter-of-a-million-acre national park offers a number of other attractions. Below the extensive snowfields that cap Rainier are such wildlife as mountain goats, black-tailed deer, black bears, and beavers. Downslope, the forests are almost like a cathedral, with enormous western and mountain hemlocks and western red cedar that tower to awesome heights thanks to the more than 100 inches of rain the area receives annually. The high spruce and fir forests are known for their summer wildflower displays, which include Columbia tiger, glacier and avalanche lilies, red columbine, monkeyflowers, subalpine buttercups, asters, blue lupine, and magenta and scarlet paintbrushes.

Summer is the best time of year to visit Mount Rainier, because the area is legendary for its deep snows. Autumn is short, with snow storms commencing in some years as early as late September. What John Muir wrote about the mountain a century ago is worth recalling: "Of all the fire mountains, which like beacons, once blazed along the Pacific Coast, Mount Rainier is the noblest."

Mesa Verde National Park Colorado

PARK INFORMATION

Southwestern Colorado
Established June 29, 1906
52,122 acres

Mesa Verde National Park
PO Box 8
Mesa Verde, CO 81330-0008
970/529-4465
www.nps.gov/meve

Visitor Center
Far View Visitor Center is open from mid-April through mid-October.

Entrance Fees
$10/vehicle for seven days.

Accommodations
Morefield Campground (800/449-2288) is open from late April to mid-October; reservations are accepted. Far View Lodge (800/449-2288) is open from mid-April through late October.

Mesa Verde National Park encompasses more than 4,000 prehistoric sites that were used by the people the Navajo call the Anasazi, or "Ancient Ones," who developed an advanced culture and suddenly disappeared hundreds of years ago. The structures and ruins include mesa-top pit houses and pueblos, as well as the ghostly, multistoried cliff villages for which the park is famous. The setting for these deserted ancient villages is what the early Spaniards called the "green tableland," or Mesa Verde.

Located just a short 35-mile drive from Durango, Colorado, Mesa Verde rises more than 2,000 feet above the surrounding Montezuma Valley. Because of its dry climate, the cliff dwellings are very well preserved. The park is a superb example of both an archaeological preserve and a splendid natural landscape. The top of the mesa is covered with forests of ponderosa, Douglas fir, Gambel's oak, and two-needled pinyon juniper. Scattered herds of mule deer are often seen among the high meadows at sunrise or sunset, as well as wild turkeys, red foxes, and coyotes. Wildflowers—columbine, Indian paintbrush, and bluebells—are abundant in the spring, and the fall colors—especially the russet red of the Gambel oak—are magnificent.

Although the "Ancient Ones" are long gone, you can still feel their spirits as you walk through these silent buildings that have stood for centuries in their rock alcoves far above the ground. The structures are startlingly intact, as if they are waiting for the return of their builders, who left suddenly about 700 years ago.

The Cliff House ruins

North Cascades National Park Washington

PARK INFORMATION

Northern Washington
Established October 2, 1968
684,302 acres

North Cascades National Park
810 State Route 20
Sedro-Woolley, WA 98284-1239
360/856-5700
www.nps.gov/noca

Visitor Center
North Cascades Visitor Center is open daily from mid-April through mid-November, weekends only the rest of the year. Golden West Visitor Center is open daily during the summer.

Entrance Fees
Admission is free.

Accommodations
Colonial Creek Campground and Goodell Creek Campground are open year-round; other campgrounds are open seasonally. North Cascades Stehekin Lodge (509/682-4494) is open year-round. Ross Lake Resort (206/386-4437) is open from early June through late October.

North Cascade Mountains

With the last light, the sun slips below the Pacific horizon and bathes the high mountains in a pink glow that warms their soaring, glacier-scoured peaks, ragged ridges, and cloud-piercing spires. These are the North Cascades, the heart of a mighty range that begins in Canada and penetrates far south into the United States.

The names of some of the peaks attest to the hardships they imposed on early trappers and prospectors: Damnation Peak, Mount Despair, Mount Fury, Forbidden Peak, and Desolation Peak. So vertical are the North Cascades that they are often called the American Alps. Like their European counterparts, these imposing peaks attract hundreds of mountaineers, hikers, and backpackers each year.

Not surprisingly, the mountain range was named for its innumerable cascades of water, fed by the melting snowfields left by lingering Pacific storms each winter. While lush forests of Douglas fir, western red cedar, and western hemlock cover the western slopes, in the great divide the eastern slopes support trees that are much smaller.

The park is joined by Lake Chelan National Recreation Area and Ross Lake National Recreation Area to be managed as one administrative unit. As with the other parks of the Pacific Northwest, the best time to visit is in middle to late summer.

Olympic National Park Washington

PARK INFORMATION

Northwestern Washington
Established June 29, 1938
922,651 acres

Olympic National Park
600 East Park Avenue
Port Angeles, WA 98362-6798
360/565-3130
www.nps.gov/olym

Visitor Center
Olympic National Park Visitor Center and Hoh Rain Forest Visitor Center are open year-round.

Entrance Fees
$10/vehicle for seven days or $5/individual for seven days.

Accommodations
The park has 16 campgrounds, some of which are open year-round. Most operate on a first-come, first-served basis, but some reservations are available (800/365-CAMP). Four in-park lodges or resorts are also available.

In Olympic National Park, visitors can behold a rain forest every bit as green and dense as any found on Earth. The rainfall that sustains this extraordinary productivity in some years exceeds 140 inches, making it the wettest area in the lower 48 states.

Take a walk in the Hoh Rain Forest, a popular hiking area on the western side of the park near the Pacific Coast, and you will find a cool northern woodland in which everything is literally covered with moss. Western hemlock, Sitka spruce, and western red cedars, some with diameters of 25 feet, tower 300 feet above you. The perpetually wet sword ferns overlap so densely on the forest floor that a person becomes soaking wet after taking just one step. Trees grow from the trunks of fallen trees, from clumps of sphagnum moss, and even from masses of flowered greenery.

Located on the Olympic Peninsula in the extreme northwest corner of Washington, Olympic is the most diverse national park in the system. Along with the Hoh and two other rain forests, the park contains a rugged wilderness seacoast, with stunning headlands and lovely beaches covered with driftwood, and the Olympic Mountains, a rugged range of high alpine meadows, great jagged ridges, and glaciers.

Rain forest

Because of this remarkably varied landscape, climatic changes within the park are unbelievably abrupt. The western side of the park has the wettest weather in the United States, averaging nearly 12 feet of precipitation each year. The eastern side of the park, which lies in the rain shadow of the mountains, is the driest area on the Pacific Coast north of Los Angeles.

But Olympic's rain forests, with trees and vegetation as lush as an Amazon jungle, may be the strangest and most fascinating sections of the park. Their richness exists only because certain conditions are met: Moisture is incredibly plentiful, and even when it is not raining, the air is humid and misty. And the temperature is mild, neither too hot nor too cold.

In the center of the park are the Olympic Mountains, a wilderness range that is nearly circular. Thirteen rivers radiate out from the Olympics' center like the spokes of a wheel. The highlands are up-and-down country, where deep valleys separate the peaks and ridges. They are accompanied by breathtaking vistas of deep canyons, towering mountain ridges, and meadows dense with wildflowers. The high mountains have some of the best alpine lily displays in the Pacific Northwest, with entire meadows covered with them by mid-July in most years. These mountains were named by an English sea captain named John Mears. In 1788 he sighted the peninsula's tallest mountain, which at 7,965 feet is not an extremely high peak, but it rises so dramatically above the sea that it looks enormous. Mears was so overwhelmed by the sight that he named the peak Mount Olympus in honor of the home of the Greek gods.

Olympic National Park is also renowned for its wild beaches, which include some rock cliffs and sea stacks, and its glaciers, of which there are more than 50, constantly fed by the moisture that comes in from the Pacific Ocean. The wild animals that roam the park range from Roosevelt elk, often seen along park trails and roads at dawn and dusk, to the great white sharks that haunt the intertidal zones of the beaches searching for seals and sea lions.

Mount Olympus

Redwood National Park California

PARK INFORMATION

Northeastern California
Established October 2, 1968
112,513 acres

Redwood National Park
1111 Second Street
Crescent City, CA 95531
707/464-6101
www.nps.gov/redw

Visitor Center
Prairie Creek Visitor Center and
Thomas H. Kuchel Visitor
Center are open year-round.
Jedediah Smith Visitor Center is
open from late May to late
September.

Entrance Fees
Admission is free.

Accommodations
Jedediah Smith Campground,
Elk Prairie Campground, and
Gold Bluffs Beach Campground
are open year-round. Some
reservations are available
(800/444-PARK). Mill Creek
Campground is open from late
May to mid-August. DeMartin
Redwood Youth Hostel
(707/482-8265) is open year-
round.

Of all the wonderful redwood groves scattered along the California coast, the finest are preserved in Redwood National Park. Here one may take a walk back in time to that distant age when redwoods were found abundantly across North America. There is a sense of timelessness in the groves, of trees that were seedlings when Julius Caesar took his ill-fated walk to the Forum and of a ground sanctified through age and beauty.

It is always twilight under the thick canopy of the redwood forests, always April cool, with the morning freshness of the biblical garden. Black-tailed deer and Roosevelt elk graze among the giant sword ferns, and hermit thrushes call out from the dense thickets. Rabbits feed in grassy clearings while bobcats watch with eyes like polished topaz.

Redwood National Park contains many of the tallest living organisms in the world, with some redwood trees growing up to 367 feet. An abundance of superb hiking trails are also found in the park. The best of these may be the Coastal Trail, which offers a quiet walk through the towering redwood groves near the Pacific shore side of the park. Inland, visitors will find many good trails among the streams and rivers. Redwood National Park also protects 40 miles of northern California sea coast, where colony-dwelling sea birds, rotund sea lions, and playful seals live.

Avenue of the Giants

Petrified Forest National Park Arizona

PARK INFORMATION

Eastern Arizona
Established December 9, 1962
93,533 acres

**Petrified Forest National
Park**
PO Box 2217
Petrified Forest, AZ 86028
928/524-6228
www.nps.gov/pefo

Visitor Center
Painted Desert Visitor Center
is open daily except December 25.

Entrance Fees
$10/vehicle for seven days or
$5/individual for seven days.

Accommodations
Camping or lodging are not
available in the park.

Quite often on cross-country airline trips, an hour or so east of Los Angeles, the pilot will come on the intercom and direct the passengers' attention to a colorful stretch of desert on the ground below. People will crowd to the windows, and there will be considerable oohing and ahhing. Much of this spectacularly eroded landscape of red, pink, yellow, bluish-gray, purple, brown, and black sand dunes and badlands is contained within Petrified Forest National Park.

The park is known both for its colorful badlands—comprised of thin layers of shale, sandstone, and gravel interbedded with bands of volcanic ash—and for its rich paleontological treasures. The fossils, some of which can be seen literally littering the ground, include petrified conifers (up to three feet in diameter) and fossilized Metoposaurs (a kind of amphibian), Phytosaurs (something like a crocodile), and Placerias (a rhinoceroslike animal).

The columns of petrified wood scattered across the desert date from 200 million years ago. Floods and lava flows originally uprooted the trees, washing them down the surrounding highlands and burying them in silt and volcanic ash. Water seeped through the wood and replaced decaying organic material, cell by cell, with multicolored silica.

The park also includes a number of early pit houses and pueblo ruins, which are up to 1,000 years old. The high desert prairie region of the park is known for its antelopes, coyotes, golden eagles, western meadowlarks, roadrunners, and white-tailed prairie dogs.

Located about one hour east of Flagstaff, Arizona, on Interstate 40, Petrified Forest National Park is one of the treasures of the Southwest. Indeed, the park attracts landscape photographers and fine artists from around the world and also served as the inspiration for the 1930s classic film *The Petrified Forest.*

Crystal Forest

Rocky Mountain National Park Colorado

PARK INFORMATION

Northern Colorado
Established January 26, 1915
265,828 acres

Rocky Mountain National Park
1000 Highway 36
Estes Park, CO 80517-8397
970/586-1206
www.nps.gov/romo

Visitor Centers
Beaver Meadows and Kawuneeche visitor centers are open daily except December 25. Fall River Visitor Center is open year-round on weekends.

Entrance Fees
$20/vehicle for seven days or $10/individual for seven days.

Accommodations
Longs Peak, Moraine Park, and Timber Creek campgrounds are open year-round. Some reservations are available (800/365-CAMP).

Much has changed about the world since pioneering writer and naturalist Isabella Byrd first climbed the 14,255-foot Long's Peak over a century ago. (Her book, *A Lady's Life in the Rocky Mountains,* is a must-read.) Thankfully, the magnificent peaks of Rocky Mountain National Park still remain unchanged.

Now, as it was then, this is high country, with sweeping vistas of a jagged skyline crowned by towering summits. Snow lingers year-round, and the highest cirques preserve remnants of glaciers left over from the last ice age.

Each year more than 3 million visitors—as many as go to Yellowstone—come to this popular park located just a couple of hours northwest of Denver, Colorado. Here they find such wonders as Glacier Gorge, where the mountain scenery rivals that of Switzerland; Trail Ridge Road, the highest continuous road in North America; and the hauntingly beautiful Kawuneeche Valley, located on the far western side of the park near Grand Lake. Whether you are an angler,

Bear Lake

mountain climber, day hiker, photographer, or artist, Rocky Mountain offers an incredibly diverse array of outdoor possibilities in the heart of the American West.

With more than 300 miles of backcountry trails, Rocky Mountain is a favorite among hikers and backpackers. One of the best areas for hiking is Wild Basin, located in the extreme southeastern corner of the park near the town of Allenspark and directly north of the legendary Indian Peaks Wilderness Area. Popular trails in Wild Basin lead to such lovely high country lakes as Thunder Lake, Snowbank Lake, and Bluebird Lake. High above Thunder Lake, on the little-traveled Boulder-Grand Pass (12,061 feet), is the lovely Lake of Many Winds, which remains frozen through much of July. Hikers in these alpine areas frequently observe Rocky Mountain bighorn sheep, elk, mule deer, and the occasional mountain goat, as well as golden eagles and ptarmigan.

Further north, in Glacier Gorge, hikers are treated to such spectacles as Hallet Peak, the Little Matterhorn, and Lake Odessa. All of these trails begin at Bear Lake, which is also a favorite among cross-country skiers and snow-shoers during the winter months. Just down the road from Bear Lake is Moraine Park. Another popular area—some might call it the center-piece of the park—is Trail Ridge Road, which leads 20 miles over the high tundra along the Continental Divide, with views as far north as Wyoming on clear days.

Lily pads in the Glacier Gorge region

Saguaro National Park Arizona

PARK INFORMATION

Southeastern Arizona
Established October 14, 1994
91,440 acres

Saguaro National Park
Headquarters
3693 South Old Spanish Trail
Tucson, AZ 85730-5601
520/733-5100
www.nps.gov/sagu

Visitor Centers
Rincon Mountain District and
Tucson Mountain District
visitor centers are open daily
except December 25.

Entrance Fees
$10/vehicle for seven days or
$5/individual for seven days.

Accommodations
Backcountry camping is
available. No lodging is available in the park.

Saguaro National Park takes its name from the saguaro cactus, the giant, many-armed symbol of southern Arizona's Sonoran Desert. Standing as high as 50 feet and weighing as much as seven or eight tons, these silent, slow-growing sentinels are a vital link in the ecology of one of the richest and most varied deserts in the world.

It is one of the few major parks located in the suburbs of a sizable city, in this case, Tucson, Arizona. First designated a national monument and then a wilderness area, Saguaro became a national park in 1994. The park preserves some amazing saguaro cacti, interspersed with other Sonoran desert flora, such as hedgehog cacti, fishhook barrel cacti, cholla, ocotillo, and prickly pear.

There are two parts to Saguaro National Park. The eastern, and larger, unit is found in the Rincon Mountains east of Tucson. The western portion, known as the Tucson Mountain District, includes similar terrain and vegetation and is located on the western side of town. For many visitors, Saguaro National Park is their first and only close view of the true Sonoran Desert. The park is a superb place for that introduction. The saguaro cactus, both aesthetically and biologically, forms the centerpiece of the desert and of the national park. Each giant cactus supports a whole community of animals, including ground-dwellers such as rodents, insects such as honey bees and harvester ants, and songbirds such as the cactus wren, Gila woodpecker, elf owl, gilded flicker, and Lucy's warbler.

Much of the best hiking in Saguaro is in the eastern portion of the park, where there are more than 120 miles of hiking trails. Most desert aficionados agree that the best time to hike in the Sonoran desert is in late March to early May when the wild-flower displays are at their peak. Last to arrive at the party are the giant saguaro cacti, which do not blossom until late May or early June.

Saguaro cactus

Shenandoah National Park Virginia

PARK INFORMATION

Northern Virginia
Established December 26, 1935
199,045 acres

Shenandoah National Park
3655 U.S. Highway 211 East
Luray, VA 22835-9036
540/999-3500
www.nps.gov/shen

Visitor Centers
Dickey Ridge Visitor Center and
Harry F. Byrd, Sr., Visitor Center
are open from mid-spring
through late fall.

Entrance Fees
$10/vehicle for seven days or
$5/individual for seven days.

Accommodations
Four campgrounds are open
from spring through late
October or late November.
Some reservations are available
(800/365-CAMP). Backcountry
camping is also available.
Skyline Resort (800/999-4714)
is open from late March to late
November. Big Mountain Lodge
(800/999-4714) is open from
late April to early November.

Shenandoah National Park, nearly 200,000 acres in size, extends about 75 miles from Front Royal, Virginia, in the north to Turk Gap near Waynesboro, Virginia, in the south. The primary focus of the park is the spectacular Skyline Drive, which follows the ridgeline crest of the Blue Ridge Mountains. On either side of the winding blacktop road, the park forms a wide buffer zone between forest and meadow. As a result, Shenandoah has often been compared in its shape to a native Blue Ridge salamander with the road constituting its spine.

Skyline Drive

Shenandoah National Park is best known for its fabulous spring flower and autumn leaf displays, as well as its numerous waterfalls. The tallest waterfall is near Mile 22 on the Skyline Drive and is nearly 100 feet in height. But it is not alone; nearly a dozen waterfalls in the park drop more than 40 feet.

The park is also known for its ancient rock formations, comprised primarily of green-stone and granite. Geologists date the rock in some of the mountain tops and side cliffs at more than one billion years old. This is quite a bit older than the surface rock normally found in the parks of the Far West. Hikers in Shenandoah will find a variety of trails, many leading to panoramic overlooks that take in the rolling Piedmont country to the east or the wide Shenandoah Valley to the west.

Sequoia National Park/Kings Canyon National Park California

PARK INFORMATION

Eastern central California
Sequoia National Park established September 25, 1890.
Kings Canyon National Park established March 4, 1940.
865,952 acres (combined)

Sequoia and Kings Canyon National Parks
47050 Generals Highway
Three Rivers, CA 93271-9700
559/565-3341
www.nps.gov/seki

Visitor Centers
Giant Forest Museum (in Sequoia) and Grant Grove Visitor Center (in Kings Canyon) are open year-round. Lodgepole Visitor Center (in Sequoia) is open daily from spring through fall, Friday-Monday during winter.

Entrance Fees
$10/vehicle for seven days or $5/individual for seven days.

Accommodations
Lodgepole, Azalea, and Potwisha campgrounds are open year-round. Eleven other campgrounds are open variously from late April to mid-November. Grant Grove Lodge (866-KCANYON) and Wuksachi Village (888-252-5757) are open year-round. Cedar Grove Lodge (866-KCANYON) is open from late April to mid-October.

Suppose national parks had themes. The theme of these two adjacent California parks, administered jointly since 1943, would probably involve the three impressive superlatives to which they lay claim.

The combined parkland of Sequoia and Kings Canyon contains the planet's most massive trees, giant sequoias so huge they far surpass the size of any other species. It's also the site of Mount Whitney, at 14,495 feet the highest mountain in the lower 48 states. Here, too, is Kings Canyon, the deepest in North America, plunging down steep granite walls more than 8,000 feet from its rim to the Kings River below.

Sequoia is America's second national park. It was established in 1890 as a wilderness sanctuary to protect groves of giant sequoia trees that were being systematically destroyed by logging. Kings Canyon, a steep-walled valley, was mandated as a national park in 1940.

The two parks encompass most of California's High Sierra country. They contain thousands of acres of sequoias and some of the nation's wildest and loveliest alpine scenery. Here are miles

Snow-covered Sequoias

LeConte Canyon

of sweeping mountain vistas, range after range of snow-capped peaks, high meadows, rocky ridges, and green forests full of pine and ponderosa.

The largest trees by weight and volume in the world, the sequoias in this park are the last relics of a species that covered much of the world before the most recent ice age. The glaciers swept over all but a few thousand acres too high in the Sierra Nevada for the ice to reach, destroying all the trees in their path.

Sequoias used to be considered a subspecies of the coastal redwood. The scientific term for the redwood tree is *Sequoia sempervirens*—a name that came from Sequoyah, the inventor of the Cherokee alphabet. The same name was at first also given to the giant trees of the Sierra

Nevada. Today, botanists realize the Sierra Nevada sequoia is a separate species. They now call it *Sequoia gigantean.*

The groves of these huge trees seem to go on forever, but they cannot compare with what existed here just a little over a century ago. Logging of what was then one of the world's finest and largest old-growth forests began in about 1862 and continued relentlessly until the turn of the 20th century. Vast stands of these giant trees were wiped out, including at least two trees larger than the park's famed General Sherman sequoia.

In the park, you can still see the Centennial Stump, the remains of a gigantic sequoia that was cut down for exhibition at the 1875 Centennial in Philadelphia. Nearby is the

Big Stump Trail, a one-mile path that leads through an incredible wasteland of downed logs, stumps, and fallen trees, sad reminders of an earlier era when these giants were only valued for their wood.

The superlative nature of these parks extends into its spectacular alpine backcountry. This is pristine wilderness encompassing most of the Sierra Nevada, the longest and highest unbroken range in North America, stretching more than 400 miles from north to south.

Parts of these parks are so remote that a backcountry hiker may not see another person for days at a time. There is one spot in the park that is said to be more distant from a road than any other location in the lower 48 states.

Theodore Roosevelt National Park North Dakota

PARK INFORMATION

Western North Dakota
Established November 10, 1978
70,447 acres

**Theodore Roosevelt
National Park**
Box 7
Medora, ND 58645-0007
701/623-4466 (South Unit
Information)
701/842-2333 (North Unit
Information)
www.nps.gov/thro

Visitor Centers
Medora Visitor Center and
North Unit Visitor Center are
open daily except January 1,
Thanksgiving Day, and Decem-
ber 25.

Entrance Fees
$5/individual ($10 maximum/
private vehicle)

Accommodations
Cottonwood Campground and
Juniper Campground are open
year-round and operate on a
first-come, first-served basis.

Oxbow Overlook

When Theodore Roo-sevelt's wife died on the same day as his mother, he believed he needed to embrace nature if he was ever to move beyond his grief. The young member of the New York assembly headed west to the Dakota Territories and bought a cattle ranch. The time was the 1880s, the same period when a cowhand named Charlie Russell was beginning to paint the land-scapes and people of the cattle country in nearby Montana. At that time, the American West was at a crossroads. Cattle ranchers were rapidly claiming the open grasslands, the old buffalo prairie that extended from Canada to Mexico. Today Theodore Roosevelt's Elkhorn Ranch on the Little Missouri River of North Dakota is protected as a national park.

In this park, visitors can still see herds of white-tailed deer, elk, antelope, and buf-falo, which Roosevelt (an avid big-game hunter) wit-nessed more than a century ago. Best of all, the park protects some of the best multicolored badland forma-tions in the region, as well as extensive surface beds of petrified wood.

Toward the end of his life, Theodore Roosevelt observed that he would never have become president had he not spent a few years out west on his beloved Elkhorn Ranch. In this unusual national park, visitors can see the landscape that turned a grieving wid-ower into the man who is now chiseled into the eternal rock of Mount Rushmore.

Voyageurs National Park Minnesota

PARK INFORMATION

Northern Minnesota
Established April 8, 1975
218,200 acres

Voyageurs National Park
3131 Highway 53 South
International Falls, MN 56649-
8904
218/283-9821
www.nps.gov/voya

Visitor Centers
Rainy Lake Visitor Center is
open daily from mid-May
through September, Wednes-
day-Sunday October through
mid-May. Ash River and
Kabetogama Lake visitor
centers are open mid-May
through September.

Entrance Fees
Admission is free.

Accommodations
Multiple campsites, as well as
backcountry camping, are
available year-round throughout
the park on a first-come, first-
served basis. Kettle Falls Hotel
(888-534-6835) is open from
early May through late September.

No one should visit this extraordinary Minnesota park without first reading one of esteemed naturalist Sigurd F. Olson's classic nature books, *The Singing Wilder-ness* or *Runes of the North*. Olson, the resident spirit of the Quetico-Superior region, wrote that Voyageurs National Park "is the most magnificent and beautiful lake and river country on the continent, possibly in the world."

Voyageurs National Park is home to beautiful landscapes, including the lovely Kabeto-

Rainy Lake

gama Peninsula and other wild lands west of the Bound-ary Waters Canoe Area. Here one may paddle up streams and across lakes to areas where moose, mink, deer, black bear, wolf, and otter still live in abundance. In the fall, the berry-picking (straw-berry, raspberry, and blue-berry) is wonderful, and the leaves on the red maples and paper birches are as bright as any found in New England. The fishing in the Voyageurs is legendary for its walleye, northern pike, smallmouth bass, trout, and even the rare lake sturgeon.

This is the country of the old French coureur-du-bois (runners of the woods), sun-burned, bug-bitten trappers who traveled by small birch and large freight canoes from Montreal to Alberta. Voyageurs is a large enough park that one can slip away across the waters, as if back down the stream of time, and visit this part of North Amer-ica when the modern age was still far off and the world was young.

Wind Cave National Park South Dakota

PARK INFORMATION

Southwest South Dakota
Established January 9, 1903
28,295 acres

Wind Cave National Park
RR I Box 190
Hot Springs, SD 57747-9430
605/745-4600
www.nps.gov/wica

Visitor Center
The visitor center is open daily
except January 1, Thanksgiving
Day, and December 25.

Entrance Fees
Admission to the park is free.
Cave tours are available for $7
to $23. Some reservations are
available (605/745-4600).

Accommodations
Elk Mountain Campground is
open year-round and operates
on a first-come, first-served
basis.

Today unspoiled remnants of the original prairie grassland are difficult to find. Wind Cave National Park, however, offers visitors a living vignette of this once widespread ecosystem. In this small but rich park, wildlife as diverse as black-tailed prairie dogs, coyotes, buffalo, pronghorn antelope, white-tailed deer, elk, western meadowlarks, and sharp-tailed grouse can be found.

Both tall and short prairie grasses blanket the park, which presents a gentle rolling landscape with miles of hiking and horseback riding trails. But underneath the quiet surface of the park is the true attraction: Pahsapa limestone, which has been dissolved and fractured into a cave system with a known length of 80 miles. The caves are unique in that, instead of traditional stalactite and stalagmite growths, there are a series of passages covered with much more fragile crystal formations.

The Wind Caves are so named because, when the barometer is falling, the air from the cave blows rapidly outward, producing a rushing sound. The park is open year-round, and cave tours are offered daily except for New Year's Day, Thanksgiving, and Christmas. The park is located near the Black Hills of western South Dakota, once the homeland of the Sioux and the same land that was disputed in a historic battle to the north at the Little Bighorn in 1876.

Rock formations

Wrangell-St. Elias National Park Alaska

PARK INFORMATION

Southeastern Alaska
Established December 2, 1980
13,175,901 acres

Wrangell-St. Elias National Park
106.8 Richardson Hwy.
PO Box 439
Copper Center, AK 99573-0439
907/822-5234
www.nps.gov/wrst

Visitor Centers
Wrangell-St. Elias Visitor
Center is open year-round.
Kennecott Visitor Center is
open daily during the summer.

Entrance Fees
Admission is free.

Accommodations
Although the National Park
Service has established no
formal campgrounds in the
park, camping is available at a
number of private camp-
grounds. A number of private
lodges are also readily available.

Wrangell-St. Elias National Park in Alaska, conjoined with the adjacent Kluane National Park in Canada's Yukon Territory, together protect 19 million acres. What was recently the exclusive domain of prospectors, trappers, and big-game hunters, Wrangell-St. Elias National Park was formally designated a World Heritage Site in 1979.

In Wrangell-St. Elias National Park, three great mountain ranges converge—Wrangell, St. Elias, and Chugach. One glacier in Wrangell-St. Elias—the Malaspina—is larger than the state of Rhode Island. The country around it resembles the frozen cordilleras of the Himalayas. Nearby, Mount St. Elias, at 18,008 feet, is one of the tallest peaks north of the Andes.

Because of its volcanic past, Wrangell-St. Elias is a landscape rich in valuable minerals, including gold, silver, and copper. In the early part of the century, the Kennicott Mining Company oper-ated a highly productive copper mine near McCarthy, an area that is, ironically, now one of the chief attractions of the park. The park also offers visitors excellent hiking and wildlife observation opportu-nities, as well as numerous sites well known to technical rock climbers. Rafters and kayakers are drawn to the pristine waters of the Chitina River. Wrangell-St. Elias is a place to come and listen to the loon sing hauntingly out on the lake, or watch the Dall sheep clamber among the high rocks, or taste the sweetness of the berry that is the essence of the Alaska outback—the mountain blueberry.

Mount Blackburn and the Crystalline Hills

Yellowstone National Park Wyoming, Montana, and Idaho

PARK INFORMATION

Northwestern Wyoming, southern Montana, and eastern Idaho
Established March 1, 1872
2,219,791 acres

Yellowstone National Park
PO Box 168
Yellowstone National Park, WY
82190-0168
307/344-7381
www.nps.gov/yell

Visitor Centers
Albright Visitor Center is open year-round. Four other visitor centers are open variously from late April through early November.

Entrance Fees
$20/vehicle for seven days, $15/motorcycle for seven days, or $10/individual for seven days.

Accommodations
Mammoth Campground is open year-round and operates on a first-come, first-served basis. Several other campgrounds are open variously from early May to early November. Some reservations are available at 307/344-7311. Abundant lodging is available during the summer months. Mammoth Hot Springs Hotel and Old Faithful Snow Lodge & Cabins are open during winter months. Reservations for all are available (307/344-7311).

Formed in 1872 as the world's first officially designated national park, Yellowstone National Park has since inspired the creation of hundreds of national parks around the world, from Israel to Indonesia, Finland to France, and Canada to Kenya. Located in the extreme northwestern corner of Wyoming, Yellowstone is a wildlife paradise and a geological wonderland.

Despite the peaceful appearance of the landscape today, the high country in Yellowstone National Park has undergone extremely violent periods over the past million years. This active past has resulted in thousands of steaming springs, geothermal pools, boiling mud pots, and explosive spurting geysers that can be found scattered throughout the Yellowstone Plateau today. No trip to the park is complete without a walk by Morning Glory Pool and Old Faithful. Morning Glory Pool is a beautiful boiling pool, reflecting an ultramarine blue, sap green, and cadmium yellow. Old Faithful attracts a crowd every hour or so when it spurts hot water 100 feet into the air.

Second to the geological splendors of Yellowstone is the wildlife. Visitors to the north entrance of the park are often greeted by the spectacle of bull elk jousting a few feet from the steps to the park library or of a bull buffalo pensively ruminating near the picnic tables by the visitor center. A few miles farther away, grizzly bears are often seen in Lamar Valley in the spring, chasing newborn elk calves. In the vicinity of the Lower Falls of Yellowstone, osprey and golden eagles dive for native cutthroat trout. Hayden Valley is one of the best spots for wildlife viewing in the park. Shiras moose abound in the meadows near the Yellowstone River, and the rare trumpeter swan is also quite often seen.

Yellowstone is a hiker's paradise as well. For those wishing to walk near the road, a day's hike up Mount Washburn, covering about three miles and reaching more than 10,000 feet in elevation, provides a wonderful panorama of the northern range of the park, from Antelope Creek at the foot of the mountain to the distant snow-covered peaks of the Absaroka Range to the north. One of the best medium-distance hikes leads from Lewis Lake to the Heart Lake Geyser Basin, which sits at the base of Mount Sheridan in the southeastern corner of the park. The Geyser Basin, about 1,000 acres in size, offers hikers a region of brilliant blue pools, boiling hot streams, and bright orange algae terraces. Heart Lake also provides some of the best fishing in the park. Longer trips generally concentrate on either the southwestern corner of the park, near Idaho, or the southeastern corner, in the wild Thorofare Country.

Increasingly, visitors are coming to Yellowstone during the winter months when snow covers the backcountry and travel is restricted to those with cross-country skis, snowshoes, or snowmobiles. Trips are also available on tracked vehicles. At that time of year, large numbers of elk, deer, buffalo, bighorn sheep, and antelope graze in the river valleys (especially the Lamar country), and the geysers and thermal pools are especially lovely, with steam clouds rising thickly into the frozen air.

Mammoth Springs

Old Faithful

Lower Falls of the Yellowstone River

Yosemite National Park California

PARK INFORMATION

Central California
Established October 1, 1890
761,266 acres

Yosemite National Park
PO Box 577
Yosemite National Park, CA
 95389
209/372-0200
www.nps.gov/yose

Visitor Centers
Yosemite Valley Visitor Center is open year-round. Tuolumne Meadows Visitor Center is open only during the summer months.

Entrance Fees
$20/vehicle for seven days or $10/individual for seven days.

Accommodations
Wawona and Hodgdon Meadow campgrounds, as well as Upper Pines and Camp 4 campgrounds in the Yosemite Valley, are open year-round. Nine other campgrounds are open variously from March through October. Some reservations are available (800/436-7275). A variety of lodges within the park are open year-round. Reservations are available (559/252-4848).

Yosemite Falls

Two of the seminal figures of the modern conservation movement—John Muir and Ansel Adams—both called the spectacular Yosemite region home. Describing Yosemite, naturalist John Muir wrote that it was "as if into this one mountain mansion Nature had gathered her choicest treasures." Landscape photographer Ansel Adams heartily agreed. He owned and operated a photographic gallery on the valley floor for many decades in the early 20th century. The fact that these two icons of conservation chose Yosemite as a base of operations for their wilderness activities says a lot about the singular scenery of the area, which was deeded by the U.S. government to the state of California for a state park.

Located in the heart of the Sierra Nevada mountain range, which Muir called "The Range of Light" because it is cloudless so many days of the year, Yosemite includes one of the greatest concentrations of natural features on the continent, if not on the planet. Here are such fabled sites as Yosemite Falls, which plunges 2,500 feet to the floor of Yosemite Valley (equal to 13 Niagaras in height), Bridalveil Falls (620 feet), and Ribbon Falls (1,612 feet). Here, too, are the Mariposa and Merced giant sequoia groves, where the largest tree is nearly 30 feet in diameter, and the quiet splendor of the Tuolumne and Merced rivers.

Half Dome is known to mountain climbers around the world and is one of the most striking sites in the park, rising in a massive, hulking shape like a medieval monk's hooded head. Nearby El Capitan, whose name means "the chief" in Spanish, is the largest piece of granite in North America and stands like a solid, broad-shouldered guard at the entrance to the valley. Across the valley from El Capitan are the fabulous Cathedral Rocks, the outcroppings of which soar upward like skyscrapers from the quiet oak groves. In the far north of the park is the Grand Canyon of the Tuolumne River, a steep and narrow barranca whose walls were carved by glaciers in ages past. Toward the south is majestic Mount Lyell, the highest point in the park at 13,114 feet.

Yosemite offers hikers more than 700 miles of trails. Short trips can be taken to Sentinel Dome, Glacier Point, and Vernal Falls. The Pacific Crest Trail traverses the highest regions of the park. On these trails hikers can walk through the same forests and meadows as John Muir, and they can share in his wonder at the magnificent splendor of this awe-inspiring park.

The park is also known for its fall colors when the oak and aspen turn and for the beauty of the dogwood blossoms in the spring. Yosemite boasts of an abundance of wildlife, which ranges from the black bears that backcountry trekkers sometimes see eating berries in the fall to the black-tailed deer of the inner valley. A person could spend a lifetime in Yosemite and never run out of places to explore—that is the mark of any crown jewel national park.

Vernal Falls

Sentinel Dome

Zion National Park Utah

PARK INFORMATION

Southwestern Utah
Established November 19, 1919
146,598 acres

Zion National Park
SR 9
Springdale, UT 84767-1099
435/772-3256
www.nps.gov/zion

Visitor Centers
Kolob Canyons and Zion
Canyon visitor centers are open
daily except December 25.

Entrance Fees
$20/vehicle for seven days or
$10/individual for seven days.

Accommodations
Watchman Campground is
open year-round. Reservations
are available (800-365-CAMP).
South Campground is open
from April through October,
and Lava Point Campground is
open from early June to mid-
October; both operate on a
first-come, first-served basis.
Zion Lodge (303/297-2757) is
open year-round.

Elongated shadows cross the floor of Zion Canyon in the early morning, while sunlight bathes the tops of massive sandstone towers. Mormon settlers gave the natural wonders they found here biblical names such as the Altar of Sacrifice, the Court of the Patriarchs, and Angels Landing. But even without these appropriately reverential names, the great figures, hulking 2,000 feet above the canyon floor, command our respect and awe. This narrow, curving gorge seems to cut through time itself.

Such wonders make Zion National Park a favorite for professional photographers. The park is a visual dream come true, with sheer canyon walls of time-scarred white limestone, red sandstone, and slickrock adorned with plunging waterfalls, hanging gardens of golden columbine and green fern, and peaceful cottonwood groves, where the wild grass is allowed to grow very deep.

Zion is a canyon of spectacular and enormous scale. Its perpendicular cliffs are nearly 3,000 feet high. Its great rock figures are imposing and monolithic, as are the monumental buttresses, deep hanging canyons, rock landings, and alcoves that have been gouged out of the cliff faces. In contrast to this grandeur, the upper end of Zion Canyon, just a few miles away, is so narrow that two people standing side by side can touch both of the canyon's rock walls. The canyon is so deep that the sun penetrates to its floor for only minutes each day.

Much of the park consists of a forested plateau deeply incised with the tributaries of ancient watercourses, such as the North and East Forks of the Virgin River. Desert and semidesert vegetation prevails at lower elevations, with big-leafed sage, prickly pear cactus flats, and tangled patches of Gambel oak, Utah and Rocky Mountain juniper, and two-needled pinyon. Elsewhere, the park is thickly forested with fir, spruce, and aspen.

Unlike other canyon parks, where many visitors view the canyons from their rims, Zion National Park draws visitors to its floor. From that vantage point, they look up at the stupendous perpendicular topography. Walking along the Virgin River, park visitors gain a unique perspective on nature.

Hikers are bound to enjoy the selection of trails in Zion.

Emerald Pool

Well-named Angels Landing is a rock pinnacle that rises 1,500 feet above the valley floor of the canyon. Visitors reach its airy and dangerous summit by following the West Rim Trail, one of the most beautiful trails in the western United States. The trail leads through a series of long switchbacks up the canyon wall to Refrigerator Canyon. Many people take a break in a glen of pine and maple before negotiating a series of steep switchbacks, called Walters Wiggles.

A narrow ridge leads to the summit of Angels Landing. The rock drops straight down on either side for more than 1,000 feet, but there are chains strung along the path and footholds cut into the rock to make the trail as safe as possible. The vista from the summit is well worth the effort. It is one of the grandest sights anywhere: a 360-degree view of Zion Canyon. A huge rock monolith, called the Great White Throne, seems to be within a stone's throw in one direction, and there is a startling view of what now appears to be a tiny Virgin River meandering through minuscule trees far below.

The Narrows